Pattern Glass

A VALUE AND IDENTIFICATION GUIDE

2ND EDITION

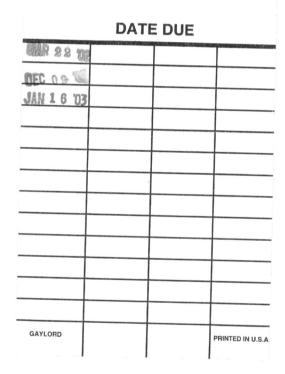

AN ILLUSTRATED REFERENCE GUIDE TO NEARLY 450 DIFFERENT TYPES OF PATTERN GLASS

EDITED BY ELLEN T. SCHROY

Published by

**krause
publications**

700 E. State Street • Iola, WI 54990-0001
Telephone: 715/445-2214

www.krause.com

Please, call or write us for our free catalog of antiques and collectibles publications.
To place an order or receive our free catalog, call 800-258-0929. For editorial comment and further information,
use our regular business telephone at (715) 445-2214

Library of Congress Catalog Number: 00-104632
ISBN: 0-87341-950-2

Printed in the United States of America

Contents

Acknowledgments

This, the second edition of *Warman's Pattern Glass*, was a pleasure to edit. It allowed me to poke around antiques shops, shows and flea markets to see that patterns and color were being offered for sale. Several interesting examples have been added to my personal collection. But it was the reading and re-reading of standard pattern glass reference books that reminded me why I write antiques price guides, because collectors want to know and deserve the best information we can provide and I love antique glass! That, coupled with a day spent with John Ahlfeld while photographing items in his inventory and personal collections. By the end of the day-long shoot, we had photographed wonderful examples and photographer Donna H. Chiarelli was becoming enthused about the forms and patterns as John and I chatted about the patterns, forms and collecting pattern glass. Instead of a conference call to chat with the advisors, we had a live meeting at the Eastern National Antiques Show, *the* place to find and purchase quality pattern glass. E-mails and telephone calls, plus generous giving of their time, has allowed this board of advisors to function well. Add to that the generous assistance of Becky Lyle, who eagerly supplied the names of patterns, which have been recently documented as made by Riverside Glass Works. Several other dealers and collectors lent their expertise, and a hearty thanks to all of them.

A special thanks to Cora A. Teter for allowing us to photograph some items from her collection that are featured in the color section.

A book such as *Warman's Pattern Glass* becomes a large project for a small operation like mine. The willingness to help with typing and proofing by my sister, Linda Fluck, and her husband, Brian, was gratefully accepted. Even dad, Lawrence R. Tischbein, got into the act, learning more about his computer in the process. Son Mark and his lovely new wife, Michelle, contributed by offering words of encouragement and letting me babble on about the wonderful patterns and colors. Pattern glass is one of those marvelous types of antiques that can be used. And, we do use our pattern glass for special occasions. Having Mark and Michelle join us for dinner was an easy excuse to use newly purchased goblets, etc. My husband Jeffrey is always supportive and has assisted with some of the line drawings for this edition. Having him by my side as we travel around seeking antiques is a treat, for he has a keen eye and loves to find interesting pieces to add to our collections.

Finishing this edition on a rainy day, it was a perfect time to re-shelve the reference books, scoop up the mountains of papers and finish the filing. Now there is a perfect space on my desk for that pretty amber string holder that I found at a flea market, in *Hanover* pattern. I'm sure it will catch my eye for sometime to come as a pleasant reminder of an interesting update to a favorite book, *Warman's Pattern Glass*.

Ellen L. Tischbein Schroy
July 2000

Introduction

Pattern glass is clear or colored glass pressed into a pattern. There are several thousand patterns. Each pattern contains a variety of useful tableware pieces and occasionally some specialized serving pieces, while others are limited to only one form, e.g. goblet. Many patterns are found only in clear, while others are found with additional adornment, such as colored staining, gilt trim, and enameled decoration.

Warman's Pattern Glass is designed to help the collector and dealer decipher the current pattern-glass market. The intent is to provide as accurate information as possible for a broad sampling of the pattern-glass market. Hopefully you will find our effort successful.

Warman's Pattern Glass is a handy reference, one that you can take comfortably to the antique shows and flea markets, shops, malls, auctions, or wherever pattern glass is sold. Use it as a reference point for pattern identification, price values, and reproduction alerts. If you want to learn more, you will find an extensive listing of the major pattern glass reference books. Refer to those when searching for additional history and complete production runs of a particular pattern.

Jacob's Ladder, compote, dolphin stem.

Jacob's Ladder, close-up of dolphin stem.

The following criteria were used to select patterns represented in *Warman's Pattern Glass*: (1) they are major patterns being collected today; (2) they represent the finest work of a particular company; and (3) they are patterns which can be used as comparables for less popular patterns. It is impossible to list every item in every pattern in this book. This is a price guide, designed to "guide" you through the exciting works of pattern-glass collecting.

What can you hope to learn by using *Warman's Pattern Glass*? If you are willing to take the time and follow up the information in this book, you will be able to (1) locate particular patterns through the alphabetical listings; (2) identify a pattern through the use of line drawings or photographs; (3) learn the manufacturer(s) of the pattern; (4) determine the value of a specific piece; (5) compare values of similar pieces; (6) be aware of modern reproductions; (7) and use the detailed cross index to locate a pattern that you may know by another name.

Names

One of the most confusing issues in collecting pattern glass is the name of the pattern. The period (original) manufacturer named or numbered each pattern. Sometimes the name reflected a design element found in the pattern, i.e., Daisy and Button. Other times it utilized a company's manufacturing name or number, i.e., Duncan & Miller #42.

The glass industry was one of the leading American industries during the late 1880s and into the early 1900s. Competition was fierce. Unfortunately, when companies went out of business, the molds were often sold to a new manufacturer, who promptly renamed the pattern. Through the years, researchers added to the confusion by renaming patterns and assigning names where they did not exist historically.

The listings in *Warman's Pattern Glass* use the name by which the pattern is commonly sold or collected. Additional names by which a pattern is known are also included.

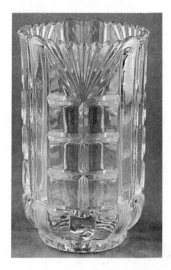

Celery vases allow more space to incorporate design elements. This vase is Skilton, flat, 6-7/8" h.

Drawings

A detailed drawing is included with every pattern. These drawings give you enough detail to adequately identify the major design components of each pattern. The pattern may differ slightly from the example shown as the design elements were incorporated into different forms. A tall slender celery vase allows more space to incorporate a design element than does an individual open salt.

Warman's has always used drawings to help identify patterns. Most of the patterns covered in this edition of *Warman's Pattern Glass* are clear. It is very difficult to photograph clear glass patterns without having the background show through the pattern. It is our belief that the use of drawings enables you to understand the design element more clearly.

Manufacturers

Each pattern listing identifies the principal manufacturers, their principal factory location, and date. Pattern glass manufacturers designed tableware lines that expanded throughout the period of production. Initial production may have been limited, e.g. a table service containing a covered butter dish, creamer, spooner, and covered sugar bowl. If the pattern was a success, the manufacturer added more pieces in the pattern, such as a water service or serving pieces. The circa date usually indicates the date when a pattern appeared in a manufacturer's catalog. Production often spanned several years or even decades for a specific pattern.

Values

The price values are only a guide for what you should expect to pay if you purchase a piece from a reputable pattern glass dealer for examples that are in excellent condition.

The listings are extensive, but may not include every form produced. If the particular form you are researching is not listed, there are enough examples to make a value judgment based on comparable prices. Just remember to be conservative.

Many of the pattern headings have information regarding how other colors and rarer items are priced. We have given specific prices and/or ranges to allow you more flexibility in determining the value of your pattern or object.

Condition is extremely important to today's pattern glass collectors. Any trim, such as gold, staining, or enameling, needs to be in excellent condition. All the values given are based on pieces in excellent condition, free of chips, cracks, flakes. Where covers are noted, these must be present and in excellent condition to achieve the full value as shown. Missing covers, worn decoration, or other types of damage will decrease the values dramatically.

Reproductions

We have tried to identify the known reproductions for each pattern with a φ symbol next to the object. In several cases, the manufacturer of these reproductions is noted. Unfortunately, many reproductions are unmarked and the manufacturers remain unknown. This is an area where active research is continuing. The number of known reproductions has increased from the first to second editions of *Warman's Pattern Glass*. The good news is that pattern glass reproductions seem to be less popular with modern manufacturers than they were in the late 1970s and 1980s. The best insurance to guard against being fooled is to know what forms were made in the pattern of your choice and carefully studying the design elements. Being familiar with known reproductions helps to keep collectors alert to reproductions. Fine publications such as *Antiques & Collectibles Reproduction News* help educate dealers and collectors about new discoveries in this sad aspect of the antiques marketplace.

Index

Because of the multiplicity of names given to pattern glass, we have provided a detailed cross-name index. Each pattern name is listed with the appropriate page number.

Pineapple & Fan #2, plate, 10-1/2" d.

Roman Rosette, compote, covered, high standard, 7-1/4" d, 11-1/2" d.

Pitcher, floral decoration.

History

Glass production in America began with the settlement of Jamestown, Virginia, shortly after the English arrived. Detailed accounts of furnaces and other glass-manufacturing tools document this attempt at early glassware production. This glassware was largely free blown. Some items were pressed using crude molds. This method of glass production predominated until the early 1820s. Press molded handles, pillar molded items, etc., did occur, but the process was time consuming and difficult. Glassblowers completed one piece of glass at a time. As America expanded, consumers wanted more and more glassware.

During the early years of the 19th century, the country enjoyed a period of prosperity and industrial growth. The demand for inexpensive utilitarian items, such as bottles, windows, and tableware, created many jobs, as new companies sprang up. Small-scale operations of blown glass, which was pressed into molds by hand, grew rapidly in the New England and Pittsburgh, PA, areas. These operations were still laborious and could not match the demand.

In the early 1820s, J. P. Bakewell of Bakewell and Company, Pittsburgh, PA, obtained a patent for the manufacture of pressed glass furniture knobs. Additional patents were issued for refinements in pressing techniques. These patents led to the production of lacy-type pressed glass. Lacy glass was still largely hand made and consisted primarily of small items. Early patterns were often ornate in design, giving the appearance of lace, hence the term lacy. Design elements of these lacy patterns were often used to disguise the fact that there were imperfections in the glass, due to the harsh, still somewhat primitive, manufacturing conditions.

While patents were being developed and advances made in the mechanical aspects of glass production, the formulas to make glass also had to be refined. The lacy patterns, although pressed, are not part of the traditional collector interpretation of pattern glass. As the technology developed, flint glass patterns were designed that were entirely machine made. These early machines worked best with newer formulas, ones requiring more expensive materials and a higher concentration of lead.

Several key companies were responsible for early advancements in the industry. One of the most important centers around Deming Jarves of the Boston and Sandwich Glass Company, who invented the first successful pressing machine in 1828. Jarves patented several processes related to mechanical glass production. His importance manifested itself as he became involved in the establishment of other glass companies, including the Mount Washington Glass Company, and later the Cape Cod Glass Company.

By the 1860s, glass-pressing machinery had been improved. Mass production of good quality matched tableware sets began in earnest. The idea of a matched glassware table service, comprising goblets, tumblers, creamers, sugars, compotes, cruets, etc., quickly found favor across America. Numerous accessory pieces, e.g., banana stands, molasses cans, and water bottles, etc. joined the more common pieces.

Americans were delighted with the variety of patterns, colors, and shapes offered for sale by numerous companies. Early patterns were designed to compete with the hand-blown patterns previously known. Design elements were simple, incorporating thumbprints, bull's eyes, and points. As the years progressed, patterns became more intricate and included ribbing, florals, and swirls. As the Brilliant Period of cut glass evolved, pattern-glass designers worked hard to develop intricate patterns which imitated the expensive cut-glass patterns.

The flint-glass formula helped initiate the production of pattern glass. The development of a non-flint formula provided the key for economical mass production and the true popularization of pattern glass. The non-flint formula was discovered around the time of the Civil War, which saw lead reserved for military purposes, not the glassware industry. A non-flint formula that used no lead allowed production to continue.

William Leighton Sr., of Hobbs, Brockunier of Wheeling, West Virginia, developed a formula that utilized soda lime instead of lead. This glass mixture could be pressed more quickly and thinner, making more detailed patterns possible. Extensive patterns were now produced utilizing the lighter non-flint formula, although some patterns continued to be produced only in flint.

By the 1880s, the American pattern glass industry reached maturity. The geographic center of the industry shifted from New England to the Pittsburgh and Ohio Valleys, rich in natural resources and having good transportation centers. A tremendous expansion occurred.

Patterns became more detailed. The production of non-flint glass in colors followed rapidly. Among the rainbow of colors available were amber, apple green, blue, emerald green, purple, and vaseline. The first patterns produced in milk glass were made in the 1880s.

New colors and decorative techniques allowed table settings to become complex. This matched similar Victorian trends in silver and ceramics. The glass industry showed few restraints in respect to form, color, staining, and a myriad of other types of ornamentation. Patterns were designed to show one's good taste, love of nature, or culture.

In 1891, a giant glass-manufacturing combine was formed. The United States Glass Company combined fifteen well-established glass companies in a single unit. The National Glass Company, the second large combine, was organized in 1899 and included nineteen glass companies. The impact of these combines on the marketplace was tremendous. They increased production, along with the sales staff, and retooled some molds. In many cases, they reissued existing patterns in new colors and with new names. One example is the United States Glass Company's states series, which was an instant hit with the American public. Today, dealers and collectors often return to the original pattern name as the popularity of the states series has waned. Today *Beaded Grape* is more often requested, rather than its later name of *California,* and *Beaded Loop* is more recognized than *Oregon #1.*

Carnival and custard glass patterns imitated expensive art glass. Simpler designs came into vogue during the early part of the 20th century, as companies such as Cambridge, Fostoria, and Heisey began production.

These new patterns mirrored the sleeker style of the Art Nouveau and Art Deco periods.

The Depression years saw a decline in the production of fine pattern glass and factories closed. When the Depression ended and World War II began, the demand for pattern glass was waning. The production of elegant etched patterns was an attempt to appeal to war brides. Many pattern-glass manufacturers closed. Those that remained were left to develop new designs for the post-War brides. These companies, such as Fostoria, Heisey, and Tiffin, owed their roots to pattern glass, but saw their future in elegant etched patterns.

Classics, compote, covered, high standard, 7-1/2" d, 9" h, manufactured by Gillinder and Sons.

Egyptian, goblet, showing Sphinx, 6" h; manufactured by Adams & Company.

Sawtooth, child's creamer, 2" d, 2-3/4" h; manufactured by New Martinsville Glass Company.

Manufacturers

The hundreds of companies, which produced pattern glass, have complex histories that include formation, expansion, personnel issues, material and supply requirements, fires, and mergers. Detailed histories have been written for some of these companies. Much more research remains to be done.

Collecting by company is an excellent alternative to collecting by pattern name or type of object. Because of the regionalism of the glass industry, many new collectors have broadened their collecting perspective and are focusing on a particular geographic area. The first significant glass-manufacturing center in America was in New England. Leading companies, which were located there, include Boston & Sandwich Glass Company, Sandwich, MA; Cape Cod Glass Company, Sandwich, MA; New England Glass Company, Boston and Cambridge, MA; Portland Glass Company, Portland, ME; Union Glass, Somerville, MA, and others.

The most prolific glass manufacturing state was Pennsylvania. Philadelphia was home to early companies such as Gillinder & Sons. However, it was the Pittsburgh area that developed as the state's leading glass manufacturing center in the late 19th century and early 20th century. Leading manufacturers were Adams & Company; Bakewell, Pears & Company; Bryce Brothers; Challinor, Taylor & Company; Curling, Robertson & Company, Doyle & Company; George Duncan & Sons; Grierson & Company, King Glass Company; James B. Lyon & Company, McKee & Brothers; O'Hara Glass Company; Pioneer Glass Company; Richards & Hartley Glass Company; Ripley and Company; United States Glass Company, and Windsor Glass Company. Other Pennsylvania manufacturers include: Co-Operative Glass Company, Beaver Falls; LaBelle Glass Company, Bridgeport; Thompson, Uniontown; and Westmoreland, Grapeville.

Ohio manufacturers include A. J. Beatty & Sons of Steubenville and Tiffin; Bellaire Goblet Company, Findlay; Cambridge Glass Company, Cambridge; Canton Glass Company, Canton; Daizell, Gilmore & Leighton, Belmont; A. H. Heisey and Company, Newark; Imperial Glass Corp., Bellaire; Model Flint Glass Company, Findlay; and Ohio Flint Glass Company, Lancaster.

West Virginia featured companies such as Central Glass Company, Wheeling; Fostoria Glass Company, Moundsville; Hobbs, Brockunier and Company, Wheeling; Jefferson, Follansbee; New Martinsville Glass Company, New Martinsville; Riverside Glass Company, Wellsburg, and Union Stopper Company, Morgantown.

Canadian glass manufacturers include Burlington Glass Company, Hamilton, Ontario; Diamond Flint Glass Company; and Syndenham Glass Company, Wallaceburg Ontario.

Cambridge Glass Company, Fenton Art Glass Company, Fostoria Glass Company, A. H. Heisey Glass Company, Imperial Glass Corp., and Westmoreland Glass Company, are among the manufacturers who dominated the pressed glass market into the twentieth century. Their enormous variety and long-term production have created a collecting interest that transcends their patterned pieces.

The United States Glass Company (1891) and the National Glass Company (1899) united small companies in Pennsylvania, Ohio, Indiana, West Virginia, and Maryland, to keep the production of glass a vital American industry. These combined pooled talents, resources, and patterns. As a result, more than one company made the same pattern. United States Glass Company has been credited with the production of 300 other different patterns.

There are several excellent reference books on specific companies. We highly recommend that you learn more about the companies that interest you. Remember that research into pattern glass and its makers is an on-going process. New discoveries and attributions about specific patterns are being made every year. In July of 2000, a Riverside Glass Company catalog was found that confirms it made patterns such as *Cabbage Leaf, Jersey Lily Ware, Grasshopper* and *Chicken (Frosted Chicken)*, plus several others. As company archives, old catalogs, advertisements, and periodicals become available to scholars, expect even more revisions to our present approach.

An exciting research area in the 1990s was the excavation of the former glass manufacturing centers, such as Boston and Sandwich Glass Company in Sandwich, Massachusetts, and the Burlington Glass Works in Hamilton, Ontario, Canada. Both sites have yielded a vast number of shards. By carefully studying these shards, which often contain handles, stems, and other bits of objects, researchers can identify patterns, colors, and production dates. This work continues. As the results are published, it will also affect how we look at pattern glass manufacturers, especially those in the early period of production. More and more glass museums, such as Corning, the National Cambridge Glass Club, and others are making their extensive libraries available to researchers. This, too, will lead a broader understanding of how important the pattern glass industry was to America.

Reproductions

Reproductions Abound

Pattern glass has been widely reproduced. While the amount made seemed to be less during the late 1990s, the large sale of molds by L. G. Wright to new glass manufacturers may have a negative impact on the pattern glass marketplace as the new millennium begins. When collecting pattern glass, it is critical to identify period forms, those that were initially made, and period colors. Know if the pattern was made in flint or non-flint, and in some cases, when flint changed to non-flint. Reproductions and reissues tend to be non-flint.

Careful attention to details is the first clue to determining if a piece is a reissue or reproduction. The stag on Westward Ho! period pieces should be well-formed, the details of the fur coat evident, and the frosting strong, but well defined in the lines and design elements. Frosting, staining, and other types of decoration will be found between well-defined lines, not trailing off or shaded in coloration. The same attention to detail is found in most period pieces. Early glass manufacturers were proud of their wares. They had no reason to sell seconds.

Glass manufacturers recycled their mistakes and damaged pieces during the 19th century. The high standards expected by the American consumers of that period were reflected in the high quality of pattern glass produced.

Pattern glass was produced using molds. Early molds were made out of wood, while later ones were cast in metals hard enough to withstand years of wear. Period pieces featured sharp relief details. Carefully examine a piece of *Beaded Loop*. The beads are sharp little points. Then check a reproduction. A reproduction *Beaded Loop* object will be much smoother. The details of the original mold were lost in the reproduction process. The small pyramid-shaped points on the period piece have become small raised dots on the reproductions. Early examples of *Daisy and Button* will feel sharp to the touch. Later examples often will be less distinct and the buttons may actually be hazy.

The key is to feel: feel for the detail; feel for weight. Reproductions are often much heavier. Look at the thickness of the stem. The thicker the stem, the more likely it is a reproduction.

Manufacturers

As research continues into who is making reproductions, several companies have emerged as leaders in that market. Some are recognized names that continue to create wonderful glassware today, such as Fenton, and Mosser. The molds accumulated by L. G. Wright of New Martinsville, WV, were sold in the late 1990s, and A. A. Importing and others who purchased the old molds are making some new reproductions. Glass created by manufacturers such as Kemple, L. E. Smith, Summit, and Degenhart Glass is now collectible in its own right.

Glass manufacturers producing new patterns made some of the earliest reproductions. Reissues are pieces made from period molds. In other cases, new molds were created using some original design elements. Look for slight variations in size from period pieces to reissues to reproductions. Many collectors include reissues and reproductions in their collections. When a form was never created in a pattern, i.e., a goblet in *Eyewinker,* the later issues are welcome additions to *Eyewinker* table services. A dangerous market trend is to assign the same value for a reissue as for a period piece. Premium prices should never be paid for the later pieces.

Companies like Westmoreland, Summit Glass, Imperial, and Fenton have and still produce vast numbers of reproductions. These companies never intended to deceive the public, merely to supplement table services with additional pieces. Some new colors are made to appeal to modern decoration tastes. Alas, novices are still fooled by them because of a lack of an identifiable mark.

Several prestigious museums, including the Metropolitan Museum of Art in New York City, the Smithsonian Institution, Washington, DC, and the Henry Ford Museum in Dearborn, Michigan, have commissioned reproductions. These were marked in the mold and should pose no problems to collectors.

Studying catalogs of these modern manufacturers can assist in learning what forms they have made, what colors, etc. As reproduction makers, such as L. G. Wright, go out of business, their catalogs become even more valuable to collectors. One of the best defenses is to know the dealer. Buyers are urged to get a sales receipt that contains the seller's name, address, telephone number and/or e-mail address. Having a description on the receipt will also help the buyer identify the piece.

A subscription to *Antiques and Collectibles Reproduction News,* P.O. Box 12130, Des Moines, IA 50312-9403, 515-274-5886, e-mail: website: www.repronews.com. is an excellent addition to a collector's library. The American Antique Association, 702 W. 76th St., Davenport, IA 52806, also assists collectors.

State of the Market

The Internet keeps making a bigger and bigger impact on the antiques and collectibles marketplace. Some dealers shake their heads and grumble how it is ruining the business. However, pattern glass is one segment of the market that is benefiting from this new tool. No longer are collectors restricted to what is available within a comfortable driving distance. Pattern glass has historically been sold at antiques shows, shops, auctions and other venues. Today, with the explosion of the Internet auctions, collectors are able to find interesting pieces to add to their collections without leaving the comfort of their home. Geographic divergences are quickly disappearing in the antiques and collectibles marketplace, the pattern glass market reflects this, too.

Activity at the last antiques show, known for fine pattern-glass dealers, saw brisk business. Collectors were seeking pieces to add to their favorite patterns, and new collectors were exploring a bright new world. Some of these young collectors are seeking specific forms, like goblets or egg cups, while others are looking for a particular company's wares, like Riverside Glass Works. The backbone of the pattern-glass market will always be the collector who is adding to his or her table settings, and those folks were at the show, too. There was excitement in the air and tables filled with sparkling glassware beckoned onlookers to come browse.

Pattern glass is not a segment of the antiques market that has wild price swings. Things are going up gradually, except for the rare items. Like in other old established collecting fields, the rare pieces are commanding higher prices in relationship to the rate of increase allotted to the middle of the market. Glass that has a chip or wear to the decoration will bring less than half the prices, sometimes even less than that. Chipped or damaged glassware is generally hard to repair and both collectors and dealers are aware of that. However, when mint or very good rare examples do surface, they are held in high esteem.

Organizations like the Early American Pattern Glass Society should take some credit for rekindling some excitement in the pattern glass market. Its organized gatherings teach collectors about this interesting field by encouraging communication and sharing of information between collectors. Its publication, the *News Journal*, is well done and contains interesting articles and information about the Society.

The pattern-glass world is fortunate in having several good auction houses that regularly schedule entire auctions of pattern glass. This is good for both the buyers and sellers. The buyer can purchase items reasonably with the assurance of the auction house's backing of age and quality. Sellers know that these auction houses will do a good job of advertising the auctions, presenting the wares in a good light, and attracting buyers from all around the country. While selling at auction does not guarantee a certain dollar amount, these large pattern-glass auctions are generally achieving high prices. The folks who are participating are anxious to add to their collections, which is why they are there. With the advent of catalogs, Internet bidding, telephone bidding and the ability to leave absentee bids, collectors today can be involved with quality auctions again from the comfort of their home.

Green Valley Auctions Inc., Mount Crawford, VA, features a large pattern glass and oil lamp auction every fall. The auction in 1999 saw bidders come from 27 states and Canada, plus 1,200 absentee and phone bids were received from 30 states and Canada. Friday's auction was a 14-hour marathon event that sold more than 5,000 pieces of glass, including goblets, wines, spooners, and all types of pattern glass. Bidding was strong the whole day. Saturday brought bidders for a collection of reference books and more than 700 pieces of early American pattern glass. Two *Beaver Band* goblets sold for $850 and $800. A *Dragon* goblet brought $1,600 and was the only one ever sold in that pattern by Green Valley Auctions Inc. A *Heart with Thumbprint* goblet with ruby-stained hearts fetched $2,500. A *Swan Mid Rushes* goblet brought $650 and an unlisted ostrich, stork and heron goblet brought $1,500. Not all the goblets sold fetched such high figures, but these are examples that collectors are willing to pay well for outstanding examples.

Additional highlights of the auction included a non-flint *Frosted Lion* milk pitcher with an applied handle that went home with a Texas collector, who outbid a California bidder at $5,100. Two telephone bidders squabbled it out over a *Three Face* hollow stem champagne, ending at $4,600, which was slightly less than a similar example that sold the year before for $5,100. Prices from the rest of the auction were also strong. Surely the auction held this year will be as great, with exciting items going up for bid and eager bidders waiting to add them to their collections.

Board of Advisors

Warman's Pattern Glass, 2nd Edition, has been a labor of love by several well-qualified advisors. This Board of Advisors contains dealers and collectors. All love pattern glass, the research involved, and the history of the pieces. Each brought a specialized area of expertise to the project. Each reviewed the prices listed, suggested additional forms, documented pieces, etc. All the members of the Board of Advisors are also members of the Early American Pattern Glass Society, an organization that brings together collectors and dealers who are fascinated with pattern glass. A special thanks is due for John and Alice Ahlfeld, 2634 Royal Road, Lancaster, PA 17603-7010, e-mail: AHLFELDS@aol.com; Mel and Roberta Lader, 8212 Glyn Street, Alexandria, VA 22309, e-mail: lader@gwu.edu; and Samuel D. Kissée, e-mail: skissee@csuchico.edu.

Comments Welcomed

Warman's Pattern Glass, 2nd Edition, is like all the other Warman's price guides published by Krause Publications. While we hope it is the finest price guide you'll ever use, we admit it was written by humans. Perhaps we've missed something you would like to tell us about, information about your favorite pattern. Or perhaps a decimal point got in the wrong place. We hope this edition will be comfortable for you to use.

Hearing from collectors is the best way to find out what's important to you, the reader. Please send comments, corrections, or suggestions to Ellen Schroy, Warman's Pattern Glass Editor, PO Box 392, Quakertown, PA 18951-0392, e-mail: Schroy@voicenet.com

Reference Books

Pattern glass, like other areas of the antiques and collectibles market, is the subject of a large number of reference books and periodicals. In the *Warman's* tradition, these books and periodicals appear below. Because out-of-print books are often a valuable tool to researchers, these titles are included also. Pattern glass is a subject where classic studies count.

Pattern glass has been blessed with a number of pioneering and contemporary researchers. Among the pioneers and their efforts were George P. and Helen McKearin, *American Glass,* Crown Publishers, 1941; E. M. Belnap, *Milk Glass,* Crown Publishers, 1949; Ruth Web Lee, *Early American Pressed Glass,* Lee Publications, 1966; 36th edition; —, *Victorian Glass,* Lee Publications, 1944, 13th edition, Alice Hulett Metz, *Early American Pattern Glass,* published by the author, 1958, revised and reprinted by Collector Books, 2000, with assistance from the Early American Pattern Glass Society; —, *Much More Early American Pattern Glass,* published by the author, 1965, revised and reprinted by Collector Books, 2000, with assistance from the Early American Pattern Glass Society; S. T. Millard, *Goblets II,* published by author, 1940, reprinted by Wallace-Homestead, 1975.

Regis F. and Mary F. Ferson, William Heacock, and Minnie Kamm continued in the footsteps of these pioneers. Contemporary research continues today with encouragement from the Early American Pattern Glass Society and the National American Glass Club.

Reference Books

The standard reference books relating to pattern glass include:

Gary Baker et al., *Wheeling Glass 1829-1939*, Oglebay Institute, 1994, distributed by Antique Publications.

E. M. Belnap, *Milk Glass,* Crown Publishers Inc., 1949.

Neila and Tom Bredehoft, *Hobbs, Brockunier & Co.,* Collector Books, 1997.

George and Linda Breeze, *Mysteries of the Moon & Star*, published by authors, 1995.

Sue C. Davis, *The Picture Book of Vaseline Glass,* Schiffer Publishing, 1999.

Shirley Dunbar, *Heisey Glass, The Early Years, 1896-1924,* Krause Publications, 2000.

Bill Edwards and Mike Carwile, *Standard Encyclopedia of Pressed glass, 1860-1930,* Collector Books, 1998.

Elaine Ezell and George Newhouse, *Cruets, Cruets, Cruets, Volume 1,* Antique Publications, 1991.

Regis F. and Mary F. Ferson, *Yesterday's Milk Glass Today,* published by the authors, 1981.

William Heacock, published a series of books which were published by Antique Publications. *Encyclopedia of Victorian Colored Pattern Glass: Book 1, Toothpick Holders from A to Z, 2nd ed.,* 1976, 1992 value update; *Book 2, Opalescent Glass from A to Z,* 1981; *Book 3, Syrups,* *Sugar Shakers & Cruets,* 1980; *Book 4, Custard Glass from A to Z,* 1980; *Book 5, U. S. Glass from A to Z,* 1980; *Book 6, Oil Cruets From A to Z,* 1981; *Book 7, Ruby Stained Glass from A To Z,* 1986; *Book 8, More Ruby Stained Glass,* 1987; *Book 9, Cranberry Opalescent Glass from A to Z,* 1981 (William Heacock and William Gamble).

—, *Old Pattern Glass*, Antique Publications, 1981.

—, *1000 Toothpick Holders*, Antique Publications, 1977.

—, *Rare and Unlisted Toothpick Holders*, Antique Publications, 1984.

William Heacock, James Measell, and Berry Wiggins, *Harry Northwood, The Early Years, 1881-1900,* Antique Publications, 1990.

—, *Harry Northwood: The Wheeling Years, 1901-1925,* Antique Publications, 1991.

Joyce A. Hicks, *Just Jenkins,* published by author, 1988.

Kyle Husfloen, *Collector's Guide to American Pressed Glass*, Wallace-Homestead, 1992.

Bill Jenks and Jerry Luna, *Early American Pattern Glass—1850 to 1910*, Wallace-Homestead, 1990.

Bill Jenks, Jerry Luna, and Darryl Reilly, *Identifying Pattern Glass Reproductions*, Wallace-Homestead, 1993.

William J. Jenks and Darryl Reilly, *American Price Guide to Unitt's Canadian & American Goblets Volumes I & II,* Author! Author! Books (P.O. Box 1964, Kingston, PA 18704), 1996.

Minnie Watson Kamm, *Pattern Glass Pitchers*, Books 1 through 8, published by author, 1970, 4th printing.

Lorraine Kovar, *Westmoreland Glass, 1950-1984,* Antique Publications, 1991.

—, *Westmoreland Glass, 1950-1984,* Volume II, Antique Publications, 1991.

Thelma Ladd and Laurence Ladd, *Portland Glass: Legacy Of A Glass House Down East,* Collector Books, 1992.

Ruth Webb Lee, *Early American Pressed Glass*, 36th ed., Lee Publications, 1966.

—, *Victorian Glass*, 13th ed., Lee Publications, 1944.

Bessie M. Lindsey, *American Historical Glass*, Charles E. Tuttle, 1967.

Robert Irwin Lucas, *Tarentum Pattern Glass*, privately printed, 1981.

Mollie H. McCain, *Collector's Encyclopedia of Pattern Glass*, Collector Books, 1982, 2000 value update.

—, *Pattern Glass Primer,* Lamplighter Books, 1979.

George P. and Helen McKearin, *American Glass*, Crown Publishers, 1941.

James Measell, *Greentown Glass*, Grand Rapids Public Museum Association, 1979, 1992-93 value update, distributed by Antique Publications.

James Measell and Don E. Smith, *Findlay Glass: The Glass Tableware Manufacturers, 1886-1902,* Antique Publications Inc., 1986.

Alice Hulett Metz, *Early American Pattern Glass*, published by author, 1958 (reprinted by Collector Books, 2000, with revisions).

——, *Much More Early American Pattern Glass*, published by author, 1965 (reprinted by Collector Books, 2000, with revisions).

S. T. Millard, *Goblets I* (1938), *Goblets II* (1940), privately printed, reprinted Wallace-Homestead, 1975.

John B. Mordock and Walter L. Adams, *Pattern Glass Mugs*, Antique Publications, 1995.

National Early American Glass Club Ltd., *Reflections on Glass,* National Early American Glass Club Ltd., 1993.

Betty Newbound, *The Glass Collector's Almanac,* published by author, 1987.

Betty and Bill Newbound, *Collector's Encyclopedia of Milk Glass,* Collector Books, 1995.

Bob Page and Dale Frederiksen, *Crystal Stemware Identification Guide,* Collector Books, 1997.

Arthur G. Peterson, *Glass Salt Shakers*, Wallace-Homestead, 1970.

Anne Geffken Pullin, *Glass Signatures, Trademarks and Trade Names From the 17th to 20th C,* Wallace-Homestead, 1986.

Jane Shadel Spillman, *American and European Pressed Glass in the Corning Museum of Glass*, Corning Museum of Glass, 1981.

——, *Knopf Collectors Guides to American Antiques, Glass,* Vol. 1 (1982), Vol. 2 (1983), Alfred A. Knopf.

Doris and Peter Unitt, *American and Canadian Goblets,* Clock House, 1970, reprinted by The Love of Glass Publishing (Box 629, Arthur, Ontario, Canada NOG 1AO), 1996.

——, *Treasury of Canadian Glass*, 2nd ed., Clock House, 1969.

Peter Unitt and Anne Worrall, *Canadian Handbook, Pressed Glass Tableware*, Clock House Productions, 1983.

Chas West Wilson, *Westmoreland Glass,* Collector Books, 1996.

Kenneth Wilson, *American Glass 1760-1930*, 2 volumes, Hudson Hills Press and The Toledo Museum of Art, 1994.

Periodical

Glass Collector's Digest, The Glass Press, P.O. Box 553, Marietta, OH 45750.

Collectors' Clubs

Early American Pattern Glass Society, P.O. Box 266, Colesburg, IA 52035, periodical: *News Journal.* The National Early American Glass Club, P.O. Box 8489, Silver Spring, MD 20907, periodicals: *Glass Club Bulletin*; *Glass Shards.*

Museums

Corning Museum of Glass, Corning, NY; Jones Museum of Glass and Ceramics, Sebago, ME; National Museum of Man, Ottawa, Ontario, Canada; Sandwich Glass Museum, Sandwich, MA; Schminck Memorial Museum, Lakeview, OR.

Websites

Early American Pattern Glass Society, www.eapgs.org; Just Glass, www.justglass.com.

Abbreviations

The following are standard abbreviations which we have used throughout this edition of *Warman's Pattern Glass, 2nd Edition.*

ah = applied handle
C = century
c = circa
circ = circular
cov = cover
d = diameter or depth
dec = decorated
dq = diamond quilted
emb = embossed
ext. = exterior
ftd = footed
GUTDODB = Give us this day our daily bread
ground = background
h = height
hp = hand painted
hs = high standard
imp = impressed
ind = individual
int. = interior
irid = iridescent
ivt = inverted thumbprint
l = length

ls = low standard
mkd = marked
mop = mother of pearl
motto = motto or saying
NE = New England
no. = Number
opal = opalescent
orig = original
os = original stopper
pat = patent
pcs = pieces
ph = pressed handle
pr = pair
rect = rectangular
sgd = signed
sngl = single
sp = silver plated
ss = sterling silver
sq = square
w = wide, width
# = numbered

Acorn

Acorn Band, Acorn Band and Loops, Paneled Acorn Band, Beaded Acorn

Acorn and the variant patterns were made in flint and non-flint, 1860s-70s. There are additional acorn variant patterns, but they were not made in table sets. Prices for all the acorn variants are similar.

Reproductions: The *Acorn* goblet is reported to be reproduced in blue. Originally it was made only in clear.

Items	Flint	Non-Flint
Bowl, cov	—	60.00
Bowl, open	—	42.00
Butter Dish, cov	65.00	—
Celery	90.00	—
Compote, cov	225.00	90.00
Compote, open	90.00	60.00
Creamer	55.00	42.00
Egg Cup	30.00	18.00
Goblet φ	48.00	30.00
Pitcher, water, ah	180.00	90.00
Sauce, flat	—	9.00
Spooner	48.00	36.00
Sugar Bowl, cov	90.00	60.00
Sugar, open, buttermilk type	42.00	24.00

Actress

Made by Adams & Company, Pittsburgh, PA, c1880, in clear and clear with frosting. Deduct 20% for only clear pieces.

Reproductions: Some pieces have been reproduced by Imperial Glass. Reproductions are found in clear, amethyst, and other colors.

Items	Frosted
Bowl, 6" or 7" d, ftd	55.00-60.00
Bowl, 8" d, Miss Neilson; or 9-1/2" d, ftd	85.00
Bread Plate, 7" x 12", HMS Pinafore	110.00
Bread Plate, 9" x 13", Miss Neilson	90.00
Butter Dish, cov	110.00
Cake Dish, 10" d	180.00
Candlesticks, pr	300.00
Celery Vase, actress head	130.00
Celery Vase, HMS Pinafore, pedestal	155.00
Cheese Dish, cov, The Lone Fisherman on cover, Two Drominos on base	300.00
Compote, cov, hs, 12" d	360.00
Compote, open, hs, 10" or 12" d	110.00-130.00
Compote, open, ls, 5" d	55.00
Creamer	90.00
Dresser Tray	72.00
Goblet, Kate Claxton, two portraits	95.00
Marmalade Jar, cov	130.00
Mug, HMS Pinafore	60.00
Pickle Dish, Love's Request is Pickles φ	55.00
Pickle/Relish, 4-1/2" x 7"; 5" x 8"; or 5-1/2" x 9"	42.00
Pitcher, milk, 6-1/2" h, HMS Pinafore	290.00
Pitcher, water, 9" h, Romeo & Juliet	300.00
Salt, master	85.00
Salt Shaker, orig pewter top	50.00
Sauce, flat	18.00
Sauce, footed	24.00
Spooner	72.00
Sugar Bowl, cov	120.00

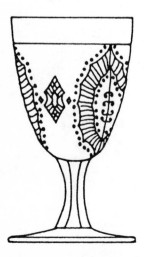

Aegis

Bead and Bar Medallion, Swiss

Made by McKee & Brothers Glass Company, Pittsburgh, PA, in the 1880s. Shards have been found at the site of the Burlington Glass Works, Hamilton, Ontario, Canada. Made in non-flint, clear.

Items	Clear
Bowl, cov, collared base, 6" d; or open, oval, flat	30.00
Butter Dish, cov	42.00
Compote, cov, hs, 7" or 8" d	55.00-60.00
Compote, cov, ls, 6", 7" or 8" d	36.00-48.00
Compote, open, hs, 6", 7" or 8" d	24.00-30.00
Compote, open, ls, 6", 7" or 8"d	24.00-30.00
Creamer	30.00
Egg Cup	30.00
Goblet	36.00
Honey Dish, flat, 3-1/2" d	9.00

Items	Clear
Pickle, 5" x 7"	18.00
Pitcher, water, ah	55.00
Salt, master	18.00
Sauce, flat, 4" d	9.00
Sauce, footed, 3-1/2" or 4" d	10.00-12.00
Spooner	24.00
Sugar Bowl, cov	110.00

Alabama

Beaded Bull's Eye and Drape, US Glass Pattern Line No. 15,062

Made by United States Glass Company, c1898. This pattern is known as one of the States patterns. Made in non-flint clear and ruby stained. Several pieces have been found in emerald green and their value would be 150% of clear. Very rare ruby and amber-stained pieces would be valued at 300% of clear.

Items	Clear	Ruby Stained
Berry Bowl, master, open, flat, 8" d	85.00	—
Bowl, rectangular	36.00	—
Butter Dish, cov	60.00	180.00
Cake Stand, hs	65.00	—
Castor Set, 4 bottles, glass frame	130.00	—
Celery Tray	55.00	—
Celery Vase	42.00	135.00
Child's Butter Dish, cov	150.00	—
Child's Creamer	65.00	—
Child's Spooner	65.00	—
Child's Sugar Bowl, cov	110.00	—
Compote, cov, 7" or 8" d	120.00-130.00	—
Creamer, individual size	24.00	42.00
Creamer, table size	55.00	72.00
Cruet, os	65.00	—
Dish, rectangular	24.00	—
Honey Dish, cov, flat	65.00	—
Jelly Compote, open, 5" d	42.00	—
Mustard Pot, cov, notched lid	120.00	—
Pickle Dish	18.00	—
Pitcher, water	90.00	—
Relish, rectangular	30.00	42.00
Salt and Pepper Shakers, pr	65.00	—
Sauce, flat or footed, 4" d	15.00	—
Spooner	36.00	—
Sugar Bowl, cov	50.00	—
Syrup, orig top	130.00	300.00
Toothpick Holder	72.00	180.00
Tumbler	55.00	—
Water Tray, 10-1/2" d	60.00	—

Alaska

Lion's Leg

Manufactured by Northwood Glass Co., 1897-1910. The forms of this pattern are square, except for the cruet, salt and pepper shakers, and tumblers. Made in a non-flint opalescent glass and some clear colors, including emerald green, clear, and blue. Some pieces have enamel decoration, which adds 75% to the clear value shown below. Sauces can be found in clear ($30); the creamer ($110) and spooner ($95) are known in clear blue.

Items	Clear Emerald Green	Blue Opalescent	Vaseline Opalescent	White Opalescent
Banana Boat	85.00	300.00	300.00	130.00
Berry Bowl, ftd	65.00	120.00	115.00	55.00
Butter Dish, cov	180.00	295.00	290.00	120.00
Celery Tray	55.00	130.00	124.00	85.00
Creamer	48.00	90.00	65.00	48.00
Cruet, os	270.00	300.00	265.00	142.00
Pitcher, water	90.00	385.00	290.00	190.00
Salt Shaker, decorated	—	60.00	55.00	55.00
Sauce	36.00	55.00	48.00	30.00
Spooner	55.00	85.00	55.00	60.00
Sugar Bowl, cov	65.00	180.00	136.00	120.00
Tumbler	55.00	90.00	65.00	55.00

All-Over Diamond

Diamond Splendor, Diamond Block #3, Duncan Pattern Line No. 556

Manufactured by George Duncan and Sons, Pittsburgh, PA, c1890-1891, and continued by United States Glass Company, c1892-1899. This pattern was made at United States Glass factory "D" and "P." This large pattern contains at least forty-five pieces, and includes fifteen different sizes of dishes and nappies, some crimped, some plain. Made in clear, clear with some pieces trimmed in gold, and ruby stained.

Items	Clear	Ruby Stained
Biscuit Jar, cov, available in three sizes	72.00	—
Bitters Bottle	36.00	—
Bowl, flat, crimped rim, 5", 7", 8" or 9" d	18.00-24.00	—
Bowl, flat, smooth rim, 7", 8" or 9" d	24.00	—
Bowl, flat, square, scalloped rim, 7", 8" or 9" d	24.00	—
Bowl, 11" d	42.00	—
Butter Dish, cov, individual size	35.00	—
Butter Dish, cov, table size	55.00	—
Cake Stand, hs	42.00	—
Candelabrum, 3 arms	130.00	—
Candelabrum, 4 arms with lusters	190.00	—
Celery Tray, flat, crimped or straight rim	24.00	—
Claret Jug	60.00	—
Celery Vase	30.00	—
Compote, cov, hs	95.00	—
Condensed Milk Jar, cov	50.00	—
Cordial	42.00	—
Creamer	24.00	—
Cruet, 1 or 2 oz, orig stopper	60.00	—
Cruet, or 4 oz, orig stopper	55.00	—
Cruet, 6 oz, orig stopper	30.00	—
Decanter, pint or quart, orig stopper	55.00	—
Egg Cup, pedestal	24.00	—
Finger Bowl	12.00	—
Goblet, round stem	30.00	—
Ice Cream Dish, 5-1/2" d, straight rim	18.00	—
Ice Cream Tray	36.00	—
Ice Tub, handles	42.00	—
Jug No. 1, No. 2, No. 3 or No. 4	42.00-72.00	—
Jug No. 5, half gallon	85.00	—
Lamp, banquet, tall stem	180.00	—
Nappy, 4" or 9" d	18.00-30.00	—
Plate, 6" or 7" d	18.00	—
Pickle Dish, long	18.00	—
Pitcher, water, bulbous, 6 sizes	72.00	—
Punch Bowl	100.00	—
Punch Cup	10.00	—
Salt Shaker, nickel plated top	18.00	—
Sauce, flat, crimped or smooth, round, 4" or 4-1/2" d	12.00	—
Sauce, flat, crimped or smooth, square, 4" d	15.00	—
Spooner	24.00	—
Sugar Bowl, cov	42.00	—
Sugar, open	25.00	—
Syrup, orig top	55.00	—
Tumbler, flat	18.00	—
Vase, 7", 8" or 9" h	24.00-30.00	—
Water Bottle	42.00	—
Water Tray	36.00	—
Wine	18.00	—
Wine Tray	36.00	—

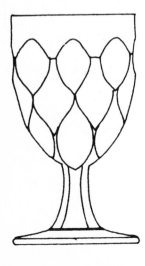

Almond Thumbprint

Pointed Thumbprint, Finger Print

Pattern attributed to Bryce, Bakewell, Pittsburgh, PA, c1865, Bakewell, Pears and Company, Pittsburgh, PA, c1860s in flint. The United States Glass Company, Pittsburgh, PA, issued the pattern in non-flint after 1891. It is an early flint pattern with variants in both flint and non-flint. Made in clear, flint and non-flint. A few milk glass pieces are known.

Items	Flint	Non-Flint
Bowl, flat, 4-1/2" d	—	24.00
Butter Dish, cov	95.00	48.00
Celery Vase	60.00	30.00
Champagne	72.00	42.00
Compote, cov, hs, 10" d	120.00	55.00
Compote, cov, ls, 4-1/2" or 7" d	55.00	36.00
Compote, open, hs, 10-1/2" d	65.00	—
Cordial	55.00	—
Creamer	72.00	48.00
Cruet, ftd, os	55.00	—
Decanter	85.00	—

Items	Flint	Non-Flint
Egg Cup, cov	55.00	30.00
Goblet	50.00	20.00
Jelly Compote, cov, hs, 4-1/2" d	72.00	48.00
Pitcher, water, half gallon	85.00	48.00
Punch Bowl	—	90.00
Salt, individual	18.00	12.00
Salt, master, flat, large	30.00	18.00
Salt, master, ftd, covered	55.00	30.00
Salt, master, ftd, open	30.00	12.00
Spooner	24.00	18.00
Sugar Bowl, cov	72.00	48.00
Sweetmeat Jar, cov	65.00	55.00
Tumbler, flat or footed	72.00	24.00
Wine	25.00	15.00

Amazon

Sawtooth, Sawtooth Band

Manufactured by Bryce Brothers, Pittsburgh, PA, c1890-91. Reissued by United States Glass Company, Pittsburgh, PA, Factory "B," c1891-1904. Made in non-flint, clear, with fern and berry etching or plain. Some pieces were made in clear amber, amethyst, blue, canary-yellow, some with ruby stain. Add 20% for those.

Items	Etched	Plain
Banana Stand, hs	115.00	65.00
Bowl, cov, oval, 6-1/2" l	—	60.00
Bowl, cov, round, 5", 6", 7" or 8" d	30.00-36.00	30.00-36.00
Bowl, cov, round, 9" d	36.00	36.00
Bowl, flared, plain rim, 5", 6", 7" or 8" d	12.00-24.00	
Bowl, scalloped, 4", 4-1/2", 5", 6", 7" or 8" d	—	12.00-30.00
Butter Dish, cov	65.00	60.00
Cake Stand, hs, 8", 9", 9-1/2" or 10" d		48.00-60.00
Celery Vase, flat or ftd	42.00	36.00
Champagne	—	42.00
Child's Butter Dish, cov, flat	60.00	—
Child's Creamer, pedestal	30.00	—
Child's Spooner, pedestal, sawtooth rim	36.00	—
Child's Sugar Bowl, cov, pedestal	36.00	—
Claret	42.00	36.00
Compote, cov, hs, 5", 6", 7" or 8" d	—	55.00-72.00
Compote, open, flared, scalloped rim, deep bowl, 4-1/2", 5", 6", 7" or 8" d	—	30.00-36.00
Compote, open, hs, smooth edge, 9-1/2" d	—	55.00
Compote, open, round, flared bowl, 5", 6", 7", 8" or 9-1/2" d	—	30.00-55.00
Compote, open, saucer bowl, sawtooth rim, 8", 9", or 10" d	—	36.00-55.00
Cordial	48.00	30.00
Creamer	36.00	30.00
Cruet, ftd, os, fist or Maltese cross stopper	60.00	55.00
Dish, cov, oval, flat, lion handles, 6", 7" or 8" l	30.00-42.00	—
Dish, open, flat, lion handles, 6", 7" or 8" l	12.00-24.00	—
Dish, open, round, shallow, lion handles, 4-1/2" or 6" d	24.00	—
Egg Cup	—	20.00
Goblet, 4-1/2", 5" or 6" h	30.00-36.00	30.00-36.00
Jelly Compote, cov, 4-1/2" d	48.00	—
Jelly Compote, open, 4-1/2" d	55.00	42.00
Pitcher, water, half gallon	72.00	55.00
Relish	36.00	30.00
Salt & Pepper Shakers, pr	60.00	48.00
Salt, individual	—	18.00
Salt, master	—	30.00
Sauce, flat, flared bowl, scalloped rim, 4" or 4-1/2" d	—	12.00
Sauce, flat, flared bowl, scalloped rim, handled, 4-1/2" d	—	18.00
Sauce, ftd, 4" or 4-1/2" d	18.00	18.00
Spooner	30.00	24.00
Sugar Bowl, cov	55.00	55.00
Syrup, orig top	60.00	50.00
Tumbler, flat	30.00	30.00
Vase, hs, ruffled rim	24.00	30.00
Wine	30.00	24.00

Anthemion

Albany

Manufactured by Model Flint Glass Company, Findlay, Ohio, c1890-1900 and by Albany Glass Company. Made in clear, amber, and blue. Prices for amber and blue would be 20% more than clear.

Items	Clear
Bowl, square, turned-in edge, 7" w	24.00
Butter Dish, cov	65.00

Items	Clear
Cake Plate, 9-1/2" d	42.00
Cake Stand	48.00
Celery Vase	42.00
Creamer	36.00
Marmalade Jar, cov	55.00
Pitcher, water	60.00
Plate, 10" d	24.00
Sauce	10.00
Spooner	30.00
Sugar Bowl, cov	42.00
Tumbler	30.00

Apollo

Canadian Horseshoe, Frosted Festal Band, Shield Band, Thumbprint and Prisms

Manufactured by Adams & Co., Pittsburgh, PA, c1875-1890 in non-flint. Reissued by United States Glass Company at Factory "A," c1891 to 1899. Made in clear, clear with frosting (acid finish), ruby stained, clear with pale yellow, dark green or blue staining. Some pieces have copper wheel engraving (etching). Frosting increases prices 20%. A lamp in blue or yellow is valued at $250.

Items	Clear
Bowl, open, flat, flared or round, 4", 5", 6", 7" or 8"d	12.00-24.00
Butter Dish, cov	48.00
Cake Stand, hs, 8", 9", 10" or 12" d	42.00-60.00
Celery Tray, rect	24.00
Celery Vase	42.00
Compote, cov, hs, 6" d	65.00
Compote, open, hs, smooth rim, 5", 6", 7" or 8" d	30.00-48.00
Compote, open, ls, smooth rim, 5", 6", 7" or 8" d	24.00-36.00
Creamer	42.00
Cruet, os	72.00
Egg Cup	36.00
Goblet	42.00
Lamp, 10" h	130.00
Pickle Dish	18.00
Pitcher, milk or water, bulbous, 1 quart; half gallon or gallon	65.00
Pitcher, water, tankard, gallon	90.00
Plate, 9-1/2" w, sq	30.00
Salad Bowl, scalloped rim	18.00
Salt, master, flat	24.00
Salt Shaker	30.00
Sauce, flat, 3-1/2" d	10.00
Sauce, flat or footed, 4" d	12.00
Sauce, footed, 5" d	15.00
Spooner	36.00
Sugar Bowl, cov, ftd	55.00
Sugar Shaker, orig top	55.00
Syrup, orig top	135.00
Tumbler	36.00
Vase	18.00
Water Tray	55.00
Wine	42.00

Arabesque

Manufactured by Bakewell, Pears and Company, Pittsburgh, PA, c1870. Made in clear, non-flint.

Items	Clear
Butter Dish, cov	60.00
Celery	48.00
Compote, cov, hs, 8" d	72.00
Compote, cov, ls, 8" d	60.00
Creamer, ah	55.00
Goblet φ	42.00
Pitcher, water, ah	90.00
Spooner	30.00
Sugar Bowl, cov	55.00
Sugar, open, buttermilk type	30.00

Arched Fleur-De-Lis

Late Fleur De-Lis

Manufactured by Bryce, Higbee and Company, c1897-88. Made in clear, clear with gilding, and ruby stained.

Items	Clear	Ruby Stained
Banana Stand	42.00	180.00
Bowl, oval, 9" l	110.00	—
Butter Dish, cov	48.00	142.00
Cake Stand	42.00	—
Creamer	36.00	72.00
Dish, shallow, 7" l	15.00	30.00
Jelly Compote	24.00	
Mug, 3-1/4" h	24.00	48.00
Olive, handle	18.00	—
Pitcher, water	130.00	360.00
Plate, square, 7" w	15.00	410.00
Relish, 8" l	18.00	—
Salt Shaker	110.00	55.00
Sauce	10.00	24.00
Spooner, double handles	24.00	65.00
Sugar Bowl, cov, double handles	42.00	120.00
Toothpick Holder	36.00	120.00
Tumbler	18.00	55.00
Vase, 10" h	42.00	90.00
Wine	30.00	65.00

Arched Grape

Manufactured by Boston and Sandwich Glass Co., Sandwich, MA, c1870. Also attributed to the Burlington Glass Works, Hamilton, Ontario, Canada. Made in clear, both flint and non-flint. Flint prices are 25% higher.

Items	Clear
Butter Dish, cov	55.00
Celery Vase	42.00
Champagne	42.00
Compote, cov, hs	60.00
Creamer	48.00
Goblet	30.00
Pitcher, water, ah	72.00
Sauce, flat	10.00
Spooner	36.00
Sugar Bowl, cov	55.00
Wine	30.00

Argus

Manufactured by Bakewell, Pears, and Company, Pittsburgh, PA, in the 1880s in flint. Earliest flint pieces have polished pontils. Made in clear, flint.

Reproductions: Copiously reproduced, some by Fostoria Glass Company, c1963-82. Some forms have a raised mark "HFM," which is the trademark for Henry Ford Museum, Dearborn, MI. Reproduction colors include clear, cobalt blue, green, and red. Forms include reproductions of covered compotes, tumblers, etc., plus pieces not originally made in the pattern, such as plates and sherbets.

Items	Clear
Ale Glass, ftd, 5-1/2" h	90.00
Beer Glass	90.00
Bitters Bottle	72.00
Bowl, cov, low collared base, 6" d	110.00
Bowl, open, flat, 5-1/2" d	36.00
Butter Dish, cov, ftd	85.00
Celery Vase, pedestal	110.00
Champagne, barrel shaped or flared bowl	65.00
Compote, cov, hs, 6" d	72.00
Compote, cov, hs, 8" d, 14" h, patterned foot	240.00
Compote, cov, hs, 8" d, 14-7/8" h	120.00
Compote, cov, hs, 9" d	180.00
Compote, cov, ls, 6" or 9" d	60.00-110.00
Compote, open, 6" d, 4-1/2" h	60.00
Compote, open, scalloped rim, 10-3/8" d	85.00
Cordial	55.00
Creamer, ah φ	120.00
Decanter, pint	90.00
Decanter, quart	85.00
Egg Cup, applied handle, ftd	95.00

Items	Clear
Egg Cup, without handle	36.00
Goblet φ	48.00
Honey Dish, flat	24.00
Lamp, oil, collared base, 4" h	72.00
Lamp, oil, footed	120.00
Mug, ah	85.00
Paperweight, solid	115.00
Pickle Jar	72.00
Pitcher, water, ah	270.00
Punch Bowl, scalloped rim, pedestal, 11-1/2" d	270.00
Punch Bowl, scalloped rim, pedestal, 14-1/4" d	245.00
Salt, individual, flat	30.00
Salt, master, open	36.00
Spooner	55.00
Sugar Bowl, cov φ	65.00
Tumbler, flat, bar type φ	65.00
Tumbler, flat, half pint	72.00
Tumbler, footed, 4" h	50.00
Tumbler, footed, 5" h	60.00
Whiskey, ah	90.00
Wine, 4" h φ	42.00

Art

Jacob's Tears, Job's Tears, Teardrop and Diamond Block

Manufactured by Adams & Company, Pittsburgh, PA, in the 1880s. Reissued by United States Glass Company, in the early 1890s. Made in non-flint clear and ruby stained.

Reproductions: A covered compote has been made in opaque milk white glass.

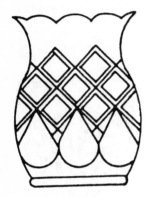

Items	Clear	Ruby Stained
Banana Stand, hs, 10" d	115.00	190.00
Biscuit Jar, cov	142.00	190.00
Berry Bowl, master, one end pointed, 8" l	60.00	85.00
Bowl, cov, collared base, belled, 6" or 7" d	36.00	—
Bowl, cov, collared base, flared rim, 6", 7" or 8" d	36.00	—
Bowl, open, collared base, flared rim, 7", 8", 9" or 10" d	42.00-48.00	—
Bowl, open, flat, flared rim, 7", 8", 8-1/2", 9" or 10" d	30.00-48.00	—
Bowl, open, footed, 6" d, 3-1/4" h	36.00	—
Bowl, low, collar base, 7" d	42.00	—
Butter Dish, cov	60.00	85.00
Cake Stand, hs, 7", 9", 10" or 10-1/2" d	55.00-65.00	—
Celery Vase	48.00	120.00
Compote, cov, hs, 6" d	55.00	120.00
Compote, cov, hs, 7" h φ	120.00	225.00
Compote, cov, hs, 8" d	60.00	225.00
Compote, open, hs, belled, 6", 7" or 8" d	48.00-60.00	—
Compote, open, hs, round bowl, 6", 7", 8", 9", 9-1/2" or 10" d	48.00-65.00	—
Compote, open, hs, shallow bowl, scalloped, 8", 9" or 10" d	55.00	—
Creamer, hotel type, large	55.00	110.00
Creamer, table	55.00	120.00
Creamer, tankard	60.00	55.00
Cruet, os, ah	130.00	300.00
Dresser Set	130.00	—
Fruit Basket, hs, 10" d	110.00	—
Goblet	510.00	—
Mug	55.00	—
Pickle Dish, flat, rect	30.00	48.00
Pitcher, milk	118.00	190.00
Pitcher, water, bulbous, half gallon	85.00	—
Pitcher, water, squatty, 2-1/2 quarts	120.00	—
Plate, 10" d	48.00	—
Preserve Dish, oblong, 8" l	42.00	—
Relish Tray, 7-3/4" x 4-1/4"	24.00	55.00
Sauce, flat or ftd, scalloped, 4" or 4-1/2" d	18.00	—
Sauce, pointed end, 4" or 4-1/2" d	20.00	—
Spooner	30.00	85.00
Sugar Bowl, cov, hotel or table size	55.00	130.00
Tumbler	55.00	—
Vinegar Jug, half pint	55.00	—
Vinegar Jug, 3 pint	90.00	—
Wine	175.00	—

Artichoke

Frosted Artichoke, Valencia

Manufactured by Fostoria Glass Company, Moundsville, WV, in 1891. Made in non-flint, clear, and frosted. Add 50% for frosted values. Limited production in opalescent and satin glass.

Reproductions: A goblet was not originally made in this pattern. However, L. G. Wright Glass Company, New Martinsville, WV, created a goblet.

Items	Clear
Bobeche	42.00
Bowl, 8" d	36.00
Butter Dish, cov	60.00
Cake Stand	50.00
Celery Vase	42.00
Compote, cov, hs	110.00
Creamer	42.00
Finger Bowl, underplate	48.00
Miniature Lamp	300.00
Pitcher, water	110.00
Rose Bowl	42.00
Sauce, flat	10.00
Spooner	30.00
Sugar Bowl, cov	55.00
Syrup, orig top	85.00
Tumbler	42.00
Water Tray	55.00

Ashburton

Barrel Ashburton, Chocked Ashburton, Dillaway, Double Flute, Double Knob Stem Ashburton, Flaring Top Ashburton, Giant Straight Stemmed Ashburton, Large Thumbprint, Near Slim Ashburton, Proxy Ashburton, Semi-Squared Ashburton, Short Ashburton, Slim Ashburton, Tailsman Ashburton

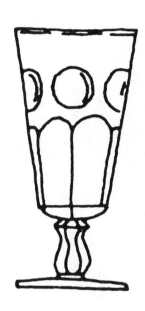

Manufactured by several companies: Bakewell Pears & Company, Pittsburgh, PA, c1875; Bellaire Goblet Company, Findlay, OH, (United States Glass Company) after 1891; Boston and Sandwich Glass Company, Sandwich, MA, c1848; Bryce, Richards & Company, Pittsburgh, PA, c1854; Bryce McKee & Company, Pittsburgh, PA, c1854; New England Glass Company, East Cambridge, MA, c1868-69. Shards have been found at the Burlington Glass Works, Hamilton, Ontario, Canada. Made in flint and non-flint. Prices listed here are for flint. Non-flint values would be 65% less. Some scarce pieces are known in color, an amber handled whiskey mug, a flint canary celery vase ($750), and a scarce emerald green wine glass ($200). A few pieces are known in fiery opalescent and are quite rare.

Reproductions: Numerous reproductions of Ashburton have been made. Some from old molds, some from new molds. Reproductions can be found in clear and colors. The Imperial glass Company was authorized by the Metropolitan Museum of Art, New York City, to reissue the following pieces with their mark of "M.M.A.": goblet, quart jug, lemonade glass, covered sugar. They also made a cornflower blue goblet with both the mark and a paper label. The L. G. Wright Company, New Martinsville, WV, reissued Ashburton in amber, Bermuda blue, clear, and green starting in 1967. The forms made include: low flared bowl, low candlestick, claret, high standard compote, creamer with a pressed handle, water pitcher with pressed handle, covered sugar bowl, and flat tumbler. The Westmoreland Glass Company, Grapeville, PA, c1966-83, created the following pieces in 1977-1978, in brown, clear, olive-green, and pink: ashtray, cake stand, candlestick, claret, covered and open compotes, creamer, goblet, water pitcher, sherbet, covered sugar bowl, old fashioned tumbler, ftd ice tea tumbler, and wine. The Libbey Glass Company, Toledo, OH, c1981, issued color and amber examples of ashtrays, bowls, goblets, salt shakers, sherbets, wines, and several sizes of tumblers. Other museums to authorize reproductions are the Smithsonian Institution, Washington, DC, the Henry Ford Museum, Dearborn, MI, and the Sandwich Glass Museum, Sandwich, MA. Each has then sold the glassware through their gift shops and catalogs. Reproduction handles tend to be pressed, rather than applied.

Items	Flint
Ale Glass, 5" h	110.00
Ale Glass, 6-1/2" h	72.00
Bar Bottle, pint or quart	55.00-90.00
Bitters Bottle	55.00
Bowl, 6-1/2" d φ	90.00
Butter Dish, cov (2 styles)	85.00
Carafe	190.00
Celery Vase, scalloped top	130.00
Celery Vase, smooth top	95.00
Champagne, flared bowl or straight bowl, cut ovals	90.00
Claret, 5-1/4" h φ	60.00
Compote, open, ls, 7-1/2"	65.00
Cordial, flared or round bowl, 4-1/4" h	90.00
Creamer, ah	255.00
Decanter, bar lip, pint or quart	190.00-300.00
Decanter, bar lip, three pints	190.00
Decanter, cut or pressed, os, half pint or pint	190.00
Decanter, cut or pressed, os, quart	300.00
Decanter, cut or pressed, os, three pints	240.00
Egg Cup, double	115.00
Egg Cup, single	30.00
Flip Glass, handle	190.00

Items	Flint
Goblet, engraved panels	55.00
Goblet, flared or straight sides φ	48.00
Honey Dish, 3-5/8" d	18.00
Jug, quart φ	110.00
Lamp	90.00
Lemonade Glass φ	55.00
Mug, 7" h	120.00
Pitcher, milk	450.00
Pitcher, water, ah	650.00
Plate, 6-5/8" d	90.00
Sauce, flat, 4-1/4" d	12.00
Spooner (2 sizes)	48.00
Sugar Bowl, cov, large φ	110.00
Sugar Bowl, cov, small φ	95.00
Toddy Jar, cov	390.00
Tumbler, bar	90.00
Tumbler, ship, half pint	55.00
Tumbler, soda	48.00
Tumbler, water φ	90.00
Tumbler, whiskey	72.00
Vase, plain top, 10-1/2" h	120.00
Water Bottle, tumble-up	115.00
Whiskey, ah	130.00
Wine, cut	65.00
Wine, pressed, flared or round bowl	48.00

Ashman

Manufactured by unknown companies, c1880. Made in clear, with some amber and blue. Pattern is distinctive in its squared shape. Flowers are sometimes found within the large ball-type finial on the butter dish.

Items	Clear
Bread Tray, motto	55.00
Bowl	24.00
Butter Dish, cov, conventional finial	310.00
Butter Dish, cov, large ball-type finial	60.00
Cake Stand, 9" d	48.00
Compote, cov, hs, 9" h or 12" d	115.00
Compote, open, hs	39.00
Creamer	42.00
Goblet	42.00
Pitcher, water, ah	65.00
Relish	18.00
Spooner	48.00
Sugar Bowl, cov	55.00
Tumbler	30.00
Water Tray	48.00
Wine	30.00

Atlanta

Clear Lion Head, Fostoria's No.500, Frosted Atlanta, Late Lion, Square Lion, Square Lion Heads

Manufactured by the Fostoria Glass Company, Moundsville, WV, c1895 to 1900. Made in non-flint clear, frosted, amber stained, ruby stained, and milk glass. Pieces are usually square in shape.

Reproductions: The goblet has been reproduced in clear, c1960.

Items	Clear	Frosted
Banana Stand, hs, folded sides	95.00	120.00
Bowl, scallop rim, 6" or 7" d	60.00-72.00	65.00-90.00
Bowl, low collar base, 8" d	55.00	85.00
Bowl, scallop rim, 8" d	72.00	85.00
Butter Dish, cov	85.00	130.00
Cake Stand, hs, sq, 9-1/4" w	115.00	148.00
Cake Stand, hs, sq, 10" w	115.00	135.00
Celery Vase	55.00	90.00
Compote, cov, hs, sq, 4-1/2", 5", 7", or 8" w, 9-1/2" h w	55.00-135.00	65.00-180.00
Compote, open, hs, scalloped, sq, 5" or 7" w	55.00-90.00	85.00-135.00
Compote, open, ls, scalloped	55.00	85.00
Creamer	60.00	65.00
Cruet, os	130.00	180.00
Egg Cup	30.00	36.00
Goblet φ	60.00	72.00
Jelly Compote, open, hs, 5" d	55.00	65.00
Marmalade Jar, cov	90.00	85.00
Pitcher, water, half gallon	130.00	190.00
Relish, oval	42.00	48.00
Salt and Pepper Shakers, pr	120.00	130.00

Items	Clear	Frosted
Salt, individual	36.00	48.00
Salt, master	60.00	85.00
Sauce, 4" d	30.00	30.00
Spooner	60.00	72.00
Sugar Bowl, cov	85.00	120.00
Syrup, orig top	180.00	240.00
Toothpick Holder	55.00	72.00
Tumbler	55.00	55.00
Wine	48.00	65.00

Atlas

Bullet, Cannon Ball, Crystal Ball, Knobby Bottom

Manufactured by Bryce Brothers, Pittsburgh, PA, c1889. Production continued by United States Glass Company at Factory "A" and Factory "B" from 1891 to 1904. The design was created and patented by Henry J. Smith of Bryce Brothers on Nov. 12, 1889. Made in non-flint, clear and clear with ruby staining.

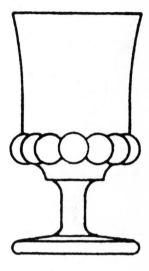

Items	Clear	Ruby Stained
Bowl, 9" d	24.00	—
Butter Dish, cov	55.00	90.00
Cake Stand, 8" d	42.00	—
Cake Stand, 9" d	48.00	115.00
Celery Vase	210.00	—
Champagne, 5-1/2" h	42.00	55.00
Compote, cov, hs, 8" d	65.00	—
Compote, open, ls, 7" d	48.00	—
Cordial	42.00	—
Creamer, table, ah	36.00	55.00
Creamer, tankard	30.00	—
Jelly Compote, cov, hs, 5" h	60.00	95.00
Goblet	55.00	65.00
Marmalade Jar, cov	55.00	—
Molasses Can	65.00	—
Pitcher, water	65.00	—
Salt and Pepper Shakers, pr	24.00	—
Salt, individual	18.00	—
Salt, master	24.00	—
Sauce, flat	12.00	—
Sauce, footed	18.00	30.00
Spooner	36.00	30.00
Sugar Bowl, cov	48.00	65.00
Syrup, orig top	65.00	—
Toothpick Holder	24.00	60.00
Tumbler	210.00	—
Water Tray	90.00	—
Whiskey	24.00	55.00
Wine	30.00	—

Aurora

Brilliant's Aurora, Diamond Horseshoe, Diamond Horse Shoe

Manufactured by the Brilliant Glass Works, 1888-1902. This company was acquired by the Greensburg Glass Company, which then continued the pattern. McKee & Brothers Glass Company, Pittsburgh, PA, c1902, made the pattern in chocolate glass only and in limited production. Pioneer Glass Company, Pittsburgh, PA, is credited with the ruby stain decoration. Made in clear and ruby stained. Also found with etching.

Items	Clear	Ruby Stained
Bowl, 5" or 6" d	12.00	24.00
Bread Plate, round, large star in center, 10" d	36.00	72.00
Bread Plate, round, plain center, 10" d	36.00	55.00
Butter Dish, cov	55.00	110.00
Cake Stand, hs	42.00	85.00
Celery Vase	42.00	72.00
Compote, cov, hs, 6" d	65.00	135.00
Compote, cov, hs, 7" d	65.00	115.00
Compote, cov, hs, 8" d	85.00	130.00
Compote, open, hs, 6", 7" or 8" d	24.00-30.00	36.00-55.00
Creamer	42.00	60.00
Decanter, os, 11-3/4" h	90.00	142.00
Goblet	60.00	65.00
Mug, handle	60.00	85.00
Olive, oval	24.00	42.00
Pickle Dish, fish shape	18.00	30.00
Pitcher, milk or water, quart or half gallon	48.00	120.00
Relish Scoop, handle	12.00	30.00
Salt and Pepper Shakers, pr	55.00	95.00
Sauce, flat or footed, sq, 4" w	10.00	18.00

Items	Clear	Ruby Stained
Spooner	30.00	410.00
Sugar Bowl, cov	55.00	65.00
Tumbler	30.00	55.00
Waste Bowl	36.00	55.00
Water Tray	55.00	65.00
Wine	30.00	60.00
Wine Tray	42.00	72.00

Austrian

Federal's No. 110, Finecut Medallion, Indiana Glass No. 200, Paneled Oval Fine Cut, Western

Manufactured by Indiana Tumbler and Goblet Company, Greentown, IN, 1897. Also made by Indiana Glass Company, Dunkirk, IN, c1907 and Federal Glass Company, Columbus, OH, c1914. Made in amber, canary, clear, clear with gilt trim, and emerald green. Experimental pieces were made in cobalt blue, and opaque colors, such as chocolate and Nile green. A Nile green 6" h vase is valued at $375.

Items	Amber	Canary	Clear	Emerald Green
Banana Stand, hs	—	—	155.00	—
Bowl, 8" d	—	180.00	55.00	—
Bowl, 7-1/4" l, 5" w, rect	—	225.00	55.00	—
Bowl, 8-3/4" l, 5-1/4" w, rect	—	—	65.00	—
Butter Dish, cov	225.00	360.00	110.00	—
Cake Stand	—	350.00	150.00	—
Child's Butter Dish, cov	—	240.00	130.00	—
Child's Creamer, 4" h	190.00	120.00	55.00	—
Child's Mug	—	—	55.00	—
Child's Spooner	—	110.00	60.00	—
Child's Sugar Bowl, cov	—	155.00	110.00	—
Compote, open, hs, 4-1/4" h	—	225.00	65.00	—
Compote, open, hs, 8" d	—	325.00	90.00	—
Compote, open, ls	—	250.00	100.00	—
Cordial	155.00	180.00	65.00	180.00
Creamer, cov, 4-1/4" h	124.00	130.00	48.00	124.00
Creamer, open, large	—	115.00	55.00	—
Creamer, open, small, pedestal	—	85.00	48.00	—
Goblet	—	180.00	48.00	—
Nappy, cov	—	142.00	55.00	—
Pitcher, water, ah	—	360.00	120.00	—
Plate, 10" d	—	—	48.00	—
Punch Cup	180.00	180.00	110.00	130.00
Rose Bowl, large	—	190.00	90.00	—
Rose Bowl, medium	—	—	90.00	—
Rose Bowl, small	—	180.00	60.00	—
Salt Shaker, orig top	—	90.00	48.00	—
Sauce, flat, 4-1/4" d	—	—	30.00	—
Sauce, flat, 4-5/8" d	—	60.00	24.00	—
Spooner	—	120.00	48.00	—
Sugar Bowl, cov, 2-1/2" d	—	85.00	30.00	—
Sugar Bowl, cov, 4" d	—	190.00	55.00	—
Tumbler	190.00	180.00	36.00	—
Vase, 6" h	250.00	145.00	55.00	250.00
Vase, 8" h	—	190.00	55.00	—
Vase, 10" d	—	270.00	90.00	—
Wine	190.00	180.00	36.00	180.00

Aztec

New Mexico

Manufactured by McKee & Brothers, Jeannette, PA, c1894 to 1915. It is considered to be a late imitation cut-glass pattern. Pieces are often found marked "PRES-CUT" in a circle on the base. This extensive pattern contains about seventy-five different forms. Made in clear and some milk white pieces.

Reproductions: Tiffin Glass Company, Tiffin, OH, produced a punch bowl set, c1955. This non-flint version does have the Pres-Cut trademark. The punch cups have a less flared shape. The Jeannette Glass Company, Jeannette, PA, issued two punch bowl sets, c1966. This punch bowl set also is reputed to be from the original molds. L. E. Smith, Mt. Pleasant, PA, reproduced the punch bowl from an original mold, but removed the Pres-Cut trademark, c1981. The Fenton Art Glass Company, Williamstown, WV, reproduced the toothpick from the original McKee mold in 1987. It was created as a limited edition for the Fenton Art Glass Collectors of America for their annual convention. The Fenton logo has replaced the McKee trademark. Also, John E. Kemple Glass Works, East Palestine, OH, and Kenova, WV, and the Summit Art Glass Co., Mogadore, OH, have reproduced items, renaming their pattern "Whirling Star."

Items	Clear
Berry Bowl	18.00
Bon Bon, ftd, 7" d	18.00

Items	Clear
Bowl, deep, flared, scalloped, 9" or 10-1/2" d	24.00
Bowl, deep, scalloped, 7" or 8" d	18.00
Bowl, deep, triangular, scalloped, 7" or 8" d	24.00
Bowl, shallow, scalloped, 7", 8" or 10-1/2" d	18.00
Butter Dish, cov, round or sq scalloped base φ	48.00
Cake Plate, trilobed	24.00
Cake Stand	36.00
Candlestick	36.00
Carafe, water	48.00
Celery Tray, 11" l	18.00
Celery Vase, 5-1/4" h	110.00
Champagne	30.00
Cologne Bottle, globular	30.00
Cologne Bottle, tall	36.00
Compote, open, hs	36.00
Condensed Milk Jar, notched lid	24.00
Cordial, 3/4 or 1 ounce	24.00
Cracker jar, cov	60.00
Creamer, individual	18.00
Creamer, regular φ	30.00
Creamer, tankard	36.00
Cruet, os	42.00
Crushed Fruit Bowl, cov, 8-1/2" d	90.00
Custard Cup	10.00
Decanter, cut stopper	40.00
Dish, flat, handle, round, sq or triangular, 5" d	18.00
Egg Nog Bowl, 2 part, flat base, 2 quart, 10-1/2" d	30.00
Finger Bowl, underplate	24.00
Goblet	30.00
Iced Tea Tumbler	30.00
Jug, ah, squatty or tall, half gallon	42.00
Lamp, 18-1/4" h	90.00
Lemonade Pitcher, half gallon	42.00
Lemon Bowl, 2 part, pedestal base, 2 quart, 10-1/2" d	30.00
Marmalade Jar, cov, ftd	24.00
Olive Tray	18.00
Pickle Jar	24.00
Pickle Tray	18.00
Pitcher, water, ah or ph, tankard, half gallon	42.00
Plate	24.00
Punch Bowl φ	90.00
Punch Cup φ	6.00
Punch Set, bowl, stand, 12 cups	130.00
Relish Tray	18.00
Rose Bowl, 4-1/2" d	18.00
Rose Bowl, 7" d	24.00
Rose Jar	30.00
Salt and Pepper Shakers, pr, bulbous or tall	42.00
Sauce, flat, round, scalloped, 4" or 4-1/2" d	12.00
Sauce, heart shape, scalloped	18.00
Sauce, triangular, deep, 4-1/2" d	12.00
Sherbet, ftd	30.00
Soda Fountain Accessory, crushed fruit jar	55.00
Soda Fountain Accessory, straw holder, glass lid	65.00
Spooner	18.00
Sugar Bowl, cov, scalloped or smooth rim	30.00
Sugar Bowl, open, scalloped rim, handle	30.00
Syrup, orig nickel or silver plated top	60.00
Toothpick Holder φ	30.00
Tumbler, water	24.00
Vase, 10" h, scalloped rim	24.00
Whiskey	15.00
Whiskey Jug, os, handle	30.00
Wine, 2 or 3 ounce	18.00

Baby Face

Cupid

Manufactured by McKee & Brothers Glass Company, Pittsburgh, PA, in the late 1870s. Made in non-flint clear with acid finished finials and stems. Forms are found plain or with copper wheel engravings.

Reproductions: Several forms in this pattern have been reproduced. To tell the difference between period and reproduction pieces, remember that the reproductions tend to be heavier, the finials and stems poorly molded and the frosting tends to be satin-like and uneven. Another clue is that the details of the baby's face are less life-like and do not exhibit the fine craftsmanship of the originals.

Items	Clear
Butter Dish, cov	300.00
Celery Vase	75.00
Champagne	120.00
Compote, cov, hs, 5-1/4" d φ, 7" or 8" d	225.00-300.00
Compote, open, ls, 7" or 8" d	115.00-120.00

Items	Clear
Cordial	120.00
Creamer	135.00
Goblet φ	120.00
Pitcher, water	360.00
Salt	60.00
Spooner	115.00
Sugar Bowl, cov φ	1,115.00
Wine φ	172.00

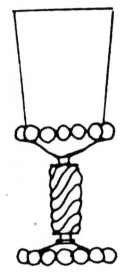

Ball and Swirl

Swirl and Ball

Manufactured by McKee Glass Company, Jeannette, PA, c1894. Made in non-flint, clear.

Reproductions: Reproductions were made by Westmoreland Glass Company, Grapeville, PA, and are known as No. 1842. Some of the reproductions are marked "WG," or have a paper label. Many are not marked. Since McKee only made this pattern in clear, the Westmoreland colored wares in amber, amethyst, blue, cerise, crimson mother-of-pearl, green marble slag, milk glass, purple carnival, and purple marble slag are easy to spot as reproductions. It's the clear Westmoreland that is hardest for collectors to distinguish from the original clear production.

Items	Clear
Butter Dish, cov	42.00
Cake Plate, flat	48.00
Cake Stand, hs φ	42.00
Candlesticks, pr φ	95.00
Compote, cov, hs, 9" d, 7-1/2" h	60.00
Compote, open, hs, 9" d, 8-1/2" h	36.00
Cordial	24.00
Cordial Tray	42.00
Creamer φ	24.00
Decanter φ	60.00
Finger Bowl	18.00
Goblet φ	24.00
Jelly Compote, open, hs	36.00
Ice Tea Tumbler, handle	18.00
Mug, small to large	12.00-18.00
Pitcher, milk, quart, tankard	60.00
Pitcher, water, half gallon, bulbous φ	48.00
Pitcher, water, half gallon, tankard	60.00
Salt and Pepper Shakers, pr	48.00
Sauce, footed	12.00
Spooner	24.00
Sugar Bowl, cov φ	30.00
Syrup, orig top	48.00
Tumbler φ	18.00
Wine φ	24.00

Baltimore Pear

Double Pear, Fig, Gipsy, Maryland Pear, Twin Pear

Manufactured originally by Adams & Company, Pittsburgh, PA, in 1874. Reissued by United States Glass Company in the 1890s, at Factory "A." There are eighteen different size compotes. Some forms were given as premiums by different manufacturers and organizations. Made in non-flint, clear.

Reproductions: Heavily reproduced in clear and cobalt blue, with the first reproductions documented in the 1930s. Imperial Glass, Jeannette Glass Company, and Westmoreland Glass Company all were making reproductions by the 1950s.

Items	Clear
Bowl, cov, 5", 6", 7", 8" or 9" d	42.00-60.00
Bowl, open, 5", 6", 7", 8" or 9" d	30.00-42.00
Bread Plate, 12-1/2" d	85.00
Butter Dish, cov φ	75.00
Cake Plate, flat	55.00
Cake Stand, 9" or 10" d φ	66.00
Celery Vase φ	60.00
Compote, cov, hs, 5", 6", 7", 8" or 8-1/2" d	55.00-95.00
Compote, cov, ls, 5", 6", 7" or 8-1/2" d	42.00-55.00
Compote, open, hs, 5", 6", 7" or 8" d	36.00-42.00
Compote, open, ls, 5", 6", 7", 8" or 8-1/2" d	24.00-42.00
Creamer φ	36.00
Goblet φ	42.00
Honey Dish, octagonal, 3-1/2" d	18.00
Honey Dish, round, 3-1/2" d, flat or footed	12.00
Jelly Compote, open	30.00

Items	Clear
Pickle	24.00
Pitcher, milk φ	95.00
Pitcher, water φ	115.00
Plate, 8-1/2" d	36.00
Plate, 9" d φ or 10" d φ	42.00-48.00
Relish	24.00
Sauce, flat φ	10.00
Sauce, footed	18.00
Spooner	48.00
Sugar Bowl, cov φ	60.00
Tray, 10-1/2" d φ	42.00

Banded Buckle

Union

Manufactured by King, Son, and Company, Pittsburgh, PA c1875. Made in non-flint, clear.

Items	Clear
Bowl	30.00
Butter Dish, cov	85.00
Compote, cov, ls, 6" d	85.00
Compote, open, ls, 7" d	55.00
Cordial	42.00
Creamer, ftd, ah	85.00
Egg Cup	60.00
Goblet	60.00
Marmalade Jar, cov	60.00
Pickle Dish	36.00
Pitcher, water, half gallon	42.00
Salt, master, flat or ftd	30.00
Spooner	42.00
Sugar Bowl, cov	60.00
Syrup, ah, orig top	190.00
Tumbler	60.00
Wine	42.00

Banded Portland

Virginia #1, Maiden's Blush

Manufactured originally as Virginia by Portland Glass Company, Portland, ME. It is considered to be one of the States Series. Made in clear and clear with painted decoration in fired-on green, yellow, blue, and possibly pink, ruby stained, and rose stained. Glass Researcher Ruth Webb Lee refers to the rose staining as Maiden's Blush. Double flashed refers to color above and below the center band. Single flashed refers to color above or below the band only.

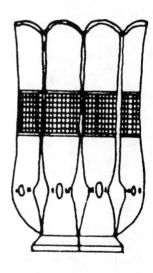

Items	Clear	Color Flashed	Maiden's Blush
Bon Bon, oval, flared, pointed ends, 5-1/2" l		24.00	—36.00
Bowl, cov, 6", 7" or 8" d	48.00-60.00	—	55.00-75.00
Bowl, open, shallow, 7-1/2", 8-1/2" or 9-1/2" d		36.00-42.00	—55.00-72.00
Bowl, open, straight sides, 6", 7" or 8" d	30.00-42.00	—	55.00-60.00
Butter Dish, cov	60.00	165.00	85.00
Cake Stand, hs	55.00	—	110.00
Candlesticks, pr	95.00	—	130.00
Carafe	95.00	—	110.00
Celery Tray	30.00	—	48.00
Celery Vase	42.00	—	55.00
Cologne Bottle, large	60.00	66.00	85.00
Cologne Bottle, small, 4 oz	48.00	—	75.00
Compote, cov, hs, 7" d	85.00	—	130.00
Compote, cov, hs, 8" d	75.00	—	118.00
Compote, open, hs, scalloped, flared, 6", 7" or 8" d	30.00-42.00	—	48.00-60.00
Compote, open, hs, straight sided, 6", 7" or 8" d	30.00-48.00	—	48.00-60.00
Creamer, individual, oval	30.00	42.00	48.00
Creamer, individual, tankard	30.00	—	48.00
Creamer, table, 6 oz	42.00	55.00	60.00
Cruet, os	55.00	55.00	66.00
Decanter, handle	72.00	110.00	130.00
Dresser Tray	60.00	—	120.00
Goblet	48.00	55.00	66.00
Jelly Compote, cov, 6" d	48.00	66.00	110.00
Lamp, oil, flat	55.00	—	—
Lamp, oil, tall	60.00	—	—
Marmalade, orig notched cover, ftd, 4-1/2" d	48.00	—	55.00
Match Holder	48.00	—	55.00

Items	Clear	Color Flashed	Maiden's Blush
Nappy, sq	18.00	55.00	66.00
Olive	110.00	—	42.00
Pin Tray	110.00	—	30.00
Pitcher, water, half gallon, tankard	75.00	115.00	248.00
Pomade Jar, cov	42.00	55.00	85.00
Puff Box, orig glass cover	48.00	—	55.00
Punch Bowl, hs	135.00	—	360.00
Punch Cup	24.00	—	36.00
Relish, 6-1/2" l	30.00	36.00	24.00
Relish, 8-1/4" l	24.00	42.00	48.00
Ring Holder	75.00	—	130.00
Salt and Pepper Shakers, pr	55.00	75.00	75.00
Sardine Box, cov	55.00	—	110.00
Sauce, oval, round, or square, flat, 4" d or 4-1/2" d	12.00	—	24.00
Spooner	210.00	—	55.00
Sugar Bowl, cov, table size	410.00	75.00	75.00
Sugar Bowl, open, individual size	30.00	—	48.00
Sugar Shaker, orig top	55.00	—	85.00
Sweetmeat Compote, cov, hs, 7" d	85.00	—	124.00
Syrup, orig top	60.00	—	142.00
Toothpick Holder	48.00	55.00	55.00
Tumbler	35.00	—	65.00
Vase, 6" h	24.00	—	310.00
Vase, 9" h	42.00	—	60.00
Wine	42.00	—	75.00

Barberry

Berry, Olive, Pepper Berry

Manufactured by McKee & Brothers Glass Company, Pittsburgh, PA, in the 1880s. Made in non-flint, clear. The 6" plates have been found in amber, canary, pale green, and pale blue and are considered scarce. The pattern has either nine berries in a bunch or twelve berries in a bunch.

Items	Clear
Bowl, cov, 6" or 8" d	48.00-55.00
Bowl, open, oval, 6", 7" or 9"l	24.00-40.00
Bowl, open, oval, 8" l	210.00
Bowl, open, round, flat, 8" d	36.00
Butter Dish, cov	60.00
Butter Dish, cov, flange, pattern on edge	95.00
Cake Stand	110.00
Celery Vase	48.00
Compote, cov, hs, 6", 7" or 8" d, shell finial	66.00-85.00
Compote, cov, ls, 6", 7" or 8" d, shell finial	66.00-75.00
Compote, open, hs, 7" or 8" d	36.00-42.00
Compote, open, ls, 7" or 8" d	36.00-42.00
Cordial	48.00
Creamer	36.00
Cup Plate	18.00
Egg Cup	110.00
Goblet	24.00
Honey Dish, flat, round	18.00
Pickle	12.00
Pitcher, water, bulbous, half gallon	120.00
Salt, master, ftd	24.00
Sauce, flat	12.00
Sauce, footed	18.00
Spooner, ftd	36.00
Sugar Bowl, cov	55.00
Syrup, orig top	18.00
Tumbler, ftd	30.00
Wine	30.00

Barley

Sprig

Manufactured by Campbell, Jones and Company, c1882. Since quality varies greatly, it is assumed other manufacturers may have also made this pattern. Made in non-flint, clear. Add 100% for color, which is hard to find.

Items	Clear
Berry Bowl, 8" d	18.00
Bowl, oval, 10" l	18.00
Bread Tray	36.00
Butter Dish, cov	55.00

Items	Clear
Cake Stand, hs, 8", 9" or 9-1/2" d	36.00-42.00
Cake Stand, hs, 10" d	30.00
Celery Vase	30.00
Compote, cov, hs or ls, 6" d	55.00
Compote, cov, hs or ls, 8-1/2" d	72.00
Compote, cov, ls, 8-1/2" d	72.00
Compote, open, hs, 8-1/2" d	30.00
Cordial	60.00
Creamer	36.00
Goblet	42.00
Honey Dish, ftd, 3-1/2" d	10.00
Marmalade Jar, cov	66.00
Pickle Castor, silver plated frame	85.00
Pickle Dish	12.00
Pitcher, water, applied handle	120.00
Pitcher, water, pressed handle	55.00
Plate, 6" d	42.00
Platter, 13" l, 8" w	36.00
Relish, flat, 8" x 6"	24.00
Relish, wheelbarrow shape, large, 8"	36.00
Relish, wheelbarrow shape, small	75.00
Sauce, flat, 4-1/2" d; or footed, 4" or 5" d	12.00
Spooner	24.00
Sugar Bowl, cov	42.00
Vegetable Dish, oval	18.00
Wine	36.00

Barred Forget Me Not

Manufactured by Canton Glass Company, Canton, OH, c1883. Made in amber, apple green, blue, clear, milk glass, and vaseline. Two goblet forms are known. The larger usually has a coarser pattern.

Items	Amber	Apple Green	Blue	Clear	Milk White	Vaseline
Butter Dish, cov	60.00	72.00	72.00	48.00	72.00	72.00
Cake Stand	55.00	66.00	66.00	55.00	66.00	66.00
Celery Vase	60.00	72.00	72.00	36.00	72.00	72.00
Compote, cov, hs	85.00	95.00	95.00	55.00	95.00	95.00
Compote, open, ls	55.00	60.00	60.00	42.00	60.00	60.00
Creamer	48.00	60.00	60.00	36.00	60.00	60.00
Goblet	55.00	72.00	72.00	36.00	72.00	72.00
Pitcher, milk	55.00	72.00	72.00	48.00	72.00	72.00
Pitcher, water	66.00	95.00	95.00	55.00	95.00	95.00
Plate, 9" d, handles	55.00	60.00	60.00	36.00	60.00	60.00
Relish	30.00	36.00	36.00	18.00	36.00	36.00
Sauce, flat	18.00	24.00	24.00	10.00	24.000	24.00
Spooner	36.00	48.00	48.00	24.00	48.00	48.00
Sugar Bowl, cov	55.00	72.00	72.00	42.00	72.00	72.00
Wine	48.00	55.00	55.00	36.00	55.00	55.00

Barred Ovals

Banded Portland, Banded Portland-Frosted, Buckle, Frosted Banded Portland, Purple Block, Oval and Crossbar, US Glass Pattern Line No. 15,004

Manufactured by George Duncan & Sons, Pittsburgh, PA, c1890. Reissued by United States Glass Company, Pittsburgh, PA, at Factory "D," c1891, as Line #15,004. Made in non-flint, clear, clear with frosting or ruby stained. This pattern is found plain or with copper wheel engraving.

Reproductions: Fenton Art Glass Company, Williamstown, WV, made new molds replicating this pattern in 1985. The glass it produced is of high quality non-flint in clear, carnival, periwinkle blue and ruby. These pieces are marked with the embossed Fenton logo. Many of the Fenton pieces are of forms not originally made, such as a basket, bell, and votive light.

Items	Clear, Plain	Ruby Stained
Bowl, open, round, 7", 8" or 9" d	24.00-30.00	42.00-48.00
Bowl, open, sq, 7" or 8" d	24.00-30.00	42.00-55.00
Butter Dish, cov	60.00	130.00
Cake Stand, hs, 10" d	55.00	120.00
Celery Tray	42.00	85.00
Celery Vase, ftd	48.00	135.00
Cheese Plate, 6" or 7" d	30.00	55.00
Compote, cov, hs, 7" d	95.00	180.00
Compote, cov, hs, 8" d	85.00	155.00
Compote, open, hs, 7" d	60.00	85.00
Compote, open, hs, 8" d	55.00	110.00

Items	Clear, Plain	Ruby Stained
Creamer	60.00	75.00
Cruet, os	55.00	300.00
Dish, oblong, 7", 8" or 9" l	24.00-30.00	42.00-48.00
Goblet	55.00	75.00
Lamp, kerosene, orig burner and chimney	130.00	—
Pickle Dish, rect, 6" l	12.00	42.00
Pitcher, milk, quart	75.00	142.00
Pitcher, water, half gallon	120.00	225.00
Salt Shaker, orig top	18.00	42.00
Sauce, flat, 4" d	12.00	30.00
Spooner	48.00	66.00
Sugar Bowl, cov φ	75.00	120.00
Tumbler	24.00	48.00

Basketweave

Unknown maker. Shards have been found at Boston and Sandwich Glass Company, Sandwich, MA, and the Burlington Glass Works, Hamilton, Ontario, Canada. Pattern dates to the mid-1880s. Made in non-flint, amber, apple green, blue, canary, clear, and vaseline. Some covered pieces have a stippled cat's head finial.

Reproductions: Goblet, water pitcher, water tray, and tumbler have been found as reproductions, some of which date from the late 1930s.

Items	Amber or Canary	Apple Green	Blue	Clear	Vaseline
Berry Bowl, master	30.00	—	30.00	110.00	—
Bread Plate, 11" d	42.00	—	42.00	12.00	—
Butter Dish, cov	42.00	72.00	48.00	36.00	48.00
Compote, cov, hs, 7" d; or cov, ls	55.00	75.00	55.00	48.00	66.00
Compote, open, hs or ls	36.00	55.00	48.00	24.00	42.00
Cordial	30.00	48.00	210.00	24.00	36.00
Creamer	36.00	60.00	42.00	210.00	42.00
Cup and Saucer	42.00	72.00	42.00	36.00	310.00
Dish, oval	15.00	24.00	18.00	12.00	18.00
Egg Cup	110.00	36.00	24.00	18.00	30.00
Finger Bowl	24.00	42.00	30.00	24.00	30.00
Goblet φ	210.00	60.00	42.00	24.00	36.00
Mug	30.00	48.00	30.00	18.00	36.00
Pickle	110.00	36.00	24.00	110.00	25.00
Pitcher, milk	48.00	72.00	55.00	42.00	60.00
Pitcher, water φ	72.00	75.00	72.00	55.00	85.00
Plate, 11" d, handles	30.00	310.00	30.00	24.00	36.00
Sauce	12.00	12.00	15.00	10.00	15.00
Spooner	36.00	310.00	36.00	24.00	36.00
Sugar Bowl, cov	42.00	48.00	42.00	36.00	48.00
Syrup, orig top	60.00	75.00	60.00	55.00	55.00
Tumbler, ftd φ	110.00	36.00	24.00	18.00	24.00
Waste Bowl	24.00	42.00	30.00	110.00	30.00
Water Tray φ w/rustic scene	42.00	55.00	48.00	36.00	60.00
Wine	36.00	60.00	36.00	24.00	36.00

Beaded Acorn Medallion

Beaded Acorn

Manufactured by Boston Silver Glass Company, East Cambridge, MA, c1869. Shards have been found at the site of the Boston and Sandwich Glass Company, Sandwich, MA. Made in non-flint, clear only. The pattern is one with heavy stippling, applied handles are typical and an interesting finial in the shape of an acorn is featured.

Items	Clear
Butter Dish, cov, acorn finial	66.00
Champagne	66.00
Compote, cov, hs, 8" d	72.00
Compote, cov, ls, 9" d	60.00
Creamer, ah	48.00
Egg Cup	30.00
Fruit Bowl	55.00
Goblet	36.00
Honey Dish, 3-1/2" d	18.00
Lamp, brass trim, orig burner and chimney	118.00
Pitcher, water, ah, bulbous	130.00
Plate, 6" d	36.00
Relish	18.00
Salt, master	36.00
Sauce, flat, 4" d	15.00
Spooner	30.00
Sugar Bowl, cov	55.00
Wine	55.00

Beaded Band

Thousand Eye Band

Attributed to Burlington Glass Company, Hamilton, Ontario, Canada, c1884, as well as by an American Midwestern factory. Made in non-flint, clear, light amber and other colors.

Items	Clear
Butter Dish, cov	42.00
Cake Stand, hs, 7-5/8" d	30.00
Compote, cov, hs, 7" d	60.00
Compote, cov, hs, 8" d	55.00
Compote, cov, ls, 9" d	95.00
Compote, open, hs, 9-1/2" or 10" d	30.00
Creamer	36.00
Doughnut Stand, hs, 7-1/2" d	24.00
Goblet	36.00
Pickle, cov	55.00
Pitcher, water, applied strap handle	75.00
Relish, double	36.00
Relish, single	18.00
Sauce, flat or footed	12.00
Spooner	30.00
Sugar Bowl, cov	48.00
Syrup, orig top, dated "June 29, '84"	115.00
Wine	36.00

Beaded Grape

Beaded Grape and Vine, California, Grape and Vine

Manufactured by United States Glass Company, Pittsburgh, PA, c1890, as one of its States series. Also attributed to Burlington Glass Works, Hamilton, Ontario, Canada, and Syndenham Glass Company, Wallaceburg, Ontario, Canada, c1910. Made in clear and emerald green. Some pieces found with gilt trim.

Reproductions: Forms in a variety of clear, milk glass, and several colors have been made by various companies, including Westmoreland Glass Co. A goblet with three beaded ovals and grape clusters on a stippled base have been made. Some are found with an amber stained or cranberry stained rims. The reproductions tend to be of heavier non-flint and the stippling is usually coarse and uneven.

Items	Clear	Emerald Green
Bowl, rect, 5-1/2" x 8"	30.00	36.00
Bowl, round, 8" d	210.00	42.00
Bowl, square, 5-1/2", 6" or 7-1/2" w	17.50-30.00	24.00-42.00
Bread Plate	30.00	55.00
Butter Dish, cov	66.00	85.00
Cake Stand, 9" d	66.00	85.00
Celery Tray	36.00	55.00
Celery Vase	48.00	72.00
Compote, cov, hs, 7" d φ, 8" d φ or 9" d φ	75.00-120.00	85.00-135.00
Compote, open, hs, 5" w, sq	55.00	75.00
Compote, open, hs, 7", 8" or 9" d	55.00-66.00	66.00-75.00
Creamer	48.00	60.00
Cruet, os	66.00	130.00
Goblet φ	42.00	60.00
Jelly Compote, open, hs	55.00	66.00
Olive, handle	24.00	42.00
Pickle	24.00	36.00
Pitcher, milk	75.00	110.00
Pitcher, water	85.00	124.00
Plate, sq, 8-1/4" w	210.00	48.00
Salt and Pepper Shakers, pr	55.00	66.00
Sauce, 4" d φ	18.00	24.00
Spooner	30.00	55.00
Sugar Bowl, cov, large, ftd, Australian	72.00	75.00
Sugar Bowl, cov, regular	55.00	55.00
Sugar Shaker	75.00	85.00
Toothpick Holder	48.00	66.00
Tumbler φ	30.00	48.00
Vase, 6" h	30.00	55.00
Wine φ	42.00	66.00

Beaded Grape Medallion

Beaded Grape Medallion Banded

Manufactured by Boston Silver Glass Company, East Cambridge, MA, c1868. Shards have been found at Boston and Sandwich Glass Company, Sandwich, MA. Made in non-flint, clear. Also found in flint. Add

40% for flint values. Several variations are known. When bands are found on this heavily stippled pattern, it is known as *Beaded Grape Medallion Banded*.

Items	Clear
Bowl, 7" d	30.00
Butter Dish, cov, acorn finial	75.00
Cake Stand, 11" d	120.00
Castor Set, 4 bottles	135.00
Celery Vase	75.00
Champagne	85.00
Compote, cov, collared base, hs	180.00
Compote, cov, ls	120.00
Compote, open, hs, collared base, 8" d	66.00
Champagne	55.00
Cordial	66.00
Creamer, ah	60.00
Dish, oval, collared base, 7" x 10"	72.00
Egg Cup	36.00
Goblet	36.00
Honey Dish, 3-1/2" d	12.00
Pickle Dish	24.00
Pitcher, water, ah, bulbous	118.00
Plate, 6" d	36.00
Relish, cov	148.00
Relish, open, mkd "Mould Pat'd May 11, 1868"	48.00
Salt, individual, flat	24.00
Salt, master, ftd	30.00
Sauce, flat, 4" d	12.00
Spooner	42.00
Sugar Bowl, cov	72.00
Sugar Bowl, open	36.00
Sweetmeat, cov	118.00
Syrup, orig top	180.00
Tumbler, ftd	55.00
Vegetable Dish, cov, ftd	75.00
Wine	55.00

Beaded Loop

Oregon #1, US Glass Pattern Line No. 15,073

Manufactured by United States Glass Company, Pittsburgh, PA. It was reissued after the 1891 merger as one of the States patterns. Made in clear.

Reproductions: Reproductions have been made by Imperial Glass in clear and colors.

Items	Clear
Berry Bowl, cov, 9" d	30.00
Berry Set, master, 6 sauces	75.00
Bowl, 3-1/2", 4", 6", 7" or 8" d	12.00-18.00
Bread Plate	42.00
Butter Dish, cov, English	66.00
Butter Dish, cov, flanged	60.00
Butter Dish, cov, flat	48.00
Cake Stand, 8", 9" or 10" d	48.00-60.00
Carafe, water	42.00
Celery Vase	36.00
Compote, cov, hs, 6" d	60.00
Compote, cov, hs, 7" d	72.00
Compote, cov, hs, 8" d	66.00
Compote, open, hs, 5", 6", 7" or 8" d	30.00-48.00
Creamer, flat	36.00
Creamer, footed	42.00
Cruet	60.00
Goblet φ	42.00
Honey Dish	12.00
Jelly Compote, cov, hs, 5" d	55.00
Mug	42.00
Pickle Dish, boat shape	18.00
Pitcher, milk	48.00
Pitcher, water	72.00
Relish	18.00
Salt and Pepper Shakers, pr	48.00
Salt, master	24.00
Sauce, flat, 3-1/2" to 4" d	6.00
Sauce, footed	12.00
Spooner, flat	30.00
Spooner, footed	210.00
Sugar Bowl, cov, flat φ	30.00
Sugar Bowl, cov, footed	36.00
Syrup, orig top	55.00
Toothpick Holder	55.00
Tumbler	30.00
Wine	60.00

Beaded Mirror

Beaded Medallion

Manufactured by Boston Silver Glass Company, East Cambridge, MA, and patented May 11, 1888. Shards have been found at Boston and Sandwich Glass Company, Sandwich, MA. Made in flint, clear.

Like its contemporary *Beaded Grape Medallion,* both have heavy stippling as a design element.

Items	Clear
Butter Dish, cov	48.00
Castor Bottle, mustard	110.00
Castor Bottle, oil	30.00
Castor Set, 5 pcs, metal frame	120.00
Celery Vase	24.00
Compote, cov, hs	60.00
Creamer	48.00
Egg Cup	24.00
Goblet	30.00
Pitcher, milk, quart	55.00
Pitcher, water, half gallon	85.00
Plate, 6" d	24.00
Relish	18.00
Salt, master, ftd	18.00
Sauce, flat or footed	10.00
Spooner	30.00
Sugar Bowl, cov	48.00

Beaded Oval Window

Argyle, Oval Medallion

Manufactured by United States Glass Company, Pittsburgh, PA, in 1891. Shards have been found at the site of the Burlington Glass Works, Hamilton, Ontario, Canada. Made in clear, amber, amethyst, blue, and vaseline. Add 50% for amber, add 100% for blue and vaseline, and 200% for amethyst.

Items	Clear
Bowl, oval	24.00
Bread Plate, motto, GUTDODB	30.00
Butter Dish, cov	48.00
Compote, cov	72.00
Creamer	36.00
Goblet	36.00
Sauce, ftd	15.00
Spooner	24.00
Sugar Bowl, cov	42.00
Wine	36.00

Beaded Swag

Bead Yoke

Manufactured by A. H. Heisey & Company, Newark, OH, c1900. Made in clear, emerald green, ruby stained, custard glass, and milk glass (called "opal" by Heisey). Prices listed are for clear. Add 25% more for custard, milk glass, and ruby stained. Emerald green would be 40% more.

Reproductions: The toothpick holder has been reproduced.

Items	Clear
Bon Bon	30.00
Bowl, 4", 4-1/2", 5", 7", 8", 9" or 10" d	24.00-60.00
Butter Dish, cov	55.00
Cake Stand, 9" or 10" d	66.00
Celery Vase	55.00
Compote, open	60.00
Creamer	42.00
Cruet	410.00
Custard Cup, handle	18.00
Finger Bowl	30.00
Finger Bowl Underplate	24.00
Goblet	30.00
Marmalade Jar, metal lid	75.00
Mug, souvenir type	36.00
Pickle Tray, rect, deep	36.00
Pitcher, water, bulbous, half gallon	75.00
Pitcher, water, tankard, half gallon	85.00
Salt Shaker	24.00
Sauce	12.00

Items	Clear
Spooner	36.00
Sugar Bowl, cov	42.00
Toothpick Holder φ	310.00
Tumbler	30.00

Beaded Swirl

Swirled Column

Manufactured by George Duncan and Sons, Pittsburgh, PA, c1890. Made in clear, emerald green and a few pieces known in milk white. Some pieces gilt trim. The dual names are for the two forms of the pattern. *Beaded Swirl* stands on flat bases and is solid in shape. *Swirled Column* stands on scrolled (sometimes gilded) feet and the shape tapers towards the base.

Items	Clear	Emerald Green
Berry Bowl, 7" d	12.00	24.00
Bowl, cov, round, 3 legs, 7" or 8" d	30.00	55.00
Bowl, cov, round, 3 legs, 9" d	36.00	72.00
Bowl, flat, oval, 7" or 8" d	18.00	30.00
Bowl, flat, oval, 9" d	110.00	30.00
Bowl, flat, round, scalloped, 7" or 8" d	18.00	30.00
Bowl, flat, round, scalloped, 9" d	110.00	30.00
Bowl, footed, round, 3 legs, 7" or 8" d	12.00	24.00
Bowl, footed, round, 3 legs, 9" d	18.00	30.00
Butter Dish, cov, flat	42.00	55.00
Butter Dish, cov, footed	55.00	75.00
Cake Stand, hs	42.00	55.00
Celery Tray	18.00	30.00
Celery Vase	36.00	55.00
Compote, cov, hs	48.00	42.00
Compote, open, ls	42.00	48.00
Creamer, flat	30.00	42.00
Creamer, footed	36.00	48.00
Cruet, os	42.00	270.00
Custard Cup, handle	6.00	12.00
Dish	12.00	18.00
Egg Cup	18.00	18.00
Goblet	36.00	30.00
Mug	12.00	15.00
Pitcher, water	48.00	66.00
Relish	18.00	30.00
Salt Shaker, orig nickel or plated top, squatty or tall		18.0030.00
Sauce, flat, 4" or 4-1/2" d	10.00	15.00
Sauce, footed, 4" or 4-1/2" d, 3 legs	12.00	18.00
Sherbet Cup	6.00	12.00
Sherbet Underplate	12.00	24.00
Spooner, flat	30.00	48.00
Spooner, footed	36.00	55.00
Sugar Bowl, cov, flat or footed	42.00	55.00
Sugar Shaker	42.00	66.00
Syrup, orig top	410.00	120.00
Tumbler	24.00	36.00
Wine	30.00	42.00

Beaded Tulip

Andes, Tulip

Manufactured by McKee & Brothers Glass Company, Pittsburgh, PA, c1894. Made in non-flint, clear, and emerald green.

Items	Clear	Emerald Green
Bowl, oval, 9-1/2" l	24.00	—
Bread Plate	55.00	—
Butter Dish, cov	60.00	130.00
Cake Stand, hs	60.00	—
Champagne	55.00	—
Compote, cov, hs, 8" d	55.00	—
Compote, open, 8" d	48.00	0
Cordial	60.00	—
Creamer	42.00	75.00
Goblet	42.00	—
Ice Cream Dish	30.00	—
Marmalade Jar, cov	48.00	—
Pickle, oval	110.00	—
Pitcher, milk, quart	55.00	66.00

Items	Clear	Emerald Green
Pitcher, water, half gallon	66.00	—
Plate, 6" d	30.00	—
Relish	24.00	—
Sauce, flat or footed, leaf shape, 4" d	12.00	—
Sauce, footed	15.00	—
Spooner	36.00	—
Sugar Bowl, cov	55.00	95.00
Tumbler	36.00	—
Water Tray	60.00	—
Wine	36.00	—
Wine Tray	60.00	—

Beautiful Lady

Manufactured by Bryce, Higbee and Company, Pittsburgh, PA, in 1905. Made in clear.

Items	Clear
Banana Stand, hs	36.00
Bowl, flat, 9" d	110.00
Bowl, low, collared base, 8" d	18.00
Butter Dish, cov	42.00
Bread Plate	18.00
Cake Plate, 9" d	30.00
Cake Stand, hs	42.00
Celery Vase	24.00
Compote, cov, hs	42.00
Compote, open, hs	30.00
Creamer	30.00
Cruet, os	36.00
Doughnut Stand, hs	55.00
Goblet	42.00
Jelly Compote, open	18.00
Pitcher, water	48.00
Plate, sq, 7" w	18.00
Plate, sq, 8" w	110.00
Plate, sq, 9" w	30.00
Plate, sq, 11" w	27.50
Salt and Pepper Shakers, pr	72.00
Spooner	18.00
Sugar Bowl, cov	30.00
Tumbler	18.00
Vase, 6-1/2" h	18.00
Wine	24.00

Bellflower

Ribbed Bellflower, Ribbed Leaf

Manufactured in the 1850s and first attributed to Boston and Sandwich Glass Company, Sandwich, MA, which made the pattern in flint. It was later produced in non-flint by McKee & Brothers Glass Company, Pittsburgh, PA, and other firms for many years. There are many variations of this pattern, single and double vine, fine and coarse rib, know and plain stems, and rayed and plain bases. Type and quality must be considered when evaluating this pattern. Very rare in color. Prices listed are for high quality flint. Made in flint, non-flint, clear. Some rare color pieces are known. Cobalt blue spoon holder sold for $7,000.

Reproductions: Reproductions have been made by the Metropolitan Museum of Art, New York City, and by Imperial Glass Company, Bellaire, OH. Museum reproductions were made in lead crystal and have a "M.M.A." monogram mold mark. Reproductions are found in clear, sapphire blue, emerald green, canary yellow, and peacock blue. Only the single vine, fine rib variety has been reproduced.

Abbreviations: DV - double vine, SV - single vine, FR - fine rib, CR - coarse rib.

Items	Flint
Bowl, 6" d, 1-3/4" h, SV; or 8" d, all types	75.00
Butter Dish, cov, SV, CR, mushroom or rose finial	85.00
Butter Dish, cov, SV, FR	190.00
Cake Stand, SV, FR, 8-1/2" d, 3" h, patterned base	1,240.00
Castor Set, 5 bottles, pewter stand	270.00
Celery Vase, SV, FR	300.00
Champagne, DV, FR, cut bellflowers	270.00
Champagne, SV, FR, knob stem, rayed base, barrel shape	130.00
Compote, cov, hs, 8" d, SV, FR	575.00
Compote, cov, ls, 7" d, SV	240.00
Compote, cov, ls, 8" d, SV	270.00
Compote, cov, ls, 8" d, SV, FR	375.00
Compote, open, ls, 7" d, DV, FR	110.00
Compote, open, ls, 7" or 8" d, SV	120.00

Items	Flint
Compote, open, ls, 9" d, SV, CR	130.00
Cordial, SV, CR, plain stem, barrel shape	130.00
Cordial, SV, FR, knob stem, rayed base, barrel shape	118.00
Creamer, DV, FR	136.00
Creamer, SV, FR φ	142.00
Decanter, pint, DV, FR, bar top	270.00
Decanter, quart, DV, FR, os; or SV, FR, bar top	475.00
Dish, flat, scalloped top, round, 8" d, SV, FR	66.00
Egg Cup, CR	42.00
Egg Cup, SV, FR	48.00
Goblet, DV, FR, cut bellflowers	236.00
Goblet, SV, CF, barrel shape	55.00
Goblet, SV, CR, straight sides	48.00
Goblet, SV, CR, knob stem, barrel shape	55.00
Goblet, SV, FR, plain stem, rayed base, barrel shape φ	36.00
Hat, SV, FR, made from tumbler mold, rare	360.00
Honey Dish, 3" d, SV, FR	42.00
Lamp, whale oil, brass stem, marble base, SV, FR	190.00
Mug, SV, FR	300.00
Paperweight Whimsy	75.00
Pitcher, milk, DV, FR; pint, DV; or quart, SV, CR	720.00
Pitcher, water, DV, CR	360.00
Pitcher, water, SV, FR φ	300.00
Plate, 6" d, SV, FR	110.00
Salt, master, flat, DV, FR	42.00
Salt, master, ftd, SV, FR	72.00
Spooner, DV	55.00
Spooner, SV, FR	42.00
Sugar Bowl, cov, DV	120.00
Sugar Bowl, cov, SV, CR; or SV, FR φ	115.00
Sweetmeat, cov, hs, 6" d, SV	360.00
Syrup, ah, ftd, 10 sides	850.00
Syrup, SV, FR	600.00
Tumbler, DV, CR	115.00
Tumbler, DV, FR, ftd	130.00
Tumbler, SV, CR, straight sides, plain base	110.00
Tumbler, SV, FR, cut bellflowers φ	240.00
Tumbler, SV, FR, footed	110.00
Whiskey, SV, CR, ah; or FR, 3-1/2" h	180.00
Wine, DV, FR, cut bellflowers, barrel shape	300.00
Wine, SV, FR, knob stem, rayed base, barrel shape	130.00
Wine, SV, FR, plain stem, rayed base, straight sided	120.00

Beveled Diamond and Star

Diamond Prism, Princeton

Manufactured by Tarentum Glass Company, Tarentum, PA, c1894. Made in non-flint, clear and clear with ruby stain.

Items	Clear	Ruby Stained
Bowl, 7" or 8" d	18.00	36.00
Bread Tray, 7" d	48.00	85.00
Butter Dish, cov	55.00	110.00
Cake Stand, hs, 9" h	48.00	110.00
Cake Stand, hs, 10" h	55.00	115.00
Celery Vase	36.00	75.00
Cheese Dish cov, flat	66.00	155.00
Compote, cov, hs, 5" or 7" d	60.00-72.00	190.00-270.00
Compote, open, serrated rim, 5" or 8" d	60.00	180.00
Compote, open, serrated rim, 7" d	55.00	172.00
Cracker Jar, cov	60.00	190.00
Creamer, tankard, 5-1/2" h	42.00	85.00
Goblet	48.00	85.00
Pickle	18.00	36.00
Pitcher, milk, quart	55.00	130.00
Pitcher, water, half gallon, ah or ph	55.00	180.00
Plate	12.00	24.00
Sauce, flat or footed	12.00	24.00
Spooner	30.00	66.00
Sugar Bowl, cov	48.00	85.00
Sugar Shaker, orig top	48.00	85.00
Syrup, orig top	55.00	180.00
Toothpick Holder	30.00	85.00
Tumbler, 3-3/4" h	18.00	36.00
Water Tray	48.00	85.00
Wine, 4" h	24.00	55.00

Bigler

Manufactured by Boston and Sandwich Glass Company, Sandwich, MA, and by other early factories. This is a scarce pattern, in which goblets are most common and vary in height, shape, and flare. Made in flint and clear, and some rare colors are also known.

Reproductions: The goblet has been reproduced as a commemorative for Biglerville, PA.

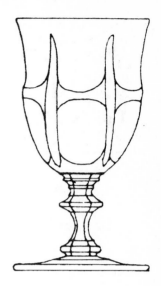

Items	Clear
Ale Glass	66.00
Bar Bottle, quart	95.00
Bowl, 6-1/2" or 10" d	48.00
Butter Dish, cov	130.00
Celery Vase	120.00
Champagne	115.00
Compote, open, 7" d	48.00
Cordial	66.00
Creamer	75.00
Cup Plate	36.00
Decanter bar lip	195.00
Egg Cup, double	60.00
Goblet, regular stem φ	410.00
Goblet, short stem	60.00
Lamp, whale oil, monument base	155.00
Mug, ah	72.00
Salt, master	24.00
Toddy Plate, 6" d	40.00
Tumbler, flat	66.00
Vase, scalloped rim, sq base, 11-1/4" h	85.00
Whiskey, ah	120.00
Wine	66.00

Bird and Strawberry

Bluebird, Flying Bird and Strawberry, Strawberry and Bird

Manufactured by Indiana Glass Company, Dunkirk, IN, c1914. Made in non-flint, clear. Pieces are occasionally highlighted by coloring the birds blue, strawberries pink, and leaves green, plus additional gilding.

Reproductions: Tiara Exclusives, Dunkirk, IN, has reproduced the flat relish, in 1978. Another unknown manufacturer reproduced the covered compote with a high standard.

Items	Clear	Colors
Bowl, 5" d	30.00	55.00
Bowl, 9-1/2" d, ftd	60.00	85.00
Bowl, 10" d; or 10-1/2" d, flared	55.00	110.00
Butter Dish, cov	120.00	190.00
Cake Stand, hs	85.00	130.00
Celery Tray	55.00	85.00
Celery Vase φ	55.00	85.00
Chop Plate, 12" d	130.00	190.00
Compote, cov, hs, 6-1/2" d φ	130.00	240.00
Compote, open, ls, ruffled, 6" d	85.00	130.00
Creamer	55.00	142.00
Cup	30.00	42.00
Goblet, barrel bowl	190.00	240.00
Goblet, flared bowl	240.00	360.00
Hat	300.00	—
Jelly Compote, cov, hs	180.00	270.00
Nappy	48.00	66.00
Pitcher, water	242.00	360.00
Plate, 6-1/2" d	85.00	—
Punch Cup	30.00	36.00
Relish φ	24.00	55.00
Sauce, round, flat or footed	24.00	42.00
Spooner	60.00	124.00
Sugar Bowl, cov	66.00	130.00
Tumbler, flat, 2 sizes	55.00	75.00
Wine	85.00	120.00

Blackberry

Manufactured by Hobbs, Brockunier & Company, Wheeling, WV, in 1870. The pattern was designed and patented by John H. Hobbs, Feb. 1, 1870. Several pieces have the date on the base. Made in non-flint, clear and milk glass.

Reproductions: Phoenix Glass Company, Monaca, PA, bought the molds from Co-Operative Glass Company, Beaver Falls, PA, in 1937. It reissued several forms in clear and milk glass. Several reproductions

are also attributed to Westmoreland Glass Company, Grapeville, PA, because of the unique colors, such as Brandywine blue, golden sunset, laurel green, and teal, as well as milk white.

Items	Clear	Milk Glass
Butter Dish, cov	72.00	85.00
Celery Vase, hs or ls	55.00	75.00
Champagne	55.00	85.00
Compote, cov, hs, 8" d	75.00	120.00
Compote, open, hs, 8" d	30.00	55.00
Creamer †	66.00	95.00
Dish, oval, 5-1/2" x 8-1/2"	24.00	48.00
Egg Cup, double †; or single	48.00	66.00
Goblet †	42.00	60.00
Honey Dish	12.00	24.00
Lamp, oil, orig burner and chimney, 8-1/2", 9-1/2" or 11-3/4" h	120.00-155.00	—
Pitcher, water, bulbous, ah, half gallon	190.00	300.00
Relish	18.00	30.00
Salt, master, ftd	30.00	55.00
Sauce, flat	15.00	30.00
Spooner †	36.00	55.00
Sugar Bowl, cov †	55.00	75.00
Syrup, orig top	180.00	240.00
Tumbler, flat	42.00	—
Wine	30.00	55.00

Blaze

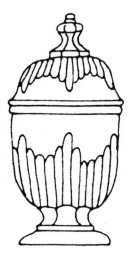

Manufactured by New England Glass Company, East Cambridge, MA, c1869. Made in flint, clear.

Items	Clear
Bowl, cov, 5-1/2", 6", 7" or 8" d	72.00-110.00
Bowl, open, 5", 5-1/2", 6" or 7" d	36.00-48.00
Butter Dish, cov	75.00
Celery Vase	95.00
Champagne	85.00
Cheese Dish, cov	66.00
Cheese Plate, 7" d	42.00
Cologne Bottle, os	66.00
Compote, cov, hs, deep bowl, 6" d	95.00
Compote, cov, hs, deep bowl, 7" or 8" d	85.00-110.00
Compote, cov, hs, shallow bowl, 6" d	95.00
Compote, cov, hs, shallow bowl, 7" or 8" d	85.00-110.00
Compote, cov, ls, deep bowl, 6" or 7"d	66.00-85.00
Compote, cov, ls, deep bowl, 8" d	75.00
Compote, cov, ls, shallow bowl, 6" or 7" d	66.00-85.00
Compote, cov, ls, shallow bowl, 8" d	75.00
Compote, open, hs, deep bowl, 6", 7" or 8" d	42.00-55.00
Compote, open, hs, shallow bowl, 6" d	60.00
Compote, open, hs, shallow bowl, 7" d	55.00
Compote, open, hs, shallow bowl, 8" d	72.00
Compote, open, hs, shallow bowl, 9" or 10" d	66.00
Compote, open, ls, deep bowl, 6", 7", 8", 9" or 10" d	42.00-60.00
Compote, open, ls, shallow bowl, 6" d	60.00
Compote, open, ls, shallow bowl, 7" d	55.00
Compote, open, ls, shallow bowl, 8" d	72.00
Cordial	66.00
Creamer	55.00
Custard Cup, handle	24.00
Dish, oval, 7", 8", 9" or 10" l	42.00-60.00
Egg Cup, ah	66.00
Goblet	55.00
Honey Dish, 3-1/2" d	18.00
Lemonade	55.00
Salt, master, flat	36.00
Sauce, flat, 4" d	12.00
Spooner	48.00
Sugar Bowl, cov	85.00
Tumbler, ftd	55.00
Wine	66.00

Bleeding Heart

King's Floral Ware, New Floral, US Glass Pattern Line No. 85

Manufactured originally by King Son and Company, Pittsburgh, PA, c1875. Reissued by United States Glass in 1898, at Factory "C." Shards have also been found at Boston and Sandwich Glass Company, Sandwich, MA, and the Burlington Glass Works, Hamilton, Ontario, Canada. The Speciality Company, East Liverpool, OH, also made only the goblet and mug in 1888. Made in non-flint, clear and some milk glass. Goblets are found with six variations. A goblet with a tin lid, containing a condiment, such as mustard, jelly, or baking powder, was also made. It is of inferior quality compared to the original goblet.

Items	Clear
Bowl, cov, 6" or 8-1/4" d	48.00-66.00
Bowl, open, oval, 5", 7", 7-1/4", 8" or 9" l	24.00-42.00
Bowl, open, round, 5", 7" or 8" d	24.00-42.00
Butter Dish, cov	75.00
Cake Stand, 9", 10" or 11" d	72.00-110.00
Cake Stand with Dessert Slots	130.00
Compote, cov, hs, 7", 8" or 9"d	75.00-115.00
Compote, cov, ls, 7" or 7-1/2" or 8" d	72.00-75.00
Compote, open, hs, 8" d	48.00
Compote, open, ls, 8-1/2" d	36.00
Creamer, applied handle, ftd	72.00
Creamer, molded handle, flat	36.00
Dish, cov, 7" d	55.00
Egg Cup	55.00
Egg Rack, cov, 3 eggs	360.00
Goblet, knob stem, barrel or straight bowl	42.00
Honey Dish, 3-1/2" d	18.00
Mug, 3-1/4" h	48.00
Pickle, 8-3/4" l, 5" w	36.00
Pitcher milk, ah, quart, bulbous	130.00
Pitcher, water, ah, half gallon, bulbous	180.00
Plate	75.00
Platter, oval	85.00
Relish, oval, 5-1/2" x 3-5/8"	42.00
Salt, master, ftd	72.00
Sauce, flat, oval or round, 3-1/2" d, 4" d, or 5" d	18.00
Spooner	30.00
Sugar Bowl, cov, ftd, short or tall	85.00
Tumbler, flat	110.00
Tumbler, footed	95.00
Waste Bowl	66.00
Wine, hexagonal stem	165.00
Wine, knob stem	190.00

Block and Fan

Red Block and Fan, Romeo

Manufactured by Richards & Hartley Glass Company, Tarentum, PA, in the late 1880s. Reissued by United States Glass, Pittsburgh, PA, after 1891. Made in non-flint, clear, and ruby-stained.

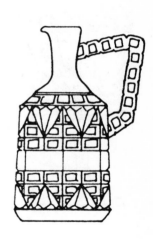

Items	Clear	Ruby Stained
Biscuit Jar, cov	66.00	180.00
Bowl, flat, 6", 7", 8", 9-1/2" or 10" d	30.00-48.00	55.00-85.00
Bowl, flat, collared base, 7", 8" or 10" d	18.00-30.00	24.00-36.00
Butter Dish, cov	60.00	85.00
Cake Stand, 9" d	42.00	—
Cake Stand, 10" d	48.00	—
Carafe	60.00	115.00
Celery Tray	36.00	—
Celery Vase	42.00	75.00
Compote, cov, hs, 7" or 8" d	55.00-60.00	190.00-195.00
Compote, open, hs, scalloped rim, 7" or 8" d	42.00-48.00	165.00-180.00
Condiment Set, salt, pepper, and cruet on tray	75.00	—
Creamer, individual	—	42.00
Creamer, regular	30.00	55.00
Creamer, large	36.00	120.00
Creamer, small	42.00	75.00
Cruet, os	42.00	—
Dish, large, rect	30.00	—
Finger Bowl	55.00	—
Goblet	410.00	124.00
Ice Cream Tray, rect	75.00	—
Ice Tub	55.00	60.00
Orange Bowl	60.00	—
Pickle Dish	24.00	
Pitcher, milk	42.00	—
Pitcher, water	410.00	142.00
Plate, 6" or 10" d	18.00-110.00	—
Relish, rect	30.00	—
Rose Bowl	30.00	—
Salt and Pepper Shakers, pr	36.00	—
Sauce, flat, 4" or 5" d	10.00	—
Sauce, footed, 3-3/4" d, 4" d, or 5" d	18.00	30.00
Spooner	30.00	—
Sugar Bowl, cov	60.00	—
Sugar Shaker	48.00	—

Items	Clear	Ruby Stained
Syrup, orig top	75.00	115.00
Tumbler	36.00	48.00
Waste Bowl	36.00	—
Wine	55.00	95.00

Blocked Arches

Berkeley

Manufactured by United States Glass Company, Pittsburgh, PA, in 1893. Made in clear, frosted, and some ruby stained.

Items	Clear	Frosted
Berry Bowl	24.00	30.00
Biscuit Jar, cov	55.00	72.00
Butter Dish, cov	55.00	60.00
Cake Stand	60.00	55.00
Creamer	36.00	42.00
Cruet, os	72.00	85.00
Cup and Saucer	60.00	72.00
Finger Bowl	30.00	36.00
Goblet	42.00	60.00
Pitcher, water	75.00	85.00
Plate, 6" d	110.00	24.00
Sugar Bowl, cov	42.00	48.00
Syrup, orig top	48.00	55.00
Tumbler	36.00	42.00
Wine	310.00	45.00

Bosworth

Star Band

Manufactured by Indiana Glass Company, Dunkirk, IN, c1907. Made in clear.

Items	Clear
Berry Bowl	15.00
Butter Dish, cov	30.00
Celery Vase, handles	20.00
Creamer	24.00
Goblet	30.00
Jelly Compote	18.00
Pitcher, water	36.00
Relish	15.00
Spooner	18.00
Sugar Bowl, cov	36.00
Tumbler	18.00
Wine	24.00

Bouquet

Narcissus Spray

Manufactured by Indiana Glass Company, Dunkirk, IN, c1918. Made in clear. Some pieces are found with flowers and leaves, with cranberry or amethyst flashing. Color-flashed pieces would be 25% higher than for the clear shown below.

Items	Clear
Berry, individual, 6" d	15.00
Berry, master, 8" d	20.00
Butter Dish, cov	48.00
Cake Plate	30.00
Creamer	30.00
Goblet	30.00
Nappy	18.00
Pitcher, water	48.00
Sauce	6.00
Spooner	24.00
Sugar Bowl, cov	36.00
Tumbler	18.00
Water Tray	30.00

Bow Tie

American Bow Tie

Manufactured by Thompson Glass Company, Uniontown, PA, c1889. Made in non-flint, clear.

Items	Clear
Bowl, 6", 7", 8" d or 10-1/4" d, 5" h	36.00-66.00
Butter Dish, cov	66.00
Butter Pat	30.00
Cake Standard, large, 9" d	72.00
Celery Vase	85.00
Compote, open, hs, scalloped rim, 7" or 8" d	55.00-72.00
Compote, open, hs, smooth rim, 5-1/4" d	72.00
Compote, open, hs, smooth rim, 9-1/4" d	66.00
Compote, open, ls, scalloped rim, 6-1/2" or 8" d	55.00
Compote, open, ls, smooth rim, 6-1/2" or 8" d	55.00
Creamer	55.00
Dish, rect, scalloped rim, 4-1/4" x 7", l5-1/4" x 8" or l5-1/2" x 9" l	24.00-36.00
Fruit Bowl, 10" d, ftd	60.00
Goblet	66.00
Honey Dish, cov	55.00
Marmalade Jar, cov	66.00
Orange Bowl, ftd, hs, 10" d	75.00
Pitcher, milk, quart, 5-1/2" h or 6-1/2" h	85.00
Pitcher, water, half gallon, 7" h, 8" h, 9" h	75.00
Punch Bowl	120.00
Relish, rect	30.00
Salt, individual	24.00
Salt, master, ftd	55.00
Salt Shaker	48.00
Sauce, flat or footed, scalloped or smooth rim, 4" d	18.00
Spooner	42.00
Sugar Bowl, cov	55.00
Sugar Bowl, open	48.00
Tumbler	55.00

Brilliant, Riverside's

Petaled Medallion, Miami

Manufactured by Riverside Glass Works, Wellsburg, WV, c1895. Made in non-flint, clear, amber stained, and ruby stained. Sometimes found with copper wheel engraving. Occasionally found with souvenir engraving.

Items	Clear	Amber or Ruby Stained
Berry Bowl, master	36.00	55.00
Butter Dish, cov	48.00	120.00
Celery Vase	42.00	110.00
Compote, cov, hs	110.00	270.00
Creamer, individual	42.00	66.00
Creamer, table	60.00	85.00
Goblet	42.00	66.00
Pitcher, water	85.00	225.00
Salt Shaker, tall, orig top	30.00	48.00
Sauce, flat	18.00	30.00
Spooner	30.00	48.00
Sugar Bowl, cov, individual	48.00	66.00
Sugar Bowl, cov, table	72.00	85.00
Tumbler	24.00	48.00
Wine	42.00	55.00

Brittanic

Manufactured by McKee & Brothers Glass Company, Pittsburgh, PA, c1902. Later made by McKee-Jeannette Glass Works, c1903. Made in non-flint, clear, amber stained, and ruby stained. A finger or waste bowl is known in emerald green. A large open compote is also documented.

Items	Amber Stained	Clear	Ruby Stained
Banana Stand	85.00	75.00	120.00
Berry Bowl	30.00	24.00	36.00
Bowl, oval, serrated rim, 7" l, 8" l, or 9" l	55.00	36.00	48.00
Bowl, round, crimped or smooth rim, 8" d	42.00	30.00	42.00
Butter Dish, cov	95.00	48.00	110.00
Cake Stand, large	—	55.00	270.00
Cake Stand, small	—	55.00	300.00
Castor Set, 4 bottles	165.00	66.00	190.00

Items	Amber Stained	Clear	Ruby Stained
Celery Tray	66.00	60.00	66.00
Celery Vase	72.00	55.00	72.00
Cologne Bottle, os	130.00	60.00	130.00
Compote, cov, hs	66.00	55.00	75.00
Compote, open, hs, scalloped rim, 7-1/2" d	95.00	42.00	95.00
Compote, open, hs, scalloped rim, 8-1/2" d	85.00	48.00	85.00
Compote, open, hs, scalloped rim, 10" d	110.00	66.00	110.00
Compote, open, hs, smooth rim, 5" d	85.00	36.00	85.00
Compote, open, hs, smooth rim, 6" d	75.00	42.00	75.00
Compote, open, hs, smooth rim, 7" d	95.00	48.00	95.00
Compote, open, hs, smooth rim, 8" d	85.00	55.00	85.00
Cracker Jar, cov	110.00	55.00	110.00
Creamer, ah, bulbous or tankard	48.00	36.00	60.00
Cruet, os	115.00	42.00	180.00
Custard Cup	—	18.00	—
Fruit Basket	—	55.00	180.00
Goblet	48.00	36.00	55.00
Honey Dish, cov, sq	—	60.00	—
Lamp, 7-1/2" h	—	66.00	—
Lamp, 8-1/2" h	—	75.00	—
Mug, 3-1/4" h	24.00	12.00	30.00
Olive Dish, handle, flat, crimped or smooth rim	42.00	24.00	42.00
Pickle, flat, crimped or smooth rim	42.00	24.00	42.00
Pitcher, water, ah, bulbous	75.00	60.00	120.00
Pitcher, water, ah, tankard	110.00	72.00	115.00
Rose Bowl	72.00	48.00	75.00
Salt and Pepper Shakers, pr	66.00	55.00	85.00
Sauce, round, flat or footed; or square, flat	36.00	12.00	36.00
Spooner	42.00	30.00	55.00
Sugar Bowl, cov	75.00	48.00	85.00
Toothpick Holder	42.00	30.00	180.00
Tumbler	36.00	24.00	55.00
Vase	75.00	55.00	75.00
Water Bottle	180.00	66.00	180.00
Wine	42.00	30.00	60.00

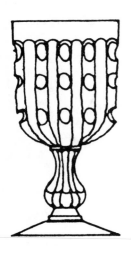

Broken Column

Bamboo, Broken Column with Red Dots, Irish Column, Notched Rib, Rattan, Ribbed Fingerprint, US Glass Pattern Line No. 15,021

Manufactured by Columbia Glass Company, Findlay, OH, c1888. Reissued by United States Glass Company, Pittsburgh, PA, after 1893 to 1900 at Factory "E" and Factory "J." Made in non-flint, clear and ruby stained. A rare cobalt blue cup is known.

Reproductions: The Metropolitan Museum of Art, New York City, and the Smithsonian Institution, Washington, DC, have both commissioned reproductions of this pattern through Imperial Glass Corp., Bellaire, OH. These reproductions are marked with a raised "M.M.A." and "S. I." mark. The L. G. Wright Glass Company, New Martinsville, WV, made a clear goblet in the 1960s. Many items have been reproduced. Generally the reproductions are heavier than the originals.

Items	Clear	Ruby Stained
Banana Stand, flat	66.00	—
Banana Stand, hs, 9" d	135.00	—
Basket, ah, 12" h 15" l	130.00	—
Biscuit Jar, cov	85.00	155.00
Berry Bowl, 4" or 6" d	18.00-24.00	24.00-55.00
Bowl, cov, deep, 5", 6", 7" or 8" d	55.00-72.00	155.00-180.00
Bowl, open, deep, 5" d	24.00	—
Bowl, open, deep, 6" d	36.00	120.00
Bowl, open, deep, 7" d	42.00	135.00
Bowl, open, deep, 8" d φ	42.00	130.00
Bowl, open, shallow, 5" d	24.00	—
Bowl, open, shallow, 6" or 7" d	36.00-42.00	120.00-130.00
Bowl, open, shallow, 8" or 9" d	48.00	—
Bread Plate	72.00	130.00
Butter Dish, cov	85.00	190.00
Cake Stand, hs, 9" d	85.00	270.00
Cake Stand, hs, 10" d	95.00	255.00
Carafe, water	75.00	180.00
Celery Tray, oval	42.00	85.00
Celery Vase	60.00	142.00
Champagne	120.00	—
Claret	75.00	—
Compote, cov, hs, 5-1/4" d, 10-1/4" h	110.00	240.00
Compote, cov, hs, 7" d, 12" h	110.00	—
Compote, cov, hs, 10" d	135.00	300.00
Compote, open, hs, belled, flared, or round bowl 6" d	55.00	180.00
Compote, open, hs, belled, flared, or round bowl 7" d	66.00	172.00
Compote, open, hs, belled, flared, or round bowl 8" d	75.00	190.00

Items	Clear	Ruby Stained
Compote, open, ls, 5" d, 6" h, flared	66.00	142.00
Creamer φ	55.00	130.00
Cruet, os	85.00	180.00
Decanter, os	115.00	—
Dish, oblong, 7" or 9" l	42.00-48.00	75.00-95.00
Finger Bowl	36.00	—
Goblet φ	60.00	120.00
Honey Dish, round	12.00	24.00
Marmalade Jar, cov	85.00	—
Olive, 5-1/2" l	30.00	66.00
Pickle Castor, silver plated frame	180.00	460.00
Pickle Dish, oblong	36.00	66.00
Plate, 4", 5", 6", 7" or 8" d	30.00-55.00	48.00-85.00
Plate, 7-1/2" d φ	55.00	115.00
Punch Cup	18.00	
Relish, 7-1/2" x 4" or 11" x 5"	30.00	118.00
Salt Shaker	55.00	66.00
Sauce, flat, 4" or 4-1/2" d φ	18.00	24.00
Spooner φ	42.00	85.00
Sugar Bowl, cov φ	85.00	142.00
Sugar Shaker	85.00	240.00
Syrup, orig top	136.00	495.00
Toothpick Holder	180.00	—
Tumbler φ	48.00	60.00
Vegetable, cov	110.00	—
Wine φ	95.00	130.00

Buckle

Early Buckle

Original flint manufacturer unknown. Shards have been found at Boston and Sandwich Glass, Sandwich, MA; Union Glass Company, Somerville, MA, and Burlington Glass Works, Hamilton, Ontario, Canada. Gillinder and Sons, Philadelphia, PA, produced non-flint in the late 1870s. Made in flint and non-flint, clear only. Rare examples are known in sapphire blue and opaque white.

Items	Flint	Non-Flint
Basket, 8-1/2" d bowl in wire basket frame	72.00	60.00
Bowl, 9" d	72.00	60.00
Bowl, 10" d	66.00	55.00
Butter Dish, cov	66.00	72.00
Cake Stand, hs, 9-3/4" h	—	42.00
Celery Vase	60.00	48.00
Champagne	72.00	—
Compote, cov, hs or ls, 6" d	110.00	48.00
Compote, open, hs or ls, 8-1/2" d	48.00	42.00
Cordial	75.00	—
Creamer, ah	135.00	55.00
Egg Cup	48.00	36.00
Goblet	48.00	30.00
Lamp, kerosene, orig burner and chimney	180.00	—
Pickle	48.00	18.00
Pitcher, water, ah	720.00	120.00
Relish	42.00	24.00
Salt, flat, oval	36.00	18.00
Salt, footed, 4" d	30.00	24.00
Sauce, flat, plain or scalloped rim, 4" d	18.00	10.00
Spooner, pedestal, scalloped	42.00	30.00
Sugar Bowl, cov	75.00	55.00
Tumbler, flat	55.00	36.00
Wine	75.00	42.00

Buckle with Star

Bryce's Orient, Buckle and Star, Late Buckle and Star, Orient

Manufactured by Bryce, Walker and Company, Pittsburgh, PA, in 1875, and United States Glass Company, Pittsburgh, PA, in 1891, at Factory "B." Shards have been found at Burlington Glass Works, Hamilton, Ontario, Canada. Made in non-flint, clear. Finials are shaped like Maltese crosses.

Items	Clear
Bowl, cov, 6" d	30.00
Bowl, oval, 7", 8" or 9" l	18.00
Bowl, oval, 10" l	110.00
Butter Dish, cov	48.00
Cake Stand, hs, 9" d	42.00
Celery Vase	36.00

Items	Clear
Cologne Bottle, os	66.00
Compote, cov, hs, 7" d	72.00
Compote, open, hs, 9-1/2" d	36.00
Creamer	42.00
Cruet, os	55.00
Goblet	36.00
Honey Dish, flat or footed, 3-1/2" d	10.00
Mug	72.00
Mustard, cov	75.00
Pickle	18.00
Pitcher, water, ah, bulbous	85.00
Relish	18.00
Salt, master, ftd	24.00
Sauce, flat, 4" d or 4-1/2" d	10.00
Sauce, footed, 4" d or 4-1/2" d	12.00
Spill Holder	55.00
Spooner	30.00
Sugar Bowl, cov	55.00
Sugar Bowl, open	30.00
Syrup, pewter or Brittania top, man's head finial, applied handle	95.00
Syrup, plain tin top, molded handle	72.00
Tumbler, handle or handleless	55.00
Wine	42.00

Budded Ivy

Manufacturer unknown. Made c1870. Contemporary of Stippled Ivy. Made in non-flint, clear. Pieces have applied handles and ivy leaf finials.

Items	Clear
Butter Dish, cov	55.00
Compote, cov, hs	72.00
Compote, cov, ls	55.00
Compote, open, hs	30.00
Creamer	36.00
Egg Cup	30.00
Goblet	36.00
Pitcher, water, ah	60.00
Relish	18.00
Salt, master, ftd	30.00
Sauce, flat or footed, 4" d	10.00
Spooner	30.00
Sugar Bowl, cov	55.00
Syrup, orig top	85.00
Wine	42.00

Bullet Emblem

Shield in Red, White and Blue

Manufactured by United States Glass Company, Pittsburgh, PA, c1898, to commemorate the Spanish-American War. Made in clear.

Items	Clear
Butter Dish, cov	266.00
Creamer	180.00
Goblet	130.00
Spooner	130.00
Sugar Bowl, cov	300.00

Bull's Eye

Manufactured by Boston and Sandwich Glass Company, Sandwich, MA, c1860s, and New England Glass Company, East Cambridge, MA, c1869. Made in flint, and non-flint, clear, also found in colors and milk glass. Add 50% to values listed below for colors and milk glass. Non-flint and colored wares are generally later.

Items	Clear
Bitters Bottle	95.00
Butter Dish, cov	180.00
Carafe	55.00
Castor Bottle	42.00
Celery Vase	85.00
Champagne, hs or ls	115.00
Cologne Bottle	85.00

Items	Clear
Cordial	75.00
Creamer, ah	130.00
Cruet, os	130.00
Decanter, pint or quart, bar lip	124.00
Egg Cup, covered	165.00
Egg Cup, open	60.00
Goblet, knob stem †	66.00
Goblet, plain stem	55.00
Lamp	120.00
Jelly Glass, flat	55.00
Mug, ah, 3-1/2" h.	135.00
Pickle Dish, oval	30.00
Pitcher, water, ah	285.00
Pomade Jar, cov	72.00
Relish, oval	30.00
Salt, individual	48.00
Salt, master, ftd, covered	120.00
Salt, master, ftd, open	55.00
Spill Holder	85.00
Spooner	48.00
Sugar Bowl, cov	130.00
Tumbler	85.00
Water Bottle, tumble-up	130.00
Whiskey	85.00
Wine	60.00

Bull's Eye and Daisy

Bull's Eye and Daisies, Knobby Bull's Eye, US Glass Pattern Line No. 15,117

Manufactured by United States Glass Company, Pittsburgh, PA, in 1909, at Factory "F" and Factory "P." Made in non-flint, clear, clear with gilt, emerald green, and ruby stained. Eyes often found stained amethyst, blue, green, or pink.

Reproductions: A goblet has been made in blue and yellow, c1950.

Items	Clear	Emerald Green	Ruby Stained
Bowl	15.00	20.00	36.00
Butter Dish, cov	30.00	210.00	110.00
Celery Vase	24.00	30.00	48.00
Creamer	30.00	30.00	60.00
Cruet, os	36.00	42.00	66.00
Decanter	—	135.00	—
Goblet φ	30.00	210.00	60.00
Jelly Dish, round, 3 handles	18.00	30.00	48.00
Olive Dish, round, flat, handle	18.00	30.00	48.00
Pitcher, water	42.00	48.00	115.00
Punch bowl	45.00	—	—
Salt Shaker	24.00	24.00	42.00
Sauce, flat	7.50	12.00	24.00
Spooner, 2 handles	24.00	30.00	48.00
Sugar Bowl, cov, 2 handles	30.00	36.00	55.00
Toothpick Holder	24.00	36.00	60.00
Tumbler	18.00	110.00	42.00
Wine	24.00	30.00	48.00

Bull's Eye and Fan

Daisies in Oval Panels

Manufactured by United States Glass Company, Pittsburgh, PA, c1904. Made in non-flint, clear, clear with amethyst stain, pink stain, or sapphire blue, and emerald green. Rare pieces in canary-yellow. Some pieces were gilted.

Items	Amethyst Stain	Clear	Emerald Green	Pink Stain	Sapphire Blue
Berry Bowl, 8" d	—	18.00	24.00	—	95.00
Bowl, 5" d, pinched ends	—	—	30.00	—	—
Butter Dish, cov	—	55.00	65.00	—	150.00
Cake Stand	—	30.00	—	—	—
Creamer, individual	—	12.00	—	—	—
Creamer, regular	—	30.00	36.00	—	95.00
Custard Cup	—	12.00	—	—	—
Goblet	30.00	24.00	55.00	30.00	55.00
Lemonade Mug, 5" h	—	55.00	—	—	—
Lemonade Pitcher, ftd	—	55.00	—	—	175.00
Pitcher, water, tankard	55.00	48.00	120.00	60.00	120.00

Items	Amethyst Stain	Clear	Emerald Green	Pink Stain	Sapphire Blue
Relish	24.00	18.00	42.00	24.00	42.00
Sauce	30.00	12.00	24.00	30.00	25.00
Spooner	30.00	24.00	55.00	30.00	70.00
Sugar Bowl, cov	48.00	42.00	72.00	36.00	125.00
Toothpick Holder	—	42.00	5.00	65.00	—
Tumbler	55.00	18.00	55.00	48.00	42.00
Wine	25.00	24.00	48.00	48.00	30.00

Bull's Eye with Diamond Point

Owl, Union

Manufactured by New England Glass Company, East Cambridge, MA, c1869. Made in flint, only in clear. Some rare examples exist in fiery opalescent and deep colors.

Items	Clear
Bowl, open, flat, 5", 6", 7" or 8" d	48.00-95.00
Butter Dish, cov	300.00
Celery Vase	180.00
Champagne	155.00
Cologne Bottle, os	110.00
Compote, open, hs, 7", 8", 9" or 10" d	120.00-172.00
Compote, open, ls, 7", 8", 9" or 10" d	110.00-180.00
Cordial	142.00
Creamer	240.00
Cruet, os	270.00
Decanter, bar lip, pint	190.00
Decanter, bar lip, quart	240.00
Egg Cup	110.00
Goblet	124.00
Honey Dish, flat	30.00
Lamp, finger, whale oil, ah	165.00
Lemonade	130.00
Pitcher, water, tankard, ah, 10-1/4" h	275.00
Salt, master, cov	120.00
Sauce, flat	24.00
Spill Holder	75.00
Spooner	130.00
Sugar Bowl, cov	190.00
Syrup, orig top	190.00
Tumbler	155.00
Tumble-Up	165.00
Whiskey	180.00
Wine	142.00

Bull's Eye with Fleur-De-Lis

Bull's Eye and Princess Feather, Bull's Eye with Fleur-de-Lis, Bull's Eye with Princess Feather, Prince's Feather, Princess Feather

Manufacture attributed to Union Glass Company, Somerville, MA, and Boston and Sandwich Glass Company, Sandwich, MA c1850. Made in flint, clear.

Items	Clear
Ale Glass	300.00
Bar Bottle, quart	135.00
Butter Dish, cov	190.00
Carafe	85.00
Celery Vase	115.00
Compote, open, hs	180.00
Compote, open, ls	130.00
Creamer	300.00
Decanter, bar lip, pint or quart	135.00
Egg Cup, pedestal	60.00
Finger Lamp	190.00
Fruit Bowl	85.00
Goblet	85.00
Honey Dish	24.00
Lamp, whale oil, all glass, 10" h	180.00
Lamp, whale oil, glass font, brass stem, marble base, 10" h	190.00
Lemonade Glass	135.00
Mug, ah	120.00
Pitcher, water, ah	495.00
Salt, master	55.00
Sauce, flat	24.00
Spooner	60.00

Items	Clear
Sugar Bowl, cov	135.00
Tumbler	120.00
Whiskey	115.00
Wine, 2 styles	75.00

Butterfly and Fan

Bird in Ring, Butterfly with Fan, Duncan's Grace, Fan, Grace, Japanese.

Manufactured by George Duncan & Sons, Pittsburgh, PA, c1880. Also made by Richards and Hartley Glass Company, Pittsburgh, PA, c1888. Made in non-flint, clear only.

Items	Clear
Berry Bowl, master	36.00
Bread Plate	60.00
Butter Dish, cov, flat	120.00
Butter Dish, cov, footed	75.00
Celery Vase	75.00
Compote, cov, hs, 7" or 8" d	115.00
Compote, open, hs	36.00
Creamer, ftd	55.00
Goblet	60.00
Marmalade Jar, cov	75.00
Pickle Castor, silver plated frame and cov	195.00
Pitcher, water	118.00
Sauce, flat or footed, 4" d	18.00
Spooner	36.00
Sugar Bowl, cov	60.00

Button Arches

Scalloped Diamond, Scalloped Daisy-Red Top, Duncan No. 39

Manufactured by Duncan and Miller Glass Company, c1898. The ruby staining was applied by the Oriental Glass Company, Pittsburgh, PA, with a wide band of gold, gilt rims, or three gold bands. Made in non-flint, clambroth, clear, and ruby stained. Pieces are found plain or with copper wheel engraving, and souvenir inscriptions. Clambroth is an unusual color in that it is semi-opaque and grayish, resembling its namesake, the broth of clams. Clambroth pieces are sometimes called "Koral," especially when trimmed in gold or used as souvenirs. A mug is documented in amethyst and a few other rare pieces exist in color.

Reproductions: Ruby stained souvenir pieces have been reproduced. The reproductions were made by Westlake Ruby Glass Works, Columbus, OH, in the 1970s. The Fenton Art Glass Company, Williamstown, WV, also reproduced a number of pieces in the 1980s, including the butter dish, open compote, and sauce dish. These pieces are not ruby stained. Reproductions have elongated ovals. Any cranberry stained example is probably a reproduction.

Items	Clambroth	Clear	Ruby Stained
Berry Bowl, master, 8" d	—	24.00	60.00
Butter Dish, cov φ	—	60.00	120.00
Cake Stand, hs, 9" d	—	42.00	195.00
Celery Vase	—	36.00	75.00
Compote, open, hs, flared rim	—	60.00	85.00
Creamer, individual φ	—	24.00	55.00
Creamer, table φ	30.00	24.00	55.00
Cruet, os	—	55.00	190.00
Custard Cup	—	18.00	30.00
Goblet φ	48.00	30.00	48.00
Jelly Compote	—	55.00	60.00
Mug φ	36.00	30.00	36.00
Mustard, cov, underplate	—	—	120.00
Pitcher, milk, tankard, quart	—	42.00	120.00
Pitcher, water, tankard, half gallon	—	75.00	130.00
Plate, 7" d	—	12.00	30.00
Punch Cup	—	18.00	30.00
Salt, individual	—	18.00	—
Salt Shaker, short or tall	35.00	18.00	36.00
Sauce, flat, 4" d φ	—	10.00	25.00
Spooner φ	—	30.00	48.00
Sugar Bowl, cov φ	—	30.00	75.00
Syrup, orig top	—	66.00	190.00
Toothpick Holder φ	—	24.00	42.00
Tumbler, handle or handleless	—	30.00	42.00
Wine, 4-1/2" h	—	18.00	30.00

Button Band

Umbilicated Hobnail, Wyandotte

Manufactured by Ripley and Company, in the late 1880s. Also reissued by United States Glass Company, after 1891, Factory "F." Made in non-flint, clear only. Some pieces are found with engraving. They are priced the same as plain clear pieces.

Items	Clear
Bowl, 10" d	36.00
Butter Dish, cov	55.00
Cake Stand, hs, 10" d	85.00
Castor Set, 5 bottles, glass stand	142.00
Celery Vase	36.00
Compote, cov, hs, 6" d	124.00
Compote, open, ls	66.00
Cordial	42.00
Creamer, ftd or tankard	36.00
Goblet	48.00
Jelly Compote, open, hs	36.00
Pitcher, milk, quart	48.00
Pitcher, water, tankard, half gallon	55.00
Plate, round	15.00
Spooner	30.00
Sugar Bowl, cov	42.00
Tumbler, flat	30.00
Water Tray	48.00
Wine	42.00

Cabbage Rose

Central's No. 140, Rose

Manufactured by Central Glass Company, Wheeling, WV, c1870. The design was patented by designer John Oesterling (No. 4,263) on July 26, 1870. Made in non-flint, clear.

Reproductions: Mosser Glass Company, Cambridge, OH, made reproductions in clear and colors during the early 1980s.

Item	Clear
Basket, 12" h	130.00
Bitters Bottle, 6-1/2" h	130.00
Bowl, cov, round, 6", 7" or 7-1/2" d	55.00-85.00
Bowl, oval, 7-1/2", 8-1/2" or 9-1/2" d	42.00-55.00
Bowl, round, 6" or 7-1/2" d	30.00-42.00
Butter Dish, cov	72.00
Cake Plate, square, flat	65.00
Cake Stand, hs, 9", 9-1/2", 10", 11", 12" or 12-1/2" d	42.00-60.00
Celery Vase, pedestal	60.00
Champagne	60.00
Compote, cov, hs, deep bowl 6", 7" or 7-1/2" d	85.00-135.00
Compote, cov, hs, deep bowl 8-1/2" d	124.00
Compote, cov, hs, deep bowl, 8" or 10" d	130.00-142.00
Compote, cov, hs, regular bowl, 8", 9" or 10" d	110.00-135.00
Compote, cov, hs, shallow bowl, 6", 7" or 8" d	90.00-115.00
Compote, cov, ls, deep bowl, 7", 8" or 9" d	120.00-124.00
Compote, cov, ls, regular bowl, 8" or 10" d	135.00
Compote, cov, ls, regular bowl, 9" d	124.00
Compote, cov, ls, shallow bowl, 6", 7" or 8" d	115.00-135.00
Compote, open, hs, 6-1/2" or 7-1/2" d	65.00-90.00
Compote, open, hs, 8-1/2" or 9-1/2" d	85.00-120.00
Cordial	55.00
Creamer, ah, 5-1/2" h	55.00
Egg Cup, with or without handle	55.00
Goblet φ (2 styles)	55.00
Mug	72.00
Pickle Dish	42.00
Pitcher, milk, quart	180.00
Pitcher, water, half gallon	130.00
Relish, 8-1/2" l, 5" w, rose filled horn of plenty center	48.00
Salt, master, ftd	30.00
Sauce, flat, 4" d	12.00
Spooner φ	30.00
Sugar Bowl, cov	55.00
Tumbler	48.00
Wine	55.00

Cable

Atlantic Cable, Cable with Ring

Manufactured by Boston and Sandwich Glass Company, Sandwich, MA, c1850, to commemorate the laying of the Atlantic Cable. Made in flint, clear. Some pieces found with amber stained panels and rarely in opaque colors.

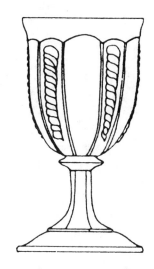

Item	Clear
Bowl, 8" d, ftd	55.00
Bowl, 9" d, flat	85.00
Butter Dish, cov	120.00
Cake Stand, hs, 9" d	120.00
Celery Vase	85.00
Champagne	300.00
Compote, open, hs, 10" d	240.00
Compote, open, ls, 7" d	60.00
Compote, open, ls, 9" d	55.00
Compote, open, ls, 11" d	90.00
Creamer, ah	240.00
Decanter, pint, os	290.00
Decanter, quart, os	325.00
Egg Cup, cov	270.00
Egg Cup, open	72.00
Goblet	85.00
Honey Dish	18.00
Jelly Compote, open, hs, 5-1/2" d	55.00
Lamp, glass base, 8-3/4" h	142.00
Lamp, marble base, 8-3/4" h	120.00
Miniature Lamp	600.00
Mug, ah	90.00
Pitcher, water, ah, half gallon, rare	600.00
Plate, 6" d	90.00
Salt, individual, flat	42.00
Salt, master, covered	115.00
Salt, master, flat	55.00
Sauce, flat	18.00
Spooner	48.00
Sugar Bowl, cov	124.00
Syrup, orig top, orig top	270.00
Tumbler, footed	240.00
Whiskey, flat	240.00
Wine	190.00

Canadian

Manufactured by Burlington Glass Works, Hamilton, Ontario, Canada, c1870. Made in non-flint, clear.

Item	Clear
Bowl, cov, flat, tab handle, 6" d	90.00
Bowl, footed, 7" d, 4-1/2" h	65.00
Bread Plate, 10" d	55.00
Butter Dish, cov	85.00
Cake Stand, hs, 9-1/4" d	85.00
Celery Vase	65.00
Compote, cov, hs, 6", 7" or 8" d	110.00-135.00
Compote, cov, hs, 10" d	130.00
Compote, cov, ls, 6", 7" or 8" d	60.00-90.00
Compote, open, hs, 6", 7" or 8" d	42.00-55.00
Compote, open, ls, 6", 7" or 8" d	42.00-48.00
Creamer	65.00
Goblet	55.00
Marmalade Jar, cov	135.00
Mug, small	55.00
Pitcher, milk, quart	110.00
Pitcher, water, half gallon	124.00
Plate, 6" d, handles	36.00
Plate, 8", 9-1/2" or 10" d	42.00-60.00
Plate, 12-1/2" d	55.00
Sauce, flat, 4" d	18.00
Sauce, footed, 4" d	24.00
Spooner	55.00
Sugar Bowl, cov	110.00
Wine	55.00

Candlewick

Banded Raindrop, Cole

Maker unknown, c1880. Made in non-flint, clear, amber, and milk glass.

Item	Amber	Clear	Milk Glass
Bowl	110.00	110.00	110.00
Cake Stand	55.00	42.00	55.00
Celery	42.00	30.00	42.00
Compote, cov	72.00	55.00	72.00
Compote, open	42.00	24.00	42.00
Creamer	36.00	24.00	36.00
Cup and Saucer	36.00	30.00	36.00
Goblet	30.00	24.00	30.00
Plate	18.00	12.00	18.00
Relish, sq	30.00	24.00	30.00
Salt and Pepper Shakers, pr	48.00	36.00	48.00
Sauce, flat	12.00	6.00	12.00
Sauce, footed	18.00	12.00	18.00
Spooner	36.00	24.00	36.00
Sugar Bowl, cov	42.00	30.00	42.00

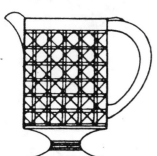

Cane

Cane Insert, Cane Seat, Hobnailed Diamond and Star, McKee's Hobnail

Manufactured by Gillinder and Sons Glass Company, Philadelphia, PA, and by McKee Brothers Glass Company, Pittsburgh, PA, c1885. Made in non-flint, amber, apple green, blue, clear, and vaseline. Goblets and toddy plates are known with inverted "buttons."

Item	Amber Amber	Apple Green	Blue	Clear	Vaseline
Berry Bowl, master	30.00	42.00	48.00	24.00	42.00
Bowl, oval, 9-1/2" l	18.00	—	—	—	—
Butter Dish, cov	55.00	72.00	90.00	48.00	72.00
Celery Vase	310.00	48.00	60.00	42.00	48.00
Compote, open, hs, 5-3/4" d	36.00	36.00	42.00	30.00	42.00
Cordial	—	—	—	30.00	—
Creamer	42.00	48.00	60.00	30.00	42.00
Finger Bowl	24.00	36.00	42.00	18.00	36.00
Goblet	30.00	48.00	42.00	24.00	48.00
Honey Dish	—	—	—	18.00	—
Match Holder, kettle shape	24.00	—	42.00	36.00	42.00
Pickle	30.00	24.00	30.00	18.00	42.00
Pitcher, milk	72.00	55.00	65.00	48.00	55.00
Pitcher, water	95.00	85.00	95.00	55.00	85.00
Relish	30.00	30.00	30.00	18.00	24.00
Salt and Pepper Shakers, pr	72.00	60.00	95.00	36.00	85.00
Sauce, flat	—	12.00	—	10.00	—
Sauce, footed	—	12.00	—	12.00	—
Slipper	36.00	—	30.00	18.00	36.00
Spooner	45.00	42.00	36.00	24.00	36.00
Sugar Bowl, cov	55.00	55.00	55.00	30.00	55.00
Toddy Plate, 4-1/2" d	24.00	30.00	36.00	24.00	30.00
Tumbler	30.00	36.00	42.00	24.00	30.00
Waste Bowl, 7-1/2" d	42.00	36.00	42.00	24.00	36.00
Water Tray	42.00	48.00	60.00	36.00	55.00
Wine	42.00	48.00	42.00	24.00	42.00

Cape Cod

Manufacture unknown. Made in non-flint, clear.

Item	Clear
Bowl, 6" d, handle	36.00
Bread Plate	48.00
Butter Dish, cov	72.00
Celery Vase	55.00
Compote, cov, hs, 6", 8" or 12" d	60.00-190.00
Compote, cov, ls, 6" d; or open, hs, 7" d	60.00
Creamer	42.00
Decanter	120.00
Goblet	55.00
Marmalade Jar, cov	85.00
Pitcher, milk	65.00
Pitcher, water	90.00

Item	Clear
Plate, 5" d, handles	36.00
Plate, 10" d	48.00
Platter, open handles	55.00
Sauce, flat, 4" d	12.00
Sauce, footed, 4" d	15.00
Spooner	36.00
Sugar Bowl, cov	42.00
Wine	36.00

Cardinal

Blue Jay, Cardinal Bird

Manufacture attributed to Ohio Flint Glass Company, Lancaster, OH, c1875. Shards have been found at Burlington Glass Works, Hamilton, Ontario, Canada. Made in non-flint, clear. There were two butter dishes made. One in the regular pattern and one with three birds on the base, labeled in script "Red Bird, Pewit, and Titmouse." The latter is less common.

Reproductions: Reproduction goblets have been made by Summit Art Glass Company, Akron, OH. These goblets can be found in blue, clear, and green.

Item	Clear
Berry Bowl	65.00
Butter Dish, cov, regular	65.00
Butter Dish, cov, three birds variation	124.00
Cake Stand, hs	90.00
Creamer φ	48.00
Goblet φ	42.00
Honey Dish, cov, 3-1/2" d	55.00
Honey Dish, open, 3-1/2" d	24.00
Pitcher, water	180.00
Sauce, flat, 4" d or 4-1/2" d	12.00
Sauce, flat, 5" d	15.00
Sauce, footed, 4" d or 4-1/2" d	18.00
Sauce, footed, 5-1/2" d	24.00
Spooner	48.00
Sugar Bowl, cov	72.00

Carolina

Inverness, Mayflower

Manufactured by Bryce Brothers, Pittsburgh, PA, c1890, and later by United States Glass Company, Pittsburgh, as part of the States series, c1900. Made in clear and ruby stained. Some ruby stained pieces are engraved as souvenirs. Other pieces have been found with gilt or purple stain.

Item	Clear	Ruby Stained
Berry Bowl	18.00	—
Bowl, oval, beaded rim, deep or shallow, 5", 6", 7", 8" or 9" d	12.00-18.00	—
Bread Tray, handles	48.00	—
Butter Dish, cov	42.00	—
Cake Stand, hs, 9-1/2", 10-1/2" or 11" d	42.00-48.00	—
Compote, cov, hs, 5", 6", 7" or 8" d	55.00-72.00	—
Compote, cov, ls, 5", 6" 7" or 8" d	42.00-48.00	—
Compote, open, hs, crimped bowl, 6", 7", 8" or 9" d	24.00-30.00	—
Compote, open, hs, deep bowl, 5", 6", 7" or 8" d	18.00-48.00	—
Compote, open, hs, saucer bowl, 8", 9" or 10" d	24.00-36.00	—
Compote, open, ls, 5", 6" or 7" d	24.00	—
Compote, open, ls, 8" d	30.00	—
Creamer, pint, tankard or table	24.00	—
Cruet, os	55.00	—
Goblet	30.00	55.00
Jelly Compote, open	12.00	—
Mug	24.00	42.00
Pitcher, milk, quart	55.00	—
Plate, 7" d or 7-1/2" d	12.00	—
Relish Tray	12.00	—
Salt and Pepper Shakers, pr	36.00	65.00
Sauce, flat, 4" d or 4-1/2" d	10.00	—
Sauce, footed, 4" d or 4-1/2" d	12.00	—
Spooner	24.00	—
Sugar Bowl, cov	30.00	—
Syrup, orig top, orig top	48.00	—
Tumbler	12.00	—
Wine	24.00	42.00

Cathedral

Orion, Waffle, and Fine Cut

Manufactured by Bryce Brothers, Pittsburgh, PA, in the 1880s and by United States Glass Company, Pittsburgh, in 1891. Made in non-flint, amber, amethyst, blue, clear, ruby stained, and vaseline. Add 50% to clear values for ruby stained.

Item	Amber	Amethyst	Blue	Clear	Vaseline
Berry Bowl, 6" d	48.00	72.00	60.00	55.00	60.00
Bowl, scalloped rim, 5" d	24.00	42.00	30.00	12.00	36.00
Bowl, scalloped rim, 6" d	30.00	48.00	36.00	18.00	42.00
Bowl, scalloped rim, 7" d	36.00	55.00	42.00	24.00	48.00
Bowl, scalloped rim, 8" d	42.00	60.00	48.00	30.00	55.00
Butter Dish, cov	72.00	135.00	48.00	55.00	72.00
Cake Stand, hs	60.00	90.00	65.00	48.00	65.00
Celery Vase	42.00	72.00	48.00	36.00	48.00
Compote, cov, hs, 8" d	95.00	150.00	120.00	85.00	110.00
Compote, open, hs, 9-1/2" d	60.00	85.00	85.00	55.00	—
Compote, open, ls, 7" d	55.00	95.00	42.00	30.00	60.00
Creamer, flat, sq	60.00	85.00	—	42.00	60.00
Creamer, tall	55.00	95.00	60.00	36.00	55.00
Cruet, os	95.00	—	—	55.00	0
Goblet	60.00	85.00	60.00	36.00	55.00
Jelly Compote, open, ruffled	—	—	—	30.00	—
Lamp, oil, orig burner and chimney, 12-3/4" h		—	—	225.00	——
Mug	—	—	—	24.00	—
Pitcher, water	90.00	135.00	90.00	72.00	120.00
Relish, fish shape	48.00	60.00	60.00	35.00	55.00
Salt, boat shape	18.00	36.00	24.00	12.00	18.00
Sauce, flat, 4" d	18.00	36.00	24.00	18.00	24.00
Sauce, footed, 4" d or 4-1/2" d	18.00	42.00	24.00	18.00	24.00
Spooner	48.00	65.00	60.00	42.00	55.00
Sugar Bowl, cov	85.00	120.00	72.00	60.00	72.00
Tumbler	48.00	48.00	42.00	30.00	48.00
Wine	48.00	72.00	55.00	36.00	60.00

Chain and Shield

Shield and Chain

Manufacturer unknown, c1875. Made in non-flint, clear.

Item	Clear
Bread Plate, handles	36.00
Butter Dish, cov	48.00
Cordial	36.00
Creamer	36.00
Goblet	36.00
Pitcher, water	60.00
Sauce, flat	12.00
Spooner	24.00
Sugar Bowl, cov	48.00
Wine	42.00

Chain with Star

Manufactured by Bryce Brothers, Pittsburgh, PA, c1882, and by United States Glass Company, Pittsburgh, PA, c1891. Shards have been found at Burlington Glass Works, Hamilton, Ontario, Canada. Made in non-flint, clear.

Item	Clear
Bowl, 7-1/2" or 9-1/2" d	30.00-36.00
Bread Plate, 11" l, handles	36.00
Butter Dish, cov	42.00
Cake Stand, hs, 8-3/4", 9-1/2" or 10-1/2" d	36.00
Celery Vase	30.00
Compote, cov, hs, 7" or 9" d	60.00
Compote, open, hs	36.00
Creamer	30.00
Dish, oval, 3-3/4" w x 7-1/2" l	24.00
Goblet	30.00
Pickle, oval	12.00
Pitcher, water	55.00
Plate, 7" or 10" d	30.00-42.00
Relish	12.00
Salt and Pepper Shakers, pr	60.00

Item	Clear
Sauce, flat or footed, 4" d	12.00
Spooner	30.00
Sugar Bowl, cov	42.00
Syrup, orig top, orig top	55.00
Wine	30.00

Champion

Fan with Cross Bars, McKee's No. 103, Seagrit

Manufactured by McKee & Brothers Glass Company, Pittsburgh, PA, c1894, McKee-Jeannette Glass Company, Jeannette, PA, and National Glass Company, Pittsburgh, PA, from c1894 to c1917. Stained items are believed to have been decorated at the Beaumont Glass Works, Pittsburgh, PA, which also sold them as its own products. Made in amber, clear, and ruby stained with limited production in emerald green. Pieces are often found with gilt trim.

Item	Amber Stained	Clear	Ruby Stained
Berry Bowl, individual, sq or round	—	—	24.00
Berry Bowl, master, sq or round	55.00	—	65.00
Butter Dish, cov	120.00	55.00	120.00
Cake Stand, hs, 7-1/2" d	120.00	42.00	110.00
Cake Stand, hs, 8-1/2" d	135.00	48.00	115.00
Cake Stand, hs, 10" d	135.00	55.00	120.00
Cake Stand, hs, 11" d	118.00	60.00	135.00
Carafe	142.00	60.00	180.00
Castor Set, 3 bottles, toothpick holder, matching glass holder	—	130.00	—
Celery Vase	120.00	48.00	120.00
Compote, cov, hs	190.00	55.00	240.00
Compote, open, belled or deep bowl, scalloped, 6" d	155.00	42.00	55.00
Compote, open, belled or deep bowl, scalloped, 7" or 8" d	180.00	48.00	72.00
Compote, open, belled or deep bowl, scalloped, 9" d	155.00	60.00	85.00
Creamer, individual	42.00	24.00	42.00
Creamer, table	60.00	30.00	72.00
Cruet, os, 4 or 5 oz	180.00	36.00	200.00
Custard Cup	30.00	12.00	30.00
Goblet	65.00	30.00	65.00
Ice Bucket	130.00	48.00	—
Jelly Compote, open, belled, deep, or shallow bowl, scalloped, 5" d	65.00	24.00	65.00
Marmalade Jar	110.00	48.00	110.00
Perfume Bottle, orig teardrop stopper, bulbous or squatty	55.00	30.00	55.00
Pickle Dish, 8" l	30.00	18.00	30.00
Pitcher, water, tankard	180.00	85.00	190.00
Plate, 6" or 8" d	60.00	30.00	90.00
Plate, 10" d	55.00	30.00	95.00
Punch Bowl, ftd, 14" d	300.00	120.00	285.00
Rose Bowl	55.00	30.00	55.00
Salt and Pepper Shakers, pr	85.00	36.00	85.00
Salt, individual	42.00	12.00	42.00
Sauce, flat, serrated rim, round or sq	24.00	6.00	24.00
Spooner	48.00	24.00	55.00
Sugar Bowl, cov, individual	72.00	42.00	90.00
Sugar Bowl, cov, table	90.00	48.00	85.00
Syrup, orig top, orig top	240.00	90.00	240.00
Toothpick Holder	65.00	24.00	85.00
Tumbler	48.00	18.00	55.00
Water Tray	—	55.00	—
Wine	55.00	24.00	55.00
Wine Tray	—	55.00	—

Chandelier

Crown Jewel

Manufactured by O'Hara Glass Company, Pittsburgh, PA, c1880. The pattern was continued by United States Glass Company, Pittsburgh, PA, after 1891. It is also attributed to a Canadian manufacturer. Made in non-flint, clear. The pattern can be found plain or with etched decoration. A sauce is known in amber ($42).

Item	Etched	Plain
Banana Stand, hs	120.00	115.00
Banana Stand, ls	110.00	90.00
Berry Bowl, master, 8" d, 3-1/4" h	60.00	48.00
Bowl, flat, 6" d or 7" d	50.00	42.00
Butter Dish, cov	85.00	65.00
Cake Stand, hs, 10" d	85.00	65.00
Celery Vase	48.00	48.00
Compote, cov, hs, 6", 7" or 8" d	90.00-110.00	85.00-95.00

Item	Etched	Plain
Compote, cov, hs, sq, 8" d	115.00	85.00
Compote, open, hs, 8" or 9-1/2"d	85.00	65.00
Creamer	72.00	55.00
Finger Bowl	48.00	36.00
Fruit Bowl, hs, scalloped rim, 9" d, 7-1/2" h	100.00	90.00
Goblet	72.00	65.00
Inkwell, dated hard rubber top	—	85.00
Nappy	—	—
Pitcher, water	130.00	118.00
Plate	—	—
Relish, sq	—	—
Salt and Pepper Shakers, pr	90.00	65.00
Salt, master	—	36.00
Sauce, flat	—	18.00
Sauce, footed	—	20.00
Sponge Dish	—	36.00
Spooner	36.00	42.00
Sugar Bowl, cov	90.00	85.00
Sugar Shaker	150.00	135.00
Toothpick Holder	—	—
Tumbler	60.00	42.00
Water Tray	100.00	80.00
Violet Bowl	—	48.00

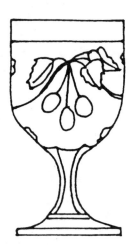

Cherry

Manufactured by Bakewell, Pears and Company, Pittsburgh, PA, c1870. The design was patented by William M. Kirchner on April 5, 1870. Made in non-flint, clear, and milk glass.

Reproductions: Reproduction of the goblet and champagne have been made and are generally of a poor quality.

Item	Clear
Butter Dish, cov	65.00
Celery Vase	48.00
Champagne φ	42.00
Compote, cov, hs, 8" d	90.00
Creamer, ah	55.00
Goblet φ	42.00
Sauce	18.00
Spooner	42.00
Sugar Bowl, cov	60.00
Wine	24.00

Cherry Thumbprint

Cherry and Cable, Paneled Cherry

Manufactured by Northwood Glass Company, Martin's Ferry, OH, c1907. Made in non-flint, clear. Some pieces are decorated with colored cherries and gilt cable.

Reproductions: Reproductions have been made by Westmoreland Glass Company, Grapeville, PA between 1967 and 1983. Mosser Glass Inc., Cambridge, OH, also reproduced this pattern, c1991. Reproduction colors include amethyst carnival and clear with decorations. A child's set is available in reproductions only, as it was never originally made.

Item	Clear	Decorated
Berry Bowl	18.00	36.00
Bowl, cov, flat	42.00	65.00
Butter Dish, cov φ	55.00	115.00
Creamer φ	42.00	72.00
Cup, pedestal	18.00	36.00
Goblet	36.00	72.00
Lemonade	42.00	55.00
Mug	30.00	60.00
Pitcher, water	95.00	135.00
Sauce, flat or footed	18.00	24.00
Spooner	42.00	60.00
Sugar Bowl, cov	65.00	85.00
Syrup, orig top, orig top	85.00	180.00
Toothpick Holder	30.00	55.00
Tumbler φ	36.00	48.00
Wine	36.00	55.00

Classic

Manufactured by Gillinder and Sons, Philadelphia, PA, c1875-1882. Made in non-flint, clear and frosted. Pieces with log feet instead of a collared base are more valuable. The finial for this pattern is a bunch of oak leaves and acorns.

Item	Clear
Berry Bowl, master	85.00
Bowl, cov, 7" d, log feet	155.00
Butter Dish, cov, log feet	225.00
Cake Stand	100.00
Celery Vase, collared	118.00
Celery Vase, log feet	130.00
Compote, cov, collared, 6-1/2", 8-1/2" or 12-1/2" d	180.00-330.00
Compote, cov, log feet, 6-1/2" d	300.00
Compote, cov, log feet, 7-1/2" d	270.00
Compote, open, log feet, 7-3/4" d	120.00
Creamer, collared	120.00
Creamer, log feet	180.00
Goblet	300.00
Marmalade Jar, cov	360.00
Pitcher, milk, log feet	460.00
Pitcher, water, collared	240.00
Pitcher, water, log feet	300.00
Plate, James G. Blaine, 10-1/2" d	225.00
Plate, President Cleveland, 10-1/2" d	195.00
Plate, Thomas H. Hendricks, 10-1/2" d	185.00
Plate, John A. Logan, 10-1/2" d	270.00
Plate, warrior, 10-1/2" d	165.00
Sauce, footed, collared, 4-1/2" d	30.00
Sauce, footed, log feet, 4-1/2" d	36.00
Spooner, collared	85.00
Spooner, log feet	130.00
Sugar Bowl, cov, collared	180.00
Sugar Bowl, cov, log feet	225.00
Sweetmeat Jar, cov	190.00

Classic Medallion

Cameo #1

Manufacturer unknown, c1870-80. Made in clear.

Item	Clear
Bowl, footed, 6-3/4" d	48.00
Bowl, straight sides, 8" d	36.00
Butter Dish, cov	48.00
Celery Vase	36.00
Compote, cov	60.00
Compote, open, 7" d, 3-3/4" h	36.00
Creamer	42.00
Goblet	42.00
Pitcher, water	95.00
Sauce, footed	18.00
Spooner	30.00
Sugar Bowl, cov	48.00

Clear Diagonal Band

Manufacturer unknown, c1880. Shards have been found at Burlington Glass Works, Hamilton, Ontario, Canada. Made in non-flint, clear. Some pieces have been found in light amber.

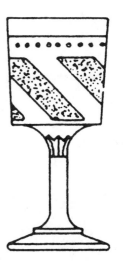

Item	Clear
Bowl, cov. ftd	36.00
Bread Plate, Eureka	48.00
Butter Dish, cov	48.00
Cake Stand, hs	48.00
Celery Vase, pedestal	30.00
Compote, cov, hs	55.00
Compote, open, hs	36.00
Cordial	30.00
Creamer, 6" h	30.00
Dish, oval	12.00
Goblet	24.00
Marmalade Jar, cov	36.00
Pitcher, water	48.00

Item	Clear
Plate	18.00
Relish, oval	12.00
Salt and Pepper Shakers, pr	36.00
Sauce, flat	6.00
Sauce, footed	12.00
Spooner	18.00
Sugar Bowl, cov	36.00
Wine	24.00

Clear Ribbon

Duncan No. 150

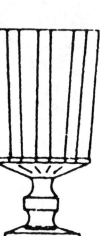

Manufactured by George Duncan and Sons, Pittsburgh, PA, c1878.

Item	Clear
Bread Plate, motto, GUTDODB, ftd	48.00
Butter Dish, cov	60.00
Cake Stand, hs, 9" d	48.00
Celery Vase	24.00
Compote, cov	65.00
Compote, open	30.00
Creamer	36.00
Dish, cov, oblong, 6" or 8" l	30.00-36.00
Goblet, fancy foot	42.00
Pickle	18.00
Pitcher, water	72.00
Sauce, footed	12.00
Spooner	30.00
Sugar Bowl, cov	48.00

Coin-Columbian

Spanish Coin

Manufacturer unknown, c1890. Made in non-flint, clear and frosted.
Reproductions: Reproductions are suspected in several forms.

Item	Clear	Frosted
Butter Dish, cov	130.00	300.00
Cake Stand	495.00	960.00
Celery	90.00	180.00
Compote, cov, 8" d	90.00	180.00
Compote, open, 7" d	72.00	124.00
Creamer	65.00	136.00
Cruet, os	65.00	136.00
Goblet φ	55.00	135.00
Lamp, oil, 8-1/2" h	130.00	300.00
Pitcher, milk	190.00	360.00
Pitcher, water	90.00	180.00
Salt and Pepper Shakers, pr	115.00	110.00
Sauce	15.00	30.00
Spooner	55.00	110.00
Sugar Bowl, cov	72.00	124.00
Sugar Bowl, open	42.00	85.00
Syrup, orig top, orig top	270.00	460.00
Toothpick Holder φ	30.00	60.00
Tumbler φ	30.00	60.00
Water Tray	130.00	300.00
Wine	85.00	148.00

Colorado

Lacy Medallion

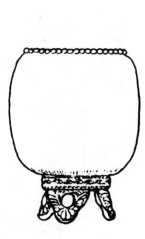

Manufactured by United States Glass Company, Pittsburgh, PA, c1898 to 1920, as one of its States series. Made in non-flint, Dewey blue, clear, clambroth, and green. The green is sometimes found with copper wheel engraving. Also made in amethyst stained, ruby stained and opaque white with enamel floral trim, all of which are scarce compared to the solid colors. Some pieces are found with ornate silver frames or feet. Purists consider these two separate patterns, with the *Lacy Medallion* restricted to souvenir pieces.
Reproductions: Many reproductions exist. The Summit Art Glass Company, Mogadore/Rootstown, OH, made a toothpick holder in clear and other original colors.

Item	Dewey Blue	Clear	Green
Banana Stand	65.00	42.00	60.00
Bowl, crimped, 5" d	36.00	24.00	30.00

Item	Dewey Blue	Clear	Green
Bowl, flared, 5" d or crimped, 6" d	42.00	30.00	36.00
Bowl, flared, 6" d or crimped, 7" d	48.00	36.00	42.00
Bowl, flared, 7" d or crimped, 8" d	55.00	42.00	48.00
Bowl, flared, 8" d	60.00	48.00	55.00
Bowl, ftd, 5" d	42.00	24.00	36.00
Bowl, ftd, 6" d	48.00	36.00	42.00
Bowl, ftd, 7" d	55.00	42.00	48.00
Bowl, ftd, 7-1/2" d	48.00	30.00	42.00
Bowl, ftd, 8" d	55.00	42.00	48.00
Bowl, ftd, 8-1/4" d	65.00	55.00	72.00
Butter Dish, cov	240.00	72.00	130.00
Cake Stand	90.00	55.00	65.00
Calling Card Tray	55.00	30.00	42.00
Celery Vase	65.00	42.00	90.00
Compote, open, ls, 5" d	42.00	24.00	36.00
Compote, open, ls, 6" d	55.00	24.00	55.00
Compote, open, ls, 9-1/2" d	115.00	42.00	65.00
Cracker Jar, cov	130.00	60.00	120.00
Creamer, individual, bulbous or tankard	55.00	36.00	48.00
Creamer, regular	115.00	48.00	85.00
Custard Cup, ah, ftd, large or small	36.00	24.00	30.00
Dresser Tray	55.00	30.00	42.00
Mug	48.00	24.00	36.00
Nappy	48.00	24.00	42.00
Olive Dish	48.00	24.00	36.00
Pickle Dish	48.00	24.00	36.00
Pitcher, milk, ah, quart	300.00	—	120.00
Pitcher, water, ah, half gallon	390.00	115.00	225.00
Plate, 6" d	60.00	20.00	55.00
Plate, 8" d	65.00	24.00	72.00
Punch Cup	36.00	20.00	30.00
Salt Shaker	65.00	36.00	48.00
Sauce, ftd, ruffled or flared rim, 4" d	36.00	18.00	30.00
Sherbet, large or small	60.00	30.00	55.00
Spooner	65.00	48.00	72.00
Sugar Bowl, cov, table	90.00	72.00	90.00
Sugar Bowl, open, individual, with or without handles	42.00	30.00	36.00
Toothpick Holder φ	72.00	36.00	55.00
Tumbler	42.00	20.00	36.00
Vase, 12" h	85.00	42.00	72.00
Violet Bowl	72.00	—	—
Wine	—	30.00	48.00

Comet

Manufacture attributed to Boston and Sandwich Glass Company, Sandwich, MA, in the early 1850s. Made in flint, clear.

Item	Clear
Butter Dish, cov	240.00
Compote, open	180.00
Creamer, ah	190.00
Goblet	175.00
Mug, ah	140.00
Pitcher, water, ah	600.00
Spooner	85.00
Sugar Bowl, cov	190.00
Tumbler	135.00
Whiskey	225.00

Connecticut

Manufactured by United States Glass Company, c1900, as one of its States series. Made in non-flint, clear, plain and engraved. Two varieties of ruby stained toothpick holders have been identified and are currently valued at $125.

Item	Clear
Basket	60.00
Biscuit Jar	30.00
Bowl, 4" d	12.00
Bowl, 6" or 8" d, pattern on rim or base	18.00
Butter Dish, cov	42.00
Cake Stand, hs, 10" d	48.00
Celery Tray	24.00
Celery Vase	42.00
Cheese, cov, plate	60.00
Compote, cov, hs, 5", 5-1/2", 6", 7" or 8" d	30.00-48.00

Item	Clear
Compote, open, hs, scalloped, 6" d	55.00
Compote, open, hs, scalloped, 7-1/2", 8-1/2" or 9-1/2" d	36.00-48.00
Compote, open, ls, 7"	30.00
Creamer	36.00
Cruet, os	30.00
Custard Cup	6.00
Dish, oblong, 8" l	24.00
Goblet	24.00
Lamp, oil, orig burner and chimney	85.00
Lemonade, handle	24.00
Marmalade Jar, cov	48.00
Pickle Jar, cov	42.00
Pitcher, milk, quart, tankard	42.00
Pitcher, water, half gallon, bulbous	48.00
Pitcher, water, half gallon, tankard	55.00
Relish	15.00
Salt and Pepper Shakers, pr	42.00
Sauce, flat, belled or straight sided, patterned base, 4" d or 4-1/2" d	12.00
Sherbet	6.00
Spooner	30.00
Sugar Bowl, cov	42.00
Toothpick Holder	55.00
Tumbler	110.00
Wine	42.00

Cord and Tassel

Manufactured by LaBelle Glass Company, Bridgeport, OH. Patented by Andrew Baggs in 1872. It was also made by Central Glass Company, Wheeling, WV, and other companies. Made in non-flint, clear.
Reproductions: It is believed that the goblet and wine have been reproduced.

Item	Clear
Bowl, oval	24.00
Butter Dish, cov	65.00
Cake Stand, hs, 10" d	65.00
Castor Bottle	30.00
Celery Vase	30.00
Compote, cov, hs, 8" d	120.00
Compote, open, ls	42.00
Cordial	55.00
Creamer	30.00
Egg Cup	42.00
Goblet φ	42.00
Lamp, ah, pedestal	120.00
Mug, ah	65.00
Mustard Jar, cov	55.00
Pickle Dish, oval	18.00
Pitcher, water, ah	115.00
Salt and Pepper Shakers, pr	55.00
Sauce, flat	12.00
Spooner	42.00
Sugar Bowl, cov	65.00
Syrup, orig top	130.00
Tumbler	55.00
Vegetable Dish, oval	30.00
Wine φ	42.00

Cord Drapery

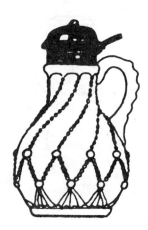

Manufactured by National Glass Combine, Greentown, IN, c1899-1903. Made by Indiana Glass Company, Dunkirk, IN, after 1907. Made in amber, blue, clear, and emerald green. Syrup, orig top also made in chocolate glass.

Item	Amber	Blue	Clear	Emerald Green
Bowl, 7-1/2" d	30.00	30.00	24.00	36.00
Butter Dish, cov	85.00	85.00	95.00	190.00
Cake Stand	60.00	55.00	55.00	90.00
Compote, open, 6" d	55.00	72.00	55.00	85.00
Compote, open, 7" d	90.00	90.00	72.00	115.00
Creamer	65.00	115.00	55.00	85.00
Cruet, os	265.00	120.00	110.00	130.00
Cup	110.00	110.00	18.00	30.00
Goblet	60.00	60.00	55.00	85.00
Jelly Compote, cov	85.00	115.00	65.00	118.00
Jelly Compote, open	—	55.00	55.00	—
Mug	130.00	155.00	72.00	—
Pickle, oval, 9-1/4" l	48.00	—	30.00	—
Pitcher, water	190.00	1,115.00	65.00	240.00

Item	Amber	Blue	Clear	Emerald Green
Plate	42.00	48.00	30.00	48.00
Punch Cup	—	130.00	36.00	—
Relish	30.00	30.00	30.00	36.00
Salt Shaker, orig top	110.00	130.00	55.00	115.00
Sauce, flat	18.00	18.00	12.00	18.00
Sauce, ftd, 3-1/2" d or 4-1/2" d	36.00	36.00	24.00	42.00
Spooner	60.00	72.00	55.00	65.00
Sugar Bowl, cov	130.00	115.00	124.00	120.00
Sweetmeat, cov, 6-1/2" d, 5-1/4" h	165.00	—	—	—
Syrup, orig top	2,115.00	—	124.00	—
Toothpick Holder	600.00	600.00	95.00	600.00
Tumbler	55.00	60.00	48.00	65.00
Water Tray	190.00	225.00	90.00	190.00
Wine	115.00	135.00	110.00	124.00

Cordova

Manufactured by O'Hara Glass Company, Pittsburgh, PA. It was exhibited for the first time at the Pittsburgh Glass Show, December, 16, 1890. Made in non-flint, clear and emerald green. Toothpick holders have been found in ruby stained (valued at $45).

Item	Clear	Emerald Green
Almond Dish, sq	24.00	—
Berry Bowl, cov	36.00	—
Bowl, cov, 6" or 7" d or 8" or 9"	30.00-36.00	—
Bowl, flared, 6" d, 7" d or 8" d or 9" d	24.00-30.00	—
Bowl, straight sides, 6" d, 7" d, 8" d, or 9" d	18.00-24.00	—
Butter Dish, cov, handle	60.00	—
Cake Stand, hs, 10" d	55.00	—
Casserole, flat, plain or flared rim, 6", 7" or 8" d	36.00	—
Catsup, cov, handle	90.00	—
Celery Vase	55.00	—
Cheese Dish	55.00	—
Cologne Bottle	36.00	—
Compote, cov, hs, 6", 7" or 8" d	42.00-55.00	—
Compote, open, hs	42.00	—
Cracker Jar, cov	55.00	—
Creamer, individual	36.00	—
Creamer, regular	42.00	55.00
Finger Bowl	18.00	—
Inkwell, metal lid	60.00	—
Marmalade Dish, handle, 5" d	18.00	—
Mug	24.00	42.00
Mustard Jar, cov	55.00	—
Nappy, handle, 6" d	15.00	—
Olive, triangular	24.00	—
Pickle Jar, cov	55.00	—
Pitcher, milk, quart, tankard	36.00	—
Pitcher, water, half gallon, tankard	72.00	—
Punch Bowl	110.00	—
Punch Cup	18.00	36.00
Salt, individual, flat	30.00	—
Salt Shaker	24.00	—
Sauce, flat, 4" d or 4-1/2" d	12.00	18.00
Spooner	42.00	55.00
Sugar Bowl, cov, regular	55.00	95.00
Sugar Bowl, open, individual	30.00	55.00
Syrup, orig top	130.00	48.00
Toothpick Holder	18.00	24.00
Tumbler	110.00	—
Vase, bud, flared or straight, 7" or 8" h	18.00	—
Vase, bud, flared or straight, 9" h	24.00	—
Water Tray	60.00	—
Wine	15.00	—

Cottage

Dinner Bell, Fine Cut Band

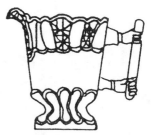

Manufactured by Adams and Company, Pittsburgh, PA, in the late 1870s and by United States Glass Company, Pittsburgh, PA, in the 1890s. Made in non-flint, clear, and ruby stained. Known to have been made in emerald green, amber, light blue, and amethyst. Add 50% for amber, 75% for other colors.

Reproductions: Reproduction stemware is of poor quality and has thicker stems.

Item	Clear	Ruby Stained
Banana Stand	55.00	—
Berry Bowl, master, 10" d	24.00	—

Item	Clear	Ruby Stained
Bowl, oval, 7-1/2" or 9-1/2" l	18.00-24.00	—
Butter Dish, cov, flat or footed	55.00	—
Cake Stand, hs, 9" or 10" d	48.00-55.00	—
Celery Vase	42.00	—
Champagne	65.00	90.00
Claret	60.00	—
Compote, cov, hs, 6" or 7" d	90.00-95.00	—
Compote, cov, hs, 8" or 8-1/4" d	85.00-110.00	—
Compote, cov, ls, 6" or 8" d	55.00	—
Compote, cov, ls, 7" d	60.00	—
Compote, open, hs, 5" d	60.00	—
Compote, open, hs or ls, 6" d	55.00	—
Compote, open, hs or ls, 7" d	72.00	—
Compote, open, hs, 8" d	65.00	—
Compote, open, ls, 8" d	72.00	—
Creamer	42.00	55.00
Cruet, os	55.00	—
Custard Cup	18.00	—
Dish, oval, deep	24.00	—
Finger Bowl	30.00	—
Goblet φ	30.00	—
Jelly Compote, open	42.00	55.00
Pitcher, milk	42.00	—
Pitcher, water	60.00	—
Plate, 5" d	12.00	24.00
Plate, 6", 7", 8" or 9" d	12.00-24.00	—
Relish	12.00	—
Salt Shaker	30.00	—
Sauce, flat, flared; or footed, 4" d or 4-1/2" d	12.00	—
Saucer	18.00	48.00
Spooner	24.00	—
Sugar Bowl, cov	55.00	—
Syrup, orig top	85.00	—
Toothpick Holder	30.00	—
Tumbler	30.00	—
Waste Bowl	24.00	—
Water Tray	42.00	—
Wine φ	42.00	—

Croesus

Manufactured by Riverside Glass Works, Wheeling, WV, in 1897. Also made by McKee and Brothers Glass in 1899. Made in clear by Riverside and amethyst and green by McKee. Some pieces were trimmed in gold.

Reproductions: Many of the reproductions of this expensive pattern are easily given away by their poor quality gold paint.

Item	Amethyst	Clear	Green
Bowl, cov, ftd, 8" d	136.00	42.00	118.00
Bowl, flat, 8" d	180.00	—	124.00
Bowl, ftd, 4" d	72.00	12.00	36.00
Bowl, ftd, 6-1/4" d	195.00	85.00	135.00
Bowl, ftd, 10" d	180.00	—	124.00
Butter Dish, cov φ	195.00	85.00	185.00
Cake Stand, hs, 10" d	195.00	48.00	148.00
Celery Vase	265.00	65.00	142.00
Compote, cov, hs, 5" d	135.00	36.00	118.00
Compote, cov, hs, 6" d	135.00	36.00	118.00
Compote, cov, hs, 7" d	118.00	36.00	130.00
Compote, open, hs, 5" d	72.00	24.00	72.00
Compote, open, hs, 6" d	65.00	30.00	65.00
Compote, open, hs, 7" d	90.00	36.00	90.00
Condiment Set, cruet, salt and pepper, small tray	240.00	190.00	190.00
Condiment Tray	90.00	30.00	36.00
Creamer, individual φ	190.00	72.00	120.00
Creamer, regular φ	180.00	55.00	124.00
Cruet, os, large	360.00	130.00	195.00
Cruet, os, small	290.00	120.00	195.00
Jelly Compote	240.00	24.00	190.00
Pickle Dish	90.00	60.00	85.00
Pitcher, water	330.00	95.00	240.00
Plate, ftd, 8" d	90.00	24.00	65.00
Relish, boat shape	85.00	36.00	72.00
Salt and Pepper Shakers, pr	118.00	48.00	130.00
Sauce, flat, 4" d	48.00	18.00	42.00
Sauce, footed, 4" d	55.00	24.00	48.00
Spooner φ	95.00	72.00	85.00
Sugar Bowl, cov, individual	185.00	30.00	85.00
Sugar Bowl, cov, regular	110.00	55.00	190.00
Toothpick Holder φ	90.00	30.00	36.00
Tumbler φ	65.00	24.00	60.00

Crystal Wedding

Collins, Crystal Anniversary

Manufactured by Adams Glass Company, Pittsburgh, PA, c1890 and by United States Glass Company in 1891. Made in non-flint, clear, frosted, amber stained, and ruby stained. Cobalt blue pieces are rare.

Reproductions: Heavily reproduced in clear, ruby stained, and milk glass with enamel trim. This pattern has been reproduced from the early 1940s. Several companies, including, Duncan, Glasscrafts & Ceramics, Jeannette, L. E. Smith and Westmoreland, have created reproductions and pieces never originally made in the pattern. Westmoreland's pattern is now collectible in it's own right, especially the decorated milk glass pieces.

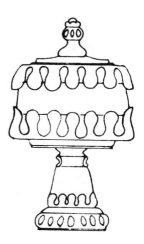

Item	Clear	Ruby Stained
Banana Stand	115.00	—
Berry Bowl, individual, 4-1/2" d	18.00	—
Berry Bowl, master, sq, 8" w	60.00	85.00
Bowl, cov, sq, 6" w	65.00	90.00
Bowl, cov, sq, 7" w	90.00	85.00
Bowl, cov, sq, 8" w	72.00	115.00
Butter Dish, cov	90.00	130.00
Cake Plate, sq, 10" w	55.00	85.00
Cake Stand, hs, 10" d	65.00	—
Celery Vase	55.00	90.00
Claret	85.00	130.00
Compote, cov, hs, 6" sq or 7" sq	90.00	118.00
Compote, cov, hs, 7" x 13"	120.00	135.00
Compote, open, hs, sq, 6" w	72.00	55.00
Compote, open, hs, sq, 7" w; or ls, sq, 7" w or 8" w	72.00	65.00
Compote, open, hs, sq, 8" d	65.00	85.00
Compote, open, ls, sq, 5" w or 6" w	60.00	55.00
Creamer	60.00	90.00
Cruet, os	130.00	240.00
Goblet φ	55.00	85.00
Ice Tub	95.00	—
Nappy, handle	30.00	—
Pickle	30.00	48.00
Pitcher, milk, round	135.00	130.00
Pitcher, milk, square	130.00	240.00
Pitcher, water, round	135.00	255.00
Pitcher, water, square	225.00	270.00
Plate, 10" d	30.00	55.00
Relish	24.00	48.00
Salt, individual	30.00	48.00
Salt, master	42.00	65.00
Salt Shaker	65.00	90.00
Sauce, sq, flat or footed, 4" d or 4-1/2" d	18.00	24.00
Spooner	36.00	72.00
Sugar Bowl, cov	85.00	85.00
Syrup, orig top	180.00	240.00
Tumbler	42.00	55.00
Vase, footed, twisted; or swung	30.00	—
Wine	55.00	85.00

Cupid and Venus

Guardian Angel

Manufactured by Richards and Hartley Glass Company, Tarentum, PA, in the late 1870s. Made in non-flint, clear, amber, and some vaseline.

Reproductions: Westmoreland Glass Company, Grapeville, PA, reproduced the plate, using the original molds.

Item	Amber	Clear
Bowl, cov, ftd, 8" d	—	42.00
Bowl, oval, 9" l	—	42.00
Bread Plate	90.00	48.00
Butter Dish, cov	—	55.00
Cake Plate, 11" d	—	55.00
Cake Stand, hs	—	72.00
Celery Vase	—	48.00
Champagne	—	110.00
Compote, cov, hs, 8" d	—	120.00
Compote, cov, ls, 7" or 9" d	—	110.00-120.00
Compote, open, ls, scalloped, 8-1/2" d	142.00	42.00
Cordial, 3-1/2" h	—	85.00
Creamer	—	42.00
Cruet, os	—	142.00
Goblet	—	90.00
Marmalade Jar, cov	—	85.00
Mug, large, 3-1/2" d	—	48.00

Item	Amber	Clear
Mug, medium, 2-1/2" h	—	42.00
Mug, miniature	—	48.00
Pickle Castor, orig silver plate frame, and tongs	165.00	—
Pitcher, milk	190.00	90.00
Pitcher, water	1,115.00	65.00
Plate, round, 10" d φ	90.00	48.00
Relish, oval, 3 sizes	18.00	—
Sauce, flat	—	12.00
Sauce, footed, 3-1/2" d, 4" d, or 4-1/2" d	—	18.00
Spooner	—	42.00
Sugar Bowl, cov	—	65.00
Wine, 3-3/4" h	—	85.00

Currant

Manufactured by Campbell, Jones and Company, Pittsburgh, PA, and patented in 1871 by Mary B. Campbell. Variations in stems and bases suggest more than one manufacturer. Shards have been found at Boston and Sandwich Glass Company, Sandwich, MA, and Burlington Glass Works, Hamilton, Ontario, Canada. Made in non-flint, clear.

Item	Clear
Bowl, oval, 5" w, 7" l	18.00
Bowl, oval, 6" w, 9" l	24.00
Butter Dish, cov	90.00
Cake Stand, hs, 9-1/2" d	72.00
Cake Stand, hs, 10-1/2" or 11" d	65.00-85.00
Celery Vase	55.00
Compote, cov, hs, 8", 9", 12" d	120.00-165.00
Compote, open, ls, 8" d	55.00
Cordial	55.00
Creamer, ah	55.00
Egg Cup	30.00
Goblet	36.00
Honey Dish, flat, 3-1/2" d	18.00
Marmalade Jar, cov	55.00
Pitcher, milk, ah	130.00
Pitcher, water, ah	115.00
Plate, oval, 5" w, 7" l	30.00
Plate, oval, 6" w, 9" l	36.00
Relish	18.00
Salt, ftd	36.00
Sauce, flat or footed, 4" d or 4-1/2" d	15.00
Spooner	30.00
Sugar Bowl, cov	55.00
Tumbler, ftd	36.00
Vegetable Bowl, 7" d	24.00
Wine	30.00

Currier and Ives

Manufactured by Bellaire Goblet Company, Findlay, OH, c1889-98. Made in non-flint, clear. Also made in colors, but rarely found. A ruby-stained decanter has been documented.

Item	Clear
Bowl, oval, canoe shape, 10" l	36.00
Bread Plate	30.00
Butter Dish, cov	60.00
Cake Stand, 10" d	90.00
Compote, cov, hs, 7-1/2" d	115.00
Compote, open, hs, scalloped, 7-1/2" d	60.00
Cordial	55.00
Creamer	36.00
Cup and Saucer	36.00
Decanter, os	42.00
Dish, oval, boat shape, 8" l	30.00
Goblet, knob stem	36.00
Goblet, plain stem	30.00
Lamp, hs, 9-1/2" h	90.00
Mug	30.00
Pitcher, milk	65.00
Pitcher, water	90.00
Plate, 10" d	24.00
Relish, boat shape or oval	110.00
Salt, master	48.00
Salt Shaker	36.00
Sauce, oval or round, flat	15.00
Spooner	36.00
Sugar Bowl, cov	55.00
Syrup, orig top	90.00

Item	Clear
Tumbler	55.00
Water Bottle, os, 12" h	55.00
Water Tray, Bulky Mule	65.00
Wine, 3-1/4" h	24.00
Wine Tray, Bulky Mule	60.00

Curtain

Sultan

Manufactured by Bryce Brothers, Pittsburgh, PA, in the late 1870s. Made in non-flint, clear.

Item	Clear
Bowl, 7-1/2" or 8" d	24.00-30.00
Butter Dish, cov	85.00
Cake Stand, 8", 8-1/2" or 9" d	48.00-60.00
Cake Stand, 10" d	55.00
Castor Set, salt, pepper, and mustard, stand	118.00
Celery Tray	36.00
Celery Vase	36.00
Compote, cov, hs, 6", 7", 8" or 9" d; or open, hs, 6", 7", 8" or 9" d	36.00-55.00
Compote, open, hs, 10" d	60.00
Creamer	30.00
Cruet, os	55.00
Finger Bowl	36.00
Goblet	36.00
Mug	30.00
Mustard Jar	55.00
Pickle	12.00
Pitcher, milk, quart	60.00
Pitcher, water, half gallon	90.00
Plate, sq, 7" w	24.00
Salt and Pepper Shakers, pr	60.00
Sauce, collared base or flat, 4-1/2" d or 4-3/4" d	12.00
Spooner	30.00
Sugar Bowl, cov	42.00
Tumbler	24.00
Water Tray	36.00

Curtain Tie Back

Manufactured by Adams and Company, Pittsburgh, PA, in the mid-1880s. Made in non-flint, clear.

Item	Clear
Bowl, square, 7-1/4" w	24.00
Bread Plate	42.00
Butter Dish, cov	48.00
Celery Tray	30.00
Celery Vase	30.00
Compote, cov, hs	48.00
Creamer	30.00
Goblet, fancy base	36.00
Goblet, flat base	24.00
Pickle	15.00
Pitcher, water	55.00
Relish	12.00
Salt and Pepper Shakers, pr	42.00
Sauce, flat	6.00
Sauce, footed	10.00
Spooner	36.00
Sugar Bowl, cov	42.00
Tumbler	18.00
Water Tray	36.00
Wine	24.00

Cut Log

Cat's Eye and Block, Ethol

Manufactured by Greensburg Glass Company, Greensburg, PA, in 1888, and by Westmoreland Specialty Glass Company, Grapeville, PA, c1896. Made in non-flint, clear. Also reported in camphor glass, but rare.

Reproductions: Jeannette Glass Company, Jeannette, PA, copied this pattern in a fruit bowl. It can be found in aqua, clear, opaque shell pink, blue to green, orange to green, red to orange, or yellow to green.

Item	Clear
Banana Stand	110.00
Biscuit Jar	85.00

Item	Clear
Bowl, deep, ftd, scalloped, 10" d	48.00
Butter Dish, cov	65.00
Cake Stand, 9" or 10" d	55.00
Celery Tray	24.00
Celery Vase	48.00
Compote, cov, hs, 7-1/4" d; 8" d, 8" h; or 12-1/2" d	85.00-115.00
Compote, open, hs, 6" d	60.00
Compote, open, hs, 8" d φ	55.00
Compote, open, hs, 10" d	85.00
Creamer, individual	18.00
Creamer, table, 5" h	48.00
Cruet, os, 3 sizes	60.00
Goblet	55.00
Honey Dish, cov	110.00
Jelly Compote, cov, hs, 6-1/4" d	55.00
Mug, large	55.00
Mustard Jar, notched lid	42.00
Olive Dish	24.00
Pitcher, water, ah, helmet shape	90.00
Pitcher, water, ah, tankard	110.00
Relish	30.00
Salt and Pepper Shakers, pr	72.00
Salt, master	85.00
Sauce, flat or footed	24.00
Spooner	42.00
Sugar Bowl, cov or open, individual	36.00
Sugar Bowl, cov, table	55.00
Tumbler	55.00
Vase	55.00
Wine	36.00

Dahlia

Manufactured by Bryce, Higbee and Company, Pittsburgh, PA, c1885. Shards have been found at Burlington Glass Works, Hamilton, Ontario, and Diamond Flint Glass Company, Montreal, Quebec, Canada. Made in non-flint, amber, apple green, blue, clear, and vaseline.

Items	Amber	Apple Green	Blue	Clear	Vaseline
Bowl, oval, 8-1/2" l	36.00	30.00	30.00	20.00	36.00
Bread Plate	65.00	60.00	72.00	55.00	55.00
Butter Dish, cov	95.00	85.00	85.00	48.00	110.00
Cake Plate	72.00	55.00	72.00	30.00	72.00
Cake Stand, hs, 9" d	75.00	60.00	60.00	30.00	75.00
Cake Stand, hs, 10" d	95.00	55.00	55.00	36.00	95.00
Champagne	65.00	85.00	75.00	55.00	75.00
Compote, cov, hs, 7" d	110.00	85.00	85.00	55.00	95.00
Compote, open, hs, 8" d	72.00	55.00	55.00	36.00	72.00
Cordial	55.00	60.00	60.00	42.00	55.00
Creamer	48.00	42.00	42.00	30.00	48.00
Egg Cup, double	95.00	65.00	65.00	60.00	95.00
Egg Cup, single	55.00	48.00	48.00	30.00	55.00
Goblet	55.00	85.00	75.00	48.00	65.00
Mug, large	55.00	55.00	55.00	42.00	55.00
Mug, small	60.00	55.00	48.00	36.00	72.00
Pickle	42.00	36.00	36.00	24.00	42.00
Pitcher, milk	85.00	55.00	55.00	55.00	85.00
Pitcher, water	120.00	110.00	110.00	55.00	110.00
Plate, 7" d	65.00	72.00	72.00	55.00	55.00
Plate, 9" d, handles	42.00	55.00	60.00	25.00	60.00
Platter, oval, fan or grape handles, 11" l	60.00	55.00	55.00	36.00	30.00
Relish Dish, 9-1/2" l	24.00	24.00	24.00	18.00	30.00
Salt, individual, ftd	42.00	36.00	36.00	6.00	42.00
Sauce, flat, 4" d	18.00	15.00	18.00	12.00	18.00
Sauce, footed, 4" d	24.00	18.00	18.00	12.00	24.00
Sugar Bowl, cov	75.00	72.00	72.00	48.00	75.00
Syrup, orig top	75.00	—	—	55.00	—
Wine	55.00	48.00	55.00	30.00	55.00

Daisy and Button

Manufactured in the 1880s by several companies in many different forms. This pattern has been in continuous production since inception. Original manufacturers include Bryce Brothers, Doyle & Company, Hobbs, Brockunier & Company, George Duncan & Sons, Beatty & Sons, and United States Glass Company. Made in amber, amber stain, amberina, apple green, light blue, clear, ruby stain, sapphire blue, and vaseline. A sapphire blue syrup is currently valued at $295.

Hobbs, Brockunier made limited pieces on amberina flint, valued at 300%.

Reproductions: Reproductions have existed since the early 1930s in original and new colors. Companies making reproductions include L. G. Wright, Imperial Glass Co., Fenton Art Glass Co., and Degenhart Glass Company.

Items	Amber	Apple Green	Blue	Clear	Vaseline
Ale Glass, 4 or 5 ounce	30.00	42.00	36.00	24.00	48.00
Bar Bottle, os	55.00	55.00	48.00	30.00	55.00
Boot	48.00	55.00	55.00	42.00	55.00
Bowl, cov, tab handles, 8" d	65.00	85.00	85.00	55.00	85.00
Bowl, open, oval, scalloped rim, 12" d	110.00	148.00	125.00	75.00	180.00
Bowl, open, round, scalloped rim, 9" d or 9-1/2" d	42.00	55.00	48.00	30.00	60.00
Bowl, open, round, shallow, 5-1/2" d or 7" d	36.00	60.00	42.00	24.00	55.00
Bowl, open, square, straight sides, 5" d or 6-1/2" d	36.00	60.00	42.00	24.00	55.00
Bowl, open, square, straight sides, 8-1/2" d	42.00	55.00	48.00	30.00	60.00
Bowl, open, triangular	48.00	55.00	55.00	30.00	65.00
Bread Plate, 13" d	42.00	72.00	42.00	24.00	48.00
Butter Dish, cov, quarter pound size φ	65.00	95.00	65.00	55.00	85.00
Butter Dish, cov, table size, round	85.00	110.00	85.00	65.00	115.00
Butter Dish, cov, table size, square	135.00	118.00	135.00	120.00	124.00
Butter Pat, round or square	36.00	48.00	42.00	30.00	42.00
Candy Basket, ah	42.00	55.00	48.00	24.00	55.00
Canoe, 4" l	15.00	30.00	18.00	12.00	30.00
Canoe, 8-1/2" l	36.00	42.00	36.00	30.00	42.00
Canoe, 12" l φ	72.00	42.00	75.00	24.00	48.00
Canoe, 14" l	36.00	48.00	42.00	30.00	48.00
Castor Set, 4 bottles, glass stand φ	110.00	85.00	115.00	65.00	75.00
Castor Set, 5 bottles, metal stand	120.00	120.00	135.00	120.00	115.00
Celery Tray	30.00	36.00	36.00	30.00	42.00
Celery Vase	55.00	55.00	48.00	36.00	55.00
Cheese Dish, underplate	120.00	130.00	130.00	75.00	142.00
Cologne Bottle, os	48.00	36.00	55.00	55.00	55.00
Compote, cov, hs, 6" d φ	42.00	60.00	55.00	30.00	60.00
Compote, open, hs, 8" d	75.00	65.00	72.00	48.00	65.00
Creamer, individual, barrel shape or round	30.00	42.00	36.00	18.00	48.00
Creamer, table size, bulbous φ	42.00	48.00	48.00	35.00	42.00
Creamer, tankard, ah	42.00	55.00	48.00	30.00	60.00
Cruet, os φ	120.00	95.00	75.00	55.00	95.00
Egg Cup	24.00	36.00	30.00	18.00	36.00
Finger Bowl	36.00	60.00	42.00	36.00	45.00
Goblet, barrel or straight-sided bowl φ	48.00	60.00	48.00	30.00	48.00
Hat, 2-1/2" d φ	36.00	42.00	48.00	24.00	48.00
Ice Cream Bowl	—	—	—	60.00	85.00
Ice Cream Tray, 14" x 9" x 2"	75.00	60.00	55.00	42.00	55.00
Ice Tub	—	42.00	—	—	75.00
Inkwell	48.00	60.00	55.00	36.00	55.00
Lamp, oil, hs	180.00	240.00	240.00	130.00	240.00
Match Safe, flat	30.00	42.00	36.00	24.00	42.00
Parfait	30.00	42.00	36.00	24.00	42.00
Pickle Castor	130.00	110.00	180.00	75.00	180.00
Pickle Dish, fish or yacht shape	36.00	48.00	42.00	30.00	48.00
Pickle Jar, cov	55.00	65.00	65.00	55.00	65.00
Pitcher, milk, ah, bulbous, quart	190.00	—	—	142.00	—
Pitcher, milk, ah, tankard	75.00	85.00	110.00	60.00	110.00
Pitcher, water, bulbous, reed handle φ	130.00	115.00	110.00	75.00	110.00
Pitcher, water, tankard	65.00	65.00	70.00	72.00	65.00
Plate, leaf shape, 5" d	24.00	30.00	20.00	15.00	30.00
Plate, round, plain rim, 6" d, 7" d, 7-1/2" d	12.00	30.00	18.00	10.00	30.00
Plate, round, plain rim, 10" d	18.00	36.00	24.00	12.00	36.00
Plate, square, 7" w	30.00	42.00	30.00	18.00	120.00
Platter, oval or rect	42.00	55.00	48.00	30.00	60.00
Punch Bowl, stand φ	110.00	120.00	115.00	85.00	42.00
Salt and Pepper Shakers, pr, straight-sided or tapered	30.00	42.00	30.00	18.00	24.00
Salt and Pepper Shakers, pr, bulbous or slender φ	36.00	48.00	36.00	24.00	30.00
Salt, individual, band master's hat	42.00	60.00	55.00	30.00	60.00
Salt, individual, hat, rect, or triangular	30.00	48.00	42.00	18.00	48.00
Salt, tub, tab handle, 1-3/4" d or 2" d	24.00	24.00	24.00	12.00	24.00
Salt, master, canoe, 5" l	24.00	36.00	30.00	18.00	36.00
Salt, master, hat	36.00	48.00	42.00	30.00	48.00
Salt, master, shoe	42.00	65.00	55.00	30.00	55.00
Salt, master, yacht	24.00	36.00	30.00	18.00	36.00
Sauce, flat, octagonal	24.00	30.00	24.00	18.00	36.00
Sauce, flat, round, 4" d φ	25.00	30.00	25.00	18.00	60.00
Sauce, flat, square, 4" w or 4-1/2" d	18.00	24.00	12.00	24.00	24.00
Sauce, flat, triangular	24.00	25.00	25.00	12.00	25.00
Shoe, baby bootie, 2-1/2" h	55.00	60.00	60.00	48.00	55.00
Sietz Bath Tub	55.00	72.00	72.00	60.00	65.00
Slipper, 5" l φ	55.00	410.00	60.00	55.00	60.00
Slipper, 11-1/2" φ	48.00	60.00	36.00	42.00	55.00
Spooner, hat shape or scalloped rim φ	48.00	48.00	55.00	42.00	60.00
Sugar Bowl, cov, table size, round, tall φ	55.00	60.00	55.00	42.00	55.00
Sugar Bowl, cov, table size, round, small	48.00	55.00	48.00	36.00	48.00
Sugar Bowl, cov, table size, square, ftd	55.00	72.00	55.00	48.00	65.00
Syrup, orig top	55.00	60.00	55.00	36.00	60.00

Items	Amber	Apple Green	Blue	Clear	Vaseline
Toothpick Holder, barrel, metal bands	30.00	48.00	42.00	24.00	42.00
Toothpick Holder, cat on pillow φ	55.00	65.00	55.00	36.00	65.00
Toothpick Holder, coal scuttle	36.00	48.00	42.00	24.00	55.00
Toothpick Holder, hat, fan or plain brim; or kettle	42.00	48.00	48.00	24.00	48.00
Toothpick Holder, round φ	48.00	55.00	30.00	48.00	55.00
Toothpick Holder, square	24.00	30.00	30.00	18.00	30.00
Toothpick Holder, urn φ	30.00	36.00	30.00	18.00	42.00
Tray, heart shape	30.00	42.00	36.00	18.00	42.00
Tray, round φ	65.00	65.00	42.00	42.00	72.00
Tray, whisk broom shape, 6-1/4" x 4" or 7-1/2" x 5"	30.00	42.00	36.00	18.00	42.00
Tumbler	25.00	36.00	42.00	18.00	30.00
Wall Pocket Vase	130.00	155.00	180.00	75.00	165.00
Water Tray, cloverleaf or triangular	85.00	130.00	135.00	65.00	130.00
Water Tray, oblong with cut corners, round	75.00	118.00	120.00	55.00	118.00
Whiskey	18.00	30.00	24.00	12.00	55.00
Wine φ	18.00	30.00	24.00	12.00	55.00

Daisy and Button with Crossbars

Daisy and Thumbprint Crossbar, Daisy and Button with Crossbar and Thumbprint Band, Daisy with Crossbar, Mikado

Manufactured by Richards & Hartley, Tarentum, PA, c1895. Reissued by United States Glass Company, Pittsburgh, PA, after 1891. Shards have been found at Burlington Glass Works, Hamilton, Ontario, Canada. Made in non-flint, amber, blue, clear, and vaseline.

Items	Amber	Blue	Clear	Vaseline
Bowl, oval, 6" l or 8" l	24.00	36.00	18.00	30.00
Bowl, oval, 9" l	48.00	48.00	30.00	42.00
Bread Plate	36.00	55.00	30.00	42.00
Butter Dish, cov, flat	55.00	55.00	55.00	55.00
Butter Dish, cov, footed	—	75.00	30.00	72.00
Celery Vase	42.00	48.00	36.00	60.00
Compote, cov, hs, 6" d	55.00	65.00	55.00	55.00
Compote, cov, hs, 8" d	65.00	75.00	55.00	65.00
Compote, cov, ls, 7" d	42.00	42.00	30.00	42.00
Compote, cov, ls, 8" d	48.00	48.00	36.00	48.00
Compote, open, hs, 7" d	48.00	55.00	30.00	48.00
Compote, open, hs, 8" d	55.00	60.00	36.00	55.00
Compote, open, ls, 7" or 8" d	36.00	42.00	24.00	55.00
Cordial	36.00	42.00	30.00	36.00
Creamer, individual	30.00	36.00	25.00	36.00
Creamer, regular	30.00	55.00	42.00	48.00
Cruet, os	75.00	85.00	42.00	120.00
Finger Bowl	55.00	48.00	36.00	42.00
Goblet	48.00	48.00	30.00	55.00
Ketchup Bottle	110.00	135.00	42.00	110.00
Lamp, oil, 4 sizes	130.00	155.00	110.00	130.00
Mug, large, 3" h; or small	18.00	35.00	15.00	24.00
Pickle Dish	24.00	24.00	12.00	24.00
Pickle Jar, cov	36.00	55.00	30.00	48.00
Pitcher, milk	65.00	72.00	55.00	110.00
Pitcher, water	115.00	85.00	65.00	130.00
Salt and Pepper Shakers, pr	48.00	5000	36.00	55.00
Sauce, flat	18.00	25.00	12.00	18.00
Sauce, footed	25.00	30.00	18.00	30.00
Spooner, ftd	42.00	42.00	30.00	42.00
Sugar Bowl, cov, individual	30.00	42.00	12.00	30.00
Sugar Bowl, cov, regular	60.00	72.00	30.00	55.00
Syrup, orig top	120.00	130.00	65.00	130.00
Toothpick Holder	48.00	48.00	85.00	42.00
Tumbler, flat	24.00	30.00	25.00	30.00
Wine	36.00	42.00	30.00	36.00

Daisy and Button with Narcissus

Daisy and Button with Clear Lily

Manufactured by Indiana Glass Company, Dunkirk, IN, c1910. Made in non-flint, clear. Sometimes found with flowers flashed with cranberry flashing. Pieces also found trimmed in gold.

Reproductions: Reproductions of this intricate pattern have been made from new molds. Colors include clear, dark blue, green, and yellow.

Items	Clear	Flashed Color
Bowl, oval, ftd, 9-1/4" l, 6" w φ	30.00	—
Bowl, round, 7-1/4" or 8-1/4" d	30.00-36.00	—

Items	Clear	Flashed Color
Butter Dish, cov	60.00	—
Celery Tray, oval	30.00	—
Celery Vase	24.00	—
Compote, open, hs	48.00	—
Compote, open, ls	42.00	—
Creamer	30.00	—
Decanter, os, quart	48.00	65.00
Goblet	30.00	—
Pickle Tray	30.00	—
Pitcher, milk	60.00	75.00
Pitcher, water	60.00	85.00
Punch Cup	12.00	25.00
Relish Dish, oval	18.00	—
Salt Shaker	35.00	—
Sauce, flat, 4" d or 4-1/2" d	12.00	—
Sauce, footed, 4" d or 4-1/2" d	18.00	—
Sherbet	12.00	18.00
Spooner	36.00	—
Sugar Bowl, cov	85.00	55.00
Tumbler	30.00	24.00
Water Tray, 10" d	36.00	48.00
Wine φ	25.00	30.00
Wine Tray	42.00	55.00

Daisy and Button with Thumbprint Panel

Daisy and Button with Amber Stripes, Daisy and Button with Thumbprint, Daisy and Button Thumbprint

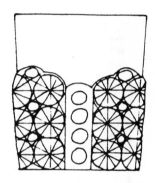

Manufactured by Adams & Company, Pittsburgh, PA, c1886. It was reissued by United States Glass Company, Pittsburgh, PA, c1891. Made in non-flint, amber, blue, clear, green, and vaseline. It can also be found with amber stain and ruby stain.

Reproductions: Reproductions have been made by L. G. Wright Glass Company, New Martinsville, WV, in amber, amethyst, amberina, amber stain, blue, clear, clear with painted panels, green, milk glass, pink, ruby, and vaseline.

Items	Amber	Blue	Clear	Ruby Stained
Bowl, cov, round, 6" d	30.00	36.00	24.00	42.00
Bowl, cov, round, 7" d	36.00	42.00	30.00	48.00
Bowl, cov, round, 8" d	42.00	48.00	36.00	55.00
Bowl, heart shape, 7" w; or oval, 9" l	36.00	42.00	30.00	55.00
Bowl, round, 5" d	12.00	18.00	12.00	24.00
Bowl, round, 6" d	18.00	24.00	12.00	30.00
Bowl, round, 7" d	24.00	30.00	18.00	36.00
Bowl, round, 8" d	30.00	36.00	24.00	42.00
Bread Plate, oval	48.00	55.00	36.00	55.00
Butter Dish, cov	18.00	18.00	48.00	85.00
Butter Pat, sq	18.00	18.00	12.00	24.00
Cake Stand, hs	55.00	72.00	55.00	75.00
Celery Vase, 10" h	55.00	72.00	42.00	85.00
Claret	36.00	42.00	24.00	55.00
Compote, cov, hs or ls, 6" d	65.00	75.00	55.00	85.00
Compote, cov, hs or ls, 7" d	85.00	95.00	60.00	110.00
Compote, cov, hs or ls, 8" d	75.00	85.00	55.00	115.00
Compote, open, hs or ls, 6" d	36.00	42.00	24.00	48.00
Compote, open, hs or ls, 7" d	42.00	48.00	30.00	55.00
Compote, open, hs or ls, 8" d	48.00	55.00	36.00	60.00
Compote, open, ls, 5" d	30.00	36.00	18.00	48.00
Compote, open, s, 11" d	55.00	60.00	42.00	55.00
Creamer, ah, 5-1/4" h	42.00	48.00	30.00	60.00
Cruet, os	180.00	180.00	110.00	165.00
Goblet φ	42.00	48.00	30.00	48.00
Lamp, oil, finger	180.00	190.00	130.00	240.00
Mug	36.00	42.00	18.00	48.00
Pickle Dish	36.00	42.00	18.00	48.00
Pitcher, water φ	130.00	142.00	85.00	190.00
Salt, master, flat	36.00	42.00	18.00	48.00
Salt Shaker, orig top	36.00	42.00	24.00	85.00
Sauce, flat, sq, 4-1/2" d	12.00	18.00	12.00	24.00
Sauce, footed, sq, 4-1/2" w	18.00	24.00	18.00	30.00
Spooner	42.00	48.00	36.00	55.00
Sugar Bowl, cov	55.00	60.00	48.00	65.00
Tumbler	36.00	42.00	18.00	36.00
Waste Bowl	24.00	36.00	18.00	42.00
Water Tray, oblong, handles	55.00	60.00	42.00	72.00
Wine φ	36.00	42.00	30.00	55.00

Daisy and Button with V Ornament

Van Dyke

Manufactured by A. J. Beatty & Company, Steubenville, OH, 1888-87. Reissued by United States Glass Company, Pittsburgh, PA, c1892. Made in non-flint, amber, blue, clear, and vaseline.

Items	Amber	Blue	Clear	Vaseline
Bowl, 9" or 10" d	36.00	48.00	30.00	42.00
Butter Dish, cov	75.00	85.00	60.00	85.00
Celery Vase, crimped, flared	60.00	55.00	60.00	55.00
Celery Vase, straight-sides	55.00	72.00	55.00	72.00
Creamer	36.00	60.00	36.00	60.00
Finger Bowl	36.00	55.00	30.00	55.00
Goblet	42.00	55.00	30.00	60.00
Ice Cream Tray, 16" l, 9" w, 2" h	75.00	—	—	—
Match Holder	36.00	48.00	42.00	30.00
Mug, 4 sizes	24.00	36.00	24.00	30.00
Pickle Castor, silver plate holder, cov, and tongs	124.00	124.00	95.00	120.00
Pitcher, milk	75.00	95.00	60.00	85.00
Pitcher, water	85.00	110.00	72.00	95.00
Plate, scalloped edge, 6" d or 7" d	30.00	30.00	42.00	24.00
Plate, scalloped edge, 8" d or 9" d	36.00	36.00	48.00	30.00
Punch Cup	18.00	24.00	18.00	30.00
Sauce, flat, 4" d	24.00	24.00	15.00	36.00
Sherbet	18.00	24.00	18.00	12.00
Spooner	48.00	48.00	42.00	55.00
Sugar Bowl, cov	60.00	75.00	55.00	65.00
Toothpick Holder	42.00	48.00	36.00	42.00
Tumbler, 2 sizes	30.00	36.00	18.00	30.00
Wine	36.00	42.00	30.00	42.00

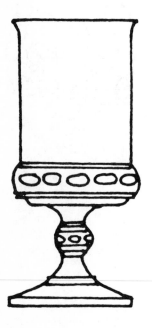

Dakota

Baby Thumbprint, Thumbprint Band

Manufactured by Ripley and Company, Pittsburgh, PA, in the late 1880s and early 1890s. It was later reissued by United States Glass Company, Pittsburgh, PA, at Factory "F" as one of the States series patterns. Made in non-flint, clear, clear etched, and ruby stained. One of the most popular etchings was named "Fern and Berry." Prices listed as "etched" below are for that etching. Another etching was known as "Fern" and has no berry. "Oak Leaf" and "Grape" etching are scarcer. Other etchings include fish, swan, peacock, bird, and insect, bird and flowers, ivy and berry, stag, spider and insect, buzzard on dead tree, and crane catching fish. Ruby stained may have the same etchings as found on clear pieces.

Reproductions: Only the tankard water pitcher has been known to be reproduced.

Items	Clear Etched	Clear Plain	Ruby Stained, Plain
Basket, metal handle, 10" x 2"	240.00	190.00	240.00
Berry Bowl, master	55.00	42.00	—
Bottle, 5-1/2" h	75.00	85.00	—
Butter Dish, cov, hotel size	85.00	410.00	180.00
Butter Dish, cov, table size	65.00	48.00	130.00
Cake Cover, high dome, 8" d	360.00	240.00	—
Cake Cover, high dome, 9" d	325.00	270.00	—
Cake Cover, high dome, 10" d	360.00	300.00	—
Cake Cover, high dome, 11" d	375.00	275.00	—
Cake Stand, hs, 8" d	60.00	42.00	—
Cake Stand, hs, 9" d	55.00	48.00	—
Cake Stand, hs, 9-1/2" d	72.00	55.00	—
Cake Stand, hs, 10" or 10-1/2" d	65.00	60.00	—
Celery Tray	42.00	30.00	—
Celery Vase, hotel size	48.00	36.00	—
Celery Vase, table size	55.00	42.00	—
Cologne Bottle, os	85.00	65.00	—
Compote, cov, hs, 5" d	72.00	60.00	—
Compote, cov, hs, 6" d	65.00	55.00	—
Compote, cov, hs, 7" d	85.00	72.00	—
Compote, cov, hs, 8" d	75.00	65.00	—
Compote, cov, hs, 9" d	95.00	85.00	—
Compote, cov, hs, 10" d	110.00	95.00	—
Compote, cov, hs, 12" d	120.00	110.00	—
Compote, open, hs, 5" d	48.00	36.00	—
Compote, open, hs, 6" or 7" d	55.00	42.00	—
Compote, open, hs, 8" d	60.00	48.00	—
Compote, open, hs, 9" d	55.00	55.00	—
Compote, open, hs, 10" d	72.00	60.00	—
Compote, open, ls, 7" d	55.00	48.00	—
Condiment Tray	—	75.00	—
Creamer, hotel size	75.00	42.00	65.00
Creamer, table size	55.00	36.00	72.00

Items	Clear Etched	Clear Plain	Ruby Stained, Plain
Cruet, os	110.00	55.00	142.00
Dish, flat, oblong, 8" l	48.00	55.00	60.00
Dish, flat, oblong, 9" l	55.00	72.00	55.00
Dish, flat, oblong, 10" l	60.00	65.00	72.00
Goblet	42.00	30.00	75.00
Honey Dish, flat or footed	24.00	30.00	36.00
Mug, ah	55.00	55.00	65.00
Pepper Sauce Bottle, os	75.00	85.00	—
Pitcher, milk, ah, jug, pint or quart	120.00	95.00	190.00
Pitcher, milk, ah, tankard, pint or quart	115.00	75.00	165.00
Pitcher, water, ah, jug, half gallon	85.00	75.00	195.00
Pitcher, water, ah, tankard, half gallon φ	130.00	85.00	270.00
Plate, 10" d	95.00	85.00	—
Plate, 12" d	85.00	75.00	—
Relish Tray	48.00	55.00	—
Salt Shaker	65.00	110.00	130.00
Sauce, flat, 4" d or 5" d	24.00	18.00	30.00
Sauce, footed, 4" d or 5" d	30.00	24.00	36.00
Spooner, hotel size	42.00	36.00	95.00
Spooner, table size	36.00	30.00	65.00
Sugar Bowl, cov, hotel size	75.00	85.00	115.00
Sugar Bowl, cov, table size	65.00	75.00	85.00
Tumbler	42.00	36.00	55.00
Waste Bowl	85.00	110.00	75.00
Water Tray, hotel size or table size, 13" d	120.00	75.00	—
Wine	36.00	24.00	55.00
Wine Tray, 10-1/2" d	115.00	85.00	—

Deer and Dog

Frosted Dog

Manufactured by unknown American makers, c1870. Shards have been found at the site of the Burlington Glass Works, Hamilton, Ontario, Canada. The pattern is identified as the frosted dog finial. Made in non-flint, clear, plain, and clear with an etched design. Deduct 33% for clear, plain.

Items	Clear, Etched
Butter Dish, cov	130.00
Celery Vase	115.00
Champagne	85.00
Cheese Dish, cov	180.00
Compote, cov, hs, 7" or 8-1/2" d	142.00-165.00
Compote, cov, ls, 7-1/2" d	120.00
Compote, open, hs	75.00
Cordial	110.00
Creamer	75.00
Goblet, bulbous or u-shaped bowl	75.00
Marmalade Jar, cov	130.00
Mug	48.00
Pitcher, water, ah	180.00
Sauce, flat or footed	24.00
Spooner	72.00
Sugar Bowl, cov	130.00
Wine	75.00

Deer and Pine Tree

Deer and Doe

Manufactured by Belmont Glass Company, and McKee & Brothers Glass Company, Pittsburgh, PA, c1888. Made in non-flint, amber, apple green, blue, and clear. Souvenir mugs with gilt are found in clear and olive green. Also made in canary (vaseline).

Reproductions: The goblet has been reproduced since 1938. L. G. Wright Glass Company, New Martinsville, WV, has reproduced the goblet using new molds.

Items	Amber	Apple Green	Blue	Clear
Bread Plate	120.00	130.00	130.00	75.00
Butter Dish, cov	130.00	430.00	130.00	115.00
Cake Stand, hs	—	—	—	75.00
Celery Vase	—	—	—	75.00
Compote, cov, hs, sq, 7" w	—	—	—	110.00
Compote, cov, hs, sq, 8" w	—	—	—	120.00
Compote, cov, hs, sq, 9" w	—	—	—	135.00
Compote, open, hs, sq, 7" or 9" w	—	—	—	—55.00
Compote, open, hs, sq, 8" w	—	—	—	60.00

Items	Amber	Apple Green	Blue	Clear
Creamer	115.00	85.00	110.00	65.00
Dish, oblong, 7-1/4" l	—	—	—	30.00
Dish, oblong, 8" l	—	—	—	36.00
Dish, oblong, 9" l	—	—	—	42.00
Finger Bowl	—	—	—	55.00
Goblet φ	—	—	—	55.00
Marmalade Jar, cov	—	—	—	110.00
Mug, large	55.00	60.00	55.00	55.00
Mug, small	48.00	55.00	60.00	48.00
Pickle	—	—	—	36.00
Pitcher, milk	—	—	—	110.00
Pitcher, water	130.00	155.00	155.00	200.00
Platter, 12" l, 8" w	75.00	—	95.00	72.00
Sauce, flat	—	—	—	24.00
Sauce, footed	—	—	—	30.00
Spooner	—	—	—	65.00
Sugar Bowl, cov	—	—	—	85.00
Waste Bowl	—	—	—	55.00
Water Tray	120.00	—	110.00	72.00

Delaware

American Beauty, Four Petal Flower

Manufactured by United States Glass Company, Pittsburgh, PA, c1889-1909. Also made by Diamond Glass Company, Montreal, Quebec, Canada, c1902. Made in non-flint, clear, green with gold trim, rose with gold trim. Rare examples are found in amethyst, clear with rose stain, custard, and milk glass.

Reproductions: Reproductions of this popular pattern are limited to a butter dish, creamer, and sugar bowl. Reproductions are found in cobalt blue (with gold trim), green, and pink. The reproductions tend to be much thicker and tend to have coarse stippling. The reproductions are marked only with paper labels reading "Made in Taiwan."

Items	Clear	Green with Gold	Rose with Gold
Banana Bowl	48.00	55.00	65.00
Bowl, 8" d	36.00	48.00	60.00
Bowl, 9" d	30.00	42.00	55.00
Bottle, os	95.00	180.00	225.00
Bride's Basket, silver plate frame	75.00	118.00	165.00
Butter Dish, cov φ	95.00	118.00	180.00
Claret Jug, tankard shape	135.00	115.00	240.00
Celery Vase, flat	75.00	110.00	115.00
Creamer, individual or table size φ	55.00	65.00	85.00
Cruet, os	110.00	240.00	300.00
Finger Bowl	30.00	60.00	75.00
Fruit Bowl, oval, 11-1/2" l	30.00	55.00	55.00
Fruit Bowl, round, 11" d	42.00	60.00	72.00
Lamp Shade, electric	85.00	—	130.00
Pin Tray	36.00	55.00	115.00
Pitcher, water	65.00	180.00	130.00
Pomade Box, jeweled	120.00	300.00	360.00
Puff Box, bulbous, jeweled	120.00	240.00	318.00
Punch Cup	30.00	24.00	42.00
Salt Shaker, orig top	75.00	130.00	180.00
Sauce, flat, boat shape, 5-1/2" d	18.00	42.00	36.00
Sauce, flat, round, 4" d	18.00	30.00	36.00
Spooner	55.00	60.00	55.00
Sugar Bowl, cov, individual	42.00	60.00	72.00
Sugar Bowl, cov, table size φ	65.00	85.00	120.00
Toothpick Holder	42.00	130.00	180.00
Tumbler	24.00	48.00	55.00
Vase, 6" or 8" h	30.00	55.00	75.00
Vase, 9-1/2" h	48.00	95.00	85.00

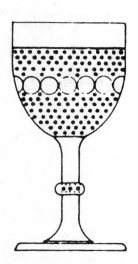

Dew and Raindrop

Dewdrop and Raindrop, Dewdrop and Rain

Manufactured by Kokomo Glass Company, Kokomo, IN, c1901. Federal Glass and others made this pattern using a lesser quality glass and without the tiny dewdrops on the stems. Made in non-flint, clear. Prices listed are for the earlier, more brilliant, pattern. A ruby stained creamer and water pitcher are documented.

Reproductions: This pattern was reproduced as early as the 1930s, with a clear wine. Colored items include cordials, sherbet cups, goblets, and wines. Colors include amber, blue, and clear with a light ruby staining.

Items	Clear
Bowl, 8" d	48.00
Butter Dish, cov	65.00

Items	Clear
Cordial φ	55.00
Creamer	42.00
Goblet φ	36.00
Mug	42.00
Pitcher, water	65.00
Salt and Pepper Shakers, pr	48.00
Sauce, flat, 4" d or 4-1/2" d	18.00
Sherbet φ	12.00
Spooner	42.00
Sugar Bowl, cov	30.00
Sugar Bowl, open	24.00
Tumbler	42.00
Wine φ	24.00

Dewdrop in Points

Manufactured by Brilliant Glass Works, Brilliant, OH, in the late 1870s, and by Greensburg Glass Company, Greensburg, PA, after 1889. Made in non-flint, clear.

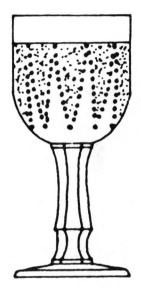

Items	Clear
Bread Plate	30.00
Butter Dish, cov	48.00
Cake Stand, hs, 10-1/2" d	48.00
Compote, cov, hs	75.00
Compote, open, hs, 7" d or 8" d	30.00
Compote, open, ls	25.00
Creamer	36.00
Goblet	30.00
Pickle Dish	18.00
Pitcher, water, ph, half gallon	42.00
Plate, 12" d	24.00
Platter, 11-3/4" l, 9" w	30.00
Sauce, flat, 4-1/2" d	12.00
Sauce, footed, 4-1/2" d	18.00
Spooner	24.00
Sugar Bowl, cov	48.00
Wine	30.00

Dewdrop with Star

Star and Dewdrop

Manufactured by Campbell, Jones, and Company, Pittsburgh, PA, in 1877. There was no goblet made in this pattern. Made in non-flint, clear.

Reproductions: Reproductions have been made in color.

Item	Clear
Bowl, 6" or 7" d	10.00-18.00
Bowl, square, ftd, 9" w	24.00
Bread Plate, motto, sheaf of wheat center	85.00
Butter Dish, dome cover	60.00
Cake Stand	48.00
Celery Vase	48.00
Cheese Dish, cov	120.00
Compote, cov, hs, dome lid	75.00
Compote, cov, ls, 5" d	72.00
Compote, open, hs	42.00
Cordial	42.00
Creamer, ah	42.00
Dish, flat, star in base, 6" d	12.00
Dish, footed, star in base, 7" d	18.00
Honey Dish, underplate	75.00
Lamp, oil, patented 1876	85.00
Pickle, oval	18.00
Pitcher, water, ah	130.00
Plate, 5". 6". 7" φ or 9" d	15.00-24.00
Relish	18.00
Salt, individual or master, footed φ	18.00-24.00
Sauce, flat, 4" d, 5" d, 5-1/2" d	12.00
Sauce, footed, 3-1/2" d, 4" d, 4-1/2" d φ	18.00
Spooner	42.00
Sugar Bowl, cov	60.00

Dewey

Flower Flange

Manufactured by Indiana Tumbler and Goblet Company, Greentown, IN, in 1894. Later made by United States Glass Company, Pittsburgh, PA, until 1904. Made in non-flint, amber, chocolate, clear, green, and vaseline. Some experimental colors were made.

Reproductions: Imperial Glass Company, Bellaire, OH, has reproduced the butter dish, some of which are marked "IG."

Items	Amber	Chocolate	Clear	Green	Nile Green	Vaseline
Bowl, ftd, 8" d	65.00	240.00	60.00	65.00	—	85.00
Butter Dish, cov, quarter lb	75.00	240.00	55.00	65.00	250.00	115.00
Butter Dish, cov, table φ	115.00	360.00	75.00	115.00	650.00	135.00
Creamer, cov, ind., 4" h	55.00	85.00	30.00	55.00	150.00	55.00
Creamer, reg., 5" h	65.00	275.00	42.00	85.00	375.00	75.00
Cruet, os	135.00	600.00	75.00	155.00	1,250.00	130.00
Mug	55.00	360.00	42.00	55.00	200.00	72.00
Parfait	65.00	180.00	55.00	65.00	250.00	75.00
Pitcher, water	110.00	—	55.00	190.00	—	190.00
Plate, ftd, 7-1/2" d	42.00	—	36.00	48.00	250.00	65.00
Relish	45.00	—	24.00	45.00	—	55.00
Salt Shaker	55.00	495.00	42.00	55.00	300.00	65.00
Sauce, flat	30.00	65.00	6.00	30.00	150.00	36.00
Spooner, 5" h	48.00	190.00	30.00	48.00	285.00	60.00
Sugar Bowl, cov, ind., 2-1/4" d	55.00	120.00	30.00	55.00	225.00	65.00
Sugar Bowl, cov, reg., 4" d	60.00	180.00	42.00	55.00	400.00	75.00
Tray, serpentine, large	55.00	—	42.00	55.00	285.00	65.00
Tray, serpentine, small	55.00	495.00	30.00	55.00	—	85.00
Tumbler	55.00	—	48.00	55.00	—	65.00

Diagonal Band

Diagonal Band and Fan

Manufactured by known American maker, c1875-85. Shards have also been found at the site of the Burlington Glass Works, Hamilton, Ontario, Canada. Made in non-flint, amber, apple green, and clear.

Items	Amber	Apple Green	Clear
Bread Plate	36.00	42.00	30.00
Butter Dish, cov	72.00	95.00	42.00
Cake Stand	48.00	55.00	36.00
Castor Bottle	55.00	60.00	36.00
Celery Vase	55.00	60.00	30.00
Champagne	—	—	30.00
Compote, cov, hs, 7" d	65.00	95.00	55.00
Compote, cov, ls, 8" d	65.00	85.00	55.00
Compote, open, ls, 7-1/2" d	55.00	60.00	24.00
Creamer	48.00	60.00	36.00
Goblet	36.00	55.00	36.00
Pickle Dish, oval	18.00	18.00	12.00
Pitcher, milk	60.00	85.00	42.00
Pitcher, water	85.00	85.00	55.00
Plate, 6" d	—	—	18.00
Relish, oval, 6-7/8" l	18.00	24.00	12.00
Sauce, flat	—	—	10.00
Sauce, footed	—	18.00	18.00
Spooner	30.00	48.00	24.00
Sugar Bowl, cov	48.00	60.00	36.00
Wine	42.00	55.00	24.00

Diamond and Sunburst

Diamond Sunburst, Plain Sunburst

Manufactured by Bryce, Walker and Company, Pittsburgh, PA, c1882. The design was patented by John Bryce in 1874. Shards have been found at the site of the Burlington Glass Works, Hamilton, Ontario, Canada. Made in non-flint, clear.

Items	Clear
Butter Dish, cov	48.00
Butter Pat	12.00
Cake Stand	42.00
Celery Vase	30.00
Champagne	30.00

Items	Clear
Compote, open, hs	60.00
Compote, open, hs	36.00
Creamer	42.00
Decanter, os	55.00
Egg Cup	30.00
Goblet	30.00
Pickle	12.00
Pitcher, water	60.00
Relish	12.00
Salt, footed	18.00
Sauce, flat	12.00
Spooner	24.00
Sugar Bowl, cov	48.00
Sugar Bowl, open	24.00
Syrup, orig top	55.00
Tumbler	30.00
Wine	36.00

Diamond Point

Diamond Point with Ribs, Pineapple, Sawtooth, Stepped Diamond Point

Manufactured by Boston and Sandwich Glass Company, Sandwich, MA, c1850, and by the New England Glass Company, East Cambridge, MA, c1880. Many other companies manufactured this pattern throughout the nineteenth century. Made in flint, and non-flint, clear. Rare in color.

Reproductions: Reproductions have been made in the goblet and wine in emerald green. Cambridge Glass Company, Cambridge, OH, produced a look-alike pattern, named Mt. Vernon, about 1920. This non-flint pattern has a similar look to *Diamond Point*, but tend to have more contemporary shapes, and it was made in amber, clear, Carmen red, forest green, Gold Krystol, Heatherbloom, light emerald green, royal blue, topaz, and violet.

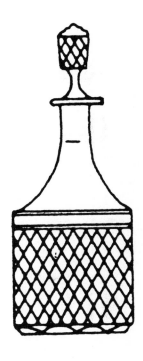

Items	Flint	Non-Flint
Ale Glass, 6-1/4" h	85.00	—
Bowl, cov, 5", 7" or 8" d	55.00-72.00	18.00-24.00
Bowl, open, 5", 6", 7" or 8" d	48.00-55.00	18.00-24.00
Butter Dish, cov	115.00	60.00
Cake Stand, hs 9", 10", 11" or 12" d	155.00-185.00	55.00-85.00
Cake Stand, hs, 14" d	225.00	—
Candlesticks, pr	155.00	
Castor Bottle	30.00	12.00
Celery Vase	75.00	36.00
Champagne	85.00	42.00
Claret	110.00	—
Compote, cov, hs, 6" d	130.00	60.00
Compote, cov, hs, 7" d	135.00	55.00
Compote, cov, hs, 8" d	142.00	72.00
Compote, cov, ls, 6" d	75.00	48.00
Compote, cov, ls, 7" d	95.00	55.00
Compote, cov, ls, 8" d	85.00	60.00
Compote, open, hs, deep bowl, 6", 7", 8", 9" or 10" d	48.00-55.00	30.00-36.00
Compote, open, hs, deep bowl, 10-1/2" d	60.00	—
Compote, open, hs, flared, 10-1/2" d	120.00	
Compote, open, hs, saucer bowl, 6", 7" or 8" d	48.00-60.00	30.00-42.00
Compote, open, hs, scalloped rim, 11" d	135.00	—
Compote, open, ls, deep bowl, 6", 7", 8", 9" or 10"	48.00-55.00	30.00-42.00
Cordial	165.00	—
Creamer, ah	118.00	—
Decanter, os, pint or quart, bar lip	180.00	—
Decanter, os, pint or quart, patterned stopper	165.00	—
Dish, oval, 7", 8", 9" or 10" l	36.00-42.00	—
Egg Cup, cov	75.00	60.00
Egg Cup, open	48.00	24.00
Goblet, gentleman's, large φ or lady's, small	55.00	42.00
Honey Dish	18.00	—
Lamp, oil, orig burner and chimney	300.00	—
Lemonade Tumbler	55.00	—
Mug, ah	130.00	—
Mustard Jar, Britannia top	42.00	—
Pepper Sauce Bottle, Britannia top	30.00	12.00
Pitcher, milk, half pint	130.00	—
Pitcher, milk, pint	225.00	—
Pitcher, milk, three pints	270.00	—
Pitcher, milk, quart	275.00	—
Pitcher, water, half gallon	300.00	—
Plate, 5", 6", 7" or 8" d	30.00-60.00	—
Salt, individual	18.00	12.00
Salt, master, cov	75.00	42.00
Sauce, flat, 4" d	18.00	—
Spill Holder	55.00	—

Items	Flint	Non-Flint
Spooner	55.00	30.00
Sugar Bowl, cov, flat or footed base	85.00	48.00
Syrup, orig top	180.00	75.00
Tumbler, bar or water	65.00	42.00
Tumbler, gill	55.00	—
Vinegar Bottle	30.00	12.00
Whiskey, ah	85.00	—
Wine φ	75.00	36.00

Diamond Quilted

Quilted Diamond

Manufactured by many companies, c1880. Made in non-flint, amber, amethyst, blue, clear, and vaseline.

Reproductions: Heavily reproduced by companies such as L. G. Wright, Fenton Art Glass, and Imperial Glass Corp.

Items	Amber	Amethyst	Blue	Clear	Vaseline
Bowl, 6" d	12.00	24.00	—	—	—
Bowl, 7" d	35.00	—	—	—	30.00
Butter Dish, cov, ftd	60.00	120.00	120.00	48.00	120.00
Celery Vase, pedestal	42.00	72.00	60.00	36.00	48.00
Champagne	—	42.00	—	24.00	42.00
Compote, cov, hs, 8" d	155.00	124.00	124.00	55.00	110.00
Compote, cov, ls, 9" d	—	—	120.00	—	—
Compote, open, hs, 8" d	65.00	95.00	65.00	42.00	65.00
Compote, open, ls, 8" d	—	—	—	18.00	42.00
Cordial	65.00	85.00	85.00	30.00	55.00
Creamer	55.00	45.00	85.00	30.00	55.00
Goblet, regular φ	48.00	48.00	48.00	36.00	42.00
Goblet, short stem	48.00	48.00	48.00	36.00	42.00
Mug	—	36.00	48.00	—	—
Pitcher, water	75.00	85.00	95.00	60.00	75.00
Salt, individual φ	24.00	30.00	24.00	12.00	24.00
Salt, master	42.00	48.00	48.00	24.00	42.00
Sauce, flat	15.00	—	20.00	10.00	25.00
Sauce, footed	20.00	25.00	25.00	15.00	25.00
Spooner, footed	42.00	48.00	48.00	36.00	60.00
Sugar Bowl, cov, footed	60.00	75.00	55.00	48.00	72.00
Tumbler φ	55.00	48.00	48.00	30.00	42.00
Vase, 9" h	—	—	—	40.00	—
Water Tray, clover leaf or round	85.00	55.00	85.00	36.00	65.00
Wine φ	24.00	48.00	42.00	18.00	24.00

Diamond Spearhead

Manufactured by Dugan Glass Company, Indiana, PA, c1900. No cruet recorded. A cake stand has been found, but it was not listed in early catalogs. Made in non-flint, canary opalescent, clear (plain), cobalt blue opalescent, green opalescent, sapphire blue opalescent, white (clear) opalescent.

Items	Canary Opalescent	Clear	Cobalt Blue Opalescent	Green Opalescent	Sapphire Blue Opalescent	White Opalescent
Berry Bowl	—	24.00	—	48.00	48.00	42.00
Butter Dish, cov	—	48.00	180.00	85.00	75.00	—
Cake Stand, hs, 10" d	85.00	—	—	—	—	—
Carafe	195.00	—	—	120.00	48.00	—
Celery Vase	—	24.00	—	55.00	36.00	42.00
Compote, cov, hs	—	—	—	42.00	60.00	40.00
Creamer	—	24.00	85.00	72.00	36.00	42.00
Cup and Saucer	—	—	—	42.00	72.00	—
Goblet	—	—	—	72.00	110.00	—
Jelly Compote, cov, ls	—	—	—	72.00	60.00	—
Mug	—	24.00	—	85.00	65.00	—
Pitcher, water	—	60.00	240.00	255.00	85.00	—
Plate, 12" d	—	—	—	95.00	—	—
Relish	—	—	—	30.00	24.00	—
Sauce	—	—	—	18.00	20.00	—
Spooner	—	24.00	—	60.00	48.00	—
Sugar Bowl, cov	—	36.00	—	60.00	55.00	—
Syrup, orig top	—	—	235.00	255.00	85.00	—
Toothpick Holder	75.00	—	130.00	85.00	—	—

Diamond Thumbprint

Diamond and Concave

Manufacture attributed to Boston and Sandwich Glass Company, Sandwich, MA, and other factories in the 1850s. Made in flint, clear.

Reproductions: Reproduction bitters bottles, celery vases, compotes, sugar bowls, and other pieces were reproduced by Viking Glass Company, New Martinsville, WV, for the Sandwich Glass Museum. Each piece is embossed with the "S. M." trademark. Colors of reproductions include amber, amethyst, blue, clear, peach, ruby, and sterling gray.

Items	Clear
Ale Glass, 6-1/4" h	110.00
Bitters Bottle, orig pewter pourer, applied lip, polished pontil φ	460.00
Bowl, cov, 6", 7" or 8" d	180.00-190.00
Bowl, open, plain rim, 5", 6", 7" or 8"d	65.00-85.00
Bowl, open, scalloped rim, 5", 6", 7" or 8" d	65.00-85.00
Butter Dish, cov φ	240.00
Cake Stand, hs, 9", 10", 11" or 12" d	300.00-450.00
Candlestick, 6-1/2" h	180.00
Castor Bottle	36.00
Celery Vase, scalloped top φ	225.00
Champagne, large	285.00
Champagne, small	300.00
Compote, cov, hs, 6", 7" or 8" d φ	225.00-275.00
Compote, cov, ls, 6", 7" or 8" d	240.00-300.00
Compote, open, hs, scalloped rim, 5", 6", 7", 8", 9" or 10" d	85.00-270.00
Compote, open, ls, scalloped rim, 5", 6", 7", 8", 9" or 10" d	65.00-110.00
Cordial, large φ	330.00
Cordial, small	360.00
Creamer, ah, footed φ	270.00
Cruet, os	495.00
Decanter, applied bar lip, pint	190.00
Decanter, applied bar lip, quart	175.00
Decanter, os, pint	190.00
Decanter, os, quart	270.00
Dish, oval, flat, 7" l or 8" l	65.00
Dish, oval, flat, 9" l or 10" l	75.00
Egg Cup	85.00
Finger Bowl	120.00
Goblet φ	360.00
Honey Dish, plain or star center φ	30.00
Mug, ah φ	240.00
Pitcher, milk, ah	460.00
Pitcher, water, ah	600.00
Sauce, flat φ	18.00
Spooner φ	85.00
Sugar Bowl, cov φ	180.00
Sweetmeat Jar, cov	300.00
Tray, rect, 11" l, 7" w	120.00
Tumbler, bar	130.00
Tumbler, water, flat	85.00
Waste Bowl	110.00
Whiskey, applied handle	360.00
Whiskey, no handle	130.00
Wine φ	300.00
Wine Jug	2,600.00

Dickson

Manufactured by Boston and Sandwich Glass Company, Sandwich, MA, c1880. Made in flint, clear.

Items	Clear
Butter Dish, cov	95.00
Compote, cov, hs, 5-1/2" d	85.00
Compote, open, ls, 7-1/4" d	55.00
Creamer, ah	55.00
Goblet	55.00
Sauce	12.00
Spooner	48.00
Sugar Bowl, cov	115.00

Dolly Madison

Jefferson's Pattern Line No. 27

Manufactured by Jefferson Glass Company, Follansbee, WV, c1907. Made in non-flint, clear (plain), blue opalescent, green, opalescent, and white (clear) opalescent. Also found in non-opalescent colors, valued at 25% less.

Items	Clear	Blue Opalescent	Green Opalescent	White Opalescent
Berry Bowl, 9-1/4" d	42.00	60.00	55.00	42.00
Butter Dish, cov	48.00	124.00	130.00	75.00
Creamer	42.00	85.00	110.00	95.00
Pitcher, water	55.00	180.00	148.00	130.00
Sauce	25.00	55.00	60.00	55.00
Spooner	36.00	75.00	85.00	75.00
Sugar Bowl, cov	55.00	65.00	120.00	55.00
Tumbler	36.00	48.00	72.00	48.00

Drapery

Lace

Manufactured by Doyle and Company, Pittsburgh, PA, in the 1870s. Originally designed and patented by Thomas B. Atterbury, c1871. Reissued by the United States Glass Company, Pittsburgh, PA, after 1891. Shards have been found at Boston and Sandwich Glass Company, Sandwich, MA. Made in non-flint, clear. Pieces with fine stippling have applied handles. Pieces with coarse stippling have pressed handles. The finials are shaped as pinecones.

Items	Clear
Butter Dish, cov	55.00
Compote, cov, hs, 7" d	65.00
Compote, open, ls, 7" d	55.00
Creamer, applied handle	36.00
Creamer, pressed handle	30.00
Dish, oval	36.00
Egg Cup, ftd	30.00
Goblet	42.00
Pitcher, water, ah	85.00
Plate, 6" d	36.00
Sauce, flat, 4" d	12.00
Spooner	30.00
Sugar Bowl, cov	48.00
Tumbler	36.00

Duncan Block

Block, Waffle Variant, Duncan's Pattern Line No. 308 and 309

Manufactured by George Duncan & Sons, Pittsburgh, PA, c1887. The pattern was continuously produced until the merger with United States Glass Company in 1891 until 1904, at Factory "D" and Factory "P." Made in non-flint, clear. Sometimes found with ruby staining and copper wheel engraving.

Items	Clear
Basket, 7" d	60.00
Basket, 8" d	72.00
Bowl, crimped rim, 8" d	30.00
Butter Dish, cov, collared base	48.00
Butter Dish, cov, flat, flanged rim	55.00
Carafe	60.00
Catsup Bottle	55.00
Celery Tray	30.00
Celery Vase, flat, scalloped rim	42.00
Celery Vase, footed, scalloped rim	48.00
Champagne	18.00
Cheese Dish, cov	60.00
Cologne Bottle, 1, 2, 4, 6, 8 or 16 oz	36.00-48.00
Creamer, individual	18.00
Creamer, table, collared base or flat	30.00
Cruet, os, round, 1 oz or 2 oz	30.00
Cruet, os, round, 4 oz or 6 oz	36.00
Cruet, os, square, 1 oz or 2 oz	36.00
Cruet, os, square, 4 oz or 6 oz	42.00
Custard Cup	12.00
Egg Cup	18.00
Finger Bowl	15.00
Goblet	24.00

Items	Clear
Ice Cream Tray, rect, with or without handles, deep or shallow	42.00
Lamp Shade, gas globe, round or ruffled	42.00
Pitcher, milk, tankard	55.00
Pitcher, water, bulbous	72.00
Pitcher, water, tankard	55.00
Plate, 7" or 8" d	12.00
Puff Box, cov, squatty or tall	42.00
Salad Bowl, crimped rim, 7" d, 8" d, or 9" d	30.00
Salad Bowl, plain rim, 7" d, 8" d, or 9" d	24.00
Salt, individual	15.00
Salt, master	18.00
Salt Shaker, orig top, 4 styles	42.00
Sauce, flat or footed, 4" d, 4-1/2" d, or 5" d	12.00
Sherbet Cup	12.00
Spooner, collared or flat base	30.00
Sugar Bowl, cov, collared base	55.00
Sugar Bowl, cov, flat base	42.00
Sugar Shaker, orig top	48.00
Syrup, orig silver plated top	48.00
Tray, round, 7" d or 8" d	30.00
Tumbler	18.00
Wine	18.00

Egg in Sand

Bean, Stippled Oval

Manufacturer unknown, c1885. Made in non-flint, clear. Rare in colors.

Items	Clear
Bread Plate, octagonal	30.00
Butter Dish, cov	48.00
Creamer	36.00
Dish, swan center	48.00
Goblet	42.00
Jelly Compote, cov	55.00
Marmalade Jar, cov	55.00
Pitcher, milk, quart	48.00
Pitcher, water, half gallon	55.00
Platter, rect, several sizes	42.00
Relish Tray	12.00
Salt and Pepper Shakers, pr	65.00
Sauce, flat	12.00
Spooner, flat rim	36.00
Sugar Bowl, cov	42.00
Tumbler	42.00
Water Tray	55.00
Wine	42.00

Egyptian

Parthenon

Manufactured by Adams & Company, Pittsburgh, PA, c1882. Made in non-flint, clear.

Reproductions: A reproduction bread tray is known and usually easily identified by the poor details in the pattern.

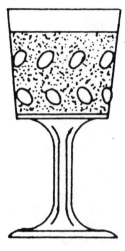

Items	Clear
Bowl, 8" d	55.00
Bowl, 8-1/2" d	60.00
Bread Plate, Cleopatra	65.00
Bread Plate, Mormon Temple φ	360.00
Butter Dish, cov	85.00
Celery Vase	75.00
Compote, cov, hs, Sphinx base, 7" d	300.00
Compote, cov, hs, Sphinx base, 8" d, 11" h	275.00
Compote, cov, ls, Sphinx base, 7" d	75.00
Compote, cov, ls, Sphinx base, 8" d	85.00
Compote, open, hs, Sphinx base, 7-1/2" d	75.00
Creamer	60.00
Goblet	55.00
Honey Dish	18.00
Pickle Dish, oval	24.00
Pitcher, water	225.00
Plate, closed handles, 6", 8" or 10" d	60.00-72.00
Plate, Pyramids, handles, 12" l	110.00
Relish Tray	24.00

Items	Clear
Sauce, flat, 4" d or 4-1/2" d	12.00
Sauce, footed, 4" d or 4-1/2" d	24.00
Spooner	48.00
Sugar Bowl, cov	95.00

Electric

Manufactured by United States Glass Company, Pittsburgh, PA, c1891. This extensive pattern was made in about forty forms. Made in non-flint, clear. Colors would be 20% more than the values shown.

Items	Clear
Berry Bowl	18.00
Biscuit Jar, cov	60.00
Butter Dish, cov	55.00
Cake Stand	42.00
Celery Vase	30.00
Compote, cov	55.00
Creamer, individual	30.00
Creamer, table	24.00
Creamer, tankard	36.00
Goblet	30.00
Jelly Compote, open	18.00
Marmalade Jar, cov	48.00
Mug	18.00
Pitcher, water	55.00
Relish	18.00
Salt Shaker	36.00
Sauce, flat, 4" d	10.00
Sauce, footed, 4" d	12.00
Spooner	30.00
Sugar Bowl, cov	48.00
Syrup, orig top	60.00
Tumbler	18.00
Water Tray	55.00

Empress

Manufactured by Riverside Glass Works, Wellsburg, WV, c1898. Made in non-flint, clear, and emerald green, both trimmed in gold. Also rarely found in amethyst.

Items	Clear w/Gold Trim	Emerald Green w/Gold Trim
Berry Bowl, 8-1/2" d	30.00	55.00
Breakfast Set, individual creamer and sugar	48.00	85.00
Butter Dish, cov	60.00	120.00
Celery Vase	55.00	—
Compote, open, hs, 6" d	42.00	75.00
Creamer, individual	42.00	75.00
Creamer, table size	48.00	95.00
Cruet, os	60.00	190.00
Lamp, oil, finger, 2 sizes	95.00	270.00
Pitcher, water, ah	65.00	135.00
Punch Cup, ftd	24.00	42.00
Salt Shaker	36.00	72.00
Sauce, footed, 4-1/2" d	18.00	30.00
Spooner	48.00	95.00
Sugar Bowl, cov	55.00	135.00
Sugar Shaker, orig top	55.00	135.00
Toothpick Holder	—	180.00
Tumbler	42.00	85.00

Esther

Tooth and Claw

Manufactured by Riverside Glass Works, Wellsburg, WV, c1896. Made in non-flint, amber stained, clear, green, and ruby stained. Some green pieces have gold trim. Stained pieces may be etched or have enamel decoration.

Items	Clear	Green	Ruby Stained
Bowl, 8" w	30.00	60.00	72.00
Butter Dish, cov	65.00	120.00	180.00
Cake Stand, hs, 10-1/2" d	72.00	95.00	115.00
Castor Set, 4 bottles	85.00	—	—

Items	Clear	Green	Ruby Stained
Celery Vase	48.00	110.00	85.00
Cheese Dish, cov	85.00	142.00	130.00
Compote, open, scalloped, 6" d	30.00	55.00	55.00
Compote, open, flared, 8" d	42.00	65.00	55.00
Cracker Jar, cov	85.00	270.00	240.00
Creamer, individual	55.00	85.00	75.00
Creamer, table size	60.00	80.00	95.00
Cruet, os	55.00	255.00	265.00
Decanter, os, gold trim	800.00	—	—
Goblet	55.00	85.00	75.00
Jelly Compote, hs	36.00	75.00	85.00
Lamp, oil	130.00	—	—
Pickle Dish	18.00	60.00	48.00
Pitcher, water	65.00	165.00	300.00
Plate, 10" d	30.00	72.00	72.00
Relish tray, oblong or oval	24.00	30.00	30.00
Salt Shaker	24.00	42.00	48.00
Sauce, flat, 4" d	12.00	18.00	24.00
Spooner	42.00	60.00	72.00
Sugar Bowl, cov	55.00	85.00	120.00
Syrup, orig top	65.00	240.00	190.00
Toothpick Holder	55.00	85.00	120.00
Tumbler	30.00	36.00	55.00
Vase	30.00	55.00	55.00
Wine	42.00	55.00	55.00

Eugenie

Manufactured by McKee & Brothers, Pittsburgh, PA, c1859. Made in flint, clear.

Items	Clear
Bowl, cov, 7" d	55.00
Bowl, cov, 9" d	65.00
Castor Bottle	30.00
Celery Vase	110.00
Champagne	85.00
Compote, cov, hs, 7" d	130.00
Compote, cov, hs, 8" d	155.00
Compote, cov, ls, 7" d	115.00
Compote, cov, ls, 8" d	118.00
Cordial	110.00
Creamer	190.00
Egg Cup	60.00
Goblet	180.00
Lamp, whale oil	180.00
Mustard Bottle	30.00
Pepper Sauce Bottle	30.00
Sugar Bowl, cov	270.00
Tumbler	55.00
Vinegar Bottle	30.00
Wine	48.00

Eureka

Manufactured by McKee & Brothers Glass Company, Pittsburgh, PA, in the late 1860s. Made in flint, and non-flint, clear. Handles are applied and finials are shaped like buds.

Items	Flint
Bowl, oval, 7" l	36.00
Bowl, oval, 8" l	42.00
Bowl, round, 6" d	30.00
Butter Dish, cov	72.00
Champagne	42.00
Compote, cov, hs, 6", 7" or 8" d	75.00-115.00
Compote, cov, ls, 6", 7" or 8" d	85.00-110.00
Compote, open, hs, 6", 7" or 8" d	72.00-95.00
Compote, open, ls, 6", 7" or 8"d	60.00-85.00
Cordial	48.00
Creamer	55.00
Dish, oval, 6", 7", 8" or 9" l	42.00-60.00
Egg Cup	36.00
Goblet	36.00
Pitcher, water	115.00
Salt, master, ftd	36.00
Sauce, flat, 4" d	12.00
Spooner	48.00
Sugar Bowl, cov	60.00
Tumbler, ftd	30.00
Wine	30.00

Everglades

Carnelian

Manufactured by Harry Northwood Company, Wheeling, WV, c1903. Made in non-flint, blue opalescent, canary opalescent, custard, green opalescent, and white (clear) opalescent.

Items	Blue Opalescent	Canary Opalescent	Custard Opalescent	Green	White Opalescent
Banana Dish	190.00	185.00	—	360.00	180.00
Berry Bowl, master	190.00	120.00	180.00	110.00	95.00
Butter Dish, cov	240.00	180.00	360.00	180.00	130.00
Creamer	110.00	75.00	155.00	120.00	55.00
Cruet, os	330.00	360.00	560.00	360.00	190.00
Jelly Compote	85.00	110.00	240.00	180.00	85.00
Pitcher, water	360.00	375.00	600.00	495.00	240.00
Salt Shaker	115.00	75.00	130.00	180.00	—
Sauce	42.00	30.00	60.00	65.00	30.00
Spooner	75.00	65.00	130.00	120.00	55.00
Sugar Bowl, cov	190.00	155.00	165.00	180.00	75.00
Tumbler	65.00	65.00	135.00	60.00	30.00

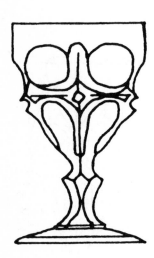

Excelsior

Manufactured by several firms, including Boston and Sandwich Glass Company, Sandwich, MA; McKee Brothers, Pittsburgh, PA, and Ihmsen and Company, Pittsburgh, PA, about 1850s-1860s. Quality and design vary from maker to maker. Made in flint, clear. Very rare in color. Prices are for high quality flint.

Reproductions: Champagnes and goblets have been reproduced since 1988 by the Dalzell-Viking Glass Company, New Martinsville, WV. They were made in azure blue, clear, cobalt blue, pink, and ruby.

Items	Flint
Ale Glass	60.00
Bar Bottle	85.00
Bitters Bottle	115.00
Bowl, cov, 12" d	130.00
Bowl, open, 10" d	55.00
Butter Dish, cov	120.00
Candlestick, 9-1/2" h	130.00
Celery Vase, scalloped top	85.00
Champagne φ	72.00
Claret	55.00
Compote, cov, ls	130.00
Compote, open, hs	85.00
Cordial	48.00
Creamer	85.00
Decanter, os, pint	85.00
Decanter, os, quart	115.00
Egg Cup, double	55.00
Egg Cup, single, cov	95.00
Egg Cup, single, open	48.00
Goblet φ	60.00
Lamp, oil, hand	115.00
Medicine Bottle	75.00
Mug	36.00
Pickle Jar, cov	55.00
Pitcher, milk, pint	300.00
Pitcher, milk, quart	450.00
Pitcher, water	360.00
Salt, master, ftd	36.00
Spill Holder	75.00
Spooner	72.00
Sugar Bowl, cov	110.00
Syrup, orig top	130.00
Tumbler, bar	60.00
Tumbler, water, flat or ftd	60.00
Tumble-Up	250.00
Water Bottle	120.00
Whiskey, Maltese Cross	65.00
Wine	55.00

Eyewinker

Cannon Ball, Crystal Ball, Winking Eye

Manufactured by Dalzell, Gilmore, and Leighton Glass Company, Findlay, OH, c1889. Made in non-flint, clear. A goblet and toothpick were not originally made in this pattern.

Reproductions: Reproductions have been made by several companies, including L. G. Wright, New Martinsville, WV, in several colors.

Items	Clear
Banana Stand, hs	130.00
Bowl, cov, 9" d	75.00
Bowl, open, 6-1/2" d	30.00
Butter Dish, cov φ	85.00
Cake Stand, hs, 8" d	60.00
Cake Stand, hs, 9-1/2" d	72.00
Cake Stand, hs, 10" d	65.00
Celery Vase φ	55.00
Compote, cov, hs, 4", 4-1/2", 5", 5-1/2", 6", 6-1/2" φ, 7", 7-1/2", 8", 8-1/2", 9", 9-1/2", 10", 10-1/2", 11", 11-1/2", 12" or 12-1/2" d	42.00-124.00
Compote, open, hs, 4", 4-1/2", 5", 5-1/2", 6", 6-1/2" d φ, 7", 7-1/2", 8", 8-1/2", 9", 9-1/2", 10", 10-1/2", 11", 11-1/2", 12" or 12-1/2" d	24.00-135.00
Compote, open, hs, fluted, 7-1/4" d φ	65.00
Creamer φ	48.00
Cruet, os	65.00
Honey Dish φ	48.00
Jelly Compote, open, 4-1/2" d φ	55.00
Lamp, kerosene	124.00
Nappy, folded sides, 7-1/2" d	36.00
Pitcher, milk, quart	95.00
Pitcher, water, half gallon φ	85.00
Plate, square, up-turned sides, 5", 6", 7", 8", 9" or 10" w	36.00-85.00
Salt Shaker φ	42.00
Sauce, flat, round or square	18.00
Spooner	42.00
Sugar Bowl, cov φ	55.00
Syrup, orig pewter lid	130.00
Tumbler φ	55.00
Vegetable Bowl, 6-1/2" d	42.00

Fancy Loops

Heisey's Pattern Line No. 1205 and 1205-1/2

Manufactured by A. H. Heisey Company, Newark, OH, c1897. Made in non-flint, clear, and emerald green. Occasionally it is found with ruby stain. Original molds did not include the Heisey "H" in a diamond trademark.

Items	Clear
Bon Bon, tri-corner	30.00
Bowl	30.00
Butter Dish, cov, individual size	55.00
Butter Dish, cov, table size	72.00
Celery Tray	40.00
Celery Vase	55.00
Champagne	55.00
Claret	55.00
Cracker Jar, cov, 2 sizes	135.00
Creamer, hotel size	42.00
Creamer, individual size	48.00
Creamer, table size	55.00
Cruet, os	85.00
Goblet	48.00
Pitcher, water, tankard	95.00
Punch Bowl, scalloped rim	150.00
Punch Cup	24.00
Relish	24.00
Salt, individual	15.00
Salt, master	35.00
Salt Shaker, orig top	45.00
Sauce, flat, round or triangular	18.00
Sherry	48.00
Spooner	42.00
Sugar Bowl, cov, hotel size	55.00
Sugar Bowl, cov, individual size	72.00
Sugar Bowl, cov, table size	65.00
Toothpick Holder	85.00
Tumbler, bar	36.00
Tumbler, water	42.00
Vase, tall, cylindrical	40.00
Wine	30.00

Fan with Diamond

Shell, McKee's Pattern Line No. 3

Manufactured by McKee and Brothers Glass Company, Pittsburgh, PA, c1880. Made in non-flint, clear.

Items	Clear
Bowl, oval, flat, 8" l, 6" w; or 9" d, 6-3/4" w	30.00
Butter Dish, cov, 4" d	60.00
Butter Dish, cov, 6" d	65.00
Compote, cov, hs, 8-1/4" d	60.00
Compote, cov, ls, 7-1/2" or 8-3/8" d	60.00
Creamer, applied handle	55.00
Creamer, pressed handle	36.00
Egg Cup	42.00
Goblet	36.00
Pitcher, water, applied strap handle	75.00
Pitcher, water, pressed handle	60.00
Sauce, flat, 4" d	15.00
Spooner	30.00
Sugar Bowl, cov	60.00
Sugar Bowl, open, buttermilk type	24.00
Syrup, ah, orig top, bird finial	120.00
Wine	42.00

Feather

Cambridge Feather, Feather and Quill, Fine Cut and Feather, Indiana Feather, Indiana Swirl, McKee's Doric, Prince's Feather, Swirl, Swirl and Feather

Manufactured by McKee and Brothers Glass Company, Pittsburgh, PA, 1896-1901; Beatty-Brady Glass Company, Dunkirk, IN, c1903, and Cambridge Glass Company, Cambridge, OH, 1902-03. Later the pattern was reissued with variations and quality differences. Made in non-flint, clear, emerald green, and some amber stained. A chocolate water pitcher is documented.

Reproductions: The wine has been reproduced from a new mold and can be found in clear and clear with a pink stain, c1950. Reproduction goblets are known in amber, blue, and clear. Fenton made goblet in pink.

Items	Clear	Emerald Green
Banana Boat, flat	75.00	190.00
Banana Boat, footed	115.00	240.00
Bowl, oval, 8-1/2" l	30.00	—
Bowl, oval, 9-1/4" l	25.00	75.00
Bowl, round, 4", 4-1/2" or 6" d	18.00-24.00	—
Bowl, round, 7" or 8" d	30.00-36.00	75.00-85.00
Bowl, square, 4-1/2" w	18.00	—
Bowl, square, 8" w	36.00	
Butter Dish, cov, flanged rim	72.00	172.00
Butter Dish, cov, plain rim	55.00	180.00
Cake Plate	65.00	
Cake Stand, hs, 8", 9-1/2" or 11" d	48.00-85.00	130.00-155.00
Celery Vase	42.00	85.00
Champagne	65.00	—
Cheese Dish, blown domed lid	180.00	
Compote, cov, hs, deep bowl, 6", 7", 8" or 8-1/2" d	120.00-135.00	224.00-300.00
Compote, cov, hs, shallow bowl, 7", 8", 9" or 10" d	120.00-135.00	224.00-300.00
Compote, cov, ls, deep bowl, 6", 7", 8" or 8-1/4" d	110.00-180.00	240.00-300.00
Compote, open, ls, 4", 6", 7" or 8" d	18.00-42.00	85.00-135.00
Cordial	130.00	180.00
Creamer	48.00	85.00
Cruet, os	55.00	300.00
Dish, 7", d 8" d and 9" d	48.00	65.00
Goblet	55.00	180.00
Honey Dish	18.00	36.00
Jelly Compote, cov, ls, 4-1/4" d	120.00	180.00
Marmalade Jar, cov	120.00	180.00
Pickle Castor	155.00	—
Pitcher, milk	60.00	165.00
Pitcher, water, tankard	75.00	300.00
Plate, 10" d	42.00	75.00
Relish Tray	24.00	48.00
Salt Shaker	42.00	75.00
Sauce, flat, round or sq, plain or scalloped rim, 4" d or 4-1/2" d	15.00	30.00
Sauce, footed, round or sq, plain or scalloped rim, 4" d or 4-1/2" d	18.00	30.00
Spooner	30.00	72.00
Sugar Bowl, cov	55.00	95.00
Syrup, orig top	130.00	360.00
Toothpick Holder	85.00	165.00
Tumbler, water, flat	55.00	85.00
Wine, scalloped border	48.00	—
Wine, straight border φ	30.00	—

Feather Duster

Rosette Medallion, Huckle, US Glass Pattern Line No. 15,043

Manufactured by United States Glass Company, Pittsburgh, PA, in 1895, and possibly by another company. A unique tray is included in this pattern. Known as the "Gold Standard Tray," it features a full-length portrait of McKinley, with a *Feather Duster* border, dated 1896. Made in non-flint, clear, and emerald green.

Items	Clear	Emerald Green
Berry Bowl, master, 8" d	18.00	24.00
Bowl, cov, 5" or 6" d or 7" or 8" d	30.00-36.00	42.00-48.00
Bowl, open, 5" or 6" d or 7" or 8" d	12.00-18.00	18.00-24.00
Bread Plate, rect	36.00	48.00
Butter Dish, cov, flanged or plain rim	48.00	72.00
Cake Stand, hs, 8", 9", 10" or 11" d	30.00-48.00	42.00-60.00
Celery Vase	24.00	36.00
Compote, cov, hs, 5" d or cov, ls, 6" d	42.00	55.00
Compote, cov, hs, 6" d or cov, ls, 7" d	48.00	60.00
Compote, cov, hs, 7" d or cov, ls, 8" d	55.00	55.00
Compote, cov, hs, 8" d	60.00	72.00
Compote, cov, ls, 5" d	36.00	48.00
Compote, open, hs, deep bowl, 5" or 6" d or 7" or 8" d	18.00-24.00	30.00-36.00
Compote, open, ls, shallow bowl, 7", 8" or 9" d	24.00-30.00	36.00-42.00
Creamer	30.00	42.00
Dish, oblong, flat, 7" l, 8" l, or 9" l	12.00	18.00
Egg Cup	30.00	42.00
Goblet	30.00	42.00
Mug, ph	36.00	48.00
Pitcher, milk, quart	48.00	60.00
Pitcher, water, half gallon	55.00	55.00
Plate, 7" d	18.00	30.00
Plate, 9" d	24.00	36.00
Relish	18.00	30.00
Salt Shaker, orig top	24.00	36.00
Sauce, flat, 4" d or 4-1/2" d	10.00	18.00
Spooner, plain form	24.00	36.00
Sugar Bowl, cov	42.00	55.00
Tray, "Gold Standard Tray"	240.00	—
Tumbler	18.00	24.00
Waste Bowl	24.00	36.00
Water Tray, round	65.00	75.00
Wine	36.00	55.00

Festoon

Manufactured by unknown American maker, c1890-94. No goblet or wine was originally made in this pattern. Made in non-flint, clear.

Items	Clear
Bowl, rect, 7" l, 4-1/2" w	30.00
Bowl, rect, 9" l	36.00
Bowl, round, 7", 8" or 9" d	24.00-36.00
Butter Dish, cov	48.00
Cake Stand, hs, 9" or 10" d	42.00-48.00
Compote, cov, hs	115.00
Compote, open, hs	85.00
Creamer	42.00
Dish, oblong, 2 sizes	24.00
Finger Bowl	36.00
Marmalade Jar, cov	72.00
Mug	42.00
Pickle Castor, silver plated frame	135.00
Pickle Dish, 9" l, 5-1/2" w, silver plated frame	55.00
Pickle Jar, cov	65.00
Pitcher, water, half gallon	65.00
Plate, 7", 8" d, or 9" d	36.00
Relish, 7-1/4" l, 4-1/2" w	36.00
Sauce, flat, 4-1/2" d	10.00
Spooner	42.00
Sugar Bowl, cov	60.00
Tumbler	25.00
Waste Bowl	36.00
Water Tray, 10" d	42.00

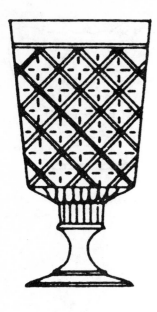

Finecut

Flower in Square, Bryce Pattern Line No. 720

Manufactured by Bryce Brothers, Pittsburgh, PA, c1885, and by United States Glass Company, Pittsburgh, PA, in 1891. Made in non-flint, amber, blue, clear, and vaseline.

Items	Amber	Blue	Clear	Vaseline
Bowl, 8-1/4" d	18.00	24.00	12.00	18.00
Bread Plate	60.00	72.00	30.00	60.00
Butter Dish, cov	55.00	75.00	55.00	95.00
Cake Stand, hs	—	—	42.00	—
Celery Tray	—	55.00	—	—
Celery Vase, silver plated holder	—	—	—	118.00
Compote, cov, hs	65.00	75.00	55.00	75.00
Creamer	310.00	48.00	42.00	75.00
Goblet	55.00	55.00	40.00	45.00
Pitcher, water	120.00	120.00	72.00	125.00
Plate, 6" d or 6-1/4" d	—	24.00	10.00	—
Plate, 7" d or 7-1/4" d	30.00	48.00	18.00	24.00
Plate, 10" d or 10-1/4" d	36.00	60.00	30.00	55.00
Relish Tray	18.00	18.00	12.00	24.00
Sauce, flat	18.00	18.00	12.00	18.00
Spooner	36.00	55.00	40.00	48.00
Sugar Bowl, cov	55.00	55.00	42.00	55.00
Tumbler	—	—	40.00	50.00
Vegetable Dish, oblong	24.00	30.00	18.00	24.00
Water Tray, 10" d	60.00	85.00	30.00	60.00
Wine	—	—	30.00	36.00

Finecut and Block

Button and Oval Medallion, Nailhead and Panel, King's Pattern Line No. 25

Manufactured by King, Son & Company, Pittsburgh, PA, c1890, and by Model Flint Glass Company, Findlay, Ohio, c1894. Made in clear, solid amber, blue, and yellow, and clear with color blocks. The solid colored pieces all have relative values.

Reproductions: This pattern has been heavily reproduced by Fenton Art Glass, Williamstown, WV.

Items	Amber Colored Blocks	Blue Colored Blocks	Clear	Pink or Yellow Colored Blocks	Solid Colored
Bowl, handle, 6" d or 7" d	42.00	42.00	24.00	42.00	42.00
Bowl, handle, 8" or 9" d	48.00	48.00	42.00	48.00	48.00
Bowl, handle, 10" d	55.00	55.00	48.00	55.00	55.00
Bowl, no handle, 6" d, 7" d, or 8" d	36.00	36.00	18.00	36.00	36.00
Butter Dish, cov, individual size	—	—	36.00	—	—
Butter Dish, cov, table size, flat	—	—	65.00	—	—
Butter Dish, cov, table size, footed	130.00	130.00	75.00	130.00	120.00
Cake Stand, hs, 8" d or 9" d	—	—	48.00	—	—
Cake Stand, hs, 10", 11" or 12" d	—	—	55.00	—	—
Celery Tray	60.00	72.00	36.00	65.00	55.00
Champagne, round or saucer bowl	60.00	60.00	30.00	60.00	—
Claret	60.00	60.00	30.00	60.00	—
Cologne Bottle, 5 sizes	115.00	115.00	65.00	115.00	75.00
Compote, cov, hs	—	—	42.00	—	—
Compote, open, ls, 8-1/2" d	55.00	55.00	36.00	55.00	65.00
Cordial	65.00	75.00	55.00	55.00	65.00
Creamer	85.00	85.00	55.00	85.00	65.00
Custard Cup	42.00	42.00	18.00	42.00	30.00
Egg Cup	55.00	55.00	24.00	55.00	30.00
Finger Bowl	55.00	55.00	24.00	55.00	48.00
Goblet, lady's	—	60.00	55.00	—	—
Goblet, regular φ	72.00	72.00	40.00	72.00	65.00
Ice Cream Tray	—	—	55.00	—	—
Jelly Compote	75.00	75.00	35.00	75.00	60.00
Lamp, oil, handle	—	—	85.00	—	—
Orange Bowl, 10" d, 12" d underplate	75.00	75.00	48.00	75.00	85.00
Perfume Bottle, 5 sizes	115.00	115.00	65.00	115.00	75.00
Pickle Jar, cov	—	—	48.00	—	—
Pitcher, milk, 3 pints	115.00	115.00	55.00	115.00	85.00
Pitcher, water, half gallon	115.00	115.00	55.00	115.00	85.00
Plate, 5-1/4" d, 6" d, or 7" d	—	—	18.00	—	—
Plate, 12" d	—	—	24.00	—	—
Punch Cup	—	24.00	15.00	—	—
Relish, rect	55.00	72.00	15.00	55.00	—
Salt, individual	24.00	24.00	15.00	24.00	18.00
Salt, master	42.00	48.00	30.00	42.00	36.00
Salt Shaker, orig top	24.00	18.00	12.00	—	24.00

Items	Amber Colored Blocks	Blue Colored Blocks	Clear	Pink or Yellow Colored Blocks	Solid Colored
Sauce, flat or footed, 4" d or 5" d	18.00	18.00	12.00	18.00	18.00
Soap Dish, rect, hanging bracket	—	—	55.00	—	—
Soap Dish, rect, flat	—	—	42.00	—	—
Spice Barrel, four wheels	—	—	115.00	—	—
Spooner	55.00	72.00	36.00	55.00	55.00
Sugar Bowl, cov	124.00	130.00	55.00	124.00	—
Tumbler	60.00	55.000	24.00	60.00	60.00
Water Tray	—	—	72.00	—	—
Wine φ	55.00	60.00	36.00	55.00	—

Finecut and Panel

Manufactured by many early Pittsburgh, PA, factories in the 1880s, including Bryce Brothers and Richard & Hartley Glass Company. Reissued in the early 1890s by United States Glass Company, Pittsburgh, PA. Made in non-flint, amber, blue, clear, and vaseline. An aqua wine is known.

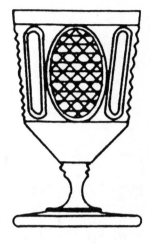

Items	Amber	Blue	Clear	Vaseline
Bowl, oval, 8" l	48.00	—	25.00	—
Bowl, round, 7" d	30.00	42.00	18.00	36.00
Bread Plate	60.00	55.00	36.00	—
Butter Dish, cov, sq	65.00	75.00	48.00	72.00
Cake Stand, hs, 10" d	60.00	75.00	36.00	60.00
Compote, cov, hs	130.00	145.00	75.00	135.00
Compote, open, ls	65.00	65.00	42.00	48.00
Cordial	36.00	42.00	30.00	48.00
Creamer	42.00	60.00	30.00	48.00
Cup	18.00	24.00	12.00	25.00
Goblet	48.00	48.00	24.00	42.00
Pickle Dish	18.00	24.00	12.00	18.00
Pitcher, milk, quart	65.00	—	—	60.00
Pitcher, water, half gallon	85.00	85.00	48.00	55.00
Plate, 6" d	15.00	24.00	12.00	18.00
Platter	36.00	60.00	30.00	36.00
Relish	24.00	30.00	18.00	36.00
Sauce, footed	12.00	30.00	10.00	18.00
Spooner	42.00	55.00	24.00	36.00
Sugar Bowl, cov	48.00	55.00	36.00	36.00
Tumbler	30.00	36.00	24.00	36.00
Vegetable Dish, oblong, 7" l, 8" l, or 9" l	36.00	42.00	24.00	42.00
Waste Bowl	36.00	42.00	24.00	36.00
Water Tray	72.00	55.00	36.00	72.00
Wine	36.00	42.00	24.00	42.00

Fine Rib

Reeded

Manufactured by the New England Glass Company, East Cambridge, MA, in the 1860s and by McKee and Brothers Glass Company, Pittsburgh, PA, 1868-69. It was made in later years in non-flint, which has limited collecting interest and is priced at approximately one third the value of flint. Made in flint, non-flint, clear. Pieces occasionally are found with variegated ovals cut into the ribs. The most common forms for this variant are decanters, stem ware, and tumblers. Expect to pay 3 times the values below for such variants.

Reproductions: Goblets and wines have been reproduced in non-flint.

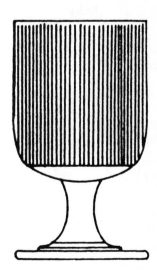

Items	Clear
Ale Glass	60.00
Bitters Bottle	65.00
Bowl, cov, 5-1/2", 6" or 7" d	60.00-65.00
Bowl, open, 5" d or 5-1/2" d	36.00
Bowl, open, 6" d, 7" d, or 8" d	42.00
Butter Dish, cov	75.00
Castor Set	240.00
Celery Vase	85.00
Champagne	130.00
Compote, cov, hs, deep bowl, 6", 7" or 8" d	75.00-135.00
Compote, cov, hs, saucer bowl, 6" or 7" d	60.00
Compote, open, hs, deep bowl, 6" d, 7" d, 8" d, 9" or 10" d	42.00-55.00
Compote, open, hs, saucer bowl, 7-3/4" d	72.00
Compote, open, ls, deep bowl, 6", 7" d, 8", 9" or 10" d	72.00-95.00
Compote, open, ls, saucer bowl, 6", 7" d	60.00
Compote, open, ls, saucer bowl, 9" d	55.00
Cordial	85.00
Creamer, ah	130.00

Items	Clear
Custard Cup, ftd	42.00
Decanter, bar lip, pint or quart	75.00
Decanter, orig stopper, pint	85.00
Decanter, orig stopper, quart	115.00
Egg Cup, pedestal, double	60.00
Egg Cup, pedestal, single	48.00
Goblet φ	72.00
Honey Dish, 3-1/2" d φ	18.00
Lamp	180.00
Lemonade Tumbler	65.00
Mug	55.00
Pitcher, milk, ah	300.00
Pitcher, water, ah	360.00
Plate, 6" or 7" d	24.00
Salt, individual, flat, round	36.00
Salt, individual, footed	42.00
Salt, master, covered, footed	85.00
Sauce, 4" d	18.00
Spooner	65.00
Sugar Bowl, cov	75.00
Tumbler, bar, half pint	75.00
Tumbler, water, half pint	65.00
Tumble-Up	130.00
Whiskey, handle	75.00
Wine	60.00

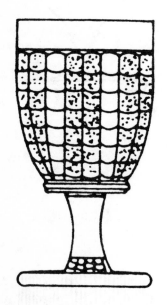

Fishscale

Coral

Manufactured by Bryce Brothers, Pittsburgh, PA, in the mid-1880s and by United States Glass Company, 1891-98. Also attributed to Burlington Glass Works, Hamilton, Ontario, Canada. Made in non-flint, clear.

Items	Clear
Bowl, cov, 6", 7" or 8" d	48.00-60.00
Bowl, cov, 9-1/2" d	55.00
Bowl, open, 6", 7", 8" or 10" d	18.00-36.00
Bread Plate	36.00
Butter Dish, cov	55.00
Cake Plate	55.00
Cake Stand, hs, 9" d or 10" d	36.00
Cake Stand, hs, 10-1/2" d or 11" d	42.00
Celery Vase	36.00
Compote, cov, hs, 6", 7", 8", 9" or 10" d	75.00-115.00
Compote, open, hs, 6", 7", 8", 9" or 10" d	24.00-60.00
Condiment Tray, rect	42.00
Creamer	36.00
Goblet	30.00
Jelly Compote, cov, 4-1/2" d	42.00
Jelly Compote, open, 4-1/2" d	24.00
Lamp, finger	75.00
Mug, large	42.00
Pickle Scoop	42.00
Pitcher, milk	42.00
Pitcher, water	55.00
Plate, square, 7" w to 10" w	36.00
Relish	18.00
Salt Shaker	65.00
Sauce, flat, 4" d	15.00
Sauce, footed, 4" d	18.00
Spooner	30.00
Sugar Bowl, cov	60.00
Syrup, orig top	120.00
Tumbler	75.00
Waste Bowl	42.00
Water Tray, round	42.00

Flamingo Habitat

Manufactured by unknown makers, c1870. The pattern design is etched. Made in non-flint, clear.

Items	Clear
Bowl, oval, 10" l	48.00
Butter Dish, cov	65.00
Celery Vase, pedestal	55.00
Champagne	55.00
Cheese Dish, blown	135.00

Items	Clear
Compote, cov, 4-1/2" d	75.00
Compote, cov, 6-1/2" d	115.00
Compote, open, 5", 6" or 6-1/2" d	48.00
Creamer	48.00
Goblet	75.00
Jelly Compote, cov, 4-1/2" d	75.00
Jelly Compote, open, 4-1/2" d	42.00
Sauce, footed	18.00
Spooner, pedestal	30.00
Sugar Bowl, cov	60.00
Tumbler	36.00
Wine	55.00

Fleur-de-Lis and Drape

Fleur-de-Lis and Tassel, US Glass Pattern Line No. 15,009

Manufactured by Adams & Company, Pittsburgh, PA, c1888. Reissued by United States Glass Company, Pittsburgh, PA, c1892. Made in non-flint, clear, emerald green, and milk white.

Items	Clear	Emerald Green
Bowl, 6" d	18.00	36.00
Bowl, 8" d	24.00	42.00
Butter Dish, cov, flat	55.00	55.00
Butter Dish, cov, footed, flanged rim	55.00	65.00
Cake Stand, hs, 9" d	42.00	55.00
Cake Stand, hs, 10" d	55.00	65.00
Celery Tray, oval	30.00	48.00
Celery Vase	36.00	55.00
Claret	42.00	60.00
Compote, cov, hs, 5", 6", 7" or 8"d	48.00-55.00	60.00-65.00
Compote, cov, ls, 5", 6", 7" or 8"d	36.00-55.00	48.00-60.00
Compote, open, hs, 5", 6", 7" or 8" d	30.00-42.00	36.00-48.00
Compote, open, ls, 5" or 6" d	24.00-30.00	30.00-36.00
Cordial	30.00	55.00
Creamer	30.00	48.00
Cruet, os	55.00	85.00
Cup and Saucer	30.00	42.00
Custard Cup	18.00	30.00
Dish, oblong, 8" l	18.00	24.00
Finger Bowl	36.00	48.00
Goblet	30.00	55.00
Honey Dish, cov	48.00	55.00
Honey Dish, open, flat or footed, 3-1/2" d	18.00	24.00
Lamp, oil	130.00	190.00
Mustard Jar, cov	42.00	60.00
Pickle Dish, boat shape	18.00	24.00
Pitcher, milk	48.00	72.00
Pitcher, water	60.00	65.00
Plate, 6", 7", 8", 9" or 10"d	12.00-30.00	30.00-48.00
Relish Tray, oval	24.00	36.00
Salt Shaker, orig top	24.00	42.00
Sauce, flat or footed, 4" d or 4-1/2" d	12.00	18.00
Spooner	30.00	48.00
Sugar Bowl, cov	36.00	55.00
Sugar Shaker, orig top	48.00	85.00
Syrup, metal top	60.00	130.00
Tumbler	24.00	36.00
Waste Bowl	36.00	48.00
Water Bottle	60.00	130.00
Water Tray, 11-1/2" d	30.00	60.00
Wine	30.00	55.00

Florida

Emerald Green Herringbone, Paneled Herringbone, Prism and Herringbone, US Glass Pattern Line No. 15,056

Manufactured by United States Glass Company, Pittsburgh, PA, in the 1890s, as one of the States series patterns. Made in non-flint, clear, and emerald green. A sapphire blue water pitcher is known and valued at $175.

Reproductions: The goblet has been reproduced in amber, amethyst, blue, emerald green, and ruby red.

Items	Clear	Emerald Green
Berry Set	75.00	135.00
Bowl, cov, 4" d	30.00	48.00

Items	Clear	Emerald Green
Bowl, open, 7-1/4" d	12.00	18.00
Bowl, open, 9" d	18.00	24.00
Butter Dish, cov	60.00	85.00
Cake Stand, large	72.00	75.00
Cake Stand, small	36.00	48.00
Celery Vase	36.00	42.00
Compote, cov, hs, sq, 6-1/2" w	48.00	60.00
Compote, open, hs, sq, 6-1/2" w	36.00	48.00
Cordial	30.00	42.00
Creamer	36.00	55.00
Cruet, os	48.00	65.00
Goblet φ	30.00	48.00
Mustard Pot, cov, attached underplate	30.00	55.00
Nappy	18.00	30.00
Pickle Dish, oval	30.00	55.00
Pitcher, water	60.00	75.00
Plate, 7-1/2" d	15.00	25.00
Plate, 9-1/4" d	18.00	30.00
Relish, square, 6" w	12.00	18.00
Relish, square, 8-1/2" w	18.00	25.00
Salt Shaker	30.00	60.00
Sauce, round, sq top, handle	10.00	15.00
Sauce, round, sq top, no handle	6.00	12.00
Spooner	24.00	42.00
Sugar Bowl, cov	42.00	60.00
Syrup, orig top	72.00	190.00
Tumbler	24.00	36.00
Wine	30.00	60.00

Flute

Manufactured by Bakewell, Pears & Company, Pittsburgh, PA, c1868, and McKee & Brothers, Pittsburgh, PA, c1859-1864, as well as other unknown companies. More than fifteen *Flute* variants were produced in flint and non-flint from the 1850s through the 1880s. Some of the flint variants are *Beaded Flute, Bessimer Flute, New England Flute*. All of these patterns have comparable prices. Made in flint, non-flint, clear. Scarce examples are known in amethyst, amber stained, cobalt blue, deep green, etc.

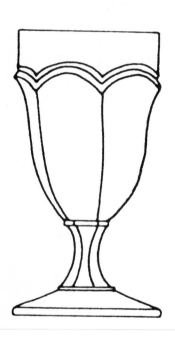

Items	Flint
Ale Glass	60.00
Beer Mug	75.00
Bitters Bottle	75.00
Butter Dish, cov, ls	72.00
Candlestick, 4" h	60.00
Champagne	30.00
Claret	55.00
Compote, open, ls, 8-1/2" d	48.00
Compote, open, ls, 9-1/2" d	55.00
Creamer	55.00
Decanter, os, bar lip	75.00
Egg Cup, double	45.00
Egg Cup, single	36.00
Goblet	30.00
Honey Dish	18.00
Jelly Glass	36.00
Lamp	75.00
Mug	42.00
Pitcher, water	110.00
Punch Cup	30.00
Sauce, flat	18.00
Sugar Bowl, cov	60.00
Syrup, orig top, ah	85.00
Tumbler, bar, 3-1/2" h	24.00
Tumbler, flip, 5-1/4" h	24.00
Tumbler, water, 4-1/4" h	24.00
Whiskey, handle	36.00
Wine	30.00

Frosted Circle

Clear Circle, Horn of Plenty, US Glass Pattern Line No. 15,007

Manufactured by Bryce Brothers, Pittsburgh, PA, c1885. Reissued by United States Glass Company, Pittsburgh, PA, in the late 1890s. Made in non-flint, clear with either a clear circle or frosted circle.

Reproductions: The goblet has been reproduced.

Items	Clear Circle	Frosted Circle
Bowl, cov, 5", 6", 7", 8" or 9" d	24.00-36.00	30.00-42.00
Bowl, open, 5" d, 6", 7", 8" or 9" d	12.00-18.00	18.00-26.00

Items	Clear Circle	Frosted Circle
Butter Dish, cov	55.00	65.00
Butter Dish, open	55.00	55.00
Cake Stand, hs, 8", 9", 9-1/2" or 10" d	36.00-55.00	42.00-55.00
Celery Vase	36.00	42.00
Champagne	42.00	55.00
Compote, cov, hs, 5", 6", 7" or 8" d	36.00-55.00	48.00-60.00
Compote, open, hs, 5", 6", 7", 8" or 10" d	18.00-55.00	24.00-55.00
Creamer	42.00	55.00
Cruet, os	55.00	65.00
Cup and Saucer	30.00	48.00
Goblet φ	42.00	55.00
Juice Tumbler	18.00	36.00
Pickle Dish, oblong	12.00	24.00
Pickle Jar, cov	42.00	60.00
Pitcher, water	55.00	95.00
Plate, 7" d	42.00	60.00
Punch Cup	18.00	24.00
Salt Shaker	30.00	36.00
Sauce	18.00	24.00
Spooner, ftd, scalloped	36.00	42.00
Sugar Bowl, cov	55.00	72.00
Sugar Shaker	48.00	72.00
Syrup, orig top	115.00	65.00
Tumbler	30.00	42.00
Wine	42.00	55.00

Frosted Stork

Flamingo, Frosted Crane

Manufactured by Crystal Glass Company, Bridgeport, OH, c1880. Shards have been found at the Burlington Glass Works, Hamilton, Ontario, Canada. Made in non-flint, clear. Details of the stork's activities differ from scene to scene on the same piece.

Reproductions: Reproduced by A. A. Importing Co., Inc., St. Louis, MO, have reproduced the bread tray, goblet, and sugar bowl from new molds.

Items	Clear
Berry Bowl, 8" d	55.00
Bowl, 9" d	60.00
Bread Plate, oval φ	85.00
Butter Dish, cov	95.00
Creamer	55.00
Dish, oval, 9" l, 6" w	36.00
Finger Bowl	60.00
Goblet φ	65.00
Marmalade Jar, cov	130.00
Pickle Jar, cov, stork finial	130.00
Pitcher, water	240.00
Plate, handle, 9" d	48.00
Platter, 101 pattern border, 11-1/2" l, 8" w	85.00
Platter, scenic border, 11-1/2" l, 8" w	75.00
Relish tray	55.00
Sauce, flat	24.00
Spooner	48.00
Sugar Bowl, cov φ	115.00
Waste Bowl	60.00
Water Tray	120.00

Galloway

Mirror Plate, U.S. Mirror, Virginia, Woodrow

Manufactured by United States Glass Company, Pittsburgh, PA, c1904 to 1918. Jefferson Glass Company, Toronto, Canada, produced it from 1900 to 1925. Made in non-flint, clear with or without gold trim, rose stain and ruby stain.

Reproductions: United States Glass Company, Tiffin, OH, reissued the punch bowl set in 1955. The toothpick holder has also been reproduced and can be found in amber, amethyst, blue, green, and orange.

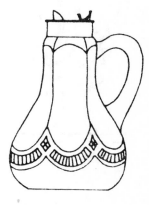

Items	Clear w/ Gold	Rose Stained
Basket, ah	75.00	130.00
Bowl, belled, 5-1/2", 6-1/2", 7-1/2", 8-1/2" or 10" d	24.00-42.00	42.00-60.00
Bowl, oval, 8" l or 8-1/2" l	42.00	55.00
Bowl, rect, 6" or 9" l	30.00-36.00	48.00-55.00
Bowl, round, 5-1/2", 6-1/2", 7-1/2", 8-1/2", 9-1/2" or 11" d	24.00-55.00	36.00-65
Butter Dish, cov, hotel or table size	65.00	130.00
Butter Dish, cov, quarter pound	60.00	120.00
Cake Stand, hs, 8-1/2", 9" or 10" d	65.00-85.00	110.00-120.00
Carafe, water	55.00	85.00

Items	Clear w/ Gold	Rose Stained
Celery Vase	42.00	75.00
Champagne	72.00	190.00
Child's Pitcher, water, 4-1/4" h	36.00	55.00
Child's Tumbler	12.00	24.00
Compote, cov, hs, 6", 7" or 8" d	110.00-120.00	130.00-142.00
Compote, open, hs, deep bowl, 5-1/2", 6-1/2", 7-1/2", 8", 8-1/2", 9", 10", or 10-1/2"	30.00-72.00	60.00-75.00
Compote, open, hs, scalloped, 10" d	55.00	75.00
Cracker Jar, cov, orig Britannia or patterned glass lid	180.00	270.00
Creamer, hotel size	36.00	60.00
Creamer, individual size	24.00	48.00
Creamer, table size, tankard	42.00	55.00
Cruet, os	55.00	130.00
Egg Cup	48.00	72.00
Finger Bowl	48.00	65.00
Goblet	75.00	115.00
Lemonade, handle	42.00	55.00
Mug	48.00	60.00
Nappy, tricorn	30.00	60.00
Olive, 6" l	24.00	36.00
Pickle Castor, silver plate holder and lid	65.00	240.00
Pickle Dish, crimped rim, 8-1/2" l, 2-1/2" h	30.00	65.00
Pickle Jar, open	42.00	55.00
Pitcher, ice jug, ah, 2 quarts	75.00	130.00
Pitcher, milk, 1 quart	72.00	95.00
Pitcher, tankard, small to large	65-85.00	118.00-130.00
Plate, 4", 5", 6" or 8" d	36.00-48.00	48.00-65.00
Punch Bowl, ftd φ	172.00	270.00
Punch Bowl Plate, 20" d φ	95.00	130.00
Punch Cup φ	12.00	18.00
Relish Tray	24.00	36.00
Rose Bowl	30.00	72.00
Salt, individual, flat, oblong	30.00	48.00
Salt, master, oblong or round, flat	42.00	72.00
Salt and Pepper Shakers, pr, squatty or tall	48.00	75.00
Sauce, flat, flared, or straight-sided, 4" d or 4-1/2" d	12.00	24.00
Sherbet, ftd, 4-1/2" d	30.00	36.00
Spooner, hotel size	36.00	95.00
Spooner, table size	42.00	85.00
Sugar Bowl, cov, hotel or table size	55.00-72.00	75.00-95.00
Sugar Bowl, open, individual, oval, flat	60.00	85.00
Sugar Shaker	48.00	120.00
Syrup, orig top, 2 sizes	65.00	142.00
Toothpick Holder φ	36.00	55.00
Tumbler, hotel size	42.00	55.00
Tumbler, water	36.00	48.00
Vase, cylindrical, pulled rim, 11" h	36.00	60.00
Vase, straight sides, 5-1/2" h	30.00	55.00
Vase, straight sides, 18" h	42.00	55.00
Waste Bowl	48.00	65.00
Water Bottle	48.00	85.00
Water Tray, 8-1/2" d	75.00	135.00
Water Tray, 10" d	85.00	124.00
Wine	55.00	65.00

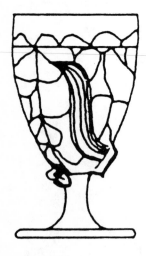

Garden of Eden

Fish, Lotus, Lotus and Serpent, Lotus with Serpent, Turtle

Manufacture unknown, c1870. Made in non-flint, clear.

Items	Clear
Bowl, oval, 7" l, 4-1/2" w	18.00
Bread Tray, motto	42.00
Butter Dish, covered	75.00
Cake Stand, hs, 11-1/2" d	60.00
Celery	30.00
Compote, cov, hs, 10" d	95.00
Compote, open, hs, scalloped rim, 9" d	55.00
Creamer, individual or table size	42.00-48.00
Dish, oval	15.00
Egg Cup	60.00
Goblet, plain stem	50.00
Goblet, serpent stem	200.00
Honey Dish	12.00
Mug	55.00
Pickle Dish, oval	18.00
Pitcher, water, half gallon	65.00
Plate, handle, 6-1/2" d	24.00
Salt, master	36.00
Sauce, flat or footed	12.00-18.00
Spooner	30.00
Sugar Bowl, covered	60.00
Toothpick Holder	55.00

Garfield Drape

Canadian Drape

Manufactured by Adams and Company, Pittsburgh, PA, in 1881, after the assassination of President Garfield. It is also believed that a Canadian glass manufacture firm also produced this commemorative pattern. Made in non-flint, clear.

Reproductions: The bread plate of this interesting commemorative pattern has been reproduced by Summit Art Glass Company, Rootstown, OH, using a new mold.

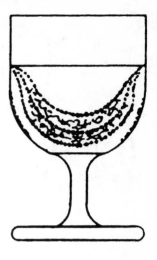

Items	Clear
Bowl	30.00
Bread Plate, memorial, portrait of Garfield φ	65.00
Bread Plate, "We Mourn Our Nation's Loss," portrait	75.00
Butter Dish, cov	72.00
Cake Stand, hs, 9-1/2" d	75.00
Celery Vase, pedestal	55.00
Compote, cov, hs, 8" d	120.00
Compote, cov, ls, 6" d	85.00
Compote, open, hs, 8-1/2" d	48.00
Creamer, ah, 5-1/2" h	48.00
Creamer, ph, 5-1/2" h	42.00
Goblet, gentleman's	48.00
Goblet, lady's	65.00
Honey Dish	18.00
Lamp, oil, orig burner and chimney	120.00
Pickle Dish, oval	24.00
Pitcher, milk, quart	85.00
Pitcher, water, applied handle, half gallon	75.00
Pitcher, water, strap handle, half gallon	120.00
Relish, oval	24.00
Sauce, flat, 3-1/2" d	12.00
Sauce, footed, 3-1/2" d	15.00
Spooner	42.00
Sugar Bowl, cov	72.00
Tumbler, flat	42.00
Tumbler, footed	55.00

Georgia

Peacock Feather

Manufactured by Richards & Hartley, Tarentum, PA, and reissued by United States Glass Company, Pittsburgh, PA, in 1902, as part of its States series. Made in non-flint clear. Rare examples are known in blue and canary. (Lamp, chamber blue, $350). No goblet is known in this pattern.

Items	Clear
Bon Bon, ftd	30.00
Bowl, 5", 6", 7" or 8" d	24.00-36.00
Butter Dish, cov, quarter pound or table size	55.00
Cake Stand, hs, 9", 9-1/2", 10" or 11" d	48.00-55.00
Castor Set, 2 bottles	72.00
Celery Tray, 11-3/4" l	42.00
Celery Vase	48.00
Child's Cake Stand	42.00
Child's Creamer	42.00
Compote, cov, hs, 5", 6", 7" or 8" d	42.00-60.00
Compote, open, hs, 5", 6", 7", 8", 9" or 10" d	24.00-55.00
Condiment Set, tray, oil cruet, salt & pepper	75.00
Creamer	42.00
Cruet, os	55.00
Decanter, os	85.00
Lamp, chamber, pedestal	85.00
Lamp, hand, oil, 7" h	95.00
Mug	30.00
Nappy	30.00
Pitcher, water	85.00
Plate, 5-1/4" d	18.00
Preserve Dish, 8" l	12.00
Relish Tray	18.00
Salt Shaker	48.00
Sauce, flat, 4" d or 4-1/2" d	12.00
Spooner	42.00
Sugar Bowl, cov	55.00
Syrup, orig top, metal lid	65.00
Tumbler	42.00

Giant Bull's Eye

Bull's Eye and Spearhead, US Glass Pattern Line No. 157

Manufactured by Bellaire Glass Company, Findlay, OH, c1889, and Model Flint Glass Company, Findlay, OH, c1891, and continued by United States Glass Company, Pittsburgh, PA, after 1891. Made in non-flint, clear.

Items	Clear
Bowl, 8" d	30.00
Brandy Bottle, os, tall, 12 oz, 16 oz, or 22 oz	55.00
Butter Dish, cov	55.00
Cake Stand, hs	36.00
Cheese Dish, cov	55.00
Claret Jug, tankard shape	72.00
Compote, cov	75.00
Compote, open, flared or scalloped rim	48.00
Condiment Set, cruet, salt and pepper shakers, mustard	85.00
Creamer	36.00
Cruet, os	72.00
Decanter, os	60.00
Goblet	55.00
Lamp, handled	130.00
Perfume Bottle, os	36.00
Pitcher, water, half gallon	75.00
Relish Tray	18.00
Sauce, flat, 4" d	10.00
Spooner, scalloped	36.00
Sugar Bowl, cov	72.00
Syrup, orig nickel top, large or small	65.00
Tumbler	36.00
Vase, 7" h, 8" h, or 9" h	42.00
Water Tray	55.00
Wine	36.00
Wine Tray, 7-1/4" d	55.00

Gothic

Cathedral

Manufacture attributed to Union Glass Company, Somerville, MA, and Boston and Sandwich Glass Company, Sandwich, MA c1860. Made in flint, clear.

Items	Clear
Bowl, scalloped, 7" d	85.00
Bowl, scalloped, 8" d	75.00
Butter Dish, cov	85.00
Castor Set, pewter frame	130.00
Celery Vase	110.00
Champagne	165.00
Compote, cov, hs, 7" or 8" d	120.00-135.00
Compote, cov, ls, 8" d	120.00
Compote, open, hs, 8" d	110.00
Compote, open, ls, 7" or 8" d	65.00-75.00
Cordial	120.00
Creamer, ah	75.00
Egg Cup	60.00
Goblet, plain or rayed base	80.00
Pickle Dish, oval, 7" l	24.00
Plate	130.00
Salt, master	72.00
Sauce, flat	18.00
Spooner	48.00
Sugar Bowl, cov	85.00
Tumbler, flat	115.00
Wine	130.00

Grand

Diamond Medallion, Fine Cut and Diamond, Fine Cut Medallion

Manufactured by Bryce, Higbee and Company, Pittsburgh, PA, in 1885. Also attributed to Diamond Glass Company, Ltd., Montreal, Canada. Made in non-flint, clear. Stemware comes in plain and roped stems.

Items	Clear
Bowl, cov, flat or footed, 6" d	36.00
Bowl, open, ftd, 6" d or 7" d	24.00
Bread Plate, 10" d	30.00
Butter Dish, cov, flat or footed	42.00-55.00

Items	Clear
Cake Stand, hs, 8", 8-1/2" or 10" d	36.00-42.00
Celery Vase, pedestal	30.00
Compote, cov, hs, 5-1/2", 6", 7", 7-1/2" or 8"d	72.00-95.00
Compote, cov, ls, 6", 7" or 8"d	65.00-85.00
Compote, open, hs or ls, 6" d	30.00
Compote, open or ls, hs, 7" d	36.00
Compote, open, hs or ls, 8" d	42.00
Compote, open, hs, 9" d	55.00
Cordial	60.00
Creamer	30.00
Decanter, os	85.00
Dish, oval, 7" l or 9" l	18.00
Goblet, plain or ring stem	30.00
Mug	30.00
Pitcher, water, ah, half gallon	48.00
Plate, 10" d or 11" d	30.00
Relish, 7-1/2" l, oval	15.00
Salt Shaker	36.00
Sauce, flat	12.00
Sauce, footed	15.00
Sherbet	18.00
Spooner	24.00
Sugar Bowl, cov, plain or scalloped rim	42.00
Syrup, orig top, metal top	110.00
Waste Bowl, collared	36.00
Water Tray, round	30.00
Wine	30.00

Grape and Festoon with Stippled Leaf

Manufactured by Doyle and Company, Pittsburgh, PA, in the early 1870s. Made in non-flint, clear.

Items	Clear
Bowl	18.00
Butter Dish, cov	60.00
Buttermilk Goblet	36.00
Celery Vase	48.00
Compote, cov, hs, 8" d	118.00
Compote, open, ls, 8" d	75.00
Creamer, ah	60.00
Egg Cup	36.00
Goblet	42.00
Lamp, oil, 7-1/2" h	65.00
Mug	24.00
Pitcher, milk, ah	75.00
Pitcher, water, ah	110.00
Plate, 6" d	35.00
Relish	15.00
Salt, ftd	30.00
Sauce, flat, 4" d	12.00
Spooner	42.00
Sugar Bowl, cov	60.00
Wine	55.00

Grape Band

Ashburton with Grape Band, Early Grape Band, Grape Vine

Manufactured by Bryce, Walker and Company, Pittsburgh, PA, in the late 1850s in flint. Non-flint was made in 1869. Made in flint, non-flint, clear.

Reproductions: Only the goblet has been reproduced in this pattern.

Items	Flint	Non-Flint
Butter Dish, cov	75.00	60.00
Compote, cov, hs	—	60.00
Compote, cov, ls	—	55.00
Compote, open, hs	—	30.00
Cordial	65.00	—
Creamer, ah	—	60.00
Egg Cup	—	24.00
Goblet φ	48.00	30.00
Pickle Dish, scoop shape	—	18.00
Pitcher, water	—	85.00
Plate, 6" d	—	24.00
Salt, individual	—	24.00
Salt, master, ftd	—	36.00
Spooner	—	36.00
Sugar Bowl, cov	—	55.00
Tumbler	42.00	24.00
Wine	42.00	30.00

Grasshopper

Locust, Long Spear, Riverside Pattern Line No. 4

Manufactured by Riverside Glass Works, Wellsburg, WV c1883. There are more than forty pieces documented. Made in non-flint, amber and clear. The creamer and sugar are known in vaseline and blue. Covered compotes and footed sauces are known in vaseline.

Reproductions: Any goblet found in this pattern is modern as none were originally made with the pattern.

Items	Amber	Clear
Bowl, cov.	55.00	42.00
Bowl, open, ftd, deep	—	30.00
Bowl, open, ftd, shallow, flared	—	42.00
Butter Dish, cov.	110.00	65.00
Celery Vase	110.00	60.00
Compote, cov, hs, 7" d	—	60.00
Compote, cov, hs, 8-1/2" d	—	65.00
Creamer	72.00	48.00
Marmalade Jar, cov.	—	130.00
Pickle	—	24.00
Pitcher, water	130.00	75.00
Plate, ftd, 8-1/2" d	—	30.00
Plate, ftd, 9" d	—	24.00
Plate, ftd, 10-1/2" d	120.00	30.00
Salt, individual	—	48.00
Salt Shaker	—	42.00
Sauce, flat	—	18.00
Sauce, footed	—	20.00
Spooner	75.00	48.00
Sugar Bowl, cov, flat	75.00	65.00
Sugar Bowl, cov, footed	95.00	85.00

Hairpin

Sandwich Loop, Gaines.

Manufactured by Boston and Sandwich Glass Company, Sandwich, MA, c1850 and McKee, 1860s. Made in flint and clear. Also produced in white (clear) opalescent. Values for opalescent would be 200%. Finials are shaped like acorns, handles are applied.

Items	Clear
Bowl, 6-1/4" d	120.00
Butter Dish, cov.	55.00
Celery Vase	48.00
Champagne	95.00
Compote, cov, hs	270.00
Compote, open, hs	180.00
Creamer, ah	65.00
Decanter, os, qt	110.00
Egg Cup, pedestal	36.00
Goblet, plain or rayed base	48.00
Lamp, all glass	250.00
Salt, cov, master, ftd	105.00
Sauce, flat	18.00
Spooner	48.00
Sugar Bowl, cov	115.00
Tumbler	60.00
Whiskey, handle	55.00
Wine	60.00

Halley's Comet

Etruria

Manufactured by Model Flint Company, Findlay, OH, c1890, and by National Glass Company, Pittsburgh, PA, c1891-1902. The tail of the comet forms continuous loops. Made in non-flint, clear and some ruby-stained pieces. Found with copper wheel engraving.

Items	Clear
Bowl, cov, 4" d, 3 ftd	48.00
Bowl, open, 8" or 9" d	30.00
Butter Dish, cov.	95.00
Cake Stand, hs	90.00
Candy Dish	24.00
Celery Vase	36.00
Compote, cov, hs, 6" or 8" d	55.00-65.00
Compote, open, hs, 6" or 8" d	36.00-48.00
Creamer	42.00
Cruet, os	72.00

Items	Clear
Goblet	42.00
Mustard, cov, ftd	55.00
Pitcher, milk, quart	90.00
Pitcher, water, half gallon	120.00
Punch Cup	30.00
Relish Tray	30.00
Salt and Pepper Shakers, pr	55.00
Sauce, flat, 4" d	12.00
Spooner	55.00
Sugar Bowl, cov	80.00
Syrup, orig top	105.00
Tumbler	30.00
Water Tray, 8" d	65.00
Wine	30.00

Hamilton

Cape Cod

Manufactured by Cape Cod Glass Company, Sandwich, MA, c1860. Shards have been found at the site of the Boston and Sandwich Glass Company, Sandwich, MA. Other companies also may have made this pattern. Made in flint, non-flint, and clear. Rare examples found in color.

Items	Flint	Non-Flint
Butter Dish, cov	90.00	30.00
Castor Set, 4 bottles, pewter standard	190.00	130.00
Celery Vase, pedestal	72.00	24.00
Compote, cov, hs	115.00	42.00
Compote, open, ls, scalloped rim, 6" d	95.00	36.00
Creamer, ah	90.00	30.00
Creamer, ph	80.00	24.00
Decanter, os	160.00	60.00
Egg Cup	60.00	18.00
Goblet	55.00	15.00
Hat, made from tumbler mold	130.00	—
Honey Dish	18.00	12.00
Lamp, hand	105.00	42.00
Pitcher, water, ah, half gallon	290.00	130.00
Plate, 6" d	55.00	15.00
Salt, master, ftd	36.00	12.00
Sauce, 4-1/2" d	36.00	12.00
Spooner	42.00	15.00
Sugar Bowl, cov	90.00	30.00
Sweetmeat Dish, hs, cov	115.00	42.00
Syrup, ah, orig top	350.00	—
Tumbler, bar	105.00	42.00
Tumbler, water	95.00	36.00
Whiskey, ah	115.00	42.00
Wine	110.00	36.00

Hand

Early Pennsylvania

Manufactured by O'Hara Glass Company, Pittsburgh, PA, c1880. Covered pieces have a finial in the shape of a hand, hence the name. Made in non-flint, clear.

Items	Clear
Bowl, 7", 9" or 10" d	36.00-48.00
Butter Dish, cov	105.00
Cake Stand, hs	65.00
Celery Vase	410.00
Compote, cov, hs, 7" or 8" d	72.00-115.00
Compote, open, hs, 7-3/4" d	42.00
Compote, open, ls, 9" d	30.00
Cordial, 3-1/2" h	105.00
Creamer, ph	48.00
Dish, oval, 7", 8", 9" or 10" d	36.00-42.00
Dish, oval, d	42.00
Goblet	55.00
Honey Dish	12.00
Marmalade Jar, cov	90.00
Mug	48.00
Pickle Tray	24.00
Pitcher, water, ph, half gallon	90.00
Platter	42.00
Sauce, flat, 4" d	15.00

Items	Clear
Sauce, footed, 4" d	18.00
Spooner	36.00
Sugar Bowl, cov	90.00
Syrup, orig top	130.00
Tumbler	105.00
Water Tray	65.00
Wine	65.00

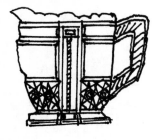

Hanover

Block with Stars, Blockhouse, Hanover Star

Manufactured by Richards & Hartley Glass Company, Tarentum, PA, c1888. Reissued by United States Glass Company, Pittsburgh, PA, after 1891. Made in amber, blue, clear, and vaseline.

Items	Amber	Blue	Clear	Vaseline
Bowl, 7" d	36.00	42.00	24.00	48.00
Bowl, 10" d	42.00	48.00	30.00	55.00
Butter Dish, cov	90.00	110.00	48.00	120.00
Cake Stand, hs, 10" d	80.00	105.00	48.00	115.00
Celery Vase	48.00	72.00	30.00	80.00
Cheese Dish, cov, 10" d	115.00	130.00	60.00	160.00
Compote, cov, hs	110.00	130.00	60.00	160.00
Compote, open, hs, 7" d	60.00	80.00	48.00	90.00
Compote, open, hs, 8" d	65.00	85.00	55.00	95.00
Compote, open, ls, 7" d	55.00	72.00	42.00	85.00
Compote, open, ls, 8" d	60.00	80.00	48.00	90.00
Creamer, ph	55.00	60.00	36.00	65.00
Cruet, os	—	—	30.00	—
Goblet	65.00	80.00	30.00	90.00
Mug, ph, large	55.00	60.00	24.00	80.00
Mug, ph, small	48.00	55.00	18.00	72.00
Pitcher, milk, ph, quart	105.00	120.00	60.00	118.00
Pitcher, water, ph, half gallon	115.00	112.00	72.00	130.00
Plate, 6" d	36.00	42.00	30.00	48.00
Plate, 10" d	42.00	48.00	36.00	42.00
Platter	65.00	80.00	36.00	90.00
Puff Box, orig glass lid	—	—	12.00	—
Sauce, footed	18.00	24.00	12.00	24.00
Spooner	42.00	48.00	30.00	55.00
String Holder	42.00	48.00	30.00	55.00
Sugar Bowl, cov	65.00	80.00	55.00	90.00
Tumbler, flat	36.00	48.00	30.00	55.00
Wine	55.00	65.00	30.00	80.00

Hartley

Paneled Diamond Cut with Fan

Manufactured by Richards and Hartley, Tarentum, PA, in the 1880s and by United States Glass Company, Pittsburgh, PA, in 1891. Made in non-flint, amber, blue, clear, and vaseline. The tri-lobed form may have either plain or engraved panels.

Items	Amber	Blue or Vaseline	Clear	Vaseline
Berry, Bowl, ftd, 7" d	36.00	42.00	18.00	48.00
Berry Bowl, 9" d	36.00	42.00	18.00	48.00
Bowl, flat, 6" d	30.00	36.00	18.00	36.00
Bowl, flat, 8" d	36.00	42.00	24.00	48.00
Bowl, flat, 9" d	36.00	42.00	24.00	55.00
Bread Plate, trilobed	36.00	48.00	24.00	48.00
Butter Dish, cov	60.00	72.00	48.00	72.00
Cake Stand, hs, 10" d	55.00	60.00	48.00	60.00
Celery Vase	36.00	48.00	30.00	60.00
Centerpiece Dish, flat	48.00	55.00	24.00	55.00
Compote, cov, hs, 7" d	65.00	90.00	48.00	90.00
Compote, cov, hs, 8" d	72.00	95.00	55.00	95.00
Compote, cov, ls, 7-3/4" d	80.00	90.00	55.00	90.00
Compote, open, 7" d	36.00	48.00	24.00	48.00
Compote, open, 8" d	42.00	55.00	30.00	55.00
Creamer	36.00	42.00	24.00	42.00
Goblet	42.00	48.00	30.00	48.00
Pitcher, milk, quart	95.00	105.00	90.00	110.00
Pitcher, water, half gallon	110.00	110.00	105.00	115.00
Plate, dinner	55.00	60.00	36.00	60.00
Relish Tray	110.00	24.00	18.00	24.00
Sauce, flat, 4" d	18.00	24.00	12.00	24.00

Items	Amber	Blue or Vaseline	Clear	Vaseline
Spooner	210.00	36.00	110.00	36.00
Sugar Bowl, cov	48.00	60.00	36.00	60.00
Tumbler	36.00	42.00	24.00	42.00
Wine	48.00	55.00	24.00	55.00

Harvard Yard

Harvard #1, Tarentum's Harvard

Manufactured by Tarentum Glass Company, Tarentum, PA, in 1896. Made in non-flint, clear. Also found in clear with gold, emerald green, pink, and ruby stained.

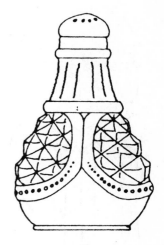

Items	Clear
Bowl, several sizes	24.00
Butter Dish, cov	36.00
Cake Stand, hs	36.00
Condiment Set	55.00
Cordial	30.00
Creamer	110.00
Egg Cup	18.00
Goblet	30.00
Jug	55.00
Pitcher, water, half gallon	48.00
Plate, 10" d	18.00
Salt, individual	18.00
Salt Shaker, orig top	18.00
Sauce, flat	6.00
Spooner	24.00
Sugar Bowl, cov	30.00
Toothpick Holder	18.00
Tray, oval	42.00
Tumbler	24.00
Wine	18.00

Heart with Thumbprint

Bull's Eye in Heart, Columbia, Columbian, Heart and Thumbprint

Manufactured by Tarentum Glass Company, Tarentum, PA, 1898-1906. Made in non-flint, clear, emerald green, and ruby stained. Some emerald green pieces have gold trim. Experimental pieces made in custard, blue custard, and opaque Nile green, as well as cobalt blue.

Items	Clear	Emerald Green	Ruby Stain
Banana Boat, large	90.00	—	155.00
Banana Boat, small	80.00	—	130.00
Barber Bottle	118.00	—	—
Bowl, round, 6" d	42.00	80.00	130.00
Bowl, round, 9" d	48.00	85.00	124.00
Bowl, sq, 7" w	42.00	120.00	118.00
Bowl, sq, 9-1/2" w	42.00	130.00	124.00
Bowl, scalloped, 10" w	55.00	120.00	120.00
Butter Dish, cov	130.00	190.00	160.00
Cake Stand, hs, 9" d	160.00	—	215.00
Carafe, water	120.00	—	190.00
Card Tray	24.00	65.00	120.00
Celery Vase	80.00	—	124.00
Cologne Bottle	120.00	—	—
Compote, open, hs, scalloped, 7-1/2" d	160.00	—	215.00
Compote, open, hs, scalloped, 8-1/2" d	120.00	—	240.00
Cordial, 3" h	130.00	190.00	190.00
Creamer, individual	36.00	55.00	90.00
Creamer, table size	72.00	112.00	125.00
Cruet, os	90.00	—	—
Finger Bowl	55.00	105.00	130.00
Goblet	510.00	130.00	148.00
Hair Receiver, lid	72.00	120.00	118.00
Ice Bucket	72.00	—	—
Lamp, finger	80.00	130.00	—
Lamp, oil, 8" h	60.00	172.00	—
Mustard, silver plate cov	115.00	120.00	—
Nappy, triangular	36.00	72.00	—
Pitcher, water, ah, bulbous	240.00	—	—
Plate, 6" d	30.00	55.00	90.00
Plate, 10" d	55.00	105.00	115.00
Powder Jar, silver plate cov	80.00	—	—
Punch Cup	24.00	42.00	72.00

Items	Clear	Emerald Green	Ruby Stain
Rose Bowl, large..	72.00	—	142.00
Rose Bowl, small	36.00	—	115.00
Salt and Pepper Shakers, pr...................................	115.00		—
Sauce, ruffled, plain, variations, 5" d......................	24.00	42.00	72.00
Spooner	60.00	105.00	115.00
Sugar Bowl, cov, table	105.00	110.00	130.00
Sugar Bowl, open, individual..................................	30.00	42.00	90.00
Syrup, orig top, large...	115.00	80.00	90.00
Syrup, orig top, small	115.00	72.00	72.00
Tray, 8-1/4" l, 4-1/4" w	36.00	80.00	90.00
Tumbler...	55.00	105.00	105.00
Vase, 6" h...	42.00	80.00	110.00
Vase, 10" h...	80.00	120.00	120.00
Wine..	55.00	160.00	160.00

Heavy Gothic

Whitton, US Glass Pattern Line No. 15,014

Manufactured by Columbia Glass Company, Findlay, OH, c1890, and continued by United States Glass Company, Pittsburgh, PA, after 1891 until 1899. Made in flint, clear, and ruby stained. Some pieces of green are known.

Reproductions: The goblet has been reproduced. It is permanently marked "© Red-Cliff C USA" for the Red-Cliff Distributing Company, Chicago, IL. Fenton Art Glass Company, Williamstown WV, produced a bell in opalescent colors in 1980.

Items	Clear	Ruby Stained
Bowl, cov, 5", 6", 7" or 8" d	36.00-48.00	80.00-90.00
Bowl, open, belled, 5-1/2", 6-1/2", 7-1/2" or 9" d........	18.00-24.00	30.00-42.00
Bowl, open, flared, 7-1/2", 8-1/2" or 10" d.................	24.00-36.00	36.00-55.00
Butter Dish, cov, 5-1/4" d	48.00	130.00
Cake Stand, hs, 9" or 10" d.......................................	55.00-60.00	72.00-80.00
Celery Vase..	30.00	110.00
Claret	42.00	80.00
Compote, cov, hs, 5" or 7" d......................................	36.00-48.00	110.00-120.00
Compote, open, hs, belled, 5-1/2" or 8-1/2" d.............	18.00-36.00	42.00-60.00
Compote, open, hs, flared, 5-1/2" or 8-1/2" d.............	18.00-36.00	42.00-72.00
Creamer, 4-1/4" h...	30.00	60.00
Dish, oblong, flat, 7", 8" or 9" l	12.00-18.00	24.00-30.00
Goblet, 6-1/4" h φ...	30.00	60.00
Honey Dish, cov, underplate, 4" d or 5" d	55.00	110.00
Lamp, oil	110.00	—
Pickle Jar, cov	60.00	112.00
Pitcher, water, half gallon	55.00	270.00
Salt Shaker, orig top...	18.00	55.00
Sauce, flat or ftd, belled or scalloped, 4-1/2" d or 5" d...	12.00	24.00
Spooner	24.00	65.00
Sugar Bowl, cov, breakfast or table size....................	30.00-42.00	55.00-80.00
Sugar Shaker...	60.00	160.00
Syrup, orig top, orig top..	60.00	190.00
Tumbler..	24.00	42.00
Wine...	18.00	42.00

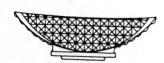

Heavy Panelled Finecut

Sequoia

Manufactured by George Duncan and Sons, Pittsburgh, PA, c1880, and by United States Glass Company, Pittsburgh, PA, in 1891. Made in non-flint, clear. Also found in amber, blue, and vaseline. Some handled pieces, such as the platter or bread tray, have small leaves on the handles.

Items	Clear
Berry Bowl, 10" d	18.00
Bread Tray	36.00
Butter Dish, cov..	48.00
Cake Stand	42.00
Castor Set, 5-bottle	90.00
Celery Boat, 11" l	36.00
Compote, cov, hs, 8" d	65.00
Creamer	42.00
Goblet	24.00
Pitcher, water	60.00
Platter..	36.00
Spooner	24.00
Sugar Bowl, cov..	42.00
Tray, small, shaped like large platter, with leaves on handles, 6-1/2" x 4-3/8"...	18.00
Tumbler, Bar	24.00

Henrietta

Big Block, Diamond Block, Hexagon Block

Manufactured by Columbia Glass Company, Findlay, OH, c1889. Reissued by United States Glass Company, Pittsburgh, PA, c1891-92. Made in non-flint, clear, emerald green, and ruby stain. Some pieces found with copper wheel engraving. Prices listed for clear plain pieces.

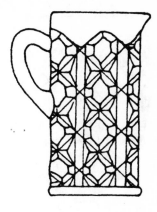

Items	Clear
Bone Dish, oval	18.00
Bon Bon	18.00
Bowl, rect, 8" l, 5" w	24.00
Bowl, round, 7" or 9" d	18.00-30.00
Bread Plate	24.00
Butter Dish, cov, 5-1/2" h	42.00
Cake Stand, hs, 8" or 10" d	48.00-55.00
Celery Tray, 8" l	24.00
Celery Vase	30.00
Compote, open, hs, scalloped	30.00
Confection Jar, cov, tall	42.00
Cracker Jar, cov	55.00
Creamer, individual or table size	24.00-30.00
Cruet, os	30.00
Custard Cup, ftd, handle	12.00
Dish, oblong, 7" or 8" l	18.00
Lamp, oil	60.00
Mustard Jar, orig nickel plated top	48.00
Pitcher, water, bulbous or tankard, ah	55.00-60.00
Olive Dish	18.00
Rose Bowl	24.00
Salt, individual	12.00
Salt, master	18.00
Salt Shaker, orig top, table or hotel size	24.00-30.00
Sauce, flat, 4-1/2" d	12.00
Spooner	30.00
Sugar Bowl, cov	36.00
Sugar Shaker, orig nickel plated top	65.00
Syrup, orig top	55.00
Tumbler, 3-5/8" h	24.00
Vase, 5" or 9" h	30.00-42.00

Hexagon Block

Manufactured by Hobbs, Brockunier & Company, Wheeling, WV, c1889. Reissued by United States Glass Company, Pittsburgh, PA, after the 1891 merger. Made in non-flint, clear, clear with amber stain, and clear with ruby stain. It is also found plain or etched with the Fern and Berry etching or Bird and Flower etching. Prices below are for plain pieces.

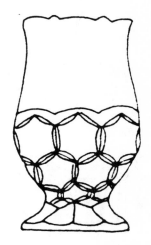

Items	Amber Stained	Clear Stained	Ruby
Bowl, deep or shallow, 7" d	24.00	18.00	24.00
Bowl, deep, 9" d	48.00	30.00	48.00
Bowl, shallow, 9" d	36.00	30.00	36.00
Butter Dish, cov	130.00	48.00	142.00
Celery Vase, ftd	90.00	42.00	105.00
Compote, cov, hs, deep bowl, 7" d	110.00	55.00	120.00
Compote, cov, hs, deep bowl, 8" d	115.00	60.00	106.00
Compote, cov, hs, saucer bowl, 8" d	105.00	48.00	115.00
Compote, cov, hs, saucer bowl, 9" d	110.00	55.00	120.00
Compote, open, hs, deep bowl, 7" d	80.00	30.00	90.00
Compote, open, hs, deep bowl, 8" d	85.00	36.00	95.00
Compote, open, hs, saucer bowl, 8" d	72.00	24.00	85.00
Compote, open, hs, saucer bowl, 9" d	80.00	30.00	90.00
Creamer, ftd, ah	80.00	48.00	90.00
Custard Cup, ftd, ah	30.00	18.00	42.00
Finger Bowl	24.00	48.00	36.00
Goblet	60.00	42.00	72.00
Pickle Jar, cov, ftd	115.00	55.00	125.00
Salt Shaker, ftd, orig top	24.00	18.00	30.00
Sauce, flat, 4" d or 4-1/2" d	24.00	12.00	18.00
Spooner, ftd	55.00	30.00	60.00
Sugar Bowl, cov, ftd	85.00	55.00	90.00
Syrup, orig top, ph	260.00	60.00	280.00
Tumbler	42.00	18.00	48.00

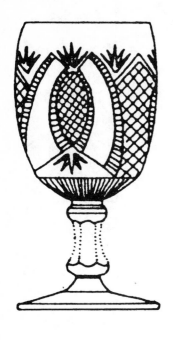

Hickman

La Clede

Manufactured by McKee & Brothers Glass Company, Pittsburgh, PA, c1897. Made in non-flint, clear, and ruby stained. Also documented in light green and two shades of amber.

Reproductions: The 10" vase and 12" h fan-shaped vase have been reproduced in amberina, clear, and milk white.

Items	Clear	Emerald Green
Banana Stand, ftd	80.00	—
Bon Bon, sq, 9" d	18.00	—
Bowl, round, or with scalloped top, 4" d	15.00	—
Bowl, round, or with scalloped top, 6" d	18.00	30.00
Bowl, round, or with scalloped top, 8" d	24.00	—
Bowl, square, 7" w	18.00	110.00
Butter Dish, cov	42.00	72.00
Celery	30.00	42.00
Champagne	30.00	—
Cologne Bottle, faceted stopper	36.00	—
Compote, cov, hs, 7" d	90.00	—
Compote, open, hs, 8" d	55.00	—
Condiment Set, handled tray, cruet, pepper sauce bottle, open salt	105.00	112.00
Cordial	30.00	—
Creamer	30.00	42.00
Cruet, os	55.00	—
Custard Cup	15.00	—
Dish, sq, 4" w	18.00	—
Goblet	36.00	48.00
Ice Bucket	72.00	—
Jelly Compote, open, ls, 4-1/2" d	48.00	55.00
Lemonade	18.00	—
Mustard Jar, underplate, cov	55.00	—
Nappy, 5" d	12.00	—
Olive, 4", handle	12.00	24.00
Pepper Sauce Bottle	30.00	—
Pickle	18.00	24.00
Pitcher, water	65.00	—
Plate, 9-1/4" d	155.00	—
Punch Bowl	190.00	390.00
Punch Cup	12.00	18.00
Punch Glass, ftd	36.00	—
Relish	24.00	18.00
Rose Bowl	30.00	36.00
Salt, individual, flat, sloping sides	12.00	—
Salt Shaker, single, round, long cut neck	18.00	—
Salt Shaker, single, round, squat	24.00	36.00
Salt Shaker, single, square	24.00	—
Sauce	10.00	12.00
Spooner	35.00	—
Sugar Bowl, cov	45.00	60.00
Sugar Shaker	55.00	—
Toothpick Holder	55.00	90.00
Tumbler	36.00	—
Vase, 10-1/4" h φ	15.00	55.00
Wine	36.00	42.00

Hidalgo

Frosted Waffle

Manufactured by Adams and Company, Pittsburgh, PA, in the 1880s and by United States Glass Company, Pittsburgh, PA, in 1891. Made in non-flint, clear, amber stained, and ruby stained. The pattern comes etched, and part of the pattern is frosted. Add 20% for frosted. Rare in color or ruby stained.

Items	Amber Stained	Clear
Bowl, sq, 10" w	42.00	24.00
Bread Plate, cupped, sq, 10" w	90.00	72.00
Butter Dish, cov	—	60.00
Celery Vase	42.00	24.00
Compote, cov, hs, 6" or 10" d	95.00-110.00	72.00-85.00
Compote, cov, ls, 6" or 7-1/2" d	—	60.00-72.00
Compote, open, hs, 6" or 11" d	—	42.00-60.00
Creamer	—	48.00
Cruet, os	—	80.00
Cup and Saucer	—	48.00
Egg Cup	—	36.00
Finger Bowl	30.00	18.00
Goblet	48.00	24.00
Nappy, handled, sq	—	110.00

Items	Amber Stained	Clear
Pickle, boat shaped... 110.00		15.00
Pitcher, milk or water... —		48.00-55.00
Plate, 10" d.. —		42.00
Salt, master, sq... —		30.00
Salt & Pepper Shakers, pr .... —		48.00
Sauce, handled.. —		12.00
Spooner.. —		24.00
Sugar Bowl, cov... —		410.00
Sugar Shaker... —		55.00
Syrup, orig top... —		72.00
Tumbler.. —		30.00
Waste Bowl.. —		30.00
Water Tray.. —		65.00

Hinoto

Diamond Point with Panels

Manufactured by Boston and Sandwich Glass Company, Sandwich, MA, in the late 1850s. Made in flint, clear. Rare in color.

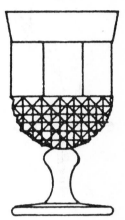

Items	Clear
Bowl, ftd 75.00
Butter Dish, cov..110.00
Celery Vase... 80.00
Champagne 90.00
Cologne Bottle, os.. 410.00
Creamer, ah 90.00
Egg Cup... 42.00
Goblet 72.00
Pitcher, tankard..115.00
Salt, master, ftd 42.00
Spooner.. 42.00
Sugar Bowl, cov... 90.00
Sweetmeat, cov, hs 110.00
Tumbler, flat 55.00
Whiskey, ftd.. 60.00
Wine... 80.00

Hobnail, Pointed

Manufacturer known, c1880. Made in non-flint, amber, apple green, blue, clear, dark green, and vaseline.

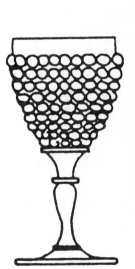

Items	Amber	Blue	Green
Bone Dish 30.00	36.00	24.00
Bowl φ... 30.00	36.00	24.00
Butter Dish, cov... 55.00	60.00	42.50
Cake Stand, hs, 10" d................................ 48.00	55.00	42.00
Celery Vase... 36.00	42.00	24.00
Compote, open, hs, 8" d 55.00	60.00	48.00
Cordial... 30.00	36.00	24.00
Creamer... 36.00	42.00	30.00
Goblet.. 36.00	42.00	30.00
Inkwell.. 36.00	42.00	30.00
Pickle... 18.00	24.00	15.00
Pitcher, water φ 48.00	55.00	42.00
Plate, 7"... 18.00	20.00	15.00
Salt, individual... 12.00	18.00	6.00
Sauce, flat φ 18.00	15.00	12.00
Spooner.. 30.00	36.00	24.00
Sugar Bowl, open φ 24.00	30.00	18.00
Water Tray, 11-1/2" d.................................. 42.00	48.00	36.00
Wine φ.. 30.00	45.00	17.50

Hobnail with Fan

Manufactured by Adams and Company, Pittsburgh, c1880. Made in non-flint, amber, blue, clear, and ruby stained.

Reproductions: Reproductions are limited to the master berry bowl and sauce bowls.

Items	Amber	Blue	Clear
Berry Bowl, master φ.................................. 42.00	48.00	30.00
Butter Dish, cov.. 65.00	72.00	48.00
Celery Vase.. 42.00	48.00	36.00

Items	Amber	Blue	Clear
Creamer	48.00	55.00	30.00
Dish, oblong	—	—	30.00
Goblet	42.00	48.00	24.00
Salt, individual	18.00	110.00	12.00
Sauce, flat, 4-3/4" d φ	18.00	110.00	8.00
Sugar Bowl, cov	55.00	60.00	36.00
Tray, 12" l	36.00	42.00	24.00

Holly

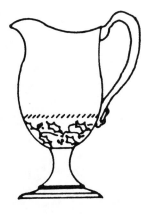

Manufacture attributed to Boston and Sandwich Glass Company, Sandwich, MA, in the late 1860s, and early 1870s. Made in non-flint, clear.

Items	Clear
Bowl, cov, 8" d	160.00
Butter Dish, cov	160.00
Cake Stand, hs, 9 or 11" d	118.00-130.00
Celery Vase, pedestal, scalloped rim	112.00
Compote, cov, hs, 8" d	180.00
Compote, open, ls, 8-1/2" d	160.00
Creamer, ah	130.00
Egg Cup	80.00
Goblet	120.00
Pickle, oval	36.00
Pitcher, water, ah	270.00
Salt, individual, flat, oval	80.00
Salt, master, ftd	95.00
Sauce, flat, 4" d	24.00
Spooner	72.00
Sugar Bowl, cov, flat or pedestal	130.00
Tumbler, flat or footed	130.00
Wine	130.00

Holly Amber

Manufactured by Indiana Tumbler and Goblet Company, Greentown, IN, c1903. The design was created and patented by Frank Jacobson, in January of 1903. The original color name, Golden Agate, reflects the gold-colored body with a marbleized onyx color on the raised design elements. All work ceased on this pattern in July 1903, when the factory was destroyed by fire. Made in Golden Agate.

Reproductions: Reproductions of this pattern are found in various color combinations.

Items	Golden Agate
Bowl, oval, 7-1/2" l	390.00
Bowl, round, 8-1/2" d	450.00
Butter Dish, cov	1,890.00
Cake Stand	3,000.00
Compote, cov, hs, 8-1/2" d, 12" h	3,000.00
Creamer, 3-1/2" w, 4" h	660.00
Cruet, os	1,860.00
Honey Dish, cov	860.00
Mug, ring handle, 4-1/2" h	600.00
Nappy	380.00
Relish, oval	360.00
Salt and Pepper Shakers, pr	600.00
Sauce	260.00
Spooner	490.00
Sugar, cov	760.00
Syrup, orig silver plate top, 5-3/4" h	2,400.00
Toothpick Holder, 2-1/4" h φ	2,750.00
Tumbler	480.00
Vase, 6" h	600.00

Honeycomb

Manufactured by numerous firms, including Bakewell Pears & Company, Pittsburgh, PA; Bellaire Goblet Company, Bellaire, OH; Doyle & Company, Pittsburgh, PA; Boston Silver and Glass Company, East Cambridge, MA; Gillinder & Sons, Philadelphia, PA; Grierson & Company, Pittsburgh, PA; New England Glass Company, East Cambridge, MA; O'Hara Glass Company, Pittsburgh; and United States Glass Company, Pittsburgh, PA, c1850-1900, resulting in minor pattern variations. Made in flint, non-flint, clear. Found with copper wheel engraving. Rare in color.

Reproductions: There are many reproduction pieces of *Honeycomb.* Fenton Art Glass Company, Williamstown, WV, created copies as early as 1930 in amber, black, clear, green, moonstone, pink, royal blue, ruby, and topaz. The Jeannette Glass Company, Jeannette, PA, c1928, made other pieces, including forms not originally created, in carnival glass, green, and pink. Viking Glass Company, New Martinsville, WV, also created new forms in 1972. They made reproductions in amber, blue, brown, green, and ruby.

Items	Flint	Non-Flint
Ale Glass	60.00	30.00
Barber Bottle	55.00	30.00
Beer Mug	30.00	18.00
Bitters Bottle	55.00	—
Bowl, cov, collared, Brittania or tin lid, 7" or 9" d	72.00-85.00	—
Bowl, cov, flat, 5-1/2", 6", 7" or 8" d	65.00-72.00	—
Bowl, cov, pat'd 1869, acorn finial, 7-1/4" d	120.00	55.00
Bowl, open, collared, deep, 6", 7", 8" or 9" d	48.00-55.00	—
Bowl, open, collared, saucer, 7", 8", 9" or 10" d	—	42.00-48.00
Butter Dish, cov φ	80.00	55.00
Cake Stand, hs, 11-1/4" d	65.00	42.00
Candlestick	160.00	
Castor Bottle	30.00	110.00
Catsup Bottle	30.00	—
Celery Vase, pedestal, scalloped rim	55.00	24.00
Celery Vase, pedestal, sawtooth rim	60.00	30.00
Champagne	60.00	30.00
Claret φ	42.00	42.00
Compote, cov, hs, deep or saucer bowl, 6" d or 7" d	110.00	55.00
Compote, cov, hs, deep bowl, 8" d or 9" d	115.00	65.00
Compote, cov, hs, saucer bowl, 9" d	120.00	—
Compote, cov, hs, 6-1/2"d, 8-1/2" h; or 9-1/4" d, 11-1/2" h	120.00-125.00	60.00-80.00
Compote, open, hs, deep bowl, 6", 7" or 10" d	42.00-55.00	30.00-42.00
Compote, open, hs, saucer bowl, 6", 7" or 8" d	42.00-48.00	30.00-36.00
Compote, open, ls, deep or saucer bowl, 6", 7", 8" or 9" d	42.00-48.00	30.00-36.00
Compote, open, ls, scalloped, 7-1/2" d	48.00	30.00
Cordial, 3-1/2" h φ	42.00	30.00
Creamer, ah or ph φ	42.00	24.00
Custard Cup, ftd, ah	80.00	—
Decanter, bar lip, pint	65.00	24.00
Decanter, bar lip, quart	90.00	—
Decanter, os, pint φ	72.00	90.00
Decanter, os, quart φ	85.00	80.00
Dish, oval, 7", 8", 9" 10" l	24.00-30.00	12.00-18.00
Egg Cup, ftd, flared or straight-sided	24.00	18.00
Finger Bowl φ	55.00	—
Goblet φ	30.00	18.00
Honey Dish, cov, 3" d or 3-1/2" d	18.00	30.00
Lamp, all glass	—	105.00
Lamp, marble base	—	110.00
Lemonade Mug, ftd, ah φ	48.00	24.00
Mug, half pint	30.00	18.00
Pepper Sauce Bottle	36.00	—
Pickle Jar, cov	110.00	80.00
Pitcher, milk, ah or ph, quart	105.00	80.00
Pitcher, water, half gallon, dated handle "Pat. 1865"	180.00	72.00
Pitcher, water, half gallon, plain handle φ	120.00	90.00
Pitcher, water, three pint	118.00	90.00
Plate, 6" d or 7" d φ	—	18.00
Pomade Jar, cov	60.00	24.00
Pony Mug	36.00	—
Punch Cup	—	18.00
Relish Dish	36.00	24.00
Salt, individual, oblong or round	18.00	12.00
Salt, master, cov, ftd	80.00	—
Salt, master, open, flat	42.00	36.00
Salt Shaker, orig top φ	—	42.00
Sauce, flat, 4" d	15.00	7.50
Spill Holder	42.00	24.00
Spooner	80.00	42.00
String Holder, two sizes	130.00	—
Sugar Bowl, cov, frosted rosebud finial	—	60.00
Sugar Bowl, cov, regular	90.00	55.00
Syrup, orig top, pint	270.00	120.00
Syrup, orig top, 3 pint	260.00	—
Syrup, orig top, quart	290.00	—
Tumble-Up	112.00	—
Tumbler, bar	42.00	
Tumbler, flat φ	48.00	12.50
Tumbler, footed φ	55.00	18.00
Vase, 7-1/2" or 10-1/2" h	55.00-90.00	—
Water Bottle	80.00	—
Whiskey, handled φ	130.00	—
Wine φ	42.00	18.00

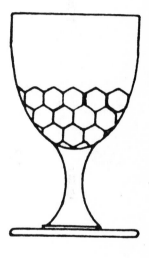

Horn of Plenty

Comet, Peacock Tail

Manufactured by Bryce, McKee & Company, Pittsburgh, PA, c1850. Also produced by McKee & Brothers, Pittsburgh, PA, c1850-60. Shards have been found at Boston and Sandwich Glass Company, Sandwich, MA. Made in flint, non-flint, clear. Handles are applied.

Reproductions: Reproductions have been made by Fostoria Glass Company, Moundsville, WV, and L. G. Wright, New Martinsville, WV.

Items	Clear Flint
Bar Bottle, pewter spout, 8" h	142.00
Bowl, flat, 7-1/2" or 8-1/2" d	142.00-155.00
Bowl, footed, 8-1/2" d	180.00
Butter Dish, cov, conventional finial	130.00
Butter Dish, cov, shape of acorn	136.00
Butter Dish, cov, Washington head finial	460.00
Butter Pat	24.00
Cake Stand, hs	415.00
Celery Vase, pedestal	200.00
Champagne, 5-1/4" h	155.00
Claret, 4-7/8" h	190.00
Compote, cov, hs, 6" or 6-1/4" d	180.00-190.00
Compote, cov, hs, oval, 8-1/4" d, 5-3/4" h	360.00
Compote, open, hs, 6", 6-1/4", 8", 8-1/4", 10" or 10-1/2" d	115.00-145.00
Compote, open, ls, 6", 6-1/4", 8", 8-1/4", 10", 10-1/4" d	60.00-115.00
Cordial	160.00
Creamer, ah, bulbous, 5-1/2" h	270.00
Creamer, ah, tall, straight-sided, 7" h	190.00
Creamer, ph, 7" h	190.00
Decanter, os, pint, quart or half gallon	490.00-600.00
Egg Cup, pedestal, flared or straight-sided	48.00
Goblet φ	90.00
Honey Dish, 3-1/4" d	24.00
Lamp, all glass, hexagonal stem φ	250.00
Lamp, glass font, brass stem, marble base	160.00
Medicine Bottle, applied lip, 4-1/4", 6", 7-1/4", 8-1/4" or 10-3/4" h	160.00-240.00
Mug, small, applied handle	160.00
Pepper Sauce Bottle, pewter top	240.00
Pickle Dish, oval, 7" l, 5" w	55.00
Pitcher, milk, ah, quart	660.00
Pitcher, water, ah, half gallon φ	690.00
Plate, 6" or 6-1/2" d	120.00
Relish Tray, 7" l, 5" w	55.00
Salt, master, oval, flat	90.00
Sauce, 4-1/2", 5", 5-1/4" or 6" d	18.00
Spill Holder	80.00
Spooner	55.00
Sugar Bowl, cov	160.00
Tumbler, bar; or water φ	90.00-105.00
Whiskey, applied handle	245.00
Whiskey, shot glass, 3" h	120.00
Wine	130.00

Horseshoe

Good Luck, Prayer Rug

Manufactured by Adams and Company, Pittsburgh, PA, and others in the 1880s. Made in non-flint, clear.
Reproductions: The bread plates have been reproduced.

Items	Clear
Bowl, cov, oval, 7" or 8" l	160.00-215.00
Bowl, open, oval, 8" l, 5" w; or 10-1/4" l, 6-1/4" d	48.00-60.00
Bread Plate, 14 x 10", double horseshoe handles φ	80.00
Bread Plate, 15 x 10", single horseshoe handles φ	48.00
Butter Dish, cov, collared lid	115.00
Butter Dish, cov, plain lid	105.00
Cake Plate	48.00
Cake Stand, hs, 8" or 12" d	80.00-95.00
Celery Dip, horseshoe shape, flat	90.00
Celery Vase, knob stem	48.00
Celery Vase, plain stem	42.00
Cheese, cov, woman churning	290.00
Compote, cov, hs, horseshoe finial, 7" d	115.00
Compote, cov, hs, 8" d, 12-1/4" h; or 11" d	130.00-142.00
Compote, cov, ls, 7-1/2" or 8" d	60.00-72.00
Creamer, 6-1/2"	65.00
Doughnut Stand	90.00
Finger Bowl	95.00

Items	Clear
Goblet, knob stem	48.00
Goblet, plain stem	310.00
Marmalade Jar, cov	112.00
Pickle Dish	18.00
Pickle Jar, cov	110.00
Pitcher, milk, quart	112.00
Pitcher, water, half gallon	105.00
Plate, 7", 7-1/2", 8-1/2" or 10" d	55.00-65.00
Platter, oval	55.00
Relish, 5" x 7"	24.00
Relish, wheelbarrow, pewter wheels, 8" l	90.00
Salt, individual, horseshoe shape	24.00
Salt, master, horseshoe shape	120.00
Salt, master, wheelbarrow, pewter wheels	90.00
Sauce, flat, 3-3/4" d, 4" d, or 4-1/2" d	12.00
Sauce, footed, 3-3/4" d, 4" d, or 4-1/2" d	18.00
Spooner	42.00
Sugar Bowl, cov	80.00
Vegetable Dish, oblong	42.00
Waste Bowl	55.00
Wine	160.00

Huber

Flaring Huber, Straight Huber

Manufactured by Bakewell Pears & Company, Pittsburgh, PA; Cape Cod Glass Company, Sandwich MA; George A. Duncan & Sons, Pittsburgh, PA; King, Son & Company, Pittsburgh, PA; J. B. Lyon & Company, Pittsburgh, PA; McKee & Brothers, Pittsburgh, PA; New England Glass Company, Cambridge, MA; and Richards and Hartley Glass Company, Pittsburgh, PA, in the 1880s. Made in flint, non-flint, clear. Some pieces are found with etching, which adds to the value. Non-flint values would be 35% less than prices shown. Rare in color.

Items	Flint
Ale Glass	24.00
Beer Mug, 1-1/2 pint	36.00
Bitters Bottle	125.00
Bowl, cov, 7" d	85.00
Bowl, cov, shallow, 6" or 8" d	48.00-60.00
Bowl, open, oval, 6", 7", 8", 9" or 10" l	24.00-30.00
Butter Dish, cov	105.00
Celery Vase, ftd	80.00
Champagne, hotel size, barrel shaped bowl	42.00
Champagne, table size, straight-sided bowl	30.00
Claret	60.00
Compote, cov, hs, shallow, 7" or 10" d	110.00-120.00
Compote, cov, ls, shallow, 6", 7" or 8" d	120.00
Compote, open, engraved, 8" d	90.00
Compote, open, hs, deep bowl, scalloped, 6", 8" or 10" d	65.00-80.00
Compote, open, ls, deep bowl, scalloped, 7" or 9" d	65.00-80.00
Compote, open, ls, shallow bowl, 6" 8" d	55.00-65.00
Cordial, hotel size, barrel shaped bowl	48.00
Cordial, table size, straight-sided bowl	55.00
Creamer	95.00
Decanter, bar lip, pint or quart	85.00-90.00
Decanter, os, pint or quart	105.00
Egg Cup, handle	48.00
Egg Cup, regular	36.00
Goblet, gentleman's, straight-sided bowl	42.00
Goblet, hotel, barrel shaped bowl or lady's, straight-sided bowl	36.00
Honey Dish, flat	18.00
Jar, ftd, 6" d	90.00
Lemonade Tumbler	30.00
Mug	42.00
Pitcher, water, ah, quart or 3 pints	124.00-160.00
Plate, 6" or 7-1/2" d	30.00-36.00
Pony Mug, ph, large	36.00
Pony Mug, ah, small	30.00
Preserve Dish, cov, 6" d	42.00
Salt, individual	18.00
Salt, master, ftd	30.00
Sauce, flat, 4" d	18.00
Spooner, large or small	42.00
Sugar Bowl, cov, ftd	85.00
Tumbler, gill	24.00
Tumbler, jelly	30.00
Tumbler, water, tapered sides	24.00
Whiskey	42.00
Wine, hotel, barrel shaped bowl	36.00
Wine, table size, straight-sided bowl	30.00

Hummingbird

Bird and Fan, Fern and Bird, Flying Robin, Hummingbird and Fern, Thunder Bird

Manufacturer unknown, c1885. Made in non-flint, amber, blue, canary, and clear.

Items	Amber	Blue	Canary	Clear
Butter Dish, cov	112.00	112.00	105.00	72.00
Celery Vase	110.00	110.00	120.00	55.00
Compote, hs, open	115.00	115.00	120.00	90.00
Creamer	90.00	90.00	72.00	48.00
Goblet	65.00	85.00	60.00	42.00
Pitcher, milk	80.00	115.00	105.00	60.00
Pitcher, water	130.00	160.00	120.00	105.00
Sauce, flat	24.00	30.00	30.00	18.00
Sauce, ftd	30.00	36.00	36.00	20.00
Spooner	48.00	90.00	55.00	36.00
Sugar Bowl, cov	120.00	120.00	80.00	65.00
Tumbler, bar	90.00	90.00	55.00	36.00
Waste Bowl, 5-1/4" d	—	—	—	42.00
Water Tray	160.00	130.00	130.00	90.00
Wine	—	—	—	80.00

Icicle

Single Icicle

Manufactured by Bakewell, Pears and Company, Pittsburgh, PA, c1874. Designed and patented by Washington Beck, Sept. 15, 1874. Made in flint, clear, and milk white. Some other rare colors are known.

Items	Clear	Milk White
Butter Dish, cov, flat or footed	90.00-105.00	112.00-130.00
Compote, cov, hs, 6" or 8" d	90.00-120.00	160.00-215.00
Compote, open, hs, 6" or 8" d	80.00-90.00	130.00-142.00
Compote, open, ls, 6" or 8" d	60.00-80.00	120.00-130.00
Creamer, ah, ftd	80.00	130.00
Dish, oval, 7" or 9" l	36.00-48.00	72.00-95.00
Goblet	72.00	124.00
Honey Dish	36.00	72.00
Lamp, oil, 9" h	120.00	200.00
Pickle Scoop	42.00	85.00
Pitcher, water, ah, half gallon	240.00	480.00
Salt, master	30.00	60.00
Sauce, flat, 4" d	18.00	36.00
Spooner, ftd	55.00	110.00
Sugar Bowl, cov	95.00	172.00

Illinois

Clarissa, Star of the East, US Glass Pattern Line No. 15,052

Manufactured by United States Glass Company, Pittsburgh, PA, c1897, as one of the States series. Made in clear, emerald green, and some ruby stained pieces, including salt ($60) and lidless straw holder ($105). Most forms are square.

Reproductions: The butter dish and celery vase have been reproduced by L. E. Smith Glass Company, Mt. Pleasant, PA.

Item	Clear	Emerald Green
Almond Stand, hs, 5" d	60.00	—
Basket, ah, 11-1/2" h	120.00	—
Bon Bon, hs, 5" or 7" d	60.00-85.00	—
Bowl, round, 5" or 8" d	24.00-30.00	—
Bowl, sq, 6" d; or 9" w	30.00-42.00	—
Butter Dish, cov φ	72.00	—
Butter Pat, sq	30.00	—
Cake Stand, hs, 11" d	80.00	—
Candlesticks, pr	115.00	—
Celery Tray, 11" l	48.00	—
Celery Vase φ	60.00	—
Cheese Dish, cov	90.00	—
Compote, open, hs, sq, 5" or 9" d	48.00-72.00	—
Creamer, individual or table	36.00-48.00	—
Cruet, os	80.00	—
Finger Bowl	30.00	—
Ice Cream Dish, rect, 5" l	42.00	—
Ice Cream Tray, rect, 12" l	60.00	—

Item	Clear	Emerald Green
Lamp, banquet, 2 sizes	760.00	—
Marmalade Jar, cov	142.00	—
Olive Dish	110.00	—
Pickle Dish, rect, 7-1/4" l	24.00	—
Pickle Jar, cov, sq	65.00	—
Pitcher, milk, round, silver plate rim	190.00	—
Pitcher, milk or water, square	80.00	—
Pitcher, water, tankard, round, silver plate rim	90.00	142.00
Plate, square or round, 7" w	30.00	—
Puff Box, cov	55.00	—
Relish, 7-1/2" x 4"	110.00	48.00
Relish, 8-1/2" x 3"	110.00	—
Relish, 9" x 3", canoe	48.00	—
Salt, individual	18.00	—
Salt, master	30.00	—
Salt & Pepper Shakers, pr	48.00	—
Sauce, flat, 4" d or 4-1/2" d	18.00	—
Spooner, hotel size	48.00	—
Spooner, table size	42.00	—
Spoon Tray, rect, 8-1/4" l	65.00	—
Straw Holder, cov	190.00	480.00
Sugar Bowl, cov, table	65.00	—
Sugar Bowl, open, hotel size	55.00	—
Sugar Bowl, open, individual	36.00	—
Sugar Shaker, orig pewter or silver plate top	90.00	—
Syrup, orig top, pewter top	115.00	—
Toothpick Holder, adv emb in base	55.00	—
Toothpick Holder, plain	36.00	—
Tray, 12" x 8", turned up sides	60.00	—
Tumbler	36.00	48.00
Vase, 6" h, sq	42.00	55.00
Vase, 9-1/2" h	—	130.00

Indiana

Doric, Prison Windows, US Glass Pattern Line No. 15,029

Manufactured by United States Glass Company, c1897, at Factory "U," Glass City, IN. Made in non-flint, clear, and rarely in ruby stained.

Items	Clear
Bowl, scalloped rim, 5", 6", 7", 8" or 9" d	18.00-24.00
Butter Dish, cov	55.00
Catsup Bottle	80.00
Celery Tray	30.00
Celery Vase	36.00
Creamer	42.00
Cruet, os, matching undertray	60.00
Dish, oval, 7", 8" or 9" l	18.00
Finger Bowl	30.00
Ice Tub	90.00
Jelly Compote, open, hs	36.00
Perfume Bottle	72.00
Pitcher, water, tankard	80.00
Salt Shaker	24.00
Sauce, flat, 4" d or 4-1/2" d	18.00
Spooner	42.00
Sugar Bowl, cov	55.00
Syrup, orig top	60.00
Tray, oblong	60.00
Tumbler	42.00
Water Bottle	72.00

Inverted Fern

Manufacture attributed to Boston and Sandwich Glass Company, Sandwich, MA, c1880. Made in flint, clear.

Reproductions: The goblets have been reproduced in color as well as non-flint clear.

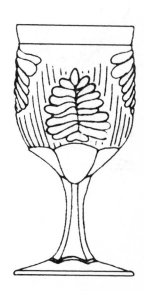

Items	Clear
Bowl, 7" d	55.00
Butter Dish, cov	115.00
Champagne	130.00
Compote, open, hs, 8" d	65.00
Creamer, ah	130.00
Egg Cup, plain base	36.00
Egg Cup, rayed base, coarse or fine ribbing	48.00

Items	Clear
Goblet, plain base	48.00
Goblet, rayed base φ	55.00
Honey Dish	110.00
Plate, 6" d	120.00
Pitcher, water, ah, half gallon	260.00
Salt, master, ftd	42.00
Sauce, flat, 4" d	12.00
Spooner	48.00
Sugar Bowl, cov	95.00
Tumbler	115.00
Wine	90.00

Inverted Strawberry

Manufactured by Cambridge Glass Company, Cambridge, OH, c1908. Made in non-flint, clear, and ruby stained. Ruby stained also found with souvenir inscriptions. No toothpick holder was originally made.

Reproductions: This pattern ahs been reproduced in amethyst, carnival glass, and green by Guernsey Glass Company, Cambridge, OH.

Items	Clear	Ruby Stained
Basket, ah φ	80.00	—
Bowl, 9" d	30.00	—
Butter Dish, cov	80.00	—
Celery Tray, handled	36.00	—
Compote, open, hs, 5" d	310.00	—
Creamer φ	30.00	—
Cruet, os φ	55.00	—
Goblet	30.00	—
Mug	24.00	36.00
Nappy φ	18.00	—
Pitcher, water φ	55.00	—
Plate, 10" d φ	30.00	48.00
Punch Cup	15.00	—
Relish Tray, 7" φ	15.00	—
Rose Bowl	36.00	—
Salt, individual	24.00	—
Sauce, flat, 4" d	110.00	—
Spooner	30.00	—
Sugar Bowl, cov φ	55.00	—
Toothpick Holder φ	30.00	—
Tumbler φ	36.00	55.00

Iowa

Paneled Zipper, US Glass Pattern Line No. 15,069

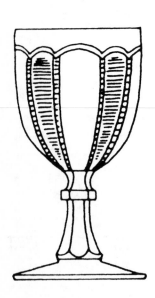

Manufactured by United States Glass Company, Pittsburgh, PA, c1902, as part of the States series. Made in non-flint, clear. Also found in clear glass with gilt trim (add 20%) and ruby or cranberry stained. Also found in amber (goblet, $85) green, canary, and blue. Add 50% to 100% for color.

Items	Clear
Berry Bowl, master	15.00
Bread Plate, motto	95.00
Butter Dish, cov	48.00
Cake Stand, hs	42.00
Carafe	42.00
Compote, cov, hs, 8" d	48.00
Corn Liquor Jug, os	72.00
Creamer	36.00
Cruet, os	36.00
Cup	18.00
Decanter, 1-1/2 pints	48.00
Goblet	210.00
Lamp, oil	130.00
Olive Tray, handle	18.00
Pitcher, water, tankard	60.00
Punch Cup	18.00
Salt Shaker, single, large or small	30.00
Sauce, 4-1/2" d	6.50
Spooner	36.00
Sugar Bowl, cov	42.00
Toothpick Holder	24.00
Tumbler	30.00
Vase, 6" or 10" h	18.00-30.00

Ivanhoe

Manufactured by Dalzell, Gilmore, and Leighton Company, Findlay, OH, c1897. Made in non-flint, clear.

Items	Clear
Butter Dish, cov	48.00
Compote, open, 7" d	42.00
Creamer	30.00
Cruet, os	80.00
Pitcher, water	72.00
Spooner	24.00
Sugar Bowl, cov	42.00
Syrup, orig metal top	90.00
Tumbler	30.00

Ivy in Snow

Ivy in Snow-Red Leaves, Forest Ware

Manufactured by Co-Operative Flint Glass Company, Beaver Falls, PA, in the 1880s. Phoenix Glass of Monaco, PA, also produced this pattern, from 1937 to 1942, and then it was called "Forest Ware." *Ivy In Snow-Red Leaves* is the name used for pieces where the leaves are ruby stained. Made in non-flint, clear, amber stained, and ruby stained. Some pieces have a ruby-stained barrel.

Reproductions: This pattern has been widely reproduced with many reproductions in white milk glass. Kemple Glass Works, East Palestine, OH, is credited with most of the milk glass reproductions, which date to the 1940s.

Items	Clear	Ruby Stained
Berry Bowl, 7" d	24.00	—
Bowl, 8" x 5-1/2" φ	36.00	—
Butter Dish, cov	65.00	
Cake Plate, round or square	36.00	80.00
Cake Stand, hs, 8" d	55.00	—
Celery Vase, pedestal φ	36.00	90.00
Champagne	42.00	65.00
Compote, cov, hs, 6" d	55.00	90.00
Compote, cov, hs, 8" d	60.00	—
Cordial	42.00	—
Creamer, regular	36.00	90.00
Creamer, tankard	42.00	142.00
Cup and Saucer φ	42.00	—
Finger Bowl	30.00	—
Goblet φ	42.00	80.00
Jelly Compote, open	42.00	65.00
Marmalade Jar	42.00	—
Mug	30.00	48.00
Pitcher, milk, quart	105.00	240.00
Pitcher, water, half gallon φ	65.00	240.00
Plate, 6" d	24.00	—
Plate, 10" d	36.00	—
Relish Tray	24.00	36.00
Sauce, flat, 4" d	18.00	24.00
Spooner	42.00	72.00
Sugar Bowl, cov φ	60.00	90.00
Syrup, orig top	85.00	290.00
Tumbler φ	30.00	55.00
Wine	40.00	65.00

Jacob's Coat

Manufacturer unknown, c1880. Made in non-flint, clear. Rarely found in colors, add 50% to the values shown.

Items	Clear
Bowl, 8" d	24.00
Butter Dish, cov	410.00
Celery	30.00
Creamer	30.00
Goblet	36.00
Goblet, milk or water	55.00
Spooner	36.00
Sugar Bowl, cov	410.00

Jacob's Ladder

Imperial, Maltese, US Glass Pattern Line No. 4,778

Manufactured by Portland Glass Company, Portland, ME, and Bryce, McKee & Company, Pittsburgh, PA, in 1876, by United States Glass Company, Pittsburgh, PA, in 1891, and the Diamond Flint Glass Company, Canada, c1902. The pattern was designed and patented by John Bryce, June 13, 1876, under the name *Imperial*. Made in non-flint, clear. A few pieces found in amber, yellow, blue, pale blue, and pale green.

Items	Clear
Berry Bowl, ornate silver plate holder, ftd, 9" d	130.00
Bowl, cov, 6" d	42.00
Bowl, oval, 5-1/2" x 7-3/4"	1,118.00
Bowl, oval, 7-1/2" x 10-3/4"	24.00
Bread Tray, oblong	55.00
Butter Dish, cov	80.00
Cake Stand, hs, 8" or 12" d	60.00-72.00
Castor Bottle	110.00
Castor Set, 4 bottles	120.00
Celery Vase	55.00
Cologne Bottle, Maltese cross stopper, ftd	105.00
Compote, cov, hs, 6" d	95.00
Compote, cov, hs, 8-1/2", 9" or 9-1/2" d	105.00-130.00
Compote, open, oblong, dolphin stem	360.00
Compote, open, hs, scalloped, 7", 9", 10-1/2" or 12" d	36.00-65.00
Creamer, pedestal	42.00
Cruet, os, ftd	105.00
Goblet, knob stem	72.00
Honey Dish, 3-1/2" d	12.00
Marmalade Jar, cov	90.00
Mug, ah	120.00
Pickle Tray, double handles	12.00
Pitcher, water, ah	160.00
Plate, 6-1/4" d	24.00
Relish, 9-1/2" x 5-1/2"	18.00
Salt, master, ftd	24.00
Sauce, flat, 4" d, 4-1/2" d, or 5" d	10.00
Sauce, footed, 4" d, 4-1/2" d, or 5" d	15.00
Spooner, pedestal	42.00
Sugar Bowl, cov	95.00
Syrup, knight's head finial	130.00
Syrup, plain top	120.00
Tumbler, bar	105.00
Wine	42.00

Jasper

Belt Buckle, Eleanor, Late Buckle

Manufactured by Bryce Brothers, Pittsburgh, PA, c1880. Reissued by United States Glass Company, Factory "B," Pittsburgh, PA, after the 1891 merger. Made in non-flint, clear.

Items	Clear
Bowl, 5" or 6"d	18.00
Butter Dish, cov	42.00
Cake Stand, hs, 8" or 11" d	30.00-42.00
Cologne Bottle, ftd, bulbous, os	80.00
Compote, cov, hs, 7" or 9" d	60.00-80.00
Compote, open, hs, scalloped rim, 7" or 12" d	24.00-42.00
Creamer, 6" h	30.00
Cruet, os	110.00
Dish, flat, oval or round, 7" or 8" l, 8" or 9" d	18.00
Goblet	30.00
Pickle Dish, handle	18.00
Pitcher, milk, 3 pint	65.00
Pitcher, water, half gallon	80.00
Salt, master, ftd, scalloped rim	18.00
Sauce, flat, 4" d or 4-1/2" d	10.00
Sauce, ftd, 4" d or 4-1/2" d	12.00
Spooner	30.00
Sugar Bowl, cov	42.00
Sweetmeat, cov, hs, 6" d	55.00
Wine	30.00

A grouping of pitchers and creamers, from left: Dakota, tankard water pitcher, Bird and Fern etching; Currier and Ives milk pitcher; Rose in Snow bulbous water pitcher; Fancy Loops individual creamer; Cupid and Venus, creamer; Dakota, tankard with Fern and Berry etching.

A grouping of Jacob's Ladder pieces, front: amethyst plate, clear wine, amber sauce dish; rear: footed vaseline celery vase, 9" h, blue relish with handles.

Mitered Diamond sauce, footed, blue, 3-1/2" w, 2-3/8" h.

Beaded Oval Window goblet and Paneled Forget Me Not, pitcher, 8-1/4" h, both in amethyst.

Pressed Diamond, compote, vaseline, 8" d, 7-1/2" h.

Ashburton, egg cup, 3-7/8" h.

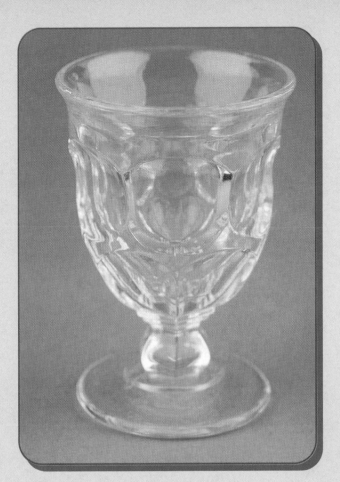

**Pressed Diamond,
salt shaker,
original top,
apple green.**

**Royal Ivy,
sauce
bowl,
rubena,
3-7/8".**

Moon and Star, from left: Jar, covered, 2-3/4" d, 6" h; perfume, 6-1/2" h; lamp, 2-3/4" h, plus top.

Celery vases, left: Jacob's Ladder, blue, footed; right: Daisy and Button with Crossbars, vaseline, footed.

This grouping shows the differences between maiden's blush (rose), ruby staining, and true cranberry. From left are: goblet, Star in Bull's Eye, maiden's blush decoration on top; center: goblet, Dakota, ruby-stained top with fern etching; right: bowl, Delaware, cranberry.

Grouping of blue pieces, back row: Hickman goblet, Teardrop creamer, Daisy and Button with Oval Panels tumbler, Hickman relish in front.

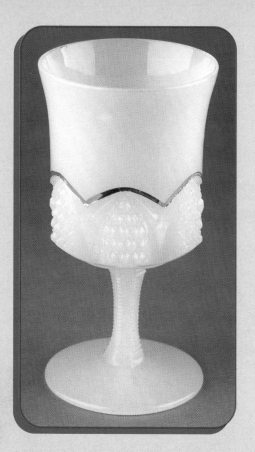

Button Arches, goblet, clambroth, 6" h.

Hickman, goblet and wine, green, gold trim.

Star in Bull's Eye and Yellow Block, goblet, left: Star in Bull's Eye, maiden's blush decoration on top; right: Yellow Block, amber stained top and blocks.

Three Panel, goblet, vaseline, 6" h

Grouping of Goblets, from left: Florida, green; Beaded Oval Window, amethyst; Two Panel, apple green; Willow Oak, amber; Cathedral, blue; Three Panel, vaseline; Teardrop, cobalt blue.

Button Arches, ruby stained souvenir wares, left: mug, engraved "Ithaca," center: goblet, engraved "Cornell," right: wine, engraved "Ithaca."

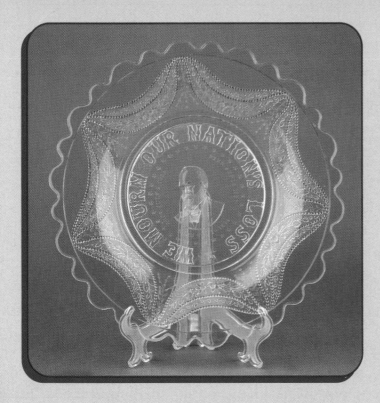

Garfield Drape, plate, 11-1/2" d.

Tree of Life, bowl, sapphire blue, 4-1/2" d, light blue, with melon ribs, 4-1/2" d.

Tree of Life, relish, leaf shape, 7" l, 4-3/4" w, green.

**Amberette,
spooner, amber
decoration, 5" h.**

**Esther, jelly
compote, green, 4" d, 5" h.**

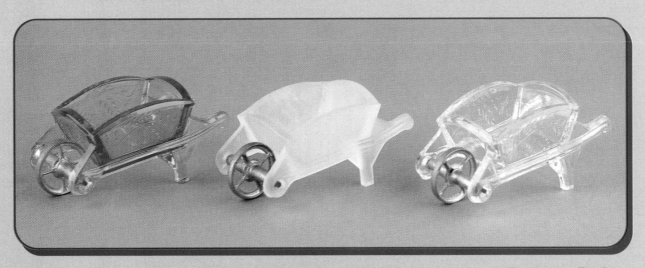

**Wheelbarrow, salts: amber, frosted, clear, 4" l, 2" w. Variously attributed to Barley
or Horseshoe patterns.**

Daisy & Button with V Ornament, celery vase, marine green, 7" h.

Ribbon, compote, open, high standard, 8" d, 8" h.

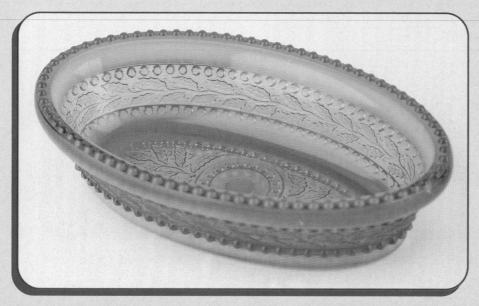

Holly Amber, bowl, 7-3/8" l, 4-1/2" h.

Louis XV, bowl, custard, 11-1/4" l, 7-1/2" w, 5" h.

New Jersey, butter dish, 9" d, 5" h.

Tree of Life, ice cream tray, apple green, 7-1/2" w, 14" l.

Grouping, left: celery vase, Daisy and Button with Crossbars, vaseline, footed, 5-3/8" h; right: spooner, Two Panel, oval, apple green.

Daisy and Button with Thumbprint Panel, cake plate, high standard, apple green, 9-1/2" w, 6-1/8" h.

Pleat Band, jelly compote, chocolate, 4-5/8" d, 4-3/4" h.

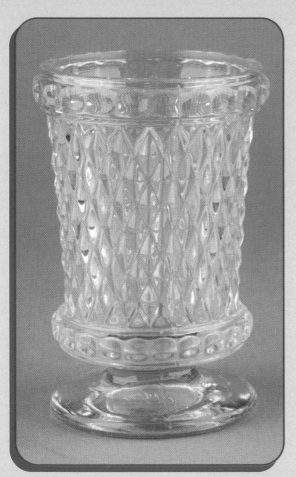

Sawtooth, spill holder, 5" h.

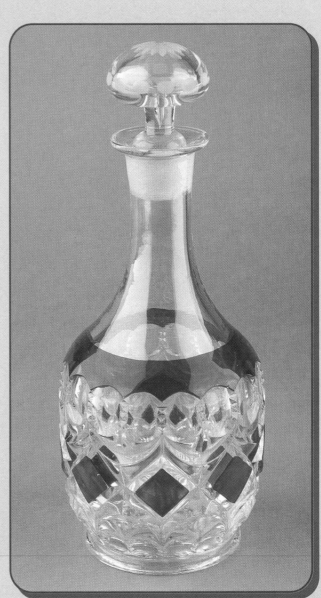

Loop and Block, decanter, 8-1/4" h.

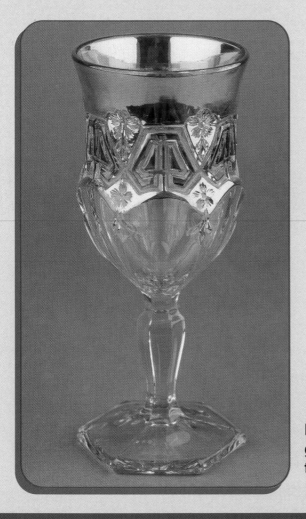

Paneled 44, goblet, gold trim, staining over the "44" motif.

Rose in Snow, pitcher, water, bulbous, 9" h.

Thousand Eye, compote, apple green, 10" d, 7" h.

Klondike, punch cup, amber stained, 2-7/8" d.

**Flower Pot, compote,
covered, high standard,
8" d, 13" h.**

**Beaded Oval Window, sauces, left: blue, flat;
right: vaseline, footed, 2" h.**

Loop, decanter, original stopper.

Jersey Swirl

Swirl, Swirl and Diamonds, Windsor Swirl, Windsor

Manufactured by Windsor Glass Company, Pittsburgh, PA, c1887. Made in non-flint, amber, blue, canary-yellow, and clear.

Reproductions: Heavily reproduced in color by L. G. Wright Company, New Martinsville, WV, from 1968 to 1974. The clear goblet is also reproduced.

Items	Amber	Blue	Canary	Clear
Bowl, 9-1/4" d	65.00	65.00	55.00	42.00
Butter Dish, cov	65.00	65.00	60.00	48.00
Cake Stand, hs, 9" d	90.00	85.00	55.00	36.00
Celery Vase	45.00	45.00	42.00	36.00
Compote, hs, 8" d	60.00	60.00	55.00	42.00
Creamer	55.00	55.00	48.00	36.00
Cruet, os	—	—	—	30.00
Goblet, buttermilk; or water φ	48.00	48.00	42.00	36.00
Marmalade Jar	—	—	—	60.00
Pickle Castor, silver plate frame and lid	—	—	—	130.00
Pitcher, water	60.00	60.00	55.00	42.00
Plate, round, 6" d	30.00	30.00	24.00	18.00
Plate, round, 10" d	310.00	310.00	42.00	36.00
Salt, individual φ	24.00	24.00	110.00	18.00
Sauce, flat, 4-1/2" d φ	24.00	24.00	18.00	12.00
Spooner	36.00	36.00	30.00	24.00
Sugar Bowl, cov	48.00	48.00	42.00	36.00
Tumbler	36.00	36.00	30.00	24.00
Wine φ	60.00	60.00	48.00	18.00

Jumbo

Manufactured by Canton Glass Company, Canton, OH, and by Aetna Glass in 1884, as a novelty pattern, also made by other companies, resulting in many variants. The unique motif was used to commemorate P. T. Barnum's famous elephant, "Jumbo." Made in non-flint, clear.

Items	Clear
Butter Dish, cov, oblong, plain Jumbo	495.00
Butter Dish, cov, round, Barnum's head	390.00
Compote, cov, 7", 10" or 12" d	495.00-960.00
Creamer, plain Jumbo	270.00
Pitcher, water	660.00
Sauce	60.00
Spoon Rack	420.00
Spooner, Barnum's head	125.00
Sugar Bowl, cov, Barnum's head	495.00

Kansas

Jewel and Dewdrop, Jewel with Dewdrop, US Glass Pattern Line No. 15,072

Manufactured by the Co-Operative Flint Glass Company, Beaver Falls, PA. Later produced as part of the States pattern series by United States Glass Company, Pittsburgh, PA, in 1901, Kokomo Glass Manufacturing Company, Kokomo, IN, c1903, Federal Glass Company, Columbus, OH, c1914, and by Jenkins Glass Company, c1915-25. Made in non-flint, clear. Also known with jewels stained in pink or gold.

Reproductions: Mugs have been reproduced in vaseline, amber, and blue. They tend to be smaller and of inferior quality.

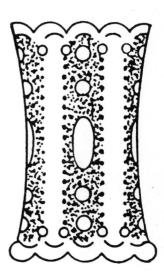

Items	Clear
Banana Stand	110.00
Bowl, oval, 7" l	42.00
Bowl, round, scalloped rim, 6" d, 6-1/2" or 8" d	30.00-48.00
Bread Plate, ODB	55.00
Butter Dish, cov, flanged, attached under plate	80.00
Butter Dish, round, no under plate	65.00
Butter Dish, notched lid	90.00
Cake Plate	80.00
Cake Stand, hs, 7-5/8" or 10" d	55.00-105.00
Cake Stand, ls, 8" or 10" d	60.00-72.00
Celery Vase	55.00
Compote, cov, hs, beading on pedestal, 7" or 8" d	80.00-105.00
Compote, cov, hs, notched lid, 6" d	65.00
Compote, cov, hs, solid lid, 5" or 6" d	55.00-60.00
Compote, open, hs, beading on pedestal, 6" or 8" d	36.00-55.00
Compote, open, ls, saucer bowl, scalloped rim, 7-1/2" or 9-1/2" d	42.00-55.00

Items	Clear
Compote, open, ls, scalloped rim, 5" d	30.00
Cordial	48.00
Creamer	48.00
Cup, handle	18.00
Goblet	65.00
Jelly Compote, 5" d	60.00
Mug, regular	55.00
Mug, tall	30.00
Pitcher, milk, quart	60.00
Pitcher, water, half gallon	72.00
Preserve Dish, 6-1/2" w, 8-1/2" l	24.00
Relish, oval, 8-1/2" l	24.00
Salt Shaker	60.00
Sauce, flat, scalloped rim, 4" d	15.00
Sugar Bowl, cov	80.00
Syrup, orig top	130.00
Toothpick Holder	80.00
Tumbler, flat	55.00
Whiskey	18.00
Wine	80.00

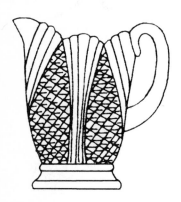

Kentucky

US Glass Pattern Line No. 150,051

Manufactured by United States Glass Company, Pittsburgh, PA, c1897 as part of the States pattern series. Made in non-flint, clear and emerald green. The goblet is found in ruby stained ($60). A footed, square sauce ($36), is known in cobalt blue with gold. A toothpick holder is also known in ruby stained ($160).

Items	Clear	Emerald Green
Bowl, 7" or 8" d	24.00	—
Butter Dish, cov	60.00	—
Cake Stand, hs, 9-1/2" or 10-1/2" d	48.00-55.00	—
Celery Tray, small or large	36.00	—
Celery Vase	42.00	—
Compote, cov, hs, 5" or 7" d	42.00-55.00	—
Compote, open, hs, 6" or 8" d	30.00-36.00	—
Creamer	30.00	—
Cruet, os	55.00	—
Custard Cup	12.00	24.00
Dish, oblong, flat, 7" or 8" l	18.00	—
Goblet	24.00	60.00
Nappy	12.00	18.00
Olive, handle	30.00	—
Pitcher, water	65.00	—
Plate, sq, 7" or 9" w	18.00	—
Punch Cup	12.00	18.00
Salt Shaker, orig top	12.00	—
Sauce, flat, sq, 4" w or 4-1/2" w	10.00	12.00
Sauce, ftd, sq, 4" w or 4-1/2" w	12.00	15.00
Spooner	42.00	—
Sugar Bowl, cov	36.00	—
Syrup, orig top	80.00	—
Toothpick Holder, sq	42.00	105.00
Tumbler	24.00	36.00
Wine	210.00	310.00

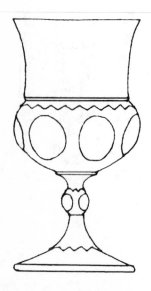

King's Crown

Blue Thumbprint, Excelsior, Ruby Thumbprint, X.L.C.R.

Manufactured by Adams & Company, Pittsburgh, PA., in the 1890s and later. Reissued by United States Glass Company, Pittsburgh, PA, at Factory "A," c1891 to 1900s. Known as Ruby Thumbprint when pieces are ruby stained. It became very popular after 1891 as ruby-stained souvenir ware. King's Crown is a large pattern, with approximately eighty-seven pieces documented. Made in non-flint, clear, green and with the thumbprints stained amethyst, gold, green, and yellow, and in clear with etching and trimmed in gold. Add 30% for engraved pieces.

Reproductions: Pattern has been copiously reproduced for the gift-trade market in milk glass, cobalt blue, and other colors. New pieces are easily distinguished. In the case of Ruby Thumbprint, the color is a very pale pinkish red. Available in amethyst stained in goblet ($36) and wine ($12) and in green stained in goblet ($30) and wine ($20).

Items	Clear	Ruby Stained
Banana Stand, ftd	105.00	142.00
Bowl, belled bowl, 5" or 7" d	18.00-30.00	30.00-42.00
Bowl, cov, collared base, 5", 6" or 9" d	42.00-55.00	65.00-80.00

Items	Clear	Ruby Stained
Bowl, flared, collared base, serrated rim, 6", d or 7" 11" d	30.00-48.00	42.00-65.00
Bowl, flared, flat, serrated rim, or pointed, 8" d or 9" d	42.00	65.00
Bowl, round, collared base, or straight sided, serrated rim,5" or 7" d	18.00-30.00	30.00-42.00
Bowl, round, collared base, 9" d	42.00	65.00
Bowl, straight sided, serrated rim, 8-1/2" or 11" d	36.00-48.00	48.00-60.00
Butter Dish, cov 7-1/2" d	60.00	110.00
Cake Stand, hs, 9" d	610.00	130.00
Cake Stand, hs, 10" d	90.00	130.00
Castor Bottle	55.00	85.00
Castor Set, glass stand, 4 bottles	190.00	360.00
Celery Vase	48.00	72.00
Champagne	30.00	42.00
Cheese Dish, cov, 7" d	120.00	270.00
Claret	42.00	60.00
Compote, cov, hs, 6", 8" or 12" d	80.00-130.00	142.00-240.00
Compote, cov, ls, 12" d	110.00	270.00
Compote, open, hs, 8-1/4" d	90.00	115.00
Compote, open, ls, 5-1/4" d	36.00	55.00
Cordial	55.00	—
Creamer, ah, 3-1/4" h, ind, tankard	30.00	42.00
Creamer, ah, 4-7/8" h, table	60.00	80.00
Cup and Saucer	65.00	85.00
Custard Cup	18.00	30.00
Fruit Basket, hs	130.00	215.00
Goblet	36.00	55.00
Honey Dish, cov, sq	120.00	190.00
Lamp, oil, 10"	142.00	—
Marmalade Jar, cov	55.00	90.00
Mustard, cov, notched lid, 4" h	42.00	90.00
Olive Dish	30.00	55.00
Orange Bowl, ftd, serrated rim	65.00	115.00
Pickle Castor, orig silver plate frame	130.00	260.00
Pickle Dish, lobed	110.00	48.00
Pitcher, milk, quart, bulbous or tankard	85.00-90.00	115.00-120.00
Pitcher, water, half gallon, bulbous	115.00	270.00
Pitcher, water, half gallon, tankard	112.00	240.00
Plate, 7" d	24.00	55.00
Preserve, 6" l or 10" l	42.00	60.00
Punch Bowl, ftd	290.00	360.00
Punch Cup	18.00	36.00
Salt, individual, rect or sq	18.00	42.00
Salt, master, rect or sq	36.00	60.00
Salt Shaker, 3-1/8" h	36.00	48.00
Sauce, flat, pointed, serrated rim or flared, 4" l or 4-1/2" l	24.00	30.00
Sauce, flat, round, belled, serrated rim or straight sides, 4" d or 4-1/2" d	18.00	24.00
Spooner, 4-1/4" h	55.00	60.00
Sugar Bowl, open, individual, 2-3/4" h	30.00	55.00
Sugar Bowl, cov, table, 6-3/4" h	65.00	115.00
Toothpick Holder, 2-3/4" h	24.00	42.00
Tumbler, 3-3/4" h	24.00	42.00
Wine, 4-3/8" h	30.00	48.00

King's #500

Bone Stem, Parrot, Swirl and Thumbprint

Manufactured by King, Son & Company Pittsburgh, PA, in 1891. Continued by United States Glass Company, Pittsburgh, PA, 1891-98, and made in a great number of pieces. Made in clear, frosted, and a rich, deep blue, known as Dewey Blue, both trimmed in gold. Values shown below are for pieces with very good gold trim. A clear goblet with frosted stem ($60) is known. Also known in dark green. A ruby stained sugar is reported ($115).

Items	Clear, Gold Trim	Dewey Blue, Gold Trim
Bowl, 7" or 9" d	12.00-20.00	36.00-55.00
Butter Dish, cov	80.00	130.00
Cake Stand, hs	48.00	72.00
Castor Set, 3 bottles	90.00	240.00
Celery Vase	24.00	80.00
Cologne Bottle, faceted stopper, 1, 2 or 8 oz	42.00-65.00	90.00-115.00
Compote, cov, hs, 8" or 9" d	60.00-65.00	90.00-95.00
Compote, open, hs, deep bowl, 8" or 9" d	30.00-42.00	48.00-60.00
Compote, open, hs, saucer, bowl, 9" or 10" d	55.00-60.00	80.00-90.00
Cracker Jar, cov	105.00	130.00
Creamer, bulbous, ah, individual or table	24.00-36.00	42.00-60.00
Cruet	55.00	190.00
Custard Cup	12.00	18.00
Decanter, locking silver plate top	250.00	—
Dish, cov, sq, flat, 7" w or 8" w	65.00	90.00
Dish, open, sq, flat, 7" w or 8" w	24.00	48.00

Items	Clear, Gold Trim	Dewey Blue, Gold Trim
Finger Bowl	18.00	42.00
Goblet	55.00	105.00
Lamp, hand	55.00	—
Lamp, stand	80.00	—
Pitcher, milk, 3 pint, bulbous or jug shape	60.00	240.00
Pitcher, water, half gallon, bulbous	90.00	240.00
Pitcher, water, half gallon, jug shape	105.00	224.00
Relish	24.00	36.00
Rose Bowl	24.00	55.00
Salt Shaker	18.00	48.00
Sauce, flat, 4" d	18.00	24.00
Spooner	36.00	85.00
Sugar Bowl, cov, individual or table	24.00-55.00	48.00-90.00
Syrup, orig top	65.00	270.00
Tumbler	30.00	42.00
Water Tray, tab handles	55.00	115.00
Wine	42.00	80.00

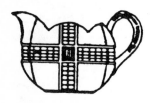

Klondike

Amberette, English Hobnail Cross, Frosted Amberette

Manufacturing attributed to A. J. Beatty and Company, Tiffin, OH, c1885. It was also made by Hobbs, Brockunier & Company, Wheeling, WV, and Daizell, Gilmore and Leighton Company, Brilliant, OH, c1880. Created to commemorate the Alaskan Gold Rush. The frosted panels depict snow; the amber bands depict the gold. Made in non-flint, clear, and frosted, with amber stained bands. Found with or without scrolls, depending on the maker. Prices are listed for frosted; clear prices would be approximately 20% of those shown.

Items	Frosted Amber Stain
Berry Bowl, sq, 8" w	240.00
Bowl, sq, 9" w	270.00
Bowl, sq, 11" w	242.00
Butter Dish, cov	360.00
Cake Stand, hs, sq, 8" w	460.00
Celery Tray	240.00
Condiment Set, cruet and shaker on tray	1,200.00
Creamer	260.00
Cruet, os	460.00
Custard Cup	130.00
Goblet	480.00
Pitcher, water, round, tankard	660.00
Punch Cup	120.00
Salt Shaker, single	120.00
Sauce, flat	90.00
Sauce, footed	95.00
Spooner	190.00
Sugar Bowl, cov	260.00
Syrup, pewter lid	660.00
Toothpick Holder	360.00
Tray, 5-1/2" sq	240.00
Vase, trumpet shape, 7" or 8" h	240.00-270.00
Vase, trumpet shape, 10" h	260.00
Wine	480.00

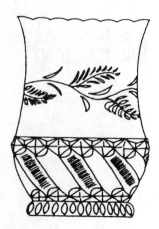

Kokomo

Bar and Diamond, R and H Swirl Band

Manufactured by Richards and Hartley, Tarentum, PA, c1885. Reissued by United States Glass Company, Pittsburgh, PA, c1891, and Kokomo Glass Company, Kokomo, IN, c1901. A large pattern, with more than fifty forms made. Made in non-flint, clear, ruby stained, and etched.

Items	Clear	Ruby Stained
Bowl, flat, 6" 7" d	24.00-30.00	—
Bowl, flat or ftd, 8" d	36.00	—
Bread Tray	36.00	72.00
Butter Dish, cov, flat	42.00	85.00
Butter Dish, cov, footed	48.00	95.00
Cake Stand, hs	55.00	180.00
Celery Vase	36.00	72.00
Compote, cov or open, hs, 5", 6" or 7" d	24.00-36.00	—
Compote, cov or open, hs, 8" d	42.00	180.00
Compote, open, ls, 5", 6", 7", 7-1/2" or 8" d	24.00-36.00	—
Condiment Set, oblong tray, salt & pepper shakers, cruet	95.00	215.00
Creamer, ah	42.00	85.00
Cruet	42.00	—

Items	Clear	Ruby Stained
Decanter, 9-3/4" h	65.00	115.00
Dish, flat, oblong, 7", 8", 9" or 10" l	18.00-24.00	—
Finger Bowl	30.00	60.00
Goblet	30.00	60.00
Lamp, hand, atypical – has no diamonds	60.00	120.00
Pickle Dish, oval	18.00	48.00
Pitcher, milk, quart, bulbous	55.00	118.00
Pitcher, milk, half pint, tankard	42.00	112.00
Pitcher, milk, quart, tankard	48.00	130.00
Pitcher, water, half gallon, bulbous or tankard	65.00	130.00
Salt, master, open, ftd	24.00	48.00
Salt Shaker	24.00	48.00
Sauce, flat, 4" d or 5" d	6.00	12.00
Sauce, ftd, 4" d or 5" d	10.00	18.00
Spooner	30.00	60.00
Sugar Bowl, cov	55.00	110.00
Sugar Shaker	42.00	90.00
Syrup, orig top	55.00	136.00
Tumbler	24.00	48.00
Water Tray	42.00	110.00
Wine	24.00	48.00

Leaf and Dart

Double Leaf and Dart, Pride

Manufactured by Richards & Hartley Flint Glass Company, Pittsburgh, PA, c1875. Reissued by United States Glass Company, Pittsburgh, PA, c1891. Shards have been found at the Boston and Sandwich Glass Works, Sandwich, MA, as well as the Burlington Glass Works, Hamilton, Ontario, Canada. Made in non-flint, clear.

Items	Clear
Bowl, footed, 8-1/4" d	30.00
Butter Dish, cov	72.00
Butter Pat	24.00
Celery Vase, pedestal	36.00
Compote, cov, ls	75.00
Compote, open, hs	42.00
Creamer, ah, pedestal	48.00
Cruet, ah, pedestal, os	120.00
Egg Cup	24.00
Goblet	28.00
Honey Dish	10.00
Lamp, finger, flat	90.00
Pitcher, milk, bulbous, ah, quart	90.00
Pitcher, water, bulbous, ah, half gallon	95.00
Relish Tray	18.00
Salt, master, ftd, cov	75.00
Salt, master, ftd, open	36.00
Sauce, flat, 4" d	8.50
Spooner	36.00
Sugar Bowl, cov	55.00
Syrup, orig top	110.00
Tumbler, ftd	30.00
Wine	36.00

Leaf and Flower

Manufactured by Hobbs, Brockunier and Company, Wheeling, WV, c1890, and United States Glass Company, Pittsburgh, PA, c1891. Made in clear and clear with amber stain. Acid etching (frosting) can be found on both clear and amber stained pieces. A few pieces have also been documented with ruby stain.

Items	Clear	Clear with Amber Stain
Bowl, scalloped, deep, 5", 7" or 8" d	30.00-36.00	36.00-48.00
Bowl, shallow, 7" or 9" d	30.00	42.00
Butter Dish, cov	72.00	110.00
Castor Set, mustard, oil bottle, salt & pepper shakers, leaf shaped tray	130.00	190.00
Celery Basket, scalloped, pressed rope handle	42.00	75.00
Celery Vase	42.00	90.00
Creamer	42.00	55.00
Finger Bowl, scalloped	65.00	100.00
Pitcher, water, tankard	75.00	120.00
Salt and Pepper Shakers, pr	48.00	72.00
Sauce, flat, 4-1/2" or 5"	18.00-30.00	36.00
Spooner	30.00	48.00
Sugar Bowl, cov	42.00	60.00
Syrup, orig top	130.00	240.00
Tumbler	24.00	42.00

Leaf and Star

Tobin, New Martinsville No. 711

Manufactured by New Martinsville Glass Manufacturing Company, New Martinsville, WV, c1910-15. Made in clear with gold trim, and ruby stained (add 100%). A toothpick holder (valued at $55) has been found in orange iridescent.

Items	Clear w/Gold
Banana Stand, ls, 8-1/2" d	55.00
Berry Bowl, master, 7" d	24.00
Bon Bon, turned up sides, 5" d	24.00
Bowl, scalloped rim, 8" d	24.00
Butter Dish, cov	42.00
Celery Tray, 11" l	24.00
Celery Vase	30.00
Creamer	25.00
Cruet, os	42.00
Custard Cup	12.00
Dresser Jar, metal top	65.00
Fruit Bowl, crimped rim, 10" d	24.00
Goblet	24.00
Hair Receiver, metal top	65.00
Humidor, orig silver plate top, 5" h, 4" d	55.00
Ice Cream Dish, 6" d	18.00
Jelly Compote, open, hs	20.00
Nut Bowl, crimped rim, ftd; cupped rim or flared rim 4" d	18.00
Pitcher, water, ice lip, half gallon	65.00
Pitcher, water, plain lip, half gallon	60.00
Plate, 6" or 8" d	12.00
Salt Shaker, orig nickel plated top	12.00
Sauce, flat, 4" d or 4-1/2" d	12.00
Sauce, footed, flared rim, 4" d or 4-1/2" d	18.00
Spooner	30.00
Sugar Bowl, cov	36.00
Toothpick Holder	18.00
Tumbler	24.00
Vase, 8-1/4" h	18.00
Wine	24.00

Lens and Star

Star and Oval

Manufactured by O'Hara Glass Company, Pittsburgh, PA, in 1880. Reissued in 1891 by United States Glass Company, Pittsburgh, PA. Made in clear with plain or frosted panels. An amber stained butter dish is known.

Items	Frosted
Butter Dish, cov	55.00
Celery	36.00
Creamer	36.00
Pitcher, water, barrel shape	60.00
Sauce	10.00
Spooner	24.00
Sugar Bowl, cov	55.00
Syrup, orig top	55.00
Tumbler	30.00
Waste Bowl	24.00

Leverne

Star in Honeycomb, Bryce Bros. No. 80

Manufactured by Bryce Brothers, Pittsburgh, PA, in the late 1880s. Reissued by United States Glass Company, Pittsburgh, PA, at Factory "B," c1891. Shards have been found at the Burlington Glass Works, Hamilton, Ontario, Canada. Made in non-flint, clear. Wines found in amber and blue. A celery vase is known in pale canary.

Items	Clear
Bowl, oval, 6-1/2" l	24.00
Butter Dish, cov	48.00
Cake Stand, hs	42.00
Celery Vase	42.00
Compote, cov, hs, 8-1/2" d	72.00
Compote, open, hs, 8-1/2" d	42.00
Creamer	42.00

Items	Clear
Cruet	60.00
Goblet	36.00
Pickle	18.00
Pitcher, milk	60.00
Pitcher, water	65.00
Relish, 5-1/4" w, 7-1/4" l	18.00
Sauce, flat, 4-1/2" d	10.00
Sauce, ftd, 4-1/2" d	15.00
Spooner	36.00
Sugar Bowl, cov	42.00
Wine	24.00

Liberty Bell

Centennial

Manufactured by Gillinder and Company, Philadelphia, c1875. James C. Gillinder registered his design patent on Sept. 28, 1875. The pattern was made at the Gillinder factory located on the grounds of the Centennial Philadelphia Exhibition of 1876. Made in clear. Some items made in milk glass. A milk glass bread plate, 13-3/8" x 9-1/2", is known and shows John Hancock's signature (valued at $360).

Reproductions: Reproductions bear the year "1876" and "200 Years" instead of the original inscriptions. The American Historical Replica Company, Grand Rapids, MI, issued reproductions for the American Bicentennial. It modified the design to include "1776-1976," and phrases such as "Declaration of Independence," etc. Its reproductions are clearly embossed "A. H.B. C. Grand Rapids, MI."

Items	Clear
Bowl, 8", ftd	100.00
Bread Plate, 13-3/8" x 9-1/2", clear, no signatures φ	100.00
Butter Dish, cov	155.00
Celery Vase, pedestal	100.00
Child's Butter Dish, cov	180.00
Child's Creamer, ph	90.00
Child's Mug, 2" h	240.00
Child's Spooner	150.00
Child's Sugar Bowl, cov	180.00
Compote, open, collared base, 6", 6-3/4" or 8" d	90.00-100.00
Creamer, applied handle	115.00
Creamer, reed handle	120.00
Goblet	48.00
Mug, snake handle	440.00
Pickle	55.00
Pitcher, water, ah	960.00
Plate, 6" d, dated	90.00
Plate, 8" or 10" d	72.00-95.00
Platter, 13" x 8", twig handles, 13 states	75.00
Relish, oval	72.00
Salt dip, individual, oval	36.00
Salt Shaker	115.00
Sauce, flat or footed, 4-1/2" d	24.00
Spooner, pedestal	72.00
Sugar Bowl, cov, pedestal	110.00

Lily of the Valley

Lily of the Valley on Legs

Manufactured by Boston and Sandwich Glass Company, Sandwich, MA, and King, Son & Company, Pittsburgh, PA, in the 1870s. Shards have also been found at Burlington Glass Works, Hamilton, Ontario, Canada. Lily of the Valley on Legs is a name frequently given to those pieces having three tall legs. Lily of the Valley on Legs pieces constitute a table set of covered butter dish, covered sugar bowl, creamer, and spooner. Add 25% for this type. Made in non-flint, clear.

Items	Clear
Berry Bowl, master	55.00
Butter Dish, cov	85.00
Buttermilk Goblet	42.00
Cake Stand, hs	75.00
Celery Tray	48.00
Celery Vase	65.00
Champagne	95.00
Compote, cov, hs, 8-1/2" d	100.00
Compote, open, hs, 8-1/2" d	60.00
Cordial	100.00
Creamer, ah	75.00
Cruet, os	135.00

Items	Clear
Egg Cup	48.00
Goblet	65.00
Honey Dish	12.00
Nappy, 4"	24.00
Pickle, scoop shape	24.00
Pitcher, milk, quart	130.00
Pitcher, water, half gallon	142.00
Relish, oval	18.00
Salt, master, cov	130.00
Salt, master, open	60.00
Sauce, flat, 4" d	15.00
Spooner, pedestal	42.00
Sugar Bowl, cov, pedestal	90.00
Sugar Bowl, open	42.00
Tumbler, flat	60.00
Tumbler, footed	75.00
Vegetable Dish, oval	36.00
Wine	120.00

Lincoln Drape with Tassel

Lincoln Drape, Oval and Lincoln Drape

Manufactured originally by Boston and Sandwich Glass Company, Sandwich, MA 1850s, and possibly continued by other companies, c1865-80. Made in flint, non-flint, clear. Some very rare pieces are known in cobalt blue. They would be valued 200% more than clear. Items without tassels are valued at 20% less.

Reproductions: The miniature lamp has been reproduced.

Items	Clear
Butter Dish, cov	120.00
Celery Vase	110.00
Compote, cov, hs, 7-1/2" or 8-1/2" d	130.00-180.00
Compote, open, hs, 7-1/2" d	90.00
Compote, open, ls, 6" or 7-1/2"d	75.00
Creamer, ah	130.00
Egg Cup	50.00
Goblet, gentleman's, large	130.00
Goblet, lady's	175.00
Honey Dish	24.00
Lamp, marble base	130.00
Miniature Lamp, orig matching shade, burner, and chimney φ	120.00
Pitcher, water, ah	360.00
Plate, 6" d	95.00
Salt, master, ftd	130.00
Sauce, 4" d	24.00
Spill Holder	60.00
Spooner	90.00
Sugar Bowl, cov	120.00
Syrup, orig top, ah	190.00
Tumbler	130.00
Wine	140.00

Lion

Frosted Lion

Manufactured by Gillinder and Sons, Philadelphia, PA, in 1876. Made in clear with frosting. Pieces made without frosting are valued at 20% less. Pieces can be found plain or with copper wheel engraving.

Reproductions: Companies such as Imperial Glass Company, Bellaire, OH, Summit Art Glass Company, Mogadore, OH, and Westmoreland Glass Company, Grapeville, PA, began to reproduce this pattern in the early 1930s. These reproductions are identified by the chalk-like feel of the frosting. In the early 1960s, Imperial Glass issued an amber compote with its mark, but a 1889 patent date. Summit Art Glass Company has also issued some pieces not originally made and in various colors.

Items	Frosted
Bowl, oblong, 7-1/2" x 4-1/4"	65.00
Bowl, oblong, 8" x 5" φ	60.00
Bread Plate, 12" d φ	110.00
Butter Dish, cov, lion's head finial	110.00
Butter Dish, cov, rampant lion finial φ	130.00
Cake Stand	100.00
Celery Vase φ	100.00
Champagne	190.00
Cheese, cov, rampant lion finial φ	440.00
Child's Cup and Saucer	55.00

Items	Frosted
Child's Table Set	600.00
Cologne Bottle, os	390.00
Compote, cov, hs, rampant lion finial, 7" d φ	180.00
Compote, cov, hs, preying lion finial, oval, collared base, 9" d	180.00
Compote, cov, hs, three lion stem, rampant lion finial, 9" d	225.00
Compote, open, ls, 8" d	90.00
Cordial	190.00
Creamer	90.00
Egg Cup, 3-1/2" h φ	75.00
Goblet φ	85.00
Marmalade Jar, preying lion finial	100.00
Pitcher, milk	390.00
Pitcher, water φ	360.00
Platter, oval, reclining lion handles, 13" l	90.00
Relish , lion handles	100.00
Salt, master, rect lid	260.00
Sauce, ftd, 4" d	30.00
Spooner φ	90.00
Sugar Bowl, cov, lion head finial φ	110.00
Sugar Bowl, cov, rampant lion finial	135.00
Syrup, orig top, dated "July 16, '72-C& W," 6-1/2" or 7-1/2" h h	360.00
Syrup, orig top, not dated, 9" h	440.00
Wine	240.00

Locket on Chain

Stippled Beaded Shield, Heisey Pattern No. 160

Manufactured by A. H. Heisey Company, Newark, OH, c1896. Ruby stain decoration added by Oriental Glass Company, Pittsburgh, PA, and sold as its one product. Made in non-flint, clear, and clear with ruby stain. Rarely found in green, milk glass, or vaseline.

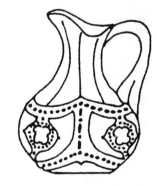

Items	Clear	Ruby Stained
Berry Bowl, 8" d	100.00	130.00
Butter, Dish, cov	120.00	260.00
Cake Stand, hs	130.00	—
Celery Vase	110.00	175.00
Compote, cov, hs, 8" d	190.00	—
Compote, open, hs, 8" d	130.00	—
Creamer, 4-5/8" h	100.00	180.00
Cruet, os	180.00	425.00
Goblet	100.00	—
Pickle	55.00	100.00
Pitcher, water	225.00	—
Plate, 8" d	75.00	—
Salt Shaker	72.00	130.00
Sauce, flat, 4" d	42.00	60.00
Spooner	90.00	180.00
Sugar Bowl, cov	120.00	260.00
Syrup, orig top	180.00	425.00
Toothpick Holder	360.00	940.00
Tumbler, flat	95.00	180.00
Wine	85.00	260.00

Log Cabin

Manufactured by Central Glass Company, Wheeling, WV, c1875. Made in non-flint, clear. Rarely found in color.

Reproductions: Reproduced creamers, spooners, and covered sugar bowls are found in clear, chocolate, and cobalt blue. Reproductions of this unique pattern usually lack details, such as door latches, etc.

Items	Clear
Bowl, cov, 8 x 5-1/4 x 3/58"	440.00
Butter Dish, cov	360.00
Compote, cov, hs, 4-1/2" or 10-1/2" d	290.00
Creamer φ	120.00
Marmalade Jar, cov	290.00
Pitcher, water	360.00
Sauce, flat	90.00
Spooner φ	124.00
Sugar Bowl, cov φ	290.00

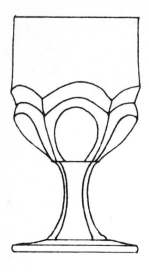

Loop

Seneca Loop, Central's No. 145, O'Hara No. 9, Portland Panel, McKee's O'Hara

Manufactured by several firms, c1850-80s, including Central Glass Company, Wheeling, WV, c1870; Challinor, Taylor & Company, Pittsburgh, PA, c1875, Doyle and Company, Pittsburgh, PA, c1875, James B. Lyon and Company, Pittsburgh, PA, c1860s, McKee Brothers, Pittsburgh, PA, c1875, O'Hara Glass Company, Pittsburgh, PA, c1860, Portland Glass Company, Portland, ME, United States Glass Company, Pittsburgh, PA, c1891. Shards found at Burlington Glass Works, Hamilton, Ontario, Canada. Later made in non-flint. Boston and Sandwich Glass Company, Sandwich, MA, also produced several forms in fiery opalescent. *Yuma Loop* is a contemporary with comparable values. Made in flint, non-flint, clear.

Items	Flint	Non-Flint
Bitters Bottle	55.00	—
Bowl, 9" d	60.00	30.00
Butter Dish, cov	72.00	48.00
Cake Stand, hs	115.00	60.00
Celery Vase, pedestal	75.00	24.00
Champagne	42.00	30.00
Compote, cov, hs, 9-1/2" d	142.00	72.00
Compote, open, hs, deep bowl, 7" d	90.00	—
Compote, open, hs, deep bowl, 9" or 10" d	118.00-130.00	48.00
Compote, open, hs, shallow bowl, 7" d	90.00	—
Cordial, 2-3/4" h	48.00	24.00
Creamer, ah	85.00	42.00
Decanter, pint, patterned stopper	75.00	—
Decanter, quart, bar lip	90.00	—
Egg Cup	36.00	24.00
Goblet, gentleman's or lady's	24.00	18.00
Lamp, oil, orig burner and chimney, 9-3/4" h	180.00	100.00
Pitcher, milk, 3 pints	180.00	100.00
Pitcher, water, ah	185.00	72.00
Plate, round	30.00	18.00
Salt, master, ftd	30.00	10.00
Spooner	36.00	30.00
Sugar Bowl, cov	85.00	36.00
Syrup, orig top	115.00	
Tumbler, flat	48.00	24.00
Tumbler, footed	30.00	18.00
Vase, 9-3/4", 10-3/4" or 11-3/4" h	48.00	24.00
Water Bottle	75.00	—
Wine	36.00	15.00

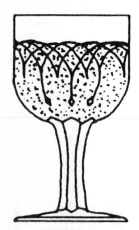

Loop and Dart, Loop and Dart with Diamond Ornament

Manufactured by the Boston and Sandwich Glass Company, Sandwich, MA, and Richards & Hartley Glass Company, Tarentum, PA in the late 1860s and early 1870s. The pattern is related to *Loop and Dart with Diamond Ornament* and *Loop and Dart with Round Ornament,* which was made by Portland Glass Company, Portland, ME. Made in non-flint, clear and stippled. Add 25% for flint prices.

Items	Loop and Dart Clear	Loop and Dart with Diamond Ornament, Clear
Bowl, oval, 9" l	25.00	24.00
Butter Dish, cov	45.00	55.00
Cake Stand, hs, 10" d	40.00	—
Celery Vase, pedestal	35.00	42.00
Compote, cov, hs, 8" d	85.00	75.00
Compote, cov, ls, 8" d	65.00	65.00
Cordial	45.00	60.00
Creamer, ah, pedestal	35.00	—
Cruet, os	95.00	—
Cup Plate	30.00	
Egg Cup	25.00	30.00
Goblet	25.00	—
Lamp, oil	85.00	—
Pickle	15.00	—
Pitcher, water	75.00	130.00
Plate, 6" d	35.00	36.00
Relish	18.00	18.00
Salt, master	50.00	20.00
Sauce	5.00	4.50
Spooner	25.00	36.00
Sugar Bowl, cov	50.00	48.00
Tumbler, footed	30.00	42.00
Tumbler, water	25.00	48.00
Wine	35.00	42.00

Loop and Dart with Round Ornament

Portland Loop and Jewel

Manufactured by the Portland Glass Company, Portland, ME, in the late 1860s and early 1870s. The pattern is related to *Loop and Dart* and *Loop and Dart with Diamond Ornament* and *Loop and Dart*, made by Boston and Sandwich Glass Company, Sandwich, MA, and Richards & Hartley Glass Company, Tarentum, PA in the late 1860s and early 1870s. Made in non-flint, clear and stippled. Add 25% for flint prices.

Items	Clear
Bowl, oval, 9" l	20.00-30..00
Butter Dish, cov	95.00
Buttermilk Goblet	24.00
Butter Pat	18.00
Celery Vase	42.00
Champagne	100.00
Compote, cov, hs, 8" d	100.00
Compote, cov, ls, 8" d	75.00
Compote, open, hs, 8" d	55.00
Creamer	42.00
Egg Cup	36.00
Goblet, water	40.00
Pitcher, water	110.00
Plate, 6" d	42.00
Relish	18.00
Salt, master	20.00-30..00
Sauce, flat	10.00
Spooner	36.00
Sugar Bowl, cov	60.00
Tumbler, footed	36.00
Tumbler, flat	42.00
Wine	42.00

Louisiana

Sharp Oval and Diamond, Granby, US Glass Pattern Line No. 15,053

Manufactured by Bryce Brothers, Pittsburgh, PA, in the 1870s. Reissued by the United States Glass Company, Pittsburgh, PA, c1898, as part of the States series. Made in clear, some forms frosted. Also found with gilt trim.

Items	Clear
Berry Bowl, 9" d	24.00
Bowl, cov, flat, 6" or 8" d	30.00-42.00
Bowl, open, round, 6" or 8" d	18.00-30.00
Bowl, open, square, 6", 7", 8" or 9" w	24.00-30.00
Butter Dish, cov	75.00
Cake Stand, hs, 7", 9" or 10" d	55.00-75.00
Celery Vase	36.00
Compote, cov, hs, 6", 7" or 8" d	65.00-90.00
Compote, open, hs, deep bowl, 6" or 8" d	18.00-30.00
Compote, open, hs, flared bowl, 6" d	24.00
Compote, open, hs, saucer bowl, 8" or 10" d	30.00-55.00
Creamer	36.00
Dish, cov, 6" d	30.00
Dish, open, flat, 6" d	24.00
Goblet	36.00
Jelly Compote, open, hs, 5" d	25.00
Match Holder	42.00
Mug, handle	30.00
Mustard, cov, matching patterned under plate	48.00
Pickle, boat shape	48.00
Nappy, cov, 4" d	36.00
Pitcher, milk or water, ph	60.00-75.00
Relish Tray	18.00
Salt Shaker	30.00
Sauce, flat, round or square, 4" d or 4-1/2" d	12.00
Spooner	36.00
Sugar Bowl, cov	55.00
Tumbler	30.00
Wine	42.00

Magnet and Grape

Magnet and Grape with Stippled Leaf

Manufactured by to Boston and Sandwich Glass Company, Sandwich, MA, c1850. Later non-flint versions have grape leaf in either clear or stippled. Made in flint and non-flint, clear.

Reproductions: Imperial Glass began producing reproductions from new molds for the Metropolitan Museum of Art, NY, in 1971 and continued through 1985. Each lead crystal piece was marked "M.M.A." By

1973, the Smithsonian Institution also authorized Imperial Glass to make reproductions of the wine glass for it. They are embossed with the museum's hallmark of "SI."

Items	Flint Frosted leaf	Non-Flint Stippled or Clear Leaf
Bowl, cov, 8" d	190.00	90.00
Butter Dish, cov	210.00	48.00
Celery Vase	180.00	30.00
Champagne	130.00	—
Compote, cov, hs, 4 –1/2" d	130.00	—
Compote, open, hs, 7-1/2" d	135.00	75.00
Cordial, 4" h	130.00	—
Creamer φ	190.00	48.00
Decanter, os, pint or quart	180.00-240.00	90.00-100.00
Egg Cup φ	90.00	24.00
Goblet, low stem	90.00	
Goblet, regular stem φ	85.00	36.00
Pitcher, milk, ah	—	90.00
Pitcher, water, ah	360.00	90.00
Relish, oval	42.00	18.00
Salt, ftd	75.00	48.00
Sauce, flat, 4" d	30.00	18.00
Spooner	120.00	60.00
Sugar Bowl, cov	180.00	90.00
Syrup, orig top	260.00	—
Tumbler, flat φ	130.00	—
Whiskey	155.00	—
Wine φ	190.00	—
Wine Jug, hs, dated, with or without inscription	3,500.00	—

Maine

Paneled Stippled Flower, Stippled Primrose, Stippled Paneled Flower

Manufactured by United States Glass Company, Pittsburgh, PA, c 1899, as part of its States series. Researchers dispute if goblet was made originally. Made in non-flint, clear, and emerald green. Sometimes found with enamel grim or overall turquoise stain.

Items	Clear	Emerald Green
Bowl, cov, round, flared, 8" d	55.00	—
Bowl, oval, 8" l, 6" w	30.00	—
Bowl, round, 6" or 8" d	24.00-36.00	32.00-48.00
Bread Plate, oval, 10" l, 7-3/4" w	36.00	—
Butter Dish, cov	65.00	—
Cake Stand, hs, 8", 10" or 11" d	48.00-72.00	72.00-90.00
Celery Vase	60.00	—
Compote, open, hs, 5", 6" or 7" d	24.00	55.00
Compote, open, hs, flared bowl, 8", 9" or 10" d	42.00-55.00	72.00-85.00
Compote, open, ls, 8" d	30.00	65.00
Compote, open, ls, 9" d	36.00	75.00
Creamer	36.00	—
Cruet	95.00	—
Goblet	115.00	—
Jelly Compote, cov	60.00	90.00
Mug	42.00	—
Pickle Tray, 8" l	18.00	36.00
Pitcher, milk, quart	75.00	100.00
Pitcher, water, half gallon	60.00	130.00
Plate, 10" d	42.00	—
Relish	18.00	—
Salt Shaker, single	36.00	—
Sauce, flat, 4" d	18.00	—
Spooner	30.00	48.00
Sugar Bowl, cov	55.00	90.00
Syrup	90.00	230.00
Toothpick Holder	130.00	—
Tumbler, flat	36.00	55.00
Wine	60.00	90.00

Manhattan

New York, US Glass Pattern Line No. 15,078

Manufactured by United States Glass Company, Pittsburgh, PA, c1902, at Factories "G" and "F." Stained decoration done by the Oriental Glass Company, Pittsburgh, PA. A Depression-era glass pattern also has the "Manhattan" name. A table-sized creamer and covered sugar are known in true ruby stained, and a goblet is known in old marigold carnival glass. Made in non-flint, clear, clear with gold trim, and green or rose stained. Rare ruby stained pieces are also found in today's antiques market.

Reproductions: Heavily reproduced by Bartlett-Collins Glass Company, Sapulpa, OK, and Tiffin Glass Company, Tiffin, OH. Reproductions are found in amber, avocado green, and clear.

Items	Clear	Rose Stained
Biscuit Jar, cov	72.00	100.00
Bowl, 6" d	20.00	—
Bowl, 8-1/4" d, scalloped	24.00	85.00
Bowl, 9-1/2", 10" or 12-1/2" d	24.00-30.00	—
Butter Dish, cov	65.00	
Cake Stand, hs, 8", 9" or 10" d	55.00-65.00	65.00-75.00
Carafe, water	48.00	75.00
Celery Tray, 8"	24.00	—
Celery Vase	30.00	—
Cheese, cov, 8-3/8" d	65.00	118.00
Compote, cov, hs, 9-1/2" d	72.00	130.00
Compote, open, hs, 9-1/2" or 10-1/2" d	55.00-60.00	115.00-120.00
Creamer, individual	24.00	48.00
Creamer, table φ	36.00	72.00
Cruet, os, large	75.00	118.00
Cruet, os, small	60.00	—
Goblet φ	30.00	60.00
Ice Bucket	42.00	75.00
Iced Tea Tumbler φ	36.00	—
Lamp Shade, electric or gas, belled or cupped	36.00	—
Marmalade Dish, round, handle	12.00	24.00
Marmalade Dish, triangular, handle	18.00	36.00
Olive Tray, Gainsborough	36.00	72.00
Pickle Castor, orig silver plate holder	120.00	240.00
Pitcher, water, half gallon, bulbous, ah	85.00	148.00
Pitcher, water, half gallon, tankard, ah	72.00	130.00
Plate, 5" d	12.00	—
Plate, 6" d φ	12.00	36.00
Plate, 8" d	18.00	42.00
Plate, 9-1/2", 10-3/4", or 11" d φ or 12" d	18.00-30.00	—
Punch Bowl φ	130.00	260.00
Punch Cup φ	12.00	24.00
Relish, 6"	15.00	30.00
Salt Shaker, single	24.00	42.00
Sauce, flat, 4" d or 4-1/2" d φ	12.00	24.00
Sauce, footed, 4" d or 4-1/2" d	18.00	—
Spooner	24.00	—
Straw Holder, cov	115.00	—
Sugar Bowl, cov, table φ	48.00	75.00
Sugar Bowl, open, individual	18.00	36.00
Syrup	110.00	190.00
Toothpick Holder	36.00	72.00
Tumbler, water φ	24.00	48.00
Vase, 6" h or 8" h	20.00	42.00
Violet Bowl	24.00	48.00
Water Bottle	48.00	95.00
Wine φ	24.00	48.00

Maple Leaf

Leaf, Maple Leaf on Trunk

Manufactured by Gillinder and Sons, Philadelphia, PA, c1880. Made in non-flint, amber, blue, canary, clear, and frosted.

Reproductions: Heavily reproduced in clear and colors by L. G. Wright Glass Company, New Martinsville, WV, and others.

Items	Amber	Blue	Canary	Clear	Frosted
Bowl, cov, oval, 5-1/2" l	55.00	65.00	55.00	30.00	42.00
Bowl, cov, oval, 11" l	75.00	90.00	42.00	30.00	65.00
Bread Plate	85.00	100.00	90.00	40.00	100.00
Butter Dish, cov	90.00	95.00	90.00	75.00	85.00
Cake Stand, hs, 11" d	72.00	75.00	72.00	55.00	60.00
Celery Vase	55.00	60.00	55.00	42.00	48.00
Compote, cov, hs, 9" d	110.00	110.00	110.00	75.00	120.00
Creamer	75.00	75.00	70.00	40.00	65.00
Cup Plate	72.00	55.00	48.00	24.00	30.00
Dish, ftd, 6" d	60.00	72.00	60.00	48.00	65.00
Goblet φ	100.00	120.00	115.00	75.00	110.00
Jelly Compote	60.00	72.00	60.00	48.00	55.00
Pitcher, milk	95.00	115.00	100.00	75.00	90.00
Pitcher, water	100.00	120.00	110.00	90.00	95.00
Platter, 10-1/2"	55.00	60.00	60.00	48.00	55.00
Sauce, leaf shape, ftd, 5" l	18.00	24.00	24.00	12.00	18.00
Sauce, leaf shape, ftd, 6" l	20.00	36.00	20.00	18.00	24.00
Spooner	72.00	90.00	72.00	48.00	55.00
Sugar Bowl, cov	95.00	120.00	95.00	60.00	90.00

Items	Amber	Blue	Canary	Clear	Frosted
Tray, leaf rim, oval, 13-1/4" l	60.00	72.00	72.00	48.00	55.00
Tray, rect, 13-1/4" l, 10" w	60.00	72.00	72.00	48.00	55.00
Tumbler	48.00	55.00	48.00	35.00	55.00

Mardi Gras

Duncan and Miller #42, Empire, Paneled English Hobnail with Prisms, Siamese Necklace

Manufactured by Duncan and Miller Glass Company, Washington, PA, c1898-1920. Made in non-flint, clear, light blue and ruby stained. Some pieces are gilt trimmed.

Reproductions: Duncan and Miller Glass Company reintroduced a two-piece punch bowl in 1943 and advertised it as made from the original molds. A division of United States Glass Company, Tiffin Glass, reissued a punch set in 1955. Indiana Glass Company, Dunkirk, IN, also reproduced the punch bowl in 1973, in addition to a vase it issued in amber and vaseline.

Items	Clear	Ruby Stained
Banana Boat, folded sides, 8" l, 5" w	60.00	130.00
Berry Bowl, 8" d	30.00	—
Bon Bon, scalloped rim, silver plated foot, 7" l	48.00	95.00
Bowl, ftd, 8" d, 4-1/4" h	30.00	—
Bowl, scalloped, 8-1/2" d, 3-1/2" h; 9" d, 3-1/4" h; or 10" d, 3-1/4" h	24.00-30.00	75.00-90.00
Butter Dish, cov	75.00	155.00
Butter Pat, 3-1/2" d	12.00	
Cake Stand, hs, 9-1/2", 10" or 11-3/4" d	65.00-90.00	—
Celery Tray, curled edges	30.00	—
Champagne, cupped or saucer bowl	40.00	—
Champagne Tumbler	24.00	—
Child's Butter Dish, cov	130.00	—
Child's Creamer	60.00	110.00
Child's Honey Jug	48.00	95.00
Child's Rose Bowl	36.00	72.00
Child's Spooner	55.00	115.00
Child's Sugar Bowl, cov	130.00	—
Claret	42.00	
Compote, cov, hs	65.00	—
Compote, open, scalloped rim, 7-3/4" d, 7" h; 8" d, 7" h; or 9-14" d, 8" h	36.00-48.00	65.00-85.00
Cordial	42.00	90.00
Creamer, individual, barrel or oval shape	24.00	60.00
Creamer, table size	42.00	75.00
Cruet, os	55.00	165.00
Egg Cup	24.00	—
Epergne, silver plated foot	180.00	—
Finger Bowl	30.00	90.00
Fruit Bowl, 10" d, 3" h	30.00	100.00
Goblet	42.00	85.00
Jelly Compote, open, 4-1/2" d	36.00	65.00
Lamp Shade, electric	42.00	85.00
Lamp Shade, gas	42.00	100.00
Mustard, cov, notched lid	48.00	—
Nappy, flat, handle, round, 5" d or 6-1/4" d	18.00	36.00
Nappy, flat, handle, triangular, 5" w or 6-1/4" w	18.00	36.00
Olive Dish, turned up sides, scalloped rim, 5" l	18.00	36.00
Pickle Dish, flat, round or square	24.00	48.00
Pitcher, milk, quart, bulbous	60.00	120.00
Pitcher, water, half gallon, straight sides, plain rim	115.00	240.00
Pitcher, water, half gallon, straight sides, silver plated rim	124.00	248.00
Pitcher, water, half gallon, tankard	120.00	240.00
Plate, 5", 6", 6-1/2", 7" or 7-1/2" d or 8" d φ	5.00-24.00	—
Pomade Jar, orig sterling silver lid	42.00	
Puff Jar, cov	42.00	—
Punch Bowl, flat φ	240.00	—
Punch Bowl, stand	295.00	—
Punch Cup φ	12.00	—
Relish Tray	12.50	
Rose Bowl	30.00	60.00
Salt, individual, oval or round	5.00	24.00
Salt, master, oval or round	30.00	75.00
Salt Shaker, bulbous or pyramid,, 2-1/2" h	30.00	60.00
Salt Shaker, straight sides, 2-1/2" h	42.00	
Sandwich Tray, handle, silver plate foot, 11-1/2" d	55.00	—
Sauce, collared, 5-3/4" d; or flat, 3-1/4", 4-1/4" or 5-1/2" d	12.00	24.00
Sherry, flared or straight	42.00	—
Spooner	30.00	
Sugar Bowl, cov	42.00	75.00
Syrup, metal lid	75.00	
Toothpick Holder	42.00	130.00
Tumbler, bar	30.00	
Tumbler, water	36.00	48.00

Items	Clear	Ruby Stained
Vase, bulbous, 9-3/4" h	24.00	—
Vase, trumpet shape, scalloped rim, 6-1/2", 8" h φ or 10" h	24.00-30.00	—
Wine	36.00	75.00

Marsh Fern

Made by Riverside Glass Works, Wellsburg, WV, c1889. Made in clear. Some items are found with copper wheel engraving.

Items	Clear
Bowl, flat, 7-1/2" d	36.00
Butter Dish, cov	48.00
Cake Stand, hs, 9-3/8" d	60.00
Celery Vase	55.00
Compote, cov, hs, 7-1/4" d	90.00
Compote, cov, ls, 6-1/8" d	85.00
Compote, open, hs, 6-1/8" d	90.00
Creamer	42.00
Goblet	48.00
Jelly Compote	36.00
Pitcher, water	95.00
Sauce, 4-1/4" d	12.00
Spooner	42.00
Sugar Bowl, cov	42.00

Maryland

Inverted Loop and Fan, Loop and Diamond, US Glass Pattern Line No. 15,049

Manufactured originally by Bryce Bros., Pittsburgh, PA. Continued by United States Glass Company, Pittsburgh, PA, as one of its States patterns. Made in non-flint, clear, clear with gilt trim, ruby stained.

Items	Clear, Gilt Trim	Ruby Stained
Banana Dish	42.00	100.00
Berry Bowl, master, 8" d	18.00	42.00
Bowl, 6" d	18.00	42.00
Bowl, 7" d	18.00	—
Bread Plate	30.00	—
Butter Dish, cov	75.00	115.00
Cake Stand, hs, 8" or 10" d	48.00-60.00	—
Celery Tray	24.00	42.00
Celery Vase	30.00	75.00
Compote, cov, hs, 6" d	30.00	—
Compote, cov, hs, 8" d	75.00	120.00
Compote, open, deep, 6" or 8" d	24.00-36.00	65.00-75.00
Compote, open, saucer bowl, 7" or 8" d	30.00-36.00	—
Creamer	30.00	65.00
Custard Cup	24.00	—
Goblet	36.00	50.00
Honey Dish, flat, 3" d	36.00	50.00
Jelly Compote, open	30.00	55.00
Olive, handle	18.00	—
Pickle, oval, flat, handle	24.00	42.00
Pitcher, milk, quart	55.00	110.00
Pitcher, water, half gallon	60.00	120.00
Plate, 7" d	30.00	—
Preserve Dish, 8" d	24.00	—
Relish, oval	18.00	40.00
Salt Shaker, single	36.00	—
Sauce, flat	12.00	18.00
Spooner	36.00	65.00
Sugar Bowl, cov	55.00	72.00
Sweetmeat, cov, 7" d	48.00	—
Toothpick Holder	130.00	190.00
Tumbler, flat	30.00	60.00
Wine	48.00	90.00

Mascotte

Dominion, Etched Fern and Waffle, Minor Block

Manufactured by Ripley and Company, Pittsburgh, PA, in the 1880s. Reissued by United States Glass Company, Pittsburgh, PA, in 1891. The butter dish shown on Plate 77 of Ruth Well Lee's Victorian Glass is said to go with this pattern. It has a horseshoe finial and was named for the famous "Maude S., Queen of the

Turf" trotting horse during the 1880s. Apothecary jar and pyramid jars were made by Tiffin Glass Co in the 1950s. Made in non-flint, clear, and clear with copper wheel etching of a fern spray. Some rare amber, blue, and milk glass pieces are known.

Items	Clear	Etched
Banana Stand, hs	36.00	72.00
Bowl, cov, 5", 6", 7", 8" or 9" d	36.00-55.00	42.00-65.00
Bowl, open, flared, 5", 6", 7", 8" or 9" d	24.00-42.00	30.00-48.00
Bowl, open, straight sides, 5", 6", 7", 8" or 9" d	18.00-36.00	24.00-42.00
Butter Dish, cov, "Maude S"	120.00	140.00
Butter Dish, cov, regular	60.00	75.00
Butter Pat	18.00	24.00
Cake Basket, handle	95.00	125.00
Cake Stand, hs, 8", 9", 10" or 11" d	36.00-55.00	55.00-72.00
Celery Tray	42.00	48.00
Celery Vase	42.00	48.00
Cheese, cov	85.00	95.00
Compote, cov, hs, 5", 7" or 9" d	42.00-75.00	48.00-110.00
Compote, open, hs, flared, 5", 6", 7", 8" or 9" d	24.00-36.00	30.00-42.00
Compote, open, hs, straight, 5", 6", 7", 8" or 9" d	24.00-36.00	30.00-42.00
Creamer	36.00	55.00
Finger Bowl	30.00	42.00
Goblet	48.00	55.00
Honey Dish, flat, 3-1/2" d	12.00	18.00
Jelly Compote, hs	30.00	36.00
Pitcher, water	65.00	75.00
Plate, turned in sides	48.00	55.00
Pyramid Jar, 7" d, one fits into other and forms tall jar-type container with lid, three sizes with flat separators ϕ	60.00	65.00
Salt, individual	30.00	—
Salt, master	36.00	48.00
Salt Shaker, orig top	30.00	55.00
Sauce, flat, 4" d	10.00	18.00
Sauce, footed, 4" d	15.00	20.00
Spooner	36.00	42.00
Sugar Bowl, cov	48.00	55.00
Tumbler	24.00	35.00
Water Tray	48.00	65.00
Wine	30.00	36.00

Masonic

Inverted Prism

Manufactured by McKee & Brothers Glass Company, Jeannette, PA, c1894-1920. Made in non-flint, clear. Rare pieces are found in emerald green (add 50%) and in ruby stained (100%).

Items	Clear
Bowl, sq or round, 4", 4-1/2", 5", 6", 7" or 8"d	24.00-36.00
Butter Dish, cov, flat or footed	55.00-72.00
Cake Stand, hs, 9" or 10" d	42.00-48.00
Celery Tray	24.00
Compote, cov, 8" d	55.00
Compote, open, 8-1/2" d	42.00
Creamer	30.00
Cruet	42.00
Custard Cup	18.00
Goblet	30.00
Honey Dish, cov, flat, sq	48.00
Nappy, heart shape	36.00
Pitcher, water, tankard	72.00
Relish, serpentine shape	18.00
Salad Bowl, sq or round, silver frame, 9"	55.00
Salt, individual, round or square	18.00
Salt Shaker, round	18.00
Salt Shaker, square	30.00
Sardine Box, rect, flat	30.00
Spooner	30.00
Syrup, jug	90.00
Sugar Bowl, cov	48.00
Toothpick Holder	36.00
Tumbler	18.00
Wine	24.00

Massachusetts

Arched Diamond Points, Cane Variant, Geneva #2, MR-131, Star and Diamonds

Manufactured in the 1880s by an unknown maker. Reissued in1898 by United States Glass Company, Pittsburgh, PA, as one of the States series. Made in non-flint, clear. A vase ($55) and wine ($55) are known in emerald green. Some pieces reported in cobalt blue and marigold carnival glass.

Reproductions: Reproduced butter dish in clear and colors.

Items	Clear
Almond Dish, flat, 5" l	24.00
Bar Bottle, metal shot glass for cover	90.00
Basket, 4-1/2", ah	60.00
Bon Bon, flat, 5" d	60.00
Bowl, sq, folded, pointed or straight sides, 6", 7", 8" or 9" w	18.00-24.00
Brandy Bottle	55.00
Butter Dish, cov φ	60.00
Candy Dish, flat, 8" l or 9" l	24.00
Celery Tray	36.00
Celery Vase	36.00
Champagne	42.00
Claret	42.00
Cocktail	42.00
Cologne Bottle, os	37.50
Compote, open, ls, cupped bowl	42.00
Condiment Set, cruet, mustard, salt shaker, tray	130.00
Cordial	65.00
Creamer, individual, medium or table	24.00-36.00
Cruet, os	55.00
Custard Cup	18.00
Decanter, os	65.00
Goblet	55.00
Gravy Boat	36.00
Hot Whiskey, stem	42.00
Juice Tumbler	30.00
Lamp, oil, orig globe, burner, and chimney, banquet size	760.00
Lamp, oil, orig globe, burner, and chimney, table size	950.00
Lemonade Tumbler, flared rim or straight sides	42.00
Mayonnaise, handle, flat	24.00
Mug, handle, small or large	24.00-30.00
Mustard Jar, cov	42.00
Olive, 6" or 8-1/2" l	8.50-15.00
Orange Tray, 9" l	42.00
Pin Tray, 5" sq	30.00
Pitcher, water, half gallon, squatty or tankard	75.00-90.00
Plate, sq, 8" w	40.00
Punch Cup	18.00
Relish Tray, 4-1/2" l, 2-3/4" w or 5-1/2" l, 3-3/4"	18.00-24.00
Rum Jug, small, medium or large	110.00
Salt Shaker, large, square; small, bulbous; or tall, round	30.00
Sauce, oval or square, 4"	18.00
Sherry	48.00
Shot Glass	18.00
Spooner, two handles	24.00
Spoon Tray, rolled sides	30.00
Sugar Bowl, cov, individual or table	30.00-48.00
Syrup	75.00
Tabasco Sauce	55.00
Toast Tray	30.00
Toothpick Holder	48.00
Tumbler, soda or pony beer, flared rim, or straight sides	42.00
Tumbler, water, round or square	48.00
Vase, trumpet, 6-1/2", 7" or 9" h	30.00-42.00
Water Bottle	42.00
Whiskey	30.00
Wine, round or square bowl	48.00
Wine Bottle	75.00

Medallion

Hearts and Spades, Spades

Manufacturer unknown, c1880. Made in non-flint, amber, apple green, blue, canary-yellow, and clear.

Reproductions: Imperial Glass Company, Bellaire, OH, has reproduced the butter dish. These reproductions can be easily detected: often the design is reversed, new colors are harsh, and the "I.G." monogram can be found on the base.

Items	Amber	Apple Green	Blue	Canary Yellow	Clear
Butter Dish, cov φ	48.00	60.00	60.00	48.00	42.00
Cake Stand, hs, 9-1/4" d	55.00	65.00	65.00	55.00	30.00

Items	Amber	Apple Green	Blue	Canary Yellow	Clear
Castor Bottle	75.00	65.00	65.00	75.00	48.00
Celery Vase	36.00	48.00	48.00	36.00	24.00
Compote, cov, hs	60.00	72.00	72.00	60.00	48.00
Compote, open, hs	48.00	60.00	60.00	48.00	36.00
Creamer	48.00	55.00	55.00	48.00	36.00
Egg Cup	30.00	48.00	48.00	30.00	24.00
Goblet	42.00	55.00	55.00	42.00	24.00
Pickle	24.00	30.00	30.00	24.00	18.00
Pitcher, water	65.00	75.00	75.00	65.00	55.00
Relish Tray	24.00	30.00	30.00	24.00	18.00
Sauce, flat, 4" d	15.00	18.00	18.00	15.00	12.00
Sauce, footed, 4" d	18.00	24.00	24.00	18.00	15.00
Spooner	30.00	48.00	48.00	30.00	24.00
Sugar Bowl, cov	48.00	60.00	60.00	48.00	30.00
Tumbler	30.00	42.00	42.00	30.00	18.00
Waste Bowl	40.00	55.00	55.00	40.00	24.00
Water Tray	65.00	75.00	75.00	65.00	48.00
Wine	36.00	48.00	48.00	36.00	24.00

Melrose

Diamond Beaded Band

Manufactured by Greensburg Glass Company, Greensburg, PA, in 1887. Reissued by Brilliant Glass Company, 1887-88; McKee & Brothers, Pittsburgh, PA, c1901; J. B. Higbee Company, Bridgeport, PA, c1907; Dugan Glass Company, (Diamond Glassware Company), Indiana, PA, c1915, and New Martinsville Glass Company, New Martinsville, WV, in 1916. Made in non-flint, clear, etched, and ruby stained. Select forms found in chocolate. Add 20% for copper wheel etching.

Items	Clear
Berry Bowl	24.00
Butter Dish, cov	55.00
Cake Plate	36.00
Cake Stand, hs	40.00
Celery Vase	30.00
Compote, cov, hs, 8" d	58.00
Compote, open, hs, 6", 7" or 9" d	24.00-36.00
Creamer, tankard	36.00
Goblet	24.00
Jelly Compote, open	24.00
Mug	18.00
Pitcher, milk, ah, bulbous, quart or half gallon	36.00-65.00
Pitcher, milk, ah, tankard, quart or half gallon	42.00-72.00
Plate, 7" d	18.00
Plate, 8" d	12.00
Salt, individual	10.00
Salt Shaker	18.00
Sauce, flat	10.00
Spooner	36.00
Sugar Bowl, cov	45.00
Tumbler	18.00
Waste Bowl	24.00
Water Tray, 11-1/2" d	55.00
Wine	24.00

Michigan

Loop and Pillar, Paneled Jewel, US Glass Pattern Line No. 15,072

Manufactured by United States Glass Company, Pittsburgh, PA, c1902, as one of the States pattern series. Made in non-flint, clear, and rose stained. The 10-1/4" bowl ($45) and punch cup ($15) are found with yellow or blue stain. Also found with painted carnations. Other colors include "Sunrise," gold, and ruby stained.

Reproductions: The toothpick holder has been reproduced by the Degenhart Glass Company, Cambridge, OH. It created a new mold and used new colors.

Items	Clear	Rose Stained
Bowl, deep, 6", 7" or 8-1/2" d	12.00-24.00	30.00-42.00
Bowl, flared rim, shallow, 5", 7-1/2", 8-1/2" or 10" d	12.00-30.00	30.00-48.00
Bowl, straight sided, shallow, 6" or 7" d	12.00-18.00	30.00-36.00
Bride's Basket, silver plated holder	72.00	130.00
Butter Dish, cov, quarter pound	75.00	—
Butter Dish, cov, table size	72.00	130.00
Candlestick	90.00	—
Celery Vase	48.00	100.00
Child's Butter Dish, cov	180.00	325.00
Child's Creamer	45.00	90.00

Items	Clear	Rose Stained
Child's Nappy, handle	36.00	—
Child's Pitcher, water	30.00	75.00
Child's Spooner	50.00	100.00
Child's Stein, 2-3/4" h	55.00	—
Child's Sugar Bowl, cov	70.00	140.00
Child's Tumbler	24.00	—
Compote, cov, hs, deep bowl, 5" d	60.00	100.00
Compote, open, hs, deep bowl, straight sided, 6" or 8" d	30.00-42.00	48.00-60.00
Compote, open, hs, flared bowl, shallow, 7-1/2" or 9-1/4" d	50.00-65.00	90.00-100.00
Creamer, individual, 6 oz, tankard	24.00	75.00
Creamer, table	36.00	60.00
Cruet, os	72.00	180.00
Crushed Fruit Bowl	90.00	—
Custard Cup	18.00	—
Dish, flat, oval, 7-1/2", 9-1/2", 10-1/2" or 12-1/2" l	18.00-30.00	—
Finger Bowl	18.00	—
Goblet	42.00	75.00
Honey Dish	12.00	—
Jelly Compote, 4-1/2" d	40.00	75.00
Lemonade Mug	30.00	48.00
Nappy, Gainsborough handle	42.00	—
Olive, two handles	12.00	30.00
Pickle Dish, oval, 2 handles	15.00	24.00
Pitcher, milk, quart, 8" h	60.00	—
Pitcher, water, three pints, helmet shape	72.00	—
Pitcher, water, half gallon, tankard, 12" h	85.00	180.00
Plate, 5-1/2" d	18.00	—
Punch Bowl, 8" d	60.00	—
Punch Cup	10.00	—
Relish Tray	24.00	42.00
Salt Shaker, single, 3 types	24.00	36.00
Sauce, flat, flared or straight sided, 4" d or 4-1/2" d	15.00	25.00
Sauce, footed, 4" d or 4-1/2" d	18.00	30.00
Sherbet Cup, handled	18.00	24.00
Spooner	50.00	80.00
Sugar Bowl, cov, table	60.00	90.00
Sugar Bowl, open, individual	18.00	—
Syrup	115.00	190.00
Toothpick Holder φ	55.00	120.00
Tumbler	36.00	48.00
Vase, bud, 8" or 12" h	42.00	48.00
Vase, bud, 16" or 17" h	48.00	—
Vase, ftd, 6" or 8" h	48.00-55.00	—
Wine	42.00	60.00

Minerva

Roman Medallion

Manufacture unknown, c1870, as well as other American companies. Shards have been found at Burlington Glass Works, Hamilton, Ontario, Canada. Made in non-flint, clear.

Items	Clear
Bowl, footed, 8" d	42.00
Bowl, rectangular, 7", 8" or 9" l	30.00-55.00
Bread Plate	75.00
Butter Dish, cov	90.00
Cake Stand, hs, 8" d	180.00
Cake Stand, hs, 9" d, 6-1/2" h; 10-1/2" d or 13" d	120.00-155.00
Champagne	100.00
Compote, cov, hs, 6" or 8" d	100.00-180.00
Compote, cov, ls, 7" or 8" d	110.00-130.00
Compote, open, hs, 10-1/2" d, octagonal base	115.00
Creamer	55.00
Goblet	85.00
Honey Dish, 3-1/2" d	12.00
Marmalade Jar, cov	180.00
Pickle Dish, oval, "Love's Request is Pickles"	30.00
Pitcher, milk, quart	190.00
Pitcher, water, half gallon, scalloped rim	200.00
Plate, 8" or 9" d or 20" d, handle	65.00-72.00
Platter, oval, 13" l	75.00
Sauce, flat or footed, 4-1/4" d or 4-1/2" d	18.50-24.00
Spooner	48.00
Sugar Bowl, cov	75.00
Waste Bowl	60.00

Minnesota

Muchness, US Glass Pattern Line No. 15,055

Manufactured by the United States Glass Company, Pittsburgh, PA, in the late 1890s, at Factory "F" and Factory "G." It is one of the States series patterns. Made in non-flint, clear, and ruby stained. Some pieces have gilt trim. A two-piece flower frog has been found in emerald green ($50).

Items	Clear	Ruby Stained
Almond Dish, oblong, pointed ends	18.00	—
Banana Stand	75.00	—
Basket, ah	75.00	—
Biscuit Jar, cov	65.00	180.00
Bon Bon, 5" l	18.00	
Bowl, boat shape, pointed ends, 5", 6", 7" or 8" l	18.00-30.00	—
Bowl, flared, round, 6", 7" or 8-1/2" d	18.00-36.00	—
Bowl, oval, 9-1/2" or 10" d	30.00	—
Bowl, square, 6" or 8" w	18.00-30.00	—
Bread Tray, 13" l	42.00	—
Butter Dish, cov	60.00	—
Candy Dish, cov, scalloped sides, pointed ends, 7" l or 8" l	24.00	—
Carafe	42.00	—
Celery Tray, oblong, 13" l; or square, 10" w	30.00	—
Cheese Plate, 7" d, turned up serrated sides	18.00	—
Compote, open, hs, deep, flared bowl, 7-1/2", 8-1/2", 9-1/2" or 10" d	55.00-72.00	—
Compote, open, hs, straight-sided bowl, 6", 7" or 8" d	42.00-55.00	—
Compote, open, hs, square, deep bowl, 6",7" or 8" d	42.00-55.00	—
Compote, open, hs, square, shallow bowl, folded sides, 8", 9" or 10" d	55.00-65.00	—
Compote, open, ls, square, 6", 8", 9" or 10" w	30.00-65.00	—
Condiment Set, cruet, salt & pepper shakers, tray	90.00	—
Confection Dish, cov, scalloped sides, pointed ends, 5" l	24.00	—
Cracker Jar, cov	65.00	—
Creamer, individual or table	24.00-36.00	—
Cruet, os	42.00	—
Crushed Fruit Jar, cov	100.00	
Custard Cup	15.00	—
Fruit Plate, 8" d, serrated rim	24.00	—
Goblet	42.00	60.00
Hair Receiver	36.00	—
Humidor, jeweled silver plate lid	180.00	—
Juice Glass	24.00	—
Lemonade Mug, ph	18.00	—
Match Safe	30.00	—
Mint Tray, 6" d	18.00	—
Mug	30.00	—
Olive Dish, 5" l or 6" l	18.00	30.00
Orange Tray, 10" l	55.00	—
Pickle Dish, 7-1/2" l	18.00	
Pitcher, water, ah, bulbous, half gallon	120.00	—
Pitcher, water, ah, bulbous, three-quarter gallon	118.00	—
Pitcher, water, ah, tankard	100.00	240.00
Plate, 5" d, turned up edges	30.00	—
Plate, 7-3/8" d	18.00	—
Pomade Jar, cov	42.00	—
Preserve Dish, rect, 9" l	24.00	—
Relish Tray	24.00	—
Salt Shaker	30.00	—
Sauce, boat shape, flared, square, or straight sided	12.00	30.00
Spooner	30.00	—
Spoon Tray, 8" l, folded sides	24.00	—
Sugar Bowl, cov	42.00	—
Sweetmeat, hs, 7-1/2" d	55.00	—
Syrup	75.00	—
Toothpick Holder, 3 handles	36.00	95.00
Tray, 8" l	18.00	—
Tumbler	24.00	—
Water Tray	55.00	—
Wine	48.00	—

Missouri

Palm and Scroll, Palm Leaf and Scroll, US Glass Pattern Line No. 15,058

Manufactured by the United States Glass Company, Pittsburgh, PA, c1898, as one of the States series patterns. Made in non-flint, clear, and emerald green. Also made in amethyst, blue, and canary.

Items	Clear	Emerald Green
Bowl, cov, 6", 7" or 8" d	42.00-60.00	—
Bowl, open, 6", 7" or 8" d	18.00-36.00	36.00-48.00
Butter Dish, cov	55.00	75.00

Items	Clear	Emerald Green
Cake Stand, hs, 8", 9", 10" or 11" d	48.00-65.00	60.00-75.00
Celery Vase	36.00	—
Compote, cov, hs, 5", 6", 7" or 8" d	42.00-60.00	—
Compote, open, hs, deep bowl, 5", 6", 7" or 8" d	30.00-55.00	—
Compote, open, hs, saucer bowl 8", 9" or 10" d	55.00-72.00	—
Cordial	42.00	72.00
Creamer	30.00	48.00
Cruet, os	65.00	120.00
Dish, cov, 6" d	75.00	90.00
Doughnut Stand, hs, 6" d	48.00	65.00
Goblet	60.00	72.00
Jelly Compote, cov, hs, 5" d, notched or plain lid	42.00	65.00
Mug	42.00	55.00
Olive Dish	18.00	30.00
Pickle Dish, rect	18.00	30.00
Pitcher, milk	48.00	100.00
Pitcher, water	90.00	100.00
Relish Dish	12.00	25.00
Salt Shaker, single	42.00	55.00
Sauce, flat, 4" d	12.00	20.00
Spooner	30.00	45.00
Sugar Bowl, cov	60.00	75.00
Syrup	100.00	190.00
Tumbler	36.00	48.00
Wine	48.00	55.00

Mitered Diamond

Pyramid, Sunken Buttons

Manufacturer unknown, believed to be of Ohio origin. Made in 1889-90. Made in amber, apple green, blue, clear, and vaseline.

Items	Amber	Apple Green	Blue	Clear	Vaseline
Bowl, square, 8" w	24.00	28.00	24.00	20.00	24.00
Bread Plate	42.00	48.00	42.00	35.00	42.00
Butter, cov	72.00	80.00	75.00	65.00	75.00
Celery Tray	30.00	36.00	36.00	24.00	36.00
Compote, ls, collared base, cov	72.00	75.00	72.00	65.00	72.00
Compote, ls, collared base, open	48.00	60.00	55.00	36.00	60.00
Creamer	36.00	48.00	42.00	30.00	42.00
Goblet	36.00	48.00	42.00	30.00	48.00
Pickle	24.00	30.00	30.00	18.00	30.00
Pitcher, water	65.00	72.00	72.00	60.00	72.00
Platter	42.00	48.00	42.00	36.00	42.00
Relish	24.00	30.00	30.00	18.00	30.00
Salt Shaker, orig top	24.00	36.00	30.00	18.00	30.00
Sauce, sq, flat	12.00	18.00	12.00	12.00	18.00
Spooner	36.00	36.00	36.00	30.00	36.00
Sugar, cov	55.00	72.00	60.00	45.00	60.00
Tumbler	28.00	35.00	30.00	24.00	30.00
Wine	55.00	42.00	42.00	36.00	42.00

Moon and Star

Bull's Eye and Star, Palace, Star and Punty

Manufactured first by Adams & Company, Pittsburgh, PA, during the 1880s, and later by several manufacturers, including Pioneer Glass, which probably decorated ruby-stained examples. Reissued by the United States Glass Company, Pittsburgh, PA, c1890-1898. Made in non-flint, clear and frosted, and clear with ruby stain. Also found with frosted highlights. Add 30% for frosted values.

Reproductions: Heavily reproduced in clear and color as early as the 1930s. L. G. Wright Company, New Martinsville, WV, made several new forms in colors. L. E. Smith Glass Company, Mt. Pleasant, PA, joined L. G. Wright in using both original and new molds. The Sturbridge Yankee Workshop, Sturbridge, MA, reissued the goblet in amber and ruby, using the original mold. Weishar Enterprises, Wheeling, WV, reproduced forms from this pattern c1991, as well as creating new forms based on the pattern design.

Items	Clear	Ruby Stained
Banana Stand φ	110.00	—
Bowl, cov, flat, flared rim, 6", 7" or 8" d; or 10" d φ	42.00-55.00	72.00-90.00
Bowl, open, flat, flared rim, 6" or 7" d, 8" d φ or 10" d	24.00-42.00	60.00-100.00
Bread Plate, rect	55.00	130.00
Butter Dish, cov φ	85.00	—
Cake Stand, hs, 9" d φ or 10" d	55.00-60.00	—
Carafe φ	48.00	—
Celery Vase	42.00	—

Items	Clear	Ruby Stained
Champagne φ	90.00	120.00
Claret	55.00	—
Compote, cov, collared base, scalloped rim, 6", 7", 8" or 10" d	65.00-75.00	110.00-120.00
Compote, cov, hs, 6", 7" d φ or 8" d φ	72.00-85.00	110.00-135.00
Compote, cov, hs, 10" d φ	90.00	118.00
Compote, cov, ls, 6-1/2" d φ	65.00	110.00
Compote, open, collared base, deep bowl 6", 7", 8" or 10" d	30.00-48.00	55.00-72.00
Compote, open, collared base, flared, scalloped bowl, 5-1/2", 7-1/2", 8-1/2", 10-1/2" d φ or 11-1/2" d	30.00-55.00	55.00-75.00
Compote, open, hs, scalloped bowl, 7-1/2", 9" or 12-1/2" d	48.00-65.00	72.00-85.00
Compote, open, ls, scalloped bowl, 7-1/2" d	30.00	55.00
Creamer φ	65.00	100.00
Cruet, os φ	130.00	—
Egg Cup φ	42.00	72.00
Fruit Bowl, 12-1/2" d, scalloped	55.00	100.00
Goblet φ	55.00	75.00
Lamp, oil, orig burner φ	148.00	—
Pickle Tray, oval	24.00	—
Pitcher, water, ah φ	190.00	260.00
Preserve Dish, rect	24.00	48.00
Relish Tray φ	24.00	48.00
Salad Bowl, 12-1/2" d, scalloped	55.00	100.00
Salt, individual φ	12.00	30.00
Salt and Pepper Shakers, pr φ	85.00	115.00
Sauce, flat, 4" d or 4-1/2" d	8.00	24.00
Sauce, footed, 4" d or 4-1/2" d φ	15.00	30.00
Spooner φ	55.00	75.00
Sugar Bowl, cov φ	75.00	110.00
Syrup, orig top φ	180.00	—
Tumbler, flat φ	55.00	75.00
Tumbler, ftd φ	60.00	85.00
Waste Bowl	75.00	110.00
Water Tray	75.00	—
Wine φ	72.00	100.00

Nail

Recessed Pillar-Red Top, Recessed Pillar-Thumbprint Band, US Glass Pattern Line No. 15,002

Manufactured by Ripley and Company, Pittsburgh, PA, c1892. Reissued by United States Glass Company, Pittsburgh, PA. Made in non-flint, clear and clear with ruby stain. Pieces can be found plain or with copper wheel engraving.

Items	Clear	Ruby Stained
Berry Bowl	30.00	55.00
Butter Dish, cov	55.00	115.00
Celery Vase	75.00	130.00
Claret	42.00	—
Compote, cov, hs, 8"d	55.00	95.00
Creamer	36.00	72.00
Cruet, os	72.00	160.00
Finger Bowl	36.00	—
Goblet	42.00	75.00
Jelly Compote, open, hs	24.00	48.00
Mustard, cov	60.00	115.00
Pitcher, water	90.00	230.00
Sauce, flat or footed	18.00	36.00
Spooner	30.00	55.00
Sugar Bowl, cov	48.00	95.00
Sugar Shaker, orig top	120.00	190.00
Syrup, orig top	90.00	130.00
Tumbler	24.00	48.00
Vase, 7" h	18.00	—
Waste Bowl	36.00	—
Water Tray	55.00	—
Wine	42.00	85.00

Nailhead

Gem

Manufactured by Bryce, Higbee and Company, Pittsburgh, PA, c1885. Shards have been found at Boston and Sandwich Glass Company, Sandwich, MA. Made in non-flint, clear. Also found in ruby stained (Goblet at $48, pitcher at $75).

Items	Clear
Bowl, 6" d	18.00
Bread Plate, 9" d	24.00

Items	Clear
Butter Dish, cov	48.00
Cake Stand, hs, 9-1/2" or 10-1/2" d	36.00-42.00
Celery Vase	36.00
Compote, cov, hs, 6", 7" or 8" d	48.00-55.00
Compote, cov, ls, 7" d	55.00
Compote, open, hs, 6-1/2" or 9-1/2" d	30.00-48.00
Cordial	30.00
Creamer	30.00
Goblet	30.00
Pitcher, water	42.00
Plate, sq, 7" w	18.00
Relish, 8-3/4" l, 5-1/4" w	12.00
Sauce, flat	12.00
Spooner	30.00
Sugar Bowl, cov	48.00
Tumbler	30.00
Wine	24.00

Nestor

Manufactured by Dugan, Indiana, PA, 1903. Made in non-flint, amethyst, blue, clear, and green. Decorated with enamel.

Items	Amethyst	Blue	Clear	Green
Berry Bowl	55.00	55.00	30.00	36.00
Butter Dish, cov	65.00	65.00	42.00	48.00
Cake Plate	65.00	65.00	42.00	48.00
Creamer	65.00	65.00	42.00	48.00
Cruet, os	72.00	72.00	48.00	55.00
Jelly Compote, open, 5" d or 6" d	72.00	72.00	48.00	55.00
Pitcher, water	85.00	85.00	60.00	65.00
Salt and Pepper Shakers, pair	85.00	85.00	60.00	65.00
Spooner	60.00	60.00	36.00	42.00
Sugar Bowl, cov	65.00	65.00	42.00	48.00
Toothpick Holder	60.00	60.00	36.00	42.00
Tumbler	72.00	72.00	48.00	55.00

Nevada

US Glass Pattern Line No. 15,075

Manufactured by United States Glass Company, Pittsburgh, PA, c1902, as part of the States pattern series. Made in non-flint, clear. Pieces are sometimes partly frosted and have enamel decoration. Add 20% for frosted forms.

Items	Clear
Biscuit Jar, cov	55.00
Bowl, cov, 6", 7" or 8" d	42.00-55.00
Bowl, open, 6", 7" or 8" d	24.00-30.00
Butter Dish, cov	72.00
Cake Stand, hs, 10" d	42.00
Celery Vase	30.00
Compote, cov, hs, 6", 7" or 8" d	48.00-65.00
Compote, open, hs, 6", 7" or 8" d	24.00-42.00
Creamer	36.00
Cruet	42.00
Custard Cup	15.00
Finger Bowl	30.00
Jug	42.00
Nappy, ftd, ah	24.00
Pickle Dish, oval	12.00
Pitcher, water, bulbous	60.00
Pitcher, water, tankard	55.00
Salt, individual or master	18.00-24.00
Salt Shaker, table size	18.00
Sauce, flat, 4" d, 4-1/2" d, or 5" d	12.00
Spooner, pedestal	42.00
Sugar Bowl, cov	42.00
Syrup, orig tin top	55.00
Toothpick Holder	48.00
Tumbler	18.00

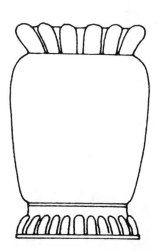

New England Pineapple

Loop and Jewel, Pineapple, Sawtooth

Manufacture attributed to Boston and Sandwich Glass Company, Sandwich, MA, or New England Glass Company, Cambridge, MA, in the early 1860s. Made in flint, and non-flint, clear, and opaque white. Rare in color.

Reproductions: Reproductions known in clear, color, and milk glass with gilt trim. The Fenton Art Glass Company, Williamstown, WV, first started reproducing the goblet about 1950, and later included a sherbet, wine, and open compote with a ruffled trim. Glasscrafts and Ceramics, Inc., Yonkers, New York, made a reproduction goblet in 1953 in clear, non-flint.

Items	Flint	Non-Flint
Berry Bowl, scalloped, 8" d	100.00	—
Butter Dish, cov	260.00	—
Cake Stand	142.00	—
Castor Bottle	60.00	—
Castor Set, 4 bottles, complete	360.00	—
Champagne	190.00	—
Compote, cov, hs, 5" or 8" d	190.00-230.00	—
Compote, open, hs, 7" or 8-1/2" d	110.00-130.00	—
Compote, open, ls, 7" or 8-1/2" d	110.00-120.00	—
Cordial	190.00	—
Creamer, ah, 6" h or 7" h	200.00	85.00
Cruet, ah, os, 2 styles	190.00	—
Decanter, os, pint or quart	230.00	—
Egg Cup	60.00	30.00
Fruit Bowl	90.00	—
Goblet, lady's	120.00	—
Goblet, regular φ	75.00	35.00
Honey Dish, 3-1/2" d	18.00	—
Mug, ah	115.00	—
Pitcher, milk, ah, quart	660.00	—
Pitcher, water, ah, half gallon	360.00	—
Plate, 6" d	110.00	—
Salt, individual	30.00	—
Salt, master	55.00	35.00
Sauce, flat	18.00	12.00
Sauce, footed	30.00	—
Spill Holder	72.00	—
Spooner	72.00	35.00
Sugar Bowl, cov, low foot	180.00	65.00
Sugar Bowl, cov, high foot	175.00	80.00
Sweetmeat, cov, hs	230.00	—
Tumbler, bar	130.00	—
Tumbler, water	100.00	—
Whiskey, ah	155.00	—
Wine φ	180.00	—

New Hampshire

Bent Buckle, Maiden's Blush, Modiste, Red Loop and Fine Cut, US Glass Pattern No. 15,084

Manufactured by United States Glass Company, Pittsburgh, PA, c1903, as one of the States pattern series. Made in non-flint, clear, clear with gilt trim, rose stained, and ruby stained.

Items	Clear with Gilt Trim	Rose Stained	Ruby Stained
Biscuit Jar, cov	90.00	—	—
Bowl, flared, 5-1/2" d	12.00	—	30.00
Bowl, flared, 6-1/2" d	18.00	42.00	—
Bowl, flared, 7-1/2" d	24.00	48.00	—
Bowl, flared, 8-1/2" d	18.00	30.00	—
Bowl, straight-sides, 6-1/2" d	18.00	42.00	—
Bowl, straight-sides, 7-1/2" d	24.00	48.00	—
Bowl, straight sides, 9-1/2" d	30.00	55.00	—
Bowl, square, 6-1/2" w	18.00	42.00	—
Bowl, square, 7-1/2" w	24.00	36.00	—
Bowl, square, 8-1/2" w	30.00	55.00	—
Butter Dish, cov	55.00	85.00	—
Cake Stand, hs, 8-1/4" d	36.00	—	—
Carafe	72.00	—	—
Celery Vase	42.00	60.00	—
Compote, cov, hs, 5", 6", 7" or 8" d	60.00-90.00	—	—
Compote, open, flared rim, 7", 8" or 9" d	42.00-55.00	60.00-72.00	—
Creamer, breakfast, individual or table	24.00-36.00	36.00-55.00	—
Cruet, os	65.00	120.00	—
Custard Cup	12.00	18.00	—
Goblet	30.00	55.00	—
Jug, ph, 3 pints	100.00	—	—
Lemonade Mug	18.00	24.00	—
Mug, large	24.00	55.00	60.00

Items	Clear with Gilt Trim	Rose Stained	Ruby Stained
Olive Dish, diamond shape, 6-3/4" l	24.00	42.00	—
Olive Dish, oblong	24.00	42.00	—
Pickle Dish, flat, oval, 7-1/2" l	18.00	36.00	—
Pitcher, water, bulbous, ah	25.00	—	—
Pitcher, water, tankard, molded handle	72.00	110.00	—
Plate, 8" d	30.00	42.00	—
Relish	110.00	—	—
Salt and Pepper Shakers, pr, hotel size; pr, small; or pr, table	42.00	48.00	—
Sauce, round or square, 4"	12.00	—	—
Sugar Bowl, cov, breakfast or table	36.00-55.00	48.00-72.00	—
Sugar Bowl, open, individual, 2 handles	24.00	30.00	—
Syrup, orig top	90.00	—	60.00
Toothpick Holder	30.00	48.00	48.00
Tumbler	24.00	42.00	48.00
Vase, 6", 8" or 9" h	42.00	50.00	—
Wine, flared or straight-sided bowl	36.00	50.00	—

New Jersey

Loops and Drops

Manufactured by United States Glass Company, Pittsburgh, PA, c1900-08, in States pattern series. Made in non-flint, clear, clear with gilt trim, and ruby stained. Items with perfect gilt trim (gold) are worth more than those with worn gold. An emerald green 11" vase is known (value $90).

Items	Clear with Gilt Trim	Ruby Stained
Bowl, deep or flared bowl, 6", 7" or 8" d	24.00-30.00	48.00-60.00
Bowl, oval, plain or pointed ends, 8", 9" or 10" d	30.00-36.00	60.00-72.00
Bowl, saucer, 9" d	32.00	75.00
Bread Plate	36.00	—
Butter Dish, cov, flat	90.00	120.00
Butter Dish, cov, footed	130.00	—
Cake Stand, hs, 8" d	75.00	—
Carafe	72.00	—
Celery Tray, rect	30.00	48.00
Compote, cov, hs, 6", 7" or 8" d	55.00-75.00	85.00-110.00
Compote, open, hs, 6", 7" or 8" d	36.00-72.00	72.00-90.00
Compote, open, hs, shallow bowl, 10-1/2" d	75.00	—
Creamer	42.00	72.00
Cruet, os	60.00	—
Dish, oval, scalloped rim, 6" or 8" l	18.00-24.00	—
Dish, oval, scalloped rim, 10" l	30.00	60.00
Fruit Bowl, hs, 12-1/2" d	65.00	100.00
Fruit Plate, 9-1/2", 10-1/2" or 12" d	24.00-36.00	—
Goblet	48.00	90.00
Jelly Compote, cov, hs, 5" d	45.00	65.00
Molasses Can	110.00	—
Olive Dish, pointed ends	18.00	—
Pickle Dish, rect	18.00	—
Pitcher, milk, ah	90.00	175.00
Pitcher, water, ah, bulbous	95.00	210.00
Pitcher, water, ph, straight sides	60.00	200.00
Plate, 8" d	36.00	55.00
Salt and Pepper Shakers, pr, small or hotel	42.00-60.00	65.00-118.00
Sauce, flat, 4" d	12.00	36.00
Spooner	35.00	90.00
Sugar Bowl, cov	72.00	95.00
Sweetmeat, cov, 8" d	75.00	110.00
Syrup, orig top	110.00	—
Toothpick Holder	65.00	230.00
Tumbler	36.00	60.00
Water Bottle	55.00	110.00
Wine, flared or straight bowl	48.00	72.00

Oaken Bucket

Wooden Pail, Bucket Set

Manufactured by Bryce, Higbee and Company, Pittsburgh, PA, c1880. Reissued by United States Glass Company, Pittsburgh, PA, after the 1891 merger. Made in non-flint, amber, amethyst, blue, canary-yellow, and clear.

Items	Amber	Amethyst	Blue	Canary Yellow	Clear
Butter Dish, cov	110.00	230.00	120.00	120.00	75.00
Child's Butter Dish, cov	—	—	—	—	75.00
Child's Creamer	—	—	—	—	48.00
Child's Spooner	—	—	—	—	42.00

Items	Amber	Amethyst	Blue	Canary Yellow	Clear
Child's Sugar Bowl, cov	—	—	—	—	55.00
Creamer	75.00	130.00	90.00	72.00	48.00
Match Holder	42.00	100.00	48.00	42.00	30.00
Pitcher, water	120.00	185.00	145.00	145.00	90.00
Spooner	72.00	120.00	75.00	65.00	42.00
Sugar Bowl, cov	85.00	160.00	95.00	85.00	55.00
Toothpick Holder	48.00	100.00	55.00	48.00	30.00
Tumbler	36.00	72.00	42.00	36.00	35.00

O'Hara Diamond

Ruby Star, Sawtooth and Star, US Glass Pattern Line No. 15,001

Manufactured by O'Hara Glass Company, Pittsburgh, PA, c1885. Reissued by United States Glass Company, Pittsburgh, PA, 1891-1904. Made in non-flint, clear and ruby stained.

Items	Clear	Ruby Stained
Berry Bowl, individual or master	12.00-30.00	30.00-90.00
Bowl, cov, 5",6", 7" or 8" d	30.00-48.00	48.00-65.00
Bowl, open, scalloped rim, 5", 6", 7" or 9" d	12.00-18.00	30.00-36.00
Butter Dish, cov, ruffled base	55.00	130.00
Cake Stand, hs, 9" or 10" d	60.00-72.00	120.00-135.00
Celery Vase	36.00	75.00
Champagne	42.00	85.00
Claret	55.00	110.00
Compote, open, hs, scalloped rim, 5", 6", 7" or 8" d	48.00-65.00	100.00-118.00
Condiment Set, salt & pepper shakers, sugar shaker, tray	130.00	260.00
Creamer	36.00	72.00
Cruet, os	65.00	160.00
Cup and Saucer	48.00	72.00
Goblet	30.00	60.00
Honey Dish, 3-1/2" d	18.00	36.00
Jelly Compote, open, hs,	40.00	100.00
Lamp, oil, orig burner and chimney	60.00	—
Pickle Dish, flat	18.00	30.00
Pitcher, water, tankard	110.00	175.00
Plate, 7", 8" or 10" d	35.00-48.00	—
Salt, master	18.00	42.00
Salt Shaker	15.00	42.00
Sauce, flat, 4" d	12.00	—
Sauce, footed, 4" d or 5" d	35.00	30.00
Spooner	35.00	65.00
Sugar Bowl, cov	42.00	110.00
Sugar Shaker	65.00	160.00
Syrup, orig top	65.00	240.00
Tumbler	36.00	55.00
Waste Bowl	18.00	36.00
Water Tray	36.00	55.00
Wine	30.00	42.00

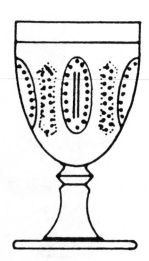

One Hundred One

Beaded 101

Manufactured by Bellaire Goblet Company, Findlay, OH, in the late 1880s. Shards have been found at the site of the Burlington Glass Works, Hamilton, Ontario, Canada. Made in non-flint, clear.

Reproductions: Only the goblet has been reproduced in this pattern. It has been reproduced in clear and colors.

Items	Clear
Bread Plate, 101 border, Farm implement center, 11" l	90.00
Butter Dish, cov	48.00
Cake Stand, hs, 9" d	75.00
Celery Vase	60.00
Compote, cov, hs, 7", 8" or 9" d	72.00-75.00
Compote, cov, ls	72.00
Creamer	55.00
Goblet φ	60.00
Lamp, oil, hand, orig burner and chimney, handle, 10" h	95.00
Lamp, oil, table, orig burner and chimney	120.00
Pickle, flat or collared base	35.00
Pitcher, water, ah	130.00
Plate, 6", 7", 8"or 9" d	18.00-30.00
Relish Tray	35.00
Salt Shaker, orig top	18.00
Sauce, flat or footed, 4" d	12.00-18.00
Spooner	30.00
Sugar Bowl, cov	55.00
Vase	30.00
Wine	72.00

Open Rose

Moss Rose

Manufacture attributed to Boston and Sandwich Glass Company, Sandwich, MA, c1870. Made in non-flint, clear.

Reproductions: Reproduced in clear and color.

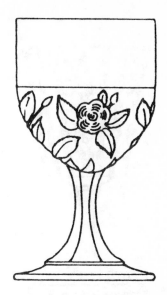

Items	Clear
Bowl, flat, 5" d	35.00
Bowl, oval, 9" x 6"	30.00
Butter Dish, cov	65.00
Cake Stand, hs	55.00
Celery Vase, pedestal	36.00
Compote, cov, hs, 6", 7", 8" or 9" d	75.00-110.00
Compote, open, ls, 6", 7", 7-1/2", 8" or 9" d	30.00-55.00
Cordial	55.00
Creamer, ah	55.00
Dish, flat, 7" d	30.00
Egg Cup	30.00
Goblet, lady's; or regular φ	36.00
Pickle Dish, oval	18.00
Pitcher, milk or water, ah, bulbous	160.00-175.00
Relish Tray	18.00
Salt, master, ftd	36.00
Sauce, flat, 4" d	12.00
Spooner φ	48.00
Sugar Bowl, cov	60.00
Tumbler	60.00

Palmette

Hearts and Spades, Spades

Manufacturer unknown, attributed to the late 1870s. Shards have been found at Burlington Glass Works, Hamilton, Ontario, Canada. Made in non-flint, clear. Syrup pitcher known in milk glass.

Items	Clear
Bowl, 8" d	30.00
Bowl, 9" d	18.00
Bread Plate, handle, 9" d	36.00
Butter Dish, cov, flat, no handles; or hexagonal knob finial	72.00
Butter Dish, cov, tab handles	75.00
Butter Pat	42.00
Cake Plate, tab handles	42.00
Cake Stand, hs, 10-1/2" d	120.00
Castor Set, 5 bottles, silver plate holder	130.00
Celery Tray	30.00
Celery Vase	65.00
Champagne	90.00
Compote, cov, hs, 7", 8-1/2" or 9-3/4" d	75.00-100.00
Compote, open, hs, 8" d	48.00
Compote, open, ls, 5-1/2" or 7" d	30.00-36.00
Cordial	120.00
Creamer, ah, pedestal	75.00
Cruet, Maltese cross finial, ah, pedestal	148.00
Cup Plate, 3-1/2" d	65.00
Egg Cup, pedestal	48.00
Goblet	42.00
Honey Dish, 3-1/2" d	18.00
Lamp, oil, orig burner, chimney, 8-1/2", 9-1/2" or 10" h	115.00-130.00
Pickle, scoop shape	25.00
Pitcher, milk, ah, bulbous	142.00
Pitcher, water, ah, bulbous	130.00
Relish	15.00
Salt, master, ftd	30.00
Salt Shaker, bulbous, orig top	65.00
Salt Shaker, saloon, oversize	95.00
Sauce, flat, 4" or 4-1/2" d	12.00
Sauce, flat, 5" d or 6" d	18.00
Spooner, pedestal	42.00
Sugar Bowl, cov	65.00
Syrup, orig top, ah	130.00
Tumbler, flat, 4" h	90.00
Tumbler, footed, 5" h	48.00
Wine	112.00

Paneled Daisy

Brazil, Daisy and Panel

Manufactured by Bryce Bros., Pittsburgh, PA, in the late 1880s. Reissued by United States Glass Company, Pittsburgh, PA, in 1891 at Factory "B." Made in non-flint, clear. Also found in amber (sugar shaker, $130) and blue (sugar shaker, $155). Milk glass pieces include 7" round plate ($48), 9" sq plate ($55), and sugar shaker ($95).

Reproductions: Both the goblet and tumbler have been reproduced by L. G. Wright Glass Company, New Martinsville, WV, c1960, in amber, blue, clear, pink, and ruby. It also reproduced the relish scoop in amber, amethyst, blue, and green. Fenton Art Glass Company, Williamstown, WV, created a high standard covered compote in carnival, clear, and opalescent colors in 1970. A toothpick holder was added in 1973.

Items	Clear
Bowl, flared rim, 6" d or 7" d	18.00
Bowl, shallow, 8" or 9" d; or square, 8" w	35.00
Bowl, square, 10-1/2" w	30.00
Butter Dish, cov, flat or footed	60.00
Cake Stand, hs, 8", 9", 10-1/4" or 11" d	36.00-60.00
Celery Vase	48.00
Compote, cov, hs, 5", 7", 8" d φ or 10" d	48.00-72.00
Compote, open, hs, 7", 9", 10" or 11"d	48.00
Creamer	42.00
Creamer, cov	75.00
Dish, oval, 9" l	35.00
Goblet φ	30.00
Jelly Compote, cov, hs, 6" d	55.00
Mug	36.00
Pickle Jar	90.00
Pickle Scoop	18.00
Pitcher, water, half gallon	72.00
Plate, round, 7" or 9" d	36.00
Plate, square, 9-1/2" or 10" w	36.00-42.00
Relish, 5"x7", wider at one end φ	25.00
Salt Shaker	30.00
Sauce, flat or footed, round, 4" d or 4-1/2" d	12.00
Spooner	30.00
Sugar Bowl, cov	48.00
Sugar Shaker	55.00
Syrup, orig top	85.00
Tumbler φ	30.00
Waste Bowl	18.00
Water Bottle	72.00
Water Tray	55.00

Paneled Forget-Me-Not

Regal

Manufactured by Bryce Brothers, Pittsburgh, PA, c1880. Reissued by United States Glass Company, c1891. Shards have been found at Burlington Glass Works, Hamilton, Ontario, Canada. Made in non-flint, amber, blue, and clear with limited production in amethyst, green, and vaseline.

Items	Amber	Blue	Clear
Bowl, cov	55.00	85.00	42.00
Bread Plate	42.00	55.00	36.00
Butter Dish, cov	110.00	150.00	55.00
Cake Stand, hs, 10" d	125.00	150.00	55.00
Celery Vase	55.00	85.00	40.00
Compote, cov, hs, 7" d	100.00	110.00	75.00
Compote, cov, hs, 8" d	95.00	120.00	85.00
Compote, open, hs, 8-1/2" d	65.00	90.00	40.00
Compote, open, hs, 10" d	72.00	95.00	48.00
Creamer	55.00	72.00	42.00
Cruet, os	—	—	55.00
Goblet	60.00	75.00	40.00
Marmalade Jar, cov	72.00	95.00	60.00
Pickle, boat shape	30.00	42.00	18.00
Pitcher, milk, quart	110.00	120.00	60.00
Pitcher, water, half gallon	150.00	250.00	75.00
Relish, scoop shape	25.00	30.00	15.00
Salt and Pepper Shakers, pr	—	—	75.00
Sauce, flat, 4" d	18.00	35.00	12.00
Sauce, ftd, 4" d	20.00	30.00	15.00
Spooner	48.00	60.00	30.00
Sugar Bowl, cov	72.00	95.00	48.00
Wine	75.00	85.00	65.00

Paneled "44"

Athenia, Reverse "44," US Glass Pattern Line No. 15,140

Manufactured by United States Glass Company, Pittsburgh, PA, c1912. Most pieces bear the intertwined United States Glass Company mark in base. Made in non-flint, clear, trimmed in gold and untarnishable platinum. Lemonade set (six-piece set, $160), basket, ($175), goblet ($100), and covered butter ($115) in rose or green stained. Some pieces in plain blue.

Items	Clear w/Platinum
Almond Dish	30.00
Basket, applied reeded handle, 6" or 7" h	120.00-130.00
Berry Bowl, master, 8" d	60.00
Bon Bon, cov, trifid ftd, handles, 4" d	100.00
Bon Bon, open, flat, 5" d	55.00
Bowl, flared, deep, 6" or 7" d	60.00-65.00
Bowl, flared, deep, footed, 5-1/2" or 8-1/2" d	65.00-75.00
Bowl, straight sides, deep, 6", 7" or 8" d	65.00-75.00
Butter Dish, cov, flat	80.00
Candlestick, 4" or 7" h	72.00-75.00
Celery Dip	30.00
Celery Tray	35.00
Celery Vase, two handles, pedestal	72.00
Compote, open, hs, 4-1/2", 5-1/2" or 6-1/2" d	40.00-55.00
Compote, open, ls, 4-1/2" or 5-1/2" d	36.00-42.00
Compote, open, ls, handle, 3", 5" or 6" d	36.00-48.00
Creamer, ph, demitasse, individual, table or tankard, ftd	36.00-55.00
Cruet, os	75.00
Custard Cup	35.00
Finger Bowl	42.00
Goblet	55.00
Iced Tea Tumbler	42.00
Lemonade Set, pitcher, 6 tumblers	240.00
Lemonade Tumbler, handle	42.00
Nut Dish, 5" d	30.00
Olive, flat, handles	36.00
Pickle Dish, 8" l	35.00
Pitcher, water, flat, bulbous, half gallon	110.00
Pitcher, water, footed, tankard	115.00
Plate, 5-1/2" d	42.00
Powdered Sugar Bowl, cov	65.00
Puff Box, cov, ftd	75.00
Puff Box, open, ftd	65.00
Rose Bowl	75.00
Salad Bowl, 6" d	42.00
Salt and Pepper Shakers, pr	90.00
Salt, master, ftd, open, double handles	55.00
Sauce, flat, flared or straight sided, 4" d or 4-1/2" d	25.00
Sherbet, ftd, handle	25.00
Sugar Basket	55.00
Sugar Bowl, cov, demitasse	42.00
Sugar Bowl, cov, table, flat, handle; or open, individual	72.00
Sundae Dish, high foot or low foot	35.00
Syrup, orig top	130.00
Toothpick Holder, ftd	65.00
Tumbler, water	36.00
Vase, loving cup shape	48.00
Wine	60.00

Paneled Grape, Late

Heavy Paneled Grape, Maple, Kokomo-Jenkins Pattern Line No. 507

Manufactured by Kokomo Glass Manufacturing Company, Kokomo, IN, c1904. Shards identified at Boston and Sandwich Glass Company, Sandwich, MA. Made in non-flint, clear. Original pattern has pink and green staining.

Reproductions: L. G. Wright Glass Company, New Martinsville, WV, has issued reproductions in many colors and clear. Westmoreland Glass Company, Grapeville, PA, made additional forms in clear and milk glass reproductions for L. G. Wright Glass Company, c1960. The Summit Art Glass Company has also made reproductions in clear and color.

Items	Clear
Ale Glass, knob stem	55.00
Bowl, cov, 8" d	42.00
Bowl, open, 8" d	30.00
Butter Dish, cov φ	48.00
Celery Vase φ	38.50
Compote, cov, hs, 4" d φ, 6-1/2", 8" or 9" d	42.00-72.00
Compote, open, ls, 6-1/2" d	36.00
Creamer φ	30.00
Goblet φ	48.00
Lemonade Tumbler	42.00

Items	Clear
Pitcher, milk, quart	42.00
Pitcher, water, half gallon φ	55.00
Relish, oval	18.00
Salt Shaker, orig top	30.00
Sauce, flat or footed φ	30.00
Sherbet, handle φ	30.00
Spooner φ	35.00
Sugar Bowl, cov φ	48.00
Syrup, orig top, glass lid	48.00
Toothpick Holder	48.00
Tumbler, water	42.00
Wine φ	48.00

Paneled Heather

Manufacturer unknown, c1890. Made in non-flint, clear. Often found with gilt.

Items	Clear
Butter Dish, cov	42.00
Cake Stand	42.00
Celery Vase	30.00
Creamer	35.00
Goblet	30.00
Spooner	36.00
Sugar Bowl, cov	42.00
Tumbler	18.00

Paneled Holly

Manufactured by Harry Northwood Glass Company, Wheeling, WV, c1905. Made in blue opalescent and white opalescent with gold trimmed holly leaves and enameling.

Items	Blue Opalescent	White Opalescent
Berry Bowl	60.00	48.00
Butter Dish, cov	120.00	75.00
Creamer	72.00	48.00
Cruet	160.00	120.00
Pitcher, water	160.00	—
Relish	55.00	42.00
Sauce	18.00	12.00
Spooner	60.00	42.00
Sugar Bowl, cov	120.00	72.00
Tumbler	42.00	36.00

Paneled Thistle

Canadian Thistle, Delta

Manufactured by J. P. Higbee Glass Company, Bridgeville, PA, c1910-20. Also made by Jefferson Glass Company, Toronto, Ontario, Canada. The Higbee Glass Company often used a bee as a trademark. Made in non-flint, clear. Occasionally found with gilt. Rare in ruby stained, with or without gilt.

Reproductions: Reproductions were made by L. G. Wright Glass Company, New Martinsville, WV, from 1969 to 1980. Reproductions are either unmarked or use an embossed elongated bee mark similar to that used by Higbee. Besides the original clear, reproductions were made in amber, amberina, blue, clear satin, pink, rubena, and ruby red.

Items	Clear
Basket, small size φ	75.00
Bowl, ftd, 6-1/2", 7" or 7-1/2" d	18.00-35.00
Bowl, ftd, 8" d, bee mark; or 8-1/2" d	30.00
Bowl, ftd, 9"d, bee mark	36.00
Bowl, rect, 7" l, 5-1/2" w	35.00
Bread Plate	48.00
Butter Dish, cov φ	72.00
Cake Stand, hs, 9" d φ	42.00
Candy Dish, cov, ftd	36.00
Celery Tray	35.00
Celery Vase φ	48.00
Champagne, bee mark	48.00
Cheese Dish, flat	42.00
Compote, open, hs, 7-1/2", 8" or 9"d	36.00-42.00
Cordial	36.00
Creamer, bee mark φ	48.00
Cruet, os φ	60.00
Doughnut Stand, hs, 6"	30.00
Goblet, flared or straight bowl φ	42.00

Items	Clear
Honey Dish, cov, sq, bee mark φ	95.00
Jelly Compote, open, hs, scalloped rim, 5" d	36.00
Mug	18.00
Pickle, 8-1/4" l	35.00
Pitcher, milk, quart	72.00
Pitcher, water, half gallon φ	85.00
Plate, 7" φ	35.00
Plate, 8-1/2" or 9-1/4" d	30.00
Plate, 10" d, bee mark	36.00
Punch Cup, bee mark	35.00
Relish, bee mark φ	30.00
Rose Bowl, 5" d	60.00
Salt, individual φ or master, ftd	35.00
Salt Shaker φ	35.00
Sauce, flared, 3-1/2" d or 4-1/2" d	15.00
Sauce, footed, 3-1/2" d or 4-1/2" d	25.00
Sherbet Cup, flared, handle	12.00
Spooner, handles φ	30.00
Sugar Bowl, cov φ	55.00
Sweetmeat, cov, ftd	55.00
Toothpick Holder, bee mark φ	55.00
Tumbler φ	30.00
Vase, 5" or 9-1/4" h	30.00
Wine, flared or straight bowl, bee mark φ	36.00

Pavonia

Pineapple Stem

Manufactured by Ripley and Company in 1885 and reissued by United States Glass Company, Pittsburgh, PA, Factory "F," in 1891-98. Made in non-flint, clear, and ruby stained. This pattern comes plain and etched.

Items	Clear	Ruby Stained
Bowl, 5", 6", 7" or 8" d	18.00-35.00	42.00-65.00
Bread Tray	55.00	110.00
Butter Dish, cov, flat, table or hotel	60.00-90.00	130.00
Cake Plate	45.00	—
Cake Stand, hs, 8", 9" or 10" d	55.00-75.00	110.00-120.00
Celery Vase, etched	55.00	90.00
Compote, cov, hs, 5", 6", 7", 8", 9" or 10" d	55.00-115.00	75.00-130.00
Compote, open, 6", 7", 8", 9" or 10" d	42.00-65.00	90.00-120.00
Creamer, hotel or table	42.00	90.00
Cup and Saucer	42.00	55.00
Custard Cup, ah	18.00	35.00
Finger Bowl, ruffled underplate	40.00	112.00
Goblet	42.00	72.00
Jelly Compote, open	40.00	—
Mug	42.00	60.00
Pitcher, lemonade, tankard	115.00	160.00
Pitcher, milk, jug, quart	75.00	—
Pitcher, milk, tankard, quart	75.00	160.00
Pitcher, water, jug, half gallon	75.00	160.00
Pitcher, water, tankard, half gallon	90.00	210.00
Plate, 6-1/2" d	17.50	—
Salt, individual	18.00	60.00
Salt, master	25.00	60.00
Salt Shaker	30.00	42.00
Sauce, flat, 3", 3-1/2", 4" or 4-1/2" d	12.00	18.00
Sauce, ftd, 3", 3-1/2", 4" or 4-1/2" d	18.00	35.00
Spooner, pedestal	55.00	60.00
Sugar Bowl, cov, hotel or table	55.00	90.00
Tray, water, etched	90.00	150.00
Tumbler	42.00	60.00
Waste Bowl	72.00	65.00
Water Tray	65.00	100.00
Wine	42.00	48.00

Peerless #1

Lady Hamilton

Manufactured by Richards & Hartley Company, Pittsburgh, PA, in 1875 and continued for a number of years. Made in a great number of pieces, many sizes of bowls, twenty-two compotes, five cake stands, and two types of goblets and creamers. Prices for similar items are all comparable to those listed. Made in clear.

Items	Clear
Bowl, 7" d	15.00
Bread Plate, oval	30.00

Items	Clear
Butter Dish, covered	48.00
Cake stand, small or large	30.00-36.00
Castor Set	90.00
Celery	30.00
Champagne	35.00
Compote, cov	60.00
Compote, open	36.00
Creamer, angular bowl	42.00
Creamer, rounded bowl	30.00
Dish, 7", 8" or 9" l	12.00-35.00
Egg Cup, saucer base	35.00
Goblet, angular sided or rounded bowl	30.00
Pickle, flat pointed shape	18.00
Pickle, round	15.00
Pickle Jar, cov	48.00
Pitcher, water, ah, half gallon	75.00
Platter, oval	30.00
Salt, cov	42.00
Salt, open, individual	12.00
Sauce, 4" or 5-1/2" d	10.00
Spooner	30.00
Sugar Bowl, cov	48.00
Tumbler	35.00
Wine	30.00

Pennsylvania

Balder, Hand, and Kamoni, US Glass Pattern Line No. 15,048

Manufactured by United States Glass Company, Pittsburgh, PA, in 1898, at Factory "O" and Factory "GP." Made in non-flint, clear and emerald green. Also known in ruby stained. A ruffled jelly compote documented in orange carnival.

Reproductions: Reproduction spooners were made in the mid-1980s.

Items	Clear w/Gold	Emerald Green
Biscuit Jar, cov	90.00	130.00
Bowl, eight-pointed, 6", 7" or 8" d	18.00-35.00	—
Bowl, scalloped, shallow, 5", 7" or 8" d	18.00-35.00	36.00-48.00
Bowl, square, 6", 7" or 8" w	18.00-35.00	36.00-48.00
Butter Dish, cov, table or hotel size	60.00-72.00	90.00-100.00
Carafe	55.00	—
Celery Tray	36.00	
Celery Vase	55.00	—
Champagne	30.00	60.00
Cheese Dish, cov	75.00	—
Child's Butter Dish, cov	65.00	235.00
Child's Creamer	75.00	150.00
Child's Spooner	60.00	125.00
Child's Sugar Bowl	75.00	200.00
Claret	42.00	—
Claret Jug, os, handle	100.00	
Creamer, individual or table	30.00-42.00	60.00-72.00
Cruet, os	55.00	—
Decanter, os, handle	120.00	—
Goblet	30.00	—
Ice Tub	55.00	—
Jelly Compote, open, hs, ruffled	60.00	—
Juice Tumbler	30.00	60.00
Molasses Can	90.00	—
Olive Dish, scalloped rim	18.00	—
Pickle Dish, scalloped rim	35.00	—
Pickle Jar, cov	55.00	—
Pitcher, water, bulbous or tankard	72.00-75.00	—
Plate, 8" d	42.00	—
Punch Bowl	190.00	—
Punch Cup	12.00	—
Salt, individual or master	35.00-36.00	—
Salt Shaker, bulbous, 3 sizes	18.00	—
Salt Shaker, straight-sided	12.00	—
Sauce, flat, eight-pointed, scalloped, square, or straight-sided bowl, 4" d	12.00	
Spooner φ	30.00	42.00
Sugar Bowl, cov	48.00	65.00
Syrup, orig top, tapered	60.00	—
Toothpick Holder	42.00	110.00
Tumbler	25.00	48.00
Whiskey	35.00	42.00
Wine	18.00	48.00

Pequot

Manufacturer unknown. Shards have been found at Burlington Glass Works, Hamilton, Ontario, Canada. Made in clear. Some items are known in blue and amber. Add 100% for colors.

Items	Clear
Bowl, 6" d, pedestal	35.00
Butter Dish, cov	60.00
Celery Vase	55.00
Champagne	55.00
Compote, cov, hs, 7-1/2" d	65.00
Compote, open, hs, 7-1/2" d	42.00
Creamer	40.00
Goblet	55.00
Marmalade Jar	60.00
Pitcher, water, applied hollow reeded handle	160.00
Spooner	40.00
Sugar Bowl, cov	50.00
Wine	42.00

Picket

London, Picket Fence

Manufactured by the King, Son & Company, Pittsburgh,, PA, c1890. Shards have been found at the site of the Burlington Glass Works, Hamilton, Ontario, Canada. Made in non-flint, clear. Toothpick holders are known in apple green, vaseline, and purple slag.

Items	Clear
Berry Bowl, sq, 9-1/2" w	36.00
Bread Plate	85.00
Butter Dish, cov	55.00
Celery Vase	48.00
Compote, cov, hs, 6", 7" or 8" d	75.00-100.00
Compote, cov, ls, 8" d	115.00
Compote, open, hs, 6", 7", 8" or 10" w, sq	36.00-85.00
Compote, open, ls, 6", 7" or 8" w, sq	55.00-65.00
Creamer	40.00
Finger Bowl	36.00
Goblet	36.00
Marmalade Jar, cov	75.00
Match Holder	65.00
Pickle Jar, cov	60.00
Pitcher, water	90.00
Salt, individual or master	12.00-42.00
Sauce, flat or footed	18.00-35.00
Spooner	36.00
Sugar Bowl, cov	55.00
Toothpick Holder	65.00
Waste Bowl	48.00
Water Tray	75.00
Wine	100.00

Pineapple and Fan #1

Pineapple with Fan, Heisey Pattern Line No. 1255

Manufactured by A. H. Heisey and Company, Newark, OH, c1897, before the Heisey trademark was used. This pattern was made in an extensive table set. Made in non-flint, clear, and emerald green. Pieces often trimmed in gold. Also known in custard and ruby stained (Toothpick Holder $130).

Items	Clear	Emerald Green
Banana Stand	60.00	—
Biscuit Jar, cov	75.00	160.00
Bowl, 5-1/2" or 10-1/2" d	18.00-48.00	36.00-100.00
Butter Dish, cov	60.00	190.00
Cake Stand, hs	55.00	90.00
Celery Tray, flat	30.00	55.00
Celery Vase	36.00	75.00
Compote, open, hs, 8"	60.00	230.00
Cracker Jar, cov	75.00	160.00
Creamer, individual, hotel or table	30.00-42.00	60.00-115.00
Cruet, os	72.00	215.00
Custard Cup	18.00	36.00
Goblet	18.00	30.00
Jelly Compote, open, 6" d	42.00	85.00
Mug	36.00	55.00

Items	Clear	Emerald Green
Pickle Tray	18.00	42.00
Pitcher, water	95.00	230.00
Rose Bowl	42.00	90.00
Salt, individual	30.00	—
Salt Shaker	35.00	75.00
Spooner	36.00	75.00
Sugar Bowl, cov, individual or table	30.00-55.00	60.00-130.00
Syrup, orig top	72.00	260.00
Toothpick Holder	90.00	160.00
Tumbler	30.00	72.00
Vase, trumpet, 10" h	30.00	55.00

Pineapple and Fan #2

Cube with Fan, Holbrook

Manufactured by Adams & Company, Pittsburgh, PA. Reissued by United States Glass Company, Pittsburgh, PA, in 1891. Made in non-flint, clear. Also found in emerald green, ruby stained, and white milk glass trimmed in gold.

Items	Clear
Bowl, 8" d	30.00
Butter Dish, cov	48.00
Cake Stand, hs, 9" d	42.00
Cologne Bottle	45.00
Creamer	30.00
Cruet, os	65.00
Decanter	48.00
Finger Bowl	30.00
Goblet	30.00
Ice Cream Tray	30.00
Pitcher, water, tankard	55.00
Plate, 6-1/2" d	18.00
Punch Bowl, 12" d	72.00
Rose Bowl	35.00
Salt, individual	15.00
Spooner	30.00
Sugar Bowl, cov	36.00
Syrup, orig top	60.00
Tumbler	18.00
Waste Bowl	18.00
Whiskey	18.00
Wine	35.00

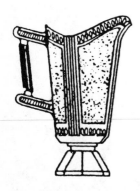

Pleat and Panel

Derby

Manufactured by Bryce Brothers, Pittsburgh, PA, in the 1880s, and later by United States Glass Company, Pittsburgh, PA, in 1891. Shards have been found at the site of the Burlington Glass Works, Hamilton, Ontario, Canada. Found in square and rectangular forms. Made in non-flint and clear. Rarely found in blue, canary, amber, and amethyst. Colored items valued at 50% to 75% higher. Do no confuse with the Depression-era Heisey pattern of the same name.

Reproductions: There are reproduction goblets and 7" plates in clear.

Items	Clear
Bowl, cov, 8" d	65.00
Bread Plate	48.00
Butter Dish, cov, flat	85.00
Butter Dish, cov, ls, handles	90.00
Butter Pat	48.00
Cake Stand, hs, sq, 8", 9" or 10" w	36.00-48.00
Celery Vase	42.00
Compote, cov, hs, sq, 6", 7", 8" or 9" w	75.00-95.00
Compote, cov, ls, sq, 6", 7", 8" or 9" w	48.00-65.00
Compote, open, hs, sq, 6", 7", 8" or 9" w	30.00-48.00
Compote, open, ls, sq, 6", 7", 8" or 9" w	35.00-42.00
Creamer	42.00
Goblet, 6" φ	36.00
Lamp, oil, orig burner, clear font, 9-1/4" h	130.00
Lamp, oil, orig burner, faceted font, 8" h	130.00
Lamp, oil, orig burner, frosted font, 7" h	120.00
Marmalade Jar, cov	60.00
Pickle Dish, 7" l	18.00
Pitcher, milk, quart	100.00
Pitcher, water, half gallon	60.00
Plate, 6" w φ; 7" w; or 7-1/2" w	35.00

Items	Clear
Plate, 8" or 8-1/2" w	30.00
Relish, 8-1/2"	25.00
Salt, master	35.00
Salt Shaker, 3-1/4" h	42.00
Sauce, flat, sq, 3-1/2" w, 4" w, 5" w	18.00
Sauce, footed, sq, 3-1/2" w, 4" or 5" w	25.00
Spooner	36.00
Sugar Bowl, cov	48.00
Syrup, patented lid	360.00
Waste Bowl, sq, 4-3/4" w	65.00
Water Tray, 14" x 9-1/4"	60.00
Wine	60.00

Plume

Manufactured by Adams & Company, Pittsburgh, PA, c1890, and by United States Glass Company in 1891. Pattern design has both horizontal and vertical plumes. Early goblets have plume motif at base of stem. Made in non-flint, clear. Also found etched. Pattern contains forty-six pieces. Some Items are frosted.

Reproductions: L. G. Wright Glass Company, New Martinsville, WV, has been reproducing goblets as early as 1960.

Items	Clear	Ruby Stained
Berry Bowl, master, sq, 8" w	55.00	90.00
Bitters Bottle	100.00	130.00
Bowl, cov, collared base, 6", 7" or 8" d	60.00-72.00	75.00-90.00
Bowl, open, belled bowl, 6" or 7" d; or flared, 7" d or 8" d	30.00	60.00
Bowl, open, scalloped rim, 6", 8" or 9" d	30.00-36.00	60.00-72.00
Butter Dish, cov	60.00	175.00
Cake Stand, hs, 9" or 10" d	55.00-60.00	118.00-130.00
Celery Vase	36.00	75.00
Compote, cov, hs, 6", 7" or 8" d	55.00-65.00	130.00-155.00
Compote, open, hs, belled bowl, scalloped rim, 7", 8" or 9" d	55.00-65.00	90.00-100.00
Compote, open, hs, belled bowl, smooth rim, 7", 8" or 9" d	55.00-65.00	90.00-100.00
Compote, open, hs, straight bowl, scalloped rim, 6", 7" or 8" d	48.00-65.00	72.00-85.00
Compote, open, hs, straight bowl, smooth rim, 8", 9" or 10" d	60.00-72.00	95.00-110.00
Creamer	42.00	60.00
Goblet φ	42.00	65.00
Ice Tub	60.00	—
Pickle Castor, silver plated holder	160.00	260.00
Pickle Dish	35.00	65.00
Pitcher, water, ah, bulbous or tankard	75.00	240.00
Sauce, flat, 4"	12.00	35.00
Sauce, footed, 4" d	18.00	30.00
Spooner	30.00	48.00
Sugar Bowl, cov	55.00	72.00
Syrup, orig top	75.00	—
Tumbler	30.00	42.00
Waste Bowl	65.00	—
Water Tray, 12-1/2" d	48.00	—

Plutec

Manufactured by McKee & Bros. Glass Company, Pittsburgh, PA, c1900. Some pieces trademarked "PRES-CUT." Made in non-flint, clear.

Items	Clear
Bowl	15.00
Butter Dish, cov	30.00
Cake Stand	30.00
Celery Vase	35.00
Compote, open, hs	30.00
Creamer	30.00
Decanter	55.00
Goblet	18.00
Pickle	18.00
Pitcher, water	55.00
Plate, 10-3/4" or 11" d	30.00
Sauce, flat	10.00
Spooner	30.00
Sugar Bowl, cov	35.00
Toothpick Holder	35.00
Tray, wine	36.00
Tumbler	18.00
Wine	18.00

Pogo Stick

Crown

Manufactured by Lancaster Glass Company, Lancaster, OH, in 1910. Made in non-flint, clear.

Items	Clear
Berry Bowl	18.00
Butter Dish, cov	48.00
Cake Stand	42.00
Celery Vase	35.00
Compote, open	35.00
Creamer	30.00
Cruet	30.00
Pitcher, water	42.00
Plate, 7" d	12.00
Relish	18.00
Sauce, flat	10.00
Spooner	35.00
Sugar Bowl, cov	42.00
Syrup, orig top Jug, metal top	55.00
Tumbler	18.00

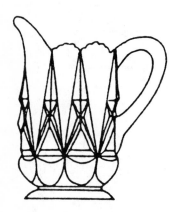

Pointed Jewel

Long Diamond, Spear Point, US Glass Pattern Line No. 15,006

Manufactured by Columbia Glass Company, Findlay, OH, c1888 and later by United States Glass Company, Pittsburgh, PA, 1892-98 at Factory "J" and Factory "N." Made in clear, although some pieces have been found with ruby stained decoration.

Reproductions: Imperial Glass Corp., Bellaire, OH, made reproduction individual creamers in milk glass. Other creamers were made in amber, heather, purple slag, and verde.

Items	Clear
Berry Bowl	35.00
Butter Dish, cov	72.00
Cake Stand	42.00
Celery	35.00
Child's Table Set	148.00
Cologne Bottle, os	60.00
Compote, cov, hs	55.00
Compote, jelly	35.00
Compote, open, ls	36.00
Creamer, table	36.00
Cup and Saucer	55.00
Dish, flat, 7-1/2"	35.00
Goblet	35.00
Honey Dish, cov, rect	55.00
Pitcher, water	55.00
Sauce	10.00
Spooner	30.00
Sugar Bowl, cov	42.00
Tray, sq	55.00
Tumbler	35.00
Wine	18.00

Polar Bear

Alaska, Arctic, Frosted Polar Bear, Ice Berg, North Pole, Polar Bear and Seal

Manufacture attributed to Crystal Glass Company, Bridgeport, OH, c1883. Made in non-flint, clear and frosted.

Reproductions: Goblets in clear, frosted, amber, blue, and heavily stippled have been made by Summit Art Glass Company, Rootstown, OH, c1977.

Items	Clear	Frosted
Bread Plate	115.00	160.00
Creamer	130.00	165.00
Goblet φ	120.00	135.00
Ice Bowl	100.00	120.00
Pickle Dish	60.00	75.00
Pitcher, water	260.00	290.00
Sauce, flat	36.00	42.00
Sugar Bowl, cov	190.00	240.00
Waste Bowl	100.00	120.00
Water Tray, oval or round	190.00	240.00

Popcorn

Manufacture attributed to Boston and Sandwich Glass Company in the late 1860s. Pieces were made with handles resembling an ear of corn, a flat oval which was filled with lines. Pieces with an outstanding ear known as "with ear" and the others "lined ear." Made in non-flint, clear.

Items	Clear
Butter Dish, cov	75.00
Cake Stand, hs, 8" or 11"	60.00-90.00
Cordial	90.00
Creamer, 4-7/8" h	48.00
Goblet, lined ear	36.00
Goblet, with ear	60.00
Pitcher, water, applied handle	75.00
Pitcher, water, applied strap handle	120.00
Sauce, flat	12.00
Spooner	42.00
Sugar Bowl, cov	55.00
Wine, with ear	75.00

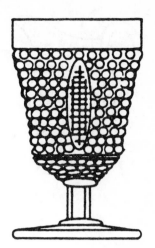

Portland

US Glass Pattern Line No. 15,121

Manufactured by Portland Glass Company, Portland, ME, late 1870s. Reissued by United States Glass Company, Pittsburgh, PA, c1910, at Factory "F" (Ripley & Co., Pittsburgh), Factory "O," (Central Glass Co., Wheeling, WV) and Factory "GP" (Glassport, PA). Made in non-flint, clear, and clear with gold trim. An oval pin tray in ruby souvenir ($35) is known and a flat sauce ($30).

Reproductions: Reproductions of this pattern have been made by Wheaton-Craft Giftware of Millville, NJ, c1976. It named the pattern *Wheaton-Craft's Cape May*. Its production was limited to clear, non-flint, creamer, nut dish, pickle tray, relish, and sugar bowl.

Items	Clear w/Gold Trim
Basket, ah	100.00
Biscuit Jar, cov	110.00
Berry Bowl, 6" or 7" d	35.00
Berry Bowl, 8" d	30.00
Bowl, cov, ftd	42.00
Butter Dish, cov	60.00
Cake Stand, hs, 10-1/2" d	55.00
Candlestick, 7" h, cupped or flared	100.00
Candlestick, 9" or 10-1/2" h	65.00-75.00
Celery Tray	30.00
Celery Vase	55.00
Compote, cov, hs, 6", 7" or 8"	72.00-85.00
Compote, open, hs, flared bowl, 7", 8-1/4" or 9-1/2" d	42.00-55.00
Compote, open, hs, straight sides, 6", 7" or 8" d	36.00-60.00
Compote, open, ls, 6", 7" or 8" d	48.00-60.00
Creamer, breakfast, table φ or tankard	35.00
Cruet, os	65.00
Custard Cup, handle	18.00
Decanter, qt, handled	60.00
Finger Bowl	30.00
Goblet	42.00
Jam Jar, silver plated cov	42.00
Lamp, oil, orig burner and chimney, 9" h	110.00
Olive Dish, oval	35.00
Pickle Dish, boat shape	18.00
Pin Tray	35.00
Pitcher, water, bulbous; or straight sides, tankard	65.00
Pomade Jar, silver plated top	36.00
Puff Box, glass lid	42.00
Punch Bowl, ftd, 13-5/8" d	160.00
Punch Cup	18.00
Relish φ	18.00
Ring Tree	100.00
Salt Shaker	18.00
Sardine Box, 4-1/2" l	36.00
Sauce, flat, oval or square	10.00
Sauce, flat, round, flared or straight sides, 4" d	10.00
Spooner, large or small	36.00
Sugar Bowl, open, breakfast; or table φ	42.00-55.00
Sugar Shaker	48.00
Syrup, orig top	60.00
Toothpick Holder	30.00
Tumbler	30.00
Vase, 6" or 9" h	36.00-42.00
Water Bottle	48.00
Wine	36.00

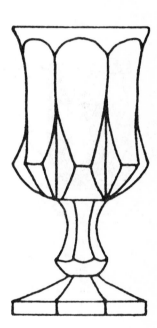

Powder and Shot

Horn of Plenty, Powder Horn and Shot

Manufacture unknown. Shards have been found at Boston and Sandwich Glass Company, Sandwich, MA, c1870, and also at Portland Glass Company, Portland, ME. Finial of covered pieces resembles a flattened upright fan or plume. Made in flint, clear.

Items	Clear
Butter Dish, cov	115.00
Castor Bottle	48.00
Celery Vase	115.00
Compote, cov, hs	120.00
Compote, open, ls	60.00
Creamer, ah, ftd	90.00
Egg Cup	60.00
Goblet	75.00
Pitcher, water, ah	160.00
Salt, master, ftd	55.00
Sauce, flat	35.00
Spooner	65.00
Sugar Bowl, cov	95.00

Pressed Diamond

Block and Diamond, Zephyr

Manufactured by Central Glass Company, Wheeling, WV, in the 1880s. Reissued by the United States Glass Company, Pittsburgh, PA, at Factory "O," c1891. Made in amber, blue, clear, light straw colored yellow, and vaseline.

Items	Amber	Blue	Clear	Yellow
Berry Bowl, 5" or 6" d	18.00	35.00	15.00	35.00
Berry Bowl, 7" d	35.00	30.00	18.00	30.00
Berry Bowl, 8" d	30.00	36.00	35.00	36.00
Butter Dish, cov	60.00	72.00	48.00	110.00
Butter Pat	18.00	35.00	12.00	18.00
Cake Stand, ls	36.00	60.00	30.00	65.00
Celery Vase	30.00	55.00	25.00	48.00
Compote, cov, hs, 11" d	90.00	120.00	55.00	90.00
Compote, open, hs, 11" d	65.00	70.00	30.00	65.00
Creamer	55.00	60.00	36.00	60.00
Cruet, os	120.00	130.00	60.00	120.00
Custard or Sherbet Cup, ah	18.00	35.00	15.00	35.00
Finger Bowl	20.00	35.00	18.00	35.00
Goblet	42.00	55.00	36.00	48.00
Pitcher, water	72.00	75.00	55.00	75.00
Plate, 11" d	55.00	65.00	42.00	55.00
Salt, individual	35.00	35.00	18.00	35.00
Salt Shaker	35.00	42.00	15.00	48.00
Sauce, flat	12.00	18.00	12.00	18.00
Spooner	55.00	72.00	30.00	55.00
Sugar Bowl, cov	65.00	90.00	42.00	75.00
Tumbler	30.00	36.00	35.00	30.00
Wine	30.00	42.00	35.00	48.00

Pressed Leaf

New Pressed Leaf

Manufactured by McKee Brothers, Pittsburgh, PA, c1868, and the Central Glass Company, Wheeling, WV, c1881. Shards have been found at Boston and Sandwich Glass Company, Sandwich, MA. The design was patented by H. S. McKee on Nov. 5, 1867. Made in flint and non-flint, clear.

Items	Non-Flint Clear
Bowl, oval	35.00
Butter Dish, cov	60.00
Cake Stand, hs	72.00
Champagne	55.00
Compote, cov, hs, 6", 7" or 8" d	65.00-75.00
Compote, cov, ls, 6", 7" or 8" d	55.00-65.00
Compote, open, hs, 6", 7" or 8" d	42.00-55.00
Compote, open, ls, 6", 7" or 8" d	42.00-55.00
Cordial	60.00
Creamer, ah	55.00
Egg Cup, ftd	30.00
Goblet	36.00

Items	Clear
Lamp, oil, orig burner and chimney	130.00
Pitcher, water, half gallon	120.00
Salt, master, open, ftd	42.00
Sauce, flat, 4" d	12.00
Spooner, ftd, scalloped	30.00
Sugar Bowl, cov	55.00
Wine	48.00

Primrose

Stippled Primrose, Canton Pattern Line No. 10

Manufactured by Canton Glass Company, Canton, OH, c1885. Made in non-flint, amber, apple green, blue, clear, and yellow. Also made in purple slag, black or white milk glass.

Items	Amber	Apple Green	Blue	Clear	Yellow
Bowl, 8"	36.00	42.00	42.00	30.00	36.00
Butter Dish, cov	60.00	72.00	72.00	42.00	60.00
Cake Plate, 9" d, handle	36.00	42.00	42.00	35.00	36.00
Cake Stand, hs, 10" d	60.00	75.00	75.00	48.00	60.00
Celery Vase	42.00	48.00	48.00	30.00	42.00
Compote, cov, hs, 6" d	75.00	90.00	90.00	55.00	75.00
Compote, cov, hs, 7-1/2" d	85.00	95.00	95.00	60.00	85.00
Compote, cov, hs, 8" d	90.00	100.00	100.00	65.00	90.00
Compote, cov, hs, 9" d	95.00	110.00	110.00	72.00	95.00
Compote, cov, ls, 6" d	48.00	55.00	55.00	36.00	48.00
Compote, cov, ls, 7-1/2" d	55.00	60.00	60.00	42.00	55.00
Compote, cov, ls, 8" d	60.00	65.00	65.00	48.00	60.00
Cordial	48.00	55.00	55.00	36.00	48.00
Creamer	42.00	48.00	48.00	36.00	42.00
Egg Cup	36.00	42.00	42.00	35.00	36.00
Goblet, knob stem	48.00	55.00	55.00	36.00	48.00
Goblet, plain stem	42.00	48.00	48.00	30.00	42.00
Lamp, finger	—	—	—	115.00	—
Pickle	30.00	35.00	35.00	18.00	30.00
Pitcher, milk	55.00	65.00	65.00	42.00	55.00
Pitcher, water	65.00	60.00	60.00	42.00	65.00
Plate, 6", 7" or 8" d	36.00	42.00	42.00	35.00	36.00
Platter, 12" l, 8" w	42.00	55.00	55.00	36.00	42.00
Relish Tray	30.00	35.00	35.00	18.00	30.00
Sauce, flat, 4" d or 5-1/2" d	18.00	25.00	25.00	12.00	18.00
Sauce, ftd, 4" d or 5-1/2" d	20.00	30.00	30.00	18.00	20.00
Spooner	40.00	45.00	45.00	35.00	40.00
Sugar Bowl, cov	48.00	65.00	65.00	42.00	48.00
Toddy Plate, 4-1/2" d	18.00	35.00	35.00	15.00	18.00
Waste Bowl	36.00	42.00	42.00	50.00	36.00
Water Tray	60.00	72.00	72.00	42.00	60.00
Wine	48.00	55.00	55.00	36.00	48.00

Princess Feather

Lacy Medallion, Princes' Feather, Rochelle

Manufactured by Bakewell, Pears and Company, Pittsburgh, PA, in the 1860s and 1870s. Later made by United States Glass Company, Pittsburgh, PA, after 1891. Shards have been identified at Boston and Sandwich Glass Company, Sandwich, MA, the Burlington Glass Works, Hamilton, Ontario, Canada, and the Diamond Glass Company, Ltd., Montreal, Quebec, Canada. Made in flint and non-flint, clear. Also made in milk glass. A rare blue opaque tumbler has been reported.

Items	Non-flint Clear
Bowl, cov, pedestal, 7" d	60.00
Bowl, flat, 6" d	30.00
Bowl, oval, 6" or 7" l	35.00
Bowl, oval, 8" or 9" l	30.00-36.00
Butter Dish, cov	60.00
Cake Plate, handles, 9" d	42.00
Celery Vase	48.00
Cheese Dish	55.00
Compote, cov, hs, 6", 7" or 8" d	55.00-60.00
Compote, cov, ls, 6", 7" or 8" d	36.00-48.00
Compote, open, ls, 8" d	42.00
Creamer, ah	65.00
Dish, oval	35.00
Egg Cup	48.00
Goblet	55.00
Honey Dish, flat, 3" d	12.00

Items	Clear
Pitcher, milk, quart	85.00
Pitcher, water, half gallon	90.00
Plate, 6", 7", 8" or 9" d	36.00-55.00
Relish	35.00
Salt, master, open, ftd	35.00
Sauce, flat, 4" d	10.00
Sauce, footed, 4" d	12.00
Spooner	36.00
Sugar Bowl, cov	65.00
Sugar, open	30.00
Wine	55.00

Priscilla #1

Alexis, Findlay, Late Moon and Star, Stelle, and Sun and Star

Manufactured by Dalzell, Gilmore and Leighton, Findlay, OH, in late 1895 and was continued by National Glass Company, Dunkirk, IN. Made in non-flint and clear. Rare examples are found with ruby stain or in color.

Reproductions: Fenton Art Glass Company, Williamstown, WV, reproduced pattern in clear, colors, and opalescent in 1951. Fenton also introduced many forms different from the original such as 12-1/2" plate, goblet, wine, 6" handled bon bon, and sugar and creamer. L. G. Wright Glass Company, New Martinsville, WV, also made reproductions of Priscilla as well as forms not original to the pattern, c1968-70.

Items	Clear
Banana Stand	95.00
Biscuit Jar, cov	155.00
Bowl, cov, flat, 7" d	60.00
Bowl, open, flat, 7-1/2" or 8" d	18.00-30.00
Bowl, open, flat, 9" d	30.00
Bowl, open, square, 8" w	35.00
Bowl, open, square, 9-1/4" w	30.00
Bowl, 10-1/4" d, straight sides φ	60.00
Butter Dish, cov	75.00
Cake Stand, hs, 9-1/2" or 10" d	72.00-75.00
Celery Vase	65.00
Compote, cov, hs, 7", 8" or 9" d	75.00-90.00
Compote, open, hs, flared rim, sq, 10" w	72.00
Compote, open, hs, scalloped, 7", 8", 9" or 10" d	55.00-72.00
Creamer, individual, 3" h	12.00
Creamer, table φ	30.00
Cruet, os	75.00
Cup	12.00
Doughnut Stand, hs	72.00
Goblet φ	48.00
Jelly Compote, cov, hs, 5" d	48.00
Mug	35.00
Pickle Dish	18.00
Pitcher, water, ah, tankard or bulbous	100.00-110.00
Plate φ	30.00
Relish	18.00
Rose Bowl	36.00
Salt Shaker, orig top	42.00
Sauce, flat, round or square, 4" d or 4-1/2" d φ	10.00
Saucer	10.00
Spooner	36.00
Sugar Bowl, cov, individual; or table φ	36.00-72.00
Syrup, orig top	110.00
Toothpick Holder	48.00
Tumbler	30.00
Wine φ	42.00

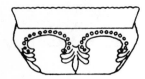

Priscilla #2

Acanthus Leaf, Fostoria Pattern Line No. 676

Made by Fostoria Glass Company, Moundsville, WV, in 1898. Made in non-flint, clear and emerald green. Some pieces have gold trim. Also made in custard with green or gold trim and white milk glass.

Items	Clear	Emerald Green
Berry Bowl, 8-1/2" d	18.00	42.00
Butter Dish, cov	75.00	115.00
Cake Stand, hs	42.00	85.00
Carafe, water	55.00	115.00
Celery Vase	42.00	72.00
Compote, cov	65.00	90.00
Compote, open	48.00	65.00

Items	Clear	Emerald Green
Creamer, ah	42.00	85.00
Cruet, os	75.00	260.00
Egg Cup	35.00	42.00
Finger Bowl	18.00	35.00
Goblet	30.00	75.00
Lamp, oil, orig burner and chimney	120.00	190.00
Marmalade Jar, cov	55.00	118.00
Pickle Dish	18.00	30.00
Pitcher, water	36.00	75.00
Salt, individual	18.00	42.00
Salt Shaker, large or small	15.00	36.00
Sauce, flat, 4-1/2" d	12.00	18.00
Sherbet	10.00	18.00
Spooner	36.00	60.00
Sugar Bowl, cov	55.00	95.00
Syrup, orig top, nickel top	65.00	160.00
Toothpick Holder, 4-1/2" h	42.00	75.00
Tumbler	30.00	42.00
Water Bottle	55.00	115.00

Prism Arc

Cross Log

Manufacturer unknown. Made in non-flint, clear.

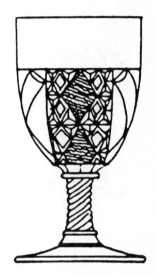

Items	Clear
Berry Bowl, 8" d	40.00
Butter Dish, cov	42.00
Cake Stand	36.00
Celery	35.00
Creamer	30.00
Cruet, os	60.00
Goblet	35.00
Mug	18.00
Pitcher, water	55.00
Plate	12.00
Sauce	10.00
Spooner	30.00
Sugar Bowl, cov	36.00
Tumbler	36.00
Wine	35.00

Prism with Diamond Points

Manufactured by Bryce Bros., Pittsburgh, PA, c1880. Reissued by United States Glass Company, Pittsburgh, PA, c1891. Shards have been found at Boston and Sandwich Glass Company, Sandwich, MA. Made in flint, clear. A flint milk glass spooner is known.

Items	Clear
Bowl	36.00
Butter Dish, cov	75.00
Celery Vase	42.00
Compote, cov, hs, 6"	110.00
Compote, open, hs, 6" d	90.00
Creamer	90.00
Egg Cup, double	65.00
Egg Cup, single	30.00
Goblet	55.00
Pickle Dish	30.00
Pitcher, water	120.00
Salt, master, cov	65.00
Spooner	55.00
Sugar Bowl, cov	60.00
Tumbler	48.00
Wine	60.00

Psyche and Cupid

Manufacturer unknown, c1870. Made in non-flint, clear.

Items	Clear
Butter Dish, cov	72.00
Celery Vase	48.00
Compote, cov, hs	90.00

Items	Clear
Compote, cov, ls	65.00
Creamer, 7"	60.00
Goblet	48.00
Marmalade Jar, cov	100.00
Pitcher, milk	72.00
Pitcher, water	90.00
Sauce, ftd, 4-1/2"	18.00
Spooner	55.00
Sugar Bowl, cov	65.00
Wine	55.00

Quartered Block

Paneled Diamond Block, Quartered Diamond, Duncan and Miller Pattern Line No. 24

Manufactured by Duncan & Miller Company, Washington, PA, c1903. Made in non-flint, clear and ruby stained.

Items	Clear	Ruby Stained
Berry Bowl, master	30.00	72.00
Butter Dish, cov	55.00	130.00
Cake Stand, 9"	60.00	—
Celery Vase	36.00	65.00
Compote, cov, hs	60.00	—
Compote, open, hs	42.00	—
Creamer	36.00	65.00
Custard Cup	12.00	18.00
Goblet	42.00	
Lamp	90.00	—
Orange Bowl	36.00	75.00
Pitcher, water	55.00	160.00
Sauce, flat	8.00	18.00
Spooner	35.00	55.00
Sugar Bowl, cov	48.00	55.00
Syrup, orig top	60.00	
Toothpick Holder	36.00	85.00
Tumbler	35.00	48.00
Vase	35.00	—
Water Bottle	42.00	—
Wine	36.00	—

Queen

Daisy and Button with Pointed Panels, Daisy with Depressed Button, Paneled Daisy and Button, Pointed Panel Daisy and Button, Sunk Daisy and Button, McKee's Pattern Line No. 2

Manufactured by McKee Glass Company, Jeannette, PA, c1894. Shards have been found at Burlington Glass Works site, Hamilton, Ontario, Canada. Made in non-flint, original production included amber, apple green, blue, canary yellow, and clear.

Reproductions: Reproductions have been made by Boyd's Crystal Art Glass Company, Cambridge, OH, and include the open low standard bowl, covered butter dish, high standard cake stand, high standard open compote, and goblet in clear, cobalt blue, and vaseline.

Items	Amber	Apple Green	Blue	Canary Yellow	Clear
Basket	130.00	130.00	142.00	118.00	90.00
Berry Bowl, 8-1/2" d	55.00	55.00	60.00	55.00	36.00
Bread Plate	55.00	60.00	60.00	55.00	42.00
Butter Dish, cov φ	100.00	100.00	115.00	95.00	65.00
Cake Stand, hs, 6-1/2" d φ	72.00	72.00	75.00	60.00	36.00
Cheese Dish, cov	120.00	120.00	130.00	115.00	90.00
Compote, cov, hs φ	90.00	90.00	110.00	85.00	55.00
Compote, open, hs	55.00	55.00	75.00	48.00	30.00
Creamer	42.00	42.00	48.00	42.00	36.00
Goblet φ	36.00	36.00	42.00	36.00	30.00
Pickle Tray, oval	18.00	35.00	30.00	35.00	12.00
Pitcher, milk	55.00	60.00	65.00	60.00	42.00
Pitcher, water	90.00	90.00	95.00	90.00	65.00
Sauce, flat, 4" d	18.00	18.00	25.00	18.00	12.00
Sauce, footed, 4" d	20.00	25.00	30.00	25.00	18.00
Spooner	36.00	36.00	42.00	36.00	30.00
Sugar Bowl, cov	70.00	75.00	75.00	70.00	60.00
Tumbler	36.00	42.00	42.00	36.00	30.00
Wine	42.00	48.00	48.00	42.00	35.00

Queen Anne

Bearded Man, Old Man, Old Man of the Woods, Santa Claus

Manufactured by LaBelle Glass Company, Bridgeport, OH, c1879. Finials are Maltese cross. Made in non-flint, clear. A table set and water pitcher are known in amber.

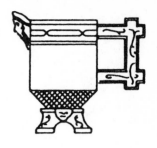

Items	Clear
Bowl, cov, oval, 8" or 9" l	55.00-65.00
Bowl, cov, round, 7" or 8" d	75.00-85.00
Bread Plate	60.00
Butter Dish, cov	75.00
Celery Vase	42.00
Compote, cov, hs, 7" or 8" d	75.00-85.00
Compote, cov, ls, 9" d	90.00
Compote, open, hs	55.00
Creamer	48.00
Egg Cup	55.00
Pitcher, milk	90.00
Pitcher, water	100.00
Salt Shaker	48.00
Sauce, ftd	18.00
Spooner	48.00
Sugar Bowl, cov	65.00
Syrup, orig top	120.00

Question Mark

Oval Loop

Manufactured by Richards & Hartley Glass Company, Pittsburgh, PA, in 1888, and later by U.S. Glass Company, Pittsburgh, PA, in 1892. A 1888 catalog lists thirty-two pieces. Made in non-flint, clear. Scarce in ruby stained.

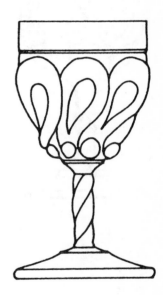

Items	Clear
Bowl, collared, round, 7" or 8" d	30.00
Bowl, oblong, 5" or 6" l	18.00
Bowl, oblong, 7" l	20.00
Bowl, oblong, 8" or 10" l	30.00
Bowl, oblong, 9" l	36.00
Bread Tray	36.00
Butter Dish, cov	45.00
Candlestick, chamber, finger loop	55.00
Celery Vase	35.00
Compote, cov, hs, 7" or 8" d	60.00-75.00
Compote, open, hs, 7" or 8" d	30.00-36.00
Compote, open, ls, 7" d	35.00
Compote, open, ls, 8" d	35.00
Cordial	35.00
Creamer	36.00
Goblet	30.00
Nappy, ftd	35.00
Pickle Jar, cov	55.00
Pitcher, milk, bulbous, quart or half gallon	48.00-60.00
Pitcher, milk, tankard, quart or half gallon	55.00-65.00
Salt Shaker	18.00
Sauce, collared or footed, 4" d	12.00
Spooner	35.00
Sugar Bowl, cov	30.00
Sugar Shaker	42.00
Sugar Bowl, cov	30.00
Tumbler	35.00
Wine	35.00

Raindrop

Manufactured by Doyle and Company, Pittsburgh, PA, c1885. Reissued by United States Glass Company, Pittsburgh, PA, in 1891. Made in non-flint, amber, blue, canary-yellow, and clear. An apple green hat ($90) and opaque blue milk glass pitcher are known. Also may have been made in white and blue milk glass.

Items	Amber	Blue	Canary-Yellow	Clear
ABC Plate	48.00	55.00	48.00	36.00
Butter Dish, cov	55.00	72.00	55.00	48.00
Cake Plate	48.00	60.00	48.00	36.00
Compote, cov, hs	65.00	75.00	65.00	55.00
Compote, cov, ls	55.00	65.00	55.00	42.00
Compote, open, hs	48.00	60.00	48.00	36.00
Compote, open, ls	42.00	55.00	42.00	35.00
Creamer	42.00	55.00	42.00	35.00

Items	Amber	Blue	Canary-Yellow	Clear
Cup and Saucer	48.00	60.00	48.00	30.00
Egg Cup, double	42.00	55.00	42.00	35.00
Finger Bowl	30.00	42.00	30.00	18.00
Lamp, miniature	100.00	—	100.00	—
Pickle Dish	30.00	42.00	30.00	35.00
Pitcher, water	55.00	65.00	55.00	42.00
Plate	48.00	60.00	48.00	36.00
Relish, oval	35.00	36.00	35.00	20.00
Sauce, flat	15.00	20.00	15.00	12.00
Sauce, footed	18.00	25.00	18.00	15.00
Spooner	48.00	60.00	48.00	36.00
Sugar Bowl, cov	55.00	72.00	55.00	42.00
Syrup, orig top	60.00	72.00	60.00	42.00
Tumbler	30.00	42.00	30.00	25.00
Water Tray	55.00	65.00	55.00	42.00
Wine	30.00	42.00	30.00	35.00

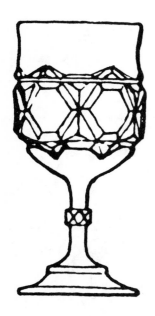

Red Block

Barrelled Block, Clear Block, Late Block, Bryce Pattern No. 175, Central's Pattern Line No. 881 and 893; Doyle's Pattern Line No. 250; Duncan Pattern Line No. 328 Fostoria's Pattern Line No. 140, Pioneer's Pattern Line No. 250

Manufactured by Doyle and Company, Pittsburgh, PA, c1885. Also made by Bryce Bothers, Pittsburgh, PA, c1898; Central Glass Co., Wheeling, WV; Fostoria Glass Company, Fostoria, OH, c1890; George Duncan & Sons, Pittsburgh, PA; Model Flint Glass Works, Albany, IN; Pioneer Glass Works, Pittsburgh, PA, c1890, as well as United States Glass Company, Pittsburgh, PA, in 1892. Because of the many manufacturers, many forms can be found, with several variations of handles, stems, and finials. Made in non-flint, clear with ruby stain, clear with amber stain. Prices for clear 50% less.

Reproductions: The goblet and wine have been reproduced in clear with amber and ruby stained blocks, as well as colors such as blue, iridescent amethyst, iridescent blue, and marigold carnival.

Items	Ruby Stained
Banana Boat	90.00
Bowl, 6", 8" or 9" d	72.00-95.00
Butter Dish, cov	120.00
Cake Stand, hs	90.00
Celery Tray	55.00
Celery Vase, 6-1/2"	100.00
Cheese Dish, cov	130.00
Creamer, individual or table	55.00-85.00
Decanter, os, 12" h	190.00
Dish, oblong, 8", 9" or 10" l	48.00-60.00
Goblet φ	42.00
Mug	40.00
Mustard, cov	65.00
Pitcher, water, bulbous, 8" h	190.00
Pitcher, water, tankard, ah, 8" h	225.00
Relish Tray	30.00
Rose Bowl	90.00
Salt, individual	60.00
Salt, master, flat	72.00
Salt Shaker	90.00
Sauce, flat, 4-1/2" d or 5" d	35.00
Sauce, footed, 4-1/2" d or 5" d	30.00
Spooner	55.00
Sugar Bowl, cov	110.00
Syrup, orig top	130.00
Tumbler	48.00
Waste Bowl	55.00
Water Tray	110.00
Wine φ	48.00

Reverse Torpedo

Bull's Eye Band, Bull's Eye with Diamond Point #2, Diamonds and Bull's Eye Band, Pointed Bull's Eye, Dalzell Pattern Line No. 490D

Manufactured by Dalzell, Gilmore and Leighton Glass Company, Findlay, OH, c1888-90. Also attributed to Burlington Glass Works, Hamilton, Ontario, Canada. Made in non-flint, clear. Sometimes found with copper wheel etching.

Items	Clear
Banana Stand, 9-3/4"	120.00
Basket	190.00

Items	Clear
Biscuit Jar, cov	142.00
Bowl, pie crust rim, 10-1/2" d	90.00
Bowl, shallow, 8-1/2" d	36.00
Bowl, smooth rim, 5-1/2" or 7-1/2" d	55.00-65.00
Bride's Basket	190.00
Butter Dish, cov, 7-1/2" d	90.00
Cake Stand, hs	100.00
Celery Vase, flat	65.00
Compote, cov, hs, 5", 6", 7", 8", 9" or 10" d	75.00-135.00
Compote, open, hs, pie crust rim, 5", 6", 7", 8", 9" or 10" d	65.00-95.00
Compote, open, hs, V shape bowl, 10-1/2" d	110.00
Compote, open, ls, 9-1/4", ruffled	100.00
Creamer, tankard, ah	55.00
Dish, flat, scalloped, metal handle, 11" d	72.00
Doughnut Tray	110.00
Fruit Basket, hs	155.00
Fruit Bowl, pie crust rim, 9" d	85.00
Goblet	100.00
Honey Dish sq, cov	155.00
Jam Jar, cov	100.00
Jelly Compote, cov, hs, 4" d	75.00
Jelly Compote, open, hs, 4" d	60.00
Lamp, oil, orig burner	190.00
Pitcher, milk, ah, tankard	110.00
Pitcher, water, ah, tankard, 10-1/4" h	172.00
Plate	42.00
Relish	36.00
Salt, master, flat	42.00
Salt Shaker, orig top	48.00
Sauce, flat, round or square, 3-3/4" d	12.00
Spooner	36.00
Sugar Bowl, cov	100.00
Syrup, orig top	175.00
Tumbler	36.00

Ribbed Ivy

Manufacture attributed to Boston and Sandwich Glass Company, Sandwich, MA, c1850. Made in flint, clear.

Items	Clear
Bowl, 6" or 8-1/2" d	18.00-35.00
Butter Dish, cov	120.00
Castor Bottle	42.00
Celery Vase	360.00
Champagne	120.00
Compote, open, hs, scalloped edge, 9" d	120.00
Cordial	90.00
Creamer	130.00
Decanter, os, pint or quart	130.00-160.00
Egg Cup, plain or rayed base	36.00
Goblet, plain or rayed base	55.00
Hat	360.00
Honey Dish, flat, 3-1/2" d	18.00
Jelly Compote, cov, hs, 6" d	130.00
Lamp, oil, brass standard, marble base	260.00
Lamp, oil, white milk glass standard	360.00
Mug, ah, small or large	95.00-120.00
Pitcher, water, ah	260.00
Salt, master, cov	130.00
Salt, master, open, beaded or scalloped rim	48.00
Sauce, flat, 4" d	15.00
Spooner	48.00
Sugar Bowl, cov	95.00
Sweetmeat, cov, on stand	175.00
Tumbler, bar	90.00
Tumbler, water	85.00
Whiskey, handle	120.00
Whiskey, plain	85.00
Wine	120.00

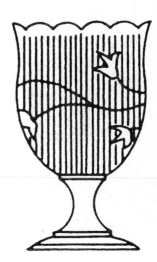

Ribbon

Frosted Ribbon, Rebecca at the Well, Simple Frosted Ribbon

Manufactured by Bakewell, Pears and Company, Pittsburgh, PA, in the late 1870s. Other Ribbon patterns are Clear Ribbon, Duncan's Frosted Ribbon, Double Ribbon, Fluted Ribbon, and Grated Ribbon. Made in non-flint, clear. Ribbon stripes are machine ground, rather than acid finished to give the appearance of frosting.

Reproductions: Compotes have been reproduced in clear and color by Fostoria for the Henry Ford Museum gift shop, and are usually marked "HFM." The Henry Ford Museum also has issued Rebecca at the Well candlesticks, which match the compotes, but were not original to the pattern. L. G. Wright Company, New Martinsville, WV, reproduced the goblet. It is unmarked, but can usually be identified by its rough-texture frosting.

Items	Frosted
Berry Bowl	65.00
Butter Dish, cov	85.00
Cake Stand, 8-1/2" d	60.00
Celery Vase, pedestal	48.00
Champagne	90.00
Cheese, cov	115.00
Cologne Bottle, os	75.00
Compote, cov, hs, 6", 7" or 8" d	75.00-90.00
Compote, cov, ls, 6", 7" or 8" d	48.00-60.00
Compote, open, hs, dolphin standard, round bowl, 10-1/2" d	260.00
Compote, open, hs, dolphin standard, oblong bowl, 8" l	290.00
Compote, open, hs, Rebecca at the Well standard	360.00
Compote, open, ls, 7" d	42.00
Creamer	36.00
Goblet φ	42.00
Pickle Jar, cov	115.00
Pitcher, milk, quart	75.00
Pitcher, water, half gallon	90.00
Plate	60.00
Platter, oblong, cut corners, 13" l, 9" w	75.00
Salt Shaker	48.00
Sauce, flat, tab handle; or footed	20.00
Spooner, ftd, scalloped	42.00
Sugar Bowl, cov	75.00
Waste Bowl	55.00
Water Tray, 15" d	120.00
Wine	130.00

Ribbon Candy

Bryce, Double Loop, Figure Eight, US Glass Pattern Line No. 15,010

Manufactured by Bryce Brothers, Pittsburgh, PA, in the 1880s. Reissued by U. S. Glass Company, Pittsburgh, PA, in the 1890s. Made in non-flint, clear. Also known in emerald green.

Items	Clear
Bowl, cov, collared base, 4" d or 5" d	35.00
Bowl, cov, collared base, 6" d or 8" d	40.00
Bowl, open, collared base, 4", 5" or 8" d	20.00-25.00
Bowl, open, flat, 6" d or 8" d	35.00
Bowl, oval, 8" l	30.00
Bread Plate, 10" d	42.00
Butter Dish, cov, flat or footed	60.00-65.00
Cake Plate, 9" d	42.00
Cake Stand, hs, 8", 9", 10" or 10-1/2" d	36.00-55.00
Celery Vase, pedestal	36.00
Child's Cake Stand, 6-1/2" d	45.00
Claret	75.00
Compote, cov, hs, 5", 6", 7" or 8" d	40.00-48.00
Compote, cov, ls, 5", 6", 7" or 8" d	40.00-48.00
Compote, open, hs, flared bowl, 6", 7", 8" or 10" d	30.00-48.00
Compote, open, hs, straight-sided bowl, 5", 6", 7", 8" or 10" d	35.00-48.00
Compote, open, ls, 3", 4", 5", 6", 7" or 8" d	20.00-35.00
Cordial	65.00
Creamer	30.00
Cruet, os	75.00
Cup and Saucer	48.00
Goblet	75.00
Honey Dish, cov, sq	90.00
Lamp, oil	90.00
Pickle Dish, boat shape	18.00
Pitcher, milk, quart	55.00
Pitcher, water, half gallon	90.00
Plate, 6" d	25.00
Plate, 7" d	35.00
Plate, 8" d	30.00
Plate, 9-1/2" or 10" d	36.00
Plate, 11" d	42.00
Relish	12.00
Salt Shaker	42.00
Sauce, flat or footed, 3-1/2" d, 4" d, or 4-1/2" d	15.00
Spooner	36.00
Sugar Bowl, cov	48.00
Syrup, orig top	110.00
Tumbler	30.00
Wine	65.00

Roanoke

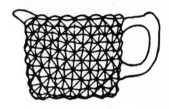

Manufactured by Ripley Glass Co., Pittsburgh, PA, c1885. Reissued by United States Glass Company, Pittsburgh, PA, after the 1891 merger. Made in non-flint, clear, emerald green, canary yellow, and ruby stained. Emerald greend and canary yellow pcs would be 30% clear.

Items	Clear	Ruby Stained
Bowl, deep or shallow, round or straight sides	30.00	55.00
Butter Dish, cov, ftd	65.00	90.00
Cake Stand, hs, curled scalloped rim, 8", 9" or 10"d	90.00	—
Compote, cov, hs, 5", 6", 7" or 8" d	48.00-60.00	100.00-115.00
Compote, open, deep bowl, 5", 6", 7" or 8" d	30.00-48.00	48.00-65.00
Compote, open, saucer bowl, 6", 7", 8" or 9" d	36.00-55.00	75.00-95.00
Creamer, flat, 3-1/2" h	42.00	60.00
Creamer, footed	48.00	72.00
Dish, flat, oblong, 7" l, 8" l, or 9" l	35.00	—
Goblet	30.00	48.00
Pitcher, water, jug or tankard, half gallon	55.00	110.00
Relish Tray	30.00	55.00
Rose Bowl	36.00	—
Salt, open, individual	12.00	36.00
Salt, open, master	20.00	60.00
Sauce, flat	12.00	35.00
Spooner, ftd	35.00	48.00
Sugar Bowl, cov, flat	48.00	72.00
Sugar Bowl, cov, footed	55.00	75.00
Tumbler	35.00	42.00
Wine	36.00	55.00

Roman Key

Frosted Roman Key, Grecian Border, Plain Roman Key.

Manufactured by Union Glass Company, Somerville, MA, c1860, and by others in several variants. Made in flint, frosted and in clear non-flint, but not as popular. Sometimes erroneously called "Greek Key."

Items	Clear	Frosted
Bowl, cable rim, 8", 9-1/2" or 10" d	36.00-42.00	55.00-60.00
Butter Dish, cov	48.00	95.00
Castor Set, silver plated holder	120.00	130.00
Celery Vase, ftd	48.00	95.00
Champagne	48.00	100.00
Compote, open, hs, cable rim, 8", 9" or 10" d	36.00-42.00	72.00-85.00
Compote, open, ls, cable rim, 7" or 8" d	40.00-42.00	75.00-85.00
Cordial	48.00	90.00
Creamer, ah, footed	110.00	125.00
Custard Cup	18.00	36.00
Decanter, os, pint or quart	—	350.00-250.00
Egg Cup	30.00	60.00
Goblet	50.00	75.00
Lamp, oil, orig burner and chimney	—	160.00
Mustard Jar, cov	—	55.00
Pickle Dish	—	55.00
Pitcher, milk, quart	—	230.00
Pitcher, water, half gallon	—	230.00
Plate, 6" d	—	42.00
Preserve Dish	—	55.00
Relish Dish, oval, cable rim	—	35.00
Salt, master, ftd	30.00	55.00
Sauce, flat, 4" d	12.00	25.00
Spooner, pedestal	30.00	55.00
Sugar Bowl, cov, hexagonal or octagonal stem	55.00	100.00
Tumbler, bar, flat or footed	30.00	55.00
Wine	—	100.00

Roman Rosette

US Glass Pattern Line No. 15,030

Manufactured by Bryce, Walker and Company, Pittsburgh, PA, c1890. Reissued by United States Glass Company, Pittsburgh, PA, in 1892 and 1898. Also attributed to Portland Glass Company, Portland, ME. Made in non-flint, clear, ruby stained and amber stained. Reproductions: Clear goblets were reproduced in the early 1960s.

Items	Clear	Ruby Stained
Bowl, 5", 5-1/2", 6", 7" or 8" d	15.00-20.00	—
Bowl, 8-1/2" d	18.00	60.00
Bread Plate	36.00	90.00

Items	Clear	Ruby Stained
Butter Dish, cov	60.00	130.00
Cake Stand, hs, 9" or 10" d	55.00	—
Castor Set, 2 bottles or 3 bottles, glass stand	60.00-75.00	—
Celery Vase	40.00	115.00
Compote, cov, hs, 5", 6", 7" or 8" d	60.00-75.00	100.00-120.00
Condiment Set, salt & pepper shakers, tray	48.00	—
Condiment Set, salt & pepper shakers, cov mustard, tray	60.00	130.00
Cordial	60.00	135.00
Creamer	40.00	55.00
Egg Cup	72.00	—
Goblet φ	48.00	75.00
Honey Dish, cov, sq	55.00	—
Jelly Compote, cov, hs, 4-1/2" d	60.00	100.00
Jug, 5 ounce	55.00	120.00
Jug, 6 ounce	60.00	125.00
Jug, 7 ounce	65.00	135.00
Mug, small or large	36.00-42.00	55.00-60.00
Mustard Jar, cov	55.00	—
Pickle Dish, boat shape	35.00	55.00
Pitcher, milk	55.00	160.00
Pitcher, water	60.00	175.00
Plate, 7" or 7-1/2" d	42.00	75.00
Platter, oval or round	42.00	90.00
Preserve Dish, oval, 7", 8" or 9" l	30.00	48.00
Relish, oval, 9"	35.00	48.00
Salt, master, footed	55.00	—
Salt and Pepper Shakers, pr	48.00	90.00
Sauce, flat, 4" d or 4-1/2" d	20.00	35.00
Sauce, footed, 4" d or 4-1/2" d	35.00	30.00
Sherbet	35.00	42.00
Spooner	30.00	55.00
Sugar Bowl, cov	48.00	95.00
Syrup, orig top	100.00	130.00
Tumbler	42.00	60.00
Wine	55.00	75.00

Rope Bands

Argent, Clear Panels with Cord Band

Manufactured by Bryce Bros., Pittsburgh, PA, c1870s. Later made by United States Glass Company, Pittsburgh, PA, after 1891. Made in non-flint, clear.

Items	Clear
Bowl	18.00
Bread Plate, medallion center	36.00
Butter Dish, cov	48.00
Cake Stand	42.00
Celery Vase	35.00
Compote, cov, double knob stem	42.00
Compote, open, double knob stem	35.00
Creamer	30.00
Goblet, double knob stem	30.00
Pitcher, water	48.00
Plate, medallion center, 6" or 7" d	18.00-35.00
Relish	18.00
Sauce, ftd	12.00
Spooner	35.00
Sugar Bowl, cov	36.00
Tumbler	35.00
Wine	30.00

Rose in Snow

Rose

Manufactured by Bryce Brothers, Pittsburgh, PA, in the square form, c1880. Also made in the more common round form by Ohio Flint Glass Company, Lancaster, OH, and after 1891 by United States Glass Company, Pittsburgh, PA. Both styles reissued by Indiana Glass Company, Dunkirk, IN. Made in non-flint, amber, blue, canary-yellow, and clear.

Reproductions: Reproductions have been made by several companies, including Imperial Glass Company, as early as 1930 and continuing through the 1970s. Colors round in reproductions include amber, blue, clear, frosted, milk white, ruby red, and vaseline.

Items	Amber	Blue	Canary-Yellow	Clear
Bitters Bottle, os	—	—	—	100.00
Bowl, cov, Items round, collared base	75.00	100.00	75.00	48.00

Items	Amber	Blue	Canary-Yellow	Clear
Bowl, sq, 8" w or 9" w	48.00	60.00	48.00	36.00
Butter Dish, cov, round	85.00	130.00	100.00	55.00
Butter Dish, cov, square	90.00	160.00	110.00	60.00
Cake Stand, hs, 9" d	130.00	190.00	130.00	110.00
Compote, cov, hs, 8" d	130.00	190.00	130.00	110.00
Compote, cov, ls, 7" d	120.00	160.00	120.00	90.00
Compote, open, ls, 5-3/4" d	48.00	135.00	48.00	42.00
Creamer, round	72.00	120.00	72.00	55.00
Creamer, square	75.00	65.00	75.00	55.00
Goblet φ	48.00	65.00	48.00	42.00
Marmalade Jar, cov	95.00	130.00	95.00	72.00
Mug, "In Fond Remembrance" φ	55.00	90.00	55.00	40.00
Pickle Dish, double, 8-1/2" x 7"	55.00	90.00	55.00	120.00
Pickle Dish, single, oval, handles at end φ	60.00	95.00	30.00	35.00
Pitcher, water, ah	190.00	240.00	190.00	25.00
Plate, 5" d	48.00	48.00	48.00	42.00
Plate, 6" d	36.00	95.00	36.00	25.00
Plate, 7" d	36.00	45.00	36.00	30.00
Plate, 9" d φ	36.00	100.00	36.00	35.00
Platter, oval	—	—	—	130.00
Sauce, flat	18.00	35.00	18.00	15.00
Sauce, footed	30.00	40.00	30.00	20.00
Spooner, round	36.00	95.00	36.00	30.00
Spooner, square	35.00	90.00	38.00	30.00
Sugar Bowl, cov, round	90.00	135.00	90.00	60.00
Sugar Bowl, cov, square	90.00	148.00	90.00	55.00
Sweetmeat, cov, 5-3/4" d	95.00	165.00	95.00	75.00
Toddy Jar, cov, underplate	160.00	165.00	160.00	130.00
Tumbler, flat	72.00	120.00	72.00	60.00

Rose Sprig

Manufactured by Campbell, Jones and Company, Pittsburgh, PA, 1886. Design patented by Henry Franz, May 25, 1886. Made in non-flint. Complete table line produced in amber, blue, canary-yellow, and clear.

Reproductions: A goblet and salt have been made from new molds, c1960. Colors of reproductions include amber, blue, canary-yellow, and clear.

Items	Amber	Blue	Canary-Yellow	Clear
Biscuit Jar, dome lid	240.00	260.00	240.00	120.00
Berry Bowl, master, sietz bath shape	55.00	75.00	60.00	30.00
Cake Stand, hs, 9" d	90.00	110.00	100.00	85.00
Celery Vase	60.00	72.00	65.00	48.00
Compote, cov, hs, 7" d	130.00	130.00	130.00	90.00
Compote, cov, hs, 8" d	136.00	136.00	136.00	100.00
Compote, cov, ls, 7" d	120.00	120.00	120.00	110.00
Compote, open, hs, 7" d	85.00	85.00	85.00	72.00
Compote, open, hs, oval, 8" l	80.00	90.00	80.00	72.00
Creamer, ph	75.00	65.00	75.00	55.00
Goblet	65.00	85.00	65.00	48.00
Mug, ph	65.00	65.00	65.00	48.00
Nappy, handle, 6" d	36.00	42.00	36.00	30.00
Pitcher, milk or water, ph	75.00	85.00	75.00	60.00
Plate, 6" d, 7" d, or 8" d	42.00	55.00	42.00	36.00
Plate, 10-1/2" d	48.00	60.00	48.00	42.00
Punch Bowl, ftd	130.00	160.00	130.00	100.00
Relish Tray, boat shape	36.00	42.00	36.00	30.00
Salt, patent date 1888	75.00	90.00	75.00	60.00
Salt, sleigh	36.00	48.00	36.00	30.00
Sauce, flat	35.00	36.00	35.00	15.00
Sauce, ftd	30.00	42.00	30.00	35.00
Spooner	36.00	42.00	36.00	30.00
Sugar Bowl, cov	65.00	85.00	65.00	55.00
Tumbler	48.00	55.00	48.00	42.00
Water Tray	65.00	85.00	65.00	55.00
Wine	65.00	90.00	65.00	60.00

Rosette

Magic

Manufactured by Bryce Bros., Pittsburgh, PA, in the late 1880s. Continued by United States Glass Company, Pittsburgh, PA, after the 1891 merger. Later made in Ohio, c1898. Made in non-flint, clear.

Items	Clear
Bowl, cov, 7-1/4" d	36.00
Bread Plate, oval, handles, 9" l	30.00
Butter Dish, cov	42.00
Cake Stand, hs, 7" d	40.00
Cake Stand, hs, 9" d	45.00
Cake Stand, hs, 10" d	45.00

Items	Clear
Cake Stand, hs, 11" d	50.00
Celery Vase, 8" d	35.00
Compote, cov, hs, 6", 7", 8" or 11-1/2" d	50.00-90.00
Compote, open, hs, 6", 7", 8", 9" or 10" d	30.00-55.00
Creamer	30.00
Goblet	30.00
Jelly Compote, open, hs, 4-1/2" d	30.00
Mug	35.00
Pickle Tray, fish shape	15.00
Pitcher, milk, quart	60.00
Pitcher, water, half gallon	75.00
Plate, 7" d	15.00
Relish, fish shape	15.00
Salt Shaker	30.00
Sauce, flat, handled	10.00
Spooner	30.00
Sugar Bowl, cov	42.00
Sugar Shaker	42.00
Syrup, orig top	50.00
Tray, 10-1/4"	42.00
Tumbler, 5"	20.00
Vegetable, open	30.00
Waste Bowl	30.00
Water Tray, 10-1/4" d	30.00
Wine	30.00

Royal Crystal

Diamond and Teardrop, Shining Diamonds, Tarentum's Atlanta

Manufactured by Tarentum Glass Company, Tarentum, PA, c1894. Made in non-flint, clear and clear with ruby stain.

Items	Clear	Ruby Stained
Bowl, flared, 5" d or 6" d	35.00	45.00
Bowl, flared, 7" d or 8" d	30.00	45.00
Bowl, square, 7-1/2" d	35.00	45.00
Bowl, straight, 5" d or 6" d	35.00	45.00
Bowl, straight, 7" d or 8" d	30.00	45.00
Bowl, triangular, handle, 6" l	30.00	20.00
Butter Dish, cov	55.00	110.00
Cake Stand, hs, 9" or 10" d	48.00-55.00	110.00-115.00
Candy Jar, cov	42.00	75.00
Celery Vase, 6-1/2" h	36.00	72.00
Cologne Bottle, os	55.00	90.00
Compote, cov, hs, 6" d or 7" d	72.00	135.00
Cracker Jar, cov	72.00	142.00
Creamer, 5-1/4" h	42.00	75.00
Cruet, os, 5 or 8 ounce	42.00-55.00	112.00-130.00
Dish, round, flat, 4" d	18.00	30.00
Goblet, 6-1/2" h	30.00	55.00
Pitcher, milk, bulbous, quart	55.00	120.00
Pitcher, water, bulbous or tankard, half gallon	75.00	135.00
Plate, 6" d	18.00	36.00
Salt Shaker, orig nickel top	18.00	42.00
Sauce, flat, 4" d or 4-1/2" d	12.00	35.00
Sauce, ftd, 4" d or 4-1/2" d	18.00	30.00
Spooner	36.00	60.00
Sugar Bowl, cov, table, 7-1/2" h	48.00	90.00
Sugar Bowl, open, individual	35.00	42.00
Syrup, orig nickel top	90.00	130.00
Toothpick Holder	36.00	72.00
Tumbler	35.00	45.00
Water Bottle	65.00	90.00
Wine	30.00	55.00

Royal Ivy

New Jewel, Northwood Pattern Line No. 287

Manufactured by Northwood Glass Company in 1889. Made in non-flint, clear with frosting (acid finish), rubena and frosted (acid finish) rubena. Also made were cased spatter, clear and frosted rainbow cracquelle, clear with amber, stained ivy, and clambroth opaline. These last mentioned were experimental pieces, not made in sets.

Items	Clear Frosted	Rubena Clear	Rubena Frosted
Berry Bowl, master	48.00	90.00	130.00
Butter Dish, cov	120.00	190.00	290.00
Creamer, ah	72.00	160.00	240.00

Items	Clear Frosted	Rubena Clear	Rubena Frosted
Cruet, os	110.00	230.00	330.00
Finger Bowl	30.00	60.00	75.00
Marmalade Jar, silver plated cov	130.00	—	—
Miniature Lamp	160.00	260.00	360.00
Pickle Castor, silver plated frame	130.00	240.00	390.00
Pitcher, water, ah	112.00	190.00	290.00
Rose Bowl	65.00	85.00	100.00
Salt Shaker, orig top	30.00	36.00	48.00
Sauce, flat	35.00	30.00	42.00
Spooner	55.00	85.00	115.00
Sugar Bowl, cov	160.00	175.00	195.00
Sugar Shaker	75.00	142.00	160.00
Syrup, orig top	135.00	230.00	360.00
Toothpick Holder	60.00	110.00	130.00
Tumbler	42.00	60.00	90.00

Royal Lady

Belmont's Royal, Royal

Manufactured by Belmont Glass Company, Bellaire, OH, c1881. Some pieces have ball feet. Made in non-flint, clear. A light amber bread plate ($90) is known.

Items	Clear
Bread Plate, crying child in center	65.00
Butter Dish, cov, 6-sided skirted base	148.00
Celery Vase	95.00
Cheese Dish, cov, base has portrait center, large dome lid	160.00
Compote, cov, hs, mkd "Fox" in lid design, 9" d	160.00
Creamer	115.00
Dish, cov, oval	112.00
Ice Cream Tray	135.00
Salt, master, 6-sided skirted base	35.00
Sauce	35.00
Spooner	115.00
Sugar Bowl, cov	115.00

Royal Oak

Acorn

Manufactured by Northwood Glass Company, Martins Ferry, Ohio, c1890. Made in non-flint, clear with frosting (acid finish), rubena and frosted (acid finish) rubena. In the early 1900s, it was made in opaque, white with colored tops and colored acorns and leaves. Milk-white pieces are rare.

Items	Clear Frosted	Rubena Clear	Rubena Frosted
Butter Dish, cov	160.00	190.00	360.00
Creamer, ah	90.00	130.00	160.00
Cruet, os	160.00	430.00	495.00
Marmalade Jar, cov	110.00	160.00	260.00
Pickle Castor, silver plated frame	120.00	160.00	230.00
Pitcher, water	120.00	360.00	360.00
Salt Shaker, orig top	48.00	55.00	75.00
Sauce, flat	18.00	35.00	50.00
Spooner	60.00	110.00	120.00
Sugar Bowl, cov, acorn finial	100.00	160.00	195.00
Sugar Shaker	90.00	142.00	175.00
Syrup, orig top	142.00	240.00	290.00
Toothpick Holder	55.00	100.00	130.00
Tumbler	48.00	72.00	95.00

Sandwich Star

Manufacture attributed to Boston & Sandwich Glass Company, Sandwich, MA, c1850. Made in flint, amethyst, clambroth, clear, electric blue, jade green, opaque blue, and opaque lavender. Colors are rare.

Items	Clear
Butter Dish, cov	360.00
Champagne	360.00
Compote, open, dolphin standard	1,000.00
Compote, open, hs, scalloped rim	360.00
Cordial	360.00

Creamer, ah	390.00
Decanter, os, pint or quart	130.00
Goblet	480.00
Lamp, whale oil, orig burner	200.00
Pitcher, water, ah	600.00
Relish Dish	85.00
Spill Holder	120.00
Spooner	120.00
Sugar Bowl, cov	430.00
Wine, large	750.00
Wine, small	175.00

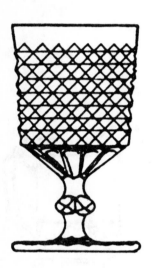

Sawtooth

Cambridge Sawtooth, Crosett Sawtooth, Diamond, Diamond Point, Lumberton Sawtooth, Mitre Diamond, Pineapple, Gillinder Pattern Line No. 56

An early clear flint made in the late 1850s by the New England Glass Company, Cambridge, MA; Boston and Sandwich Glass Company, Sandwich, MA; James B. Lyon & Co., Pittsburgh, PA, early 1860s; McKee & Brothers, Pittsburgh, PA, c1859-1865; Gillinder & Sons, Philadelphia, PA; Union Glass Company, Somerville, MA. Later made in non-flint by Bryce Brothers, Pittsburgh, PA, and United States Glass Company, Pittsburgh, PA. Because this pattern was made for more than forty years and by many manufacturers, there are many variations. Made in flint, non-flint, clear. Also known in milk glass, amethyst, amber, blue, fiery opalescent, jade green, medium blue, clear deep sapphire blue, opaque blue, and canary yellow. Flint colors are rare.

Reproductions: Westmoreland Glass Company, Grapeville, PA, reissued the covered compote with high standard in milk white, c1977-78, using the old mold. New molds were created to make a flat covered butter dish, 6" d covered compote, 9" d covered compote, 6-1/2" d covered dish, goblet, iced tea, sherbet, and wine. The Westmoreland reissued usually are marked with its "W. G." monogram. L. G. Wright Glass Company, New Martinsville, WV, reproduced the 6-1/2" d covered butter dish in clear in 1967. It also created a sherbet and wine.

Items	Flint	Non-Flint
Bowl, cov, 6" or 7" d	65.00-75.00	—
Bowl, open, flat, 6", 7", 8", 9" or 10" d	24.00-48.00	—
Butter Dish, cov	90.00	55.00
Cake Stand, hs, 9", 10" or 11" d	95.00-110.00	55.00-72.00
Cake Stand, hs, 12" or 14" d	115.00-120.00	—
Celery Vase, pedestal, 10" h	72.00	36.00
Champagne	75.00	36.00
Child's Butter Dish, cov	—	55.00
Child's Creamer, ph	—	30.00
Child's Spooner	—	45.00
Child's Sugar Bowl	—	45.00
Compote, cov, hs, deep bowl, 6", 7", 8", 9", 9-1/2" or 10" d	90.00-115.00	55.00-72.00
Compote, cov, hs, shallow bowl, 6" or 7" d	90.00-95.00	55.00-60.00
Compote, open, hs, flared deep bowl, sawtooth rim, 6", 7", 8", 9" ot 10" d	45.00-72.00	36.00-60.00
Compote, open, hs, flared shallow bowl, sawtooth rim, 6" or 7" d	45.00	36.00
Compote, open, ls, deep bowl, 6", 7", 8", 9" or 10" d	45.00-55.00	36.00-48.00
Cordial	60.00	36.00
Creamer, applied handle	90.00	48.00
Creamer, pressed handle	55.00	36.00
Cruet, acorn stopper	120.00	60.00
Decanter, os, quart	65.00	45.00
Dish, flat, oval, 5" l, 6" l, or 7" l	36.00	24.00
Egg Cup	55.00	30.00
Fruit Dish, 6", 7", 8", 9", 10", 11" or 12" d	36.00-48.00	24.00-36.00
Goblet, knob or plain stem	60.00	24.00
Honey Dish	18.00	12.00
Lamp, oil, orig burner and chimney	160.00	—
Lamp Shade, gas	—	45.00
Pitcher, milk, ah, quart	115.00	75.00
Pitcher, milk, ph, quart	90.00	55.00
Pitcher, water, ah, half gallon	160.00	115.00
Pitcher, water, ph, half gallon	—	65.00
Plate, 6-1/2" d	55.00	36.00
Pomade Jar, cov	60.00	45.00
Salt, master, cov, ftd	75.00	48.00
Salt, master, open, smooth edge	30.00	24.00
Sauce, flat, 4" d, 4-1/2" d, or 5" d	18.00	12.00
Spill Holder	60.00	—
Spooner, plain or rayed base	85.00	36.00
Sugar Bowl, cov	75.00	45.00
Tumbler, bar	60.00	30.00
Tumble-Up, water bottle and tumbler	72.00	—
Tumbler, water, flat or footed	55.00	30.00
Water Tray, 10", 11", 12" or 14" d	—	75.00-100.00
Wine, knob or plain stem	45.00	24.00

Sawtoothed Honeycomb

Sawtooth Honeycomb, Serrated Block and Loop, Steimer's Diamond, Union's Radiant

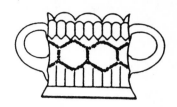

Manufactured by Steimer Glass Company, Buckhannon, WV, c1906. The molds were sold to Union Stopper Company, Morgantown, WV, c1908. Made in non-flint, clear and ruby stained. Some pieces have gilt trim.

Items	Clear	Ruby Stained
Berry Bowl, flat	24.00	55.00
Bon Bon	30.00	45.00
Bowl, 9" d	18.00	55.00
Butter Dish, cov	48.00	120.00
Celery Vase	30.00	95.00
Compote, open, hs	45.00	60.00
Creamer, 4" h, ph	30.00	48.00
Cruet, os	60.00	130.00
Goblet	30.00	72.00
Orange Bowl, 14-1/2" d	75.00	130.00
Pitcher, water, ph, two pints or half gallon	36.00-60.00	115.00-155.00
Salt Shaker, orig top	24.00	45.00
Sauce, flat or ftd,, 4"d or 4-1/2" d	12.00-15.00	24.00-30.00
Spooner	36.00	55.00
Sugar Bowl, cov	55.00	90.00
Sugar, open, double handles	45.00	60.00
Syrup, orig top	72.00	190.00
Toothpick Holder	30.00	160.00
Tumbler, flat, 3-3/4" h	24.00	48.00

Scalloped Diamond Point

Late Diamond Point Band, Panel with Diamond Point, Diamond Point with Flute

Manufactured by Central Glass Company, Wheeling, WV. Also made by United States Glass Company, Pittsburgh, PA, after 1891. Made in non-flint, clear. A wine ($90) is known in electric blue and in amber ($60).

Items	Clear
Bowl, oval, 9" l	24.00
Butter Dish, cov	65.00
Cake Stand, hs, 8" or 12" d	45.00-55.00
Cheese Dish, cov, 8" d	60.00
Compote, cov, hs, 8" d	90.00
Compote, open, hs, 7" d	48.00
Creamer	60.00
Goblet	36.00
Jelly Compote, cov, 5" d	45.00
Mustard Jar, cov	36.00
Pickle Dish, oval	24.00
Pickle Jar, cov	55.00
Plate, 5" or 9" d	15.00-24.00
Sauce, ftd, 4" d	12.00
Spooner	30.00
Sugar Bowl, cov	48.00
Wine	45.00

Scalloped Six Points

Divided Medallion with Diamond Cut, Duncan's Pattern Line No. 30

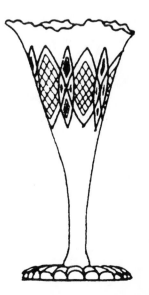

Manufactured by George Duncan & Sons, Washington, PA, c1897 to 1912. Made in non-flint, clear, and rarely in clear with ruby stain. Goblets, clarets, and wines made in both a cupped and straight bowl form. Both forms have the same value.

Items	Clear
Bowl, round, 9" d; or square, 9" w	36.00
Butter Dish, cov	55.00
Butter Pat	12.00
Cake Stand, hs, round or square	48.00-55.00
Celery Tray	30.00
Celery Vase	36.00
Champagne	36.00
Claret	36.00
Cocktail	36.00
Compote, open, hs	45.00
Compote, open, ls	36.00

Items	Clear
Cordial	36.00
Cracker Jar, cov	72.00
Creamer, individual or table size	36.00-45.00
Custard Cup	18.00
Egg Cup	30.00
Goblet	48.00
Mustard Jar, cov	24.00
Nappy, handle	18.00
Pickle Dish	24.00
Pickle Jar, cov	60.00
Pitcher, water, bulbous or tankard	55.00-60.00
Plate	24.00
Rose Bowl	55.00
Salt, individual	18.00
Salt Shaker, orig top	30.00
Sherbet	18.00
Sherry	30.00
Spooner	36.00
Sugar Bowl, cov, individual or table size	45.00
Syrup, orig top	55.00
Toothpick Holder	55.00
Tumbler	30.00
Vase, 6" or 8" h	24.00
Wine	30.00

Scroll

Lilly, Stippled Scroll

Manufactured by George Duncan & Sons Company, Pittsburgh, PA, c1870. Made in non-flint, clear. Also made in milk glass and light blue opaque.

Items	Clear
Butter Dish, cov	60.00
Celery Vase	36.00
Compote, cov, hs, 7" d	75.00
Compote, cov, ls, 7" d	72.00
Compote, open, hs, 7" d	45.00
Creamer, ah	48.00
Egg Cup, pedestal	36.00
Goblet	45.00
Pitcher, water, ah	90.00
Salt, individual or master, footed	24.00-30.00
Sauce	12.00
Spooner	36.00
Sugar Bowl, cov	55.00
Sugar Bowl, open	30.00
Tumbler, ftd	30.00
Wine	36.00

Scroll with Flowers

Manufacture attributed to Central Glass Company, Wheeling, WV, in the 1870s and the Canton Glass Company, Canton, OH, c1880. Made in non-flint, clear. Occasionally found in amber, apple green, and blue.

Items	Clear
Butter Dish, cov	48.00
Cake Plate, handle, 10-1/2" d	30.00
Celery Vase	45.00
Compote, cov, ls	55.00
Cordial	45.00
Creamer	48.00
Egg Cup, handle	24.00
Goblet	30.00
Mustard Jar, cov	60.00
Pickle Tray, handle	20.00
Pitcher, water, half gallon	55.00
Plate, double-handles, 10-1/2" d	48.00
Sauce, double-handles	12.00
Spooner	28.50
Sugar Bowl, cov	55.00
Syrup, orig top	90.00
Wine	36.00

Sedan

Paneled Star and Button

Manufacturer unknown, c1870. Made in non-flint, clear.

Items	Clear
Berry Bowl, master	24.00
Butter Dish, cov	36.00
Celery Tray	18.00
Celery Vase	30.00
Compote, cov, hs, 8-1/2" d	45.00
Compote, open, hs, scalloped rim	24.00
Creamer	24.00
Goblet	18.00
Mug	18.00
Pickle Tray, double handles	20.00
Pitcher, water	45.00
Relish Tray	12.00
Salt Shaker	24.00
Sauce, flat	10.00
Spooner	18.00
Sugar Bowl, cov	45.00
Tumbler	24.00
Wine	18.00

Shell and Jewel

Jewel and Shell, Victor, Nugget, Late Nugget, Fostoria Pattern Line No. 618

Manufactured by Westmoreland Glass Company, Grapeville, PA, c1893. Made by Fostoria Glass Company, Moundsville, WV, in 1898. Also attributed to Sydenham Glass Company, Wallaceburg, Ontario, Canada, c1895, and Jefferson Glass Company, Toronto, Ontario, Canada, c1920. American-made items have more rounded shell decorations. Canadian-made items have pointed shells sometimes with rows of balls between fans. Made in non-flint, amber, blue, and clear. Limited production in amber, cobalt blue, green, and carnival glass.

Items	Amber	Blue	Clear
Banana Stand, 10" d	—	—	75.00
Berry Bowl, 8" d	45.00	—	24.00
Bowl, 6" d	—	—	24.00
Butter Dish, cov, large or small	—	—	72.00
Cake Stand, hs, 10" d	—	—	60.00
Compote, cov, hs, 7" d	—	—	60.00
Compote, open, hs, 7" d	—	—	45.00
Creamer, ftd	—	—	48.00
Dish, oval, 7" or 8" l	—	—	24.00
Honey Dish, cov	—	—	30.00
Orange Bowl	—	—	75.00
Pitcher, water	60.00	72.00	55.00
Sauce, flat, 4-1/2" d	—	—	15.00
Spooner	—	—	24.00
Sugar Bowl, cov	—	—	60.00
Tumbler	45.00	48.00	30.00
Water Set, 8 pcs	360.00	360.00	240.00
Water Tray	—	—	60.00

Shell and Tassel

Shell and Spike, Duncan Pattern Line No. 555

Manufactured by George A. Duncan and Sons, Pittsburgh, PA, in the 1880s. It was patented by Augustus Heisey on July 26, 1881 in two forms. Patent No. 12,371 was for frosted corner shells, and Patent No. 12,372 was for clear corner shells. Shards have also been found at the site of the Burlington Glass Works, Hamilton, Ontario, Canada. There is a square form that has shell-shaped finials, scalloped rims. Some cake stands and compotes in this shape are sometimes marked "Duncan & Sons" on the bases. The round form has frosted dog finials and smooth rims. Made in non-flint, clear. Also made in azure blue, amber, and canary, but colored forms are rare.

Reproductions: L. G. Wright Glass Company, New Martinsville, WV, made a clear goblet, c1970.

Items	Round	Square
Bowl, cov, 6", 7" or 8" d	—	112.00-124.00
Bowl, oval, 12" l	100.00	75.00
Bread Plate	65.00	75.00
Butter Dish, cov	130.00	130.00
Butter Pat, shell shaped	—	30.00
Cake Stand, hs, 5", 6", 7", 8", 9", 10" or 11" d	—	65.00-100.00

Items	Round	Square
Cake Stand, hs, 12" d	72.00	110.00
Celery Vase	65.00	65.00
Compote, cov, hs, 6" d	—	100.00
Compote, open, hs, 6", 7", 8" or 9" d		55.00-72.00
Compote, open, hs, 10" d	90.00	75.00
Creamer	48.00	65.00
Goblet φ	48.00	55.00
Jelly Compote, open, 4-1/2" d		55.00
Ice Cream Tray	75.00	—
Nappy	24.00	30.00
Oyster Plate	230.00	
Pickle Jar, cov		160.00
Pitcher, water	100.00	100.00
Plate, fan shape, 12" w	—	130.00
Salt, individual	—	18.00
Salt Shaker	60.00	120.00
Sauce, flat or ftd, 4" d or 4-1/2" d	12.00	12.00-18.00
Soda Tumbler, 10, 15 or 18 oz	—	48.00-60.00
Spooner	42.00	48.00
Sugar Bowl, cov	120.00	100.00
Tumbler, 9 oz	—	48.00
Vase, scalloped rim, 7-1/2" h	—	120.00

Sheraton

Ida

Manufactured by Bryce, Higbee and Company, Pittsburgh, PA, c1885. Also attributed to Burlington Glass Works, Hamilton, Ontario, Canada. Made in non-flint, amber, blue, and clear.

Items	Amber	Blue	Clear
Bowl, 8"	45.00	48.00	18.00
Bread Plate	55.00	60.00	30.00
Butter Dish, cov	48.00	60.00	30.00
Celery Vase	36.00	45.00	28.50
Compote, cov, hs, 7" d	55.00	65.00	45.00
Compote, open, hs, 7" d	36.00	45.00	30.00
Compote, open, ls, 7" d	30.00	36.00	24.00
Creamer	45.00	55.00	36.00
Goblet	48.00	60.00	45.00
Pitcher, milk	48.00	60.00	36.00
Pitcher, water	55.00	65.00	45.00
Relish, handle	30.00	36.00	18.00
Sauce, flat or footed, 3-1/2" d	18.00	20.00	12.00
Spooner	30.00	36.00	20.00
Sugar Bowl, cov	48.00	65.00	36.00
Tumbler	45.00	48.00	36.00
Wine	45.00	48.00	36.00

Shosone

Blazing Pinwheels, Floral Diamond, Victor, US Glass Pattern Line No. 15,046

Manufactured by United States Glass Company, Pittsburgh, PA, c1895-96. Westmoreland Glass Company, Grapeville, PA, copied the pattern and sold it through its Sterling line. Made in non-flint, clear, emerald green, and amber stained or ruby stained.

Items	Amber Stained	Clear	Green	Ruby Stained
Banana Stand, hs	100.00	75.00	85.00	100.00
Bowl, collared base, 7" d or 8" d	55.00	36.00	48.00	55.00
Bowl, flat, flared, 5" d or 6" d	48.00	30.00	45.00	48.00
Bowl, flat, flared, 7" or 8" d	55.00	36.00	48.00	55.00
Bowl, flat, straight sides, 6" d or 7" d	48.00	30.00	45.00	48.00
Bowl, flat, straight sides, 8" d	55.00	36.00	48.00	55.00
Butter, domed cov	90.00	55.00	75.00	100.00
Cake Stand, hs, 9", 10" or 11" d	—	45.00-55.00	60.00-72.00	—
Celery Vase	100.00	45.00	75.00	100.00
Compote, cov, hs, 6" or 7" d	100.00	60.00	65.00	100.00
Compote, cov, hs, 8" d	110.00	65.00	72.00	110.00
Compote, cov, ls, 7" d	—	60.00	72.00	—
Compote, open, ls, 8" d	—	65.00	—	—
Compote, open, ls, 4-1/2" d	90.00	45.00	55.00	90.00
Compote, open, ls, 7" d	100.00	55.00	60.00	100.00
Compote, open, ls, 9" d	110.00	60.00	72.00	110.00
Compote, open, ls, 10" d	120.00	65.00	75.00	120.00

Items	Amber Stained	Clear	Green	Ruby Stained
Creamer, individual	45.00	30.00	36.00	45.00
Creamer, table, 5" h	55.00	30.00	55.00	55.00
Goblet, 6-1/2" h	65.00	36.00	—	72.00
Horseradish, cov	—	36.00	—	72.00
Ice Tub, tab handles	90.00	45.00	75.00	90.00
Jelly Dish, double handles, 5-1/2" w	30.00	18.00	30.00	30.00
Olive Tray, 7-3/4" l	30.00	18.00	30.00	30.00
Pickle Tray	30.00	24.00	30.00	30.00
Pitcher, water, ah, bulbous or tankard, half gallon	190.00	60.00	160.00	190.00
Plate, 7" d, sq	—	36.00	—	45.00
Salt, master	65.00	30.00	—	75.00
Salt Shaker, orig top	55.00	24.00	48.00	55.00
Sauce, flat, 4" d	24.00	24.00	12.00	24.00
Spooner	48.00	30.00	45.00	65.00
Sugar Bowl, cov, individual	65.00	45.00	65.00	75.00
Sugar Bowl, cov, table	75.00	48.00	75.00	90.00
Toothpick Holder, 2-3/4" h	230.00	48.00	100.00	230.00
Tumbler, 2-3/4" h	55.00	45.00	48.00	55.00
Wine, 4-1/2" h	45.00	36.00	45.00	55.00

Shrine

Jewel with Moon and Star, Little Shrine, Orient

Manufactured by Beatty & Indiana Glass Company, Dunkirk, IN, around the late 1880s. Made in non-flint, clear.

Items	Clear
Bowl, 4", 6-1/2" or 9-1/2" d	18.00-36.00
Butter Dish, cov	60.00
Cake Stand, hs, 8-1/2" d	48.00
Celery	55.00
Creamer	48.00
Goblet	55.00
Jelly Compote, hs	24.00
Lemonade Tumbler	48.00
Mug	30.00
Pickle Tray	24.00
Pitcher, water, normal or jumbo size	60.00-120.00
Platter	48.00
Relish	18.00
Salt Shaker, squatty or tall	36.00
Sauce, flat, 4" d	18.00
Spooner	36.00
Sugar Bowl, cov	60.00
Toothpick Holder	110.00
Tumbler, water	45.00

Shuttle

Hearts of Loch Haven

Manufactured by Indiana Tumbler and Goblet Company, Greentown, IN, c1896, and Indiana Glass Company, Dunkirk, IN, c1898. Made in non-flint, clear, and some forms in chocolate glass.

Items	Clear	Chocolate
Berry Bowl, master	30.00	550.00
Butter Dish, cov	60.00	1,120.00
Cake Stand	118.00	—
Celery Vase	36.00	—
Champagne	95.00	900.00
Cordial	40.00	75.00
Creamer, table size	36.00	650.00
Creamer, tankard	45.00	130.00
Cruet, os	30.00	—
Custard Cup	12.00	
Goblet	72.00	950.00
Mug	30.00	85.00
Nappy	40.00	190.00
Pitcher, water	60.00	3,500.00
Punch Cup	10.00	110.00
Salt Shaker, orig top	55.00	350.00
Sauce, flat	12.00	—
Spooner	24.00	500.00
Sugar Bowl, cov	48.00	850.00
Tumbler	30.00	140.00
Wine	24.00	1,250.00

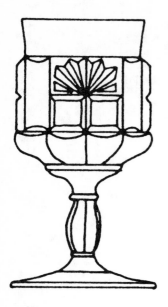

Skilton

Early Oregon

Manufactured by Richards & Hartley of Tarentum, PA, in 1888, and by United States Glass Company, Pittsburgh, PA, after 1891. This is not one of the United States Glass States pattern series and should not be confused with Beaded Loop, which is Oregon #1, named by United States Glass Company. It is better known as Skilton (named by Millard) to avoid confusion with Beaded Loop. Made in non-flint, clear, and clear with ruby stain.

Items	Clear	Ruby Stained
Bowl, rect, 7", 8" or 9" l	24.00-36.00	—
Bowl, round, 4" or 5" d	12.00-18.00	—
Bowl, round, 6" or 8" d	24.00-30.00	45.00-48.00
Butter Dish, cov	55.00	112.00
Cake Stand, hs	45.00	
Celery Vase	45.00	115.00
Compote, cov, hs, 7" or 8" d	55.00	
Compote, open, hs, 7" or 8" d	30.00-36.00	—
Compote, open, ls, 4" or 7" d	12.00-30.00	
Compote, open, ls, 8"d	36.00	90.00
Creamer	36.00	65.00
Dish, oblong, sq	30.00	—
Goblet	45.00	60.00
Jelly Compote, hs, 4-1/2" d	12.00	45.00
Olive, handle	24.00	—
Pickle Tray	18.00	—
Pitcher, milk, bulbous	55.00	130.00
Pitcher, water, bulbous or tankard	60.00-65.00	130.00-136.00
Salt and Pepper Shakers, pr	55.00	—
Sauce, flat or ftd, 4" d	12.00-15.00	24.00
Spooner, flat	30.00	65.00
Sugar Bowl, cov	45.00	100.00
Tumbler	30.00	48.00
Water Tray	55.00	—
Wine	45.00	60.00

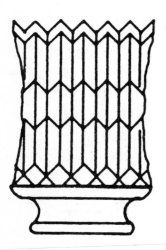

Smocking

Manufactured by Boston and Sandwich Glass Company, Sandwich, MA, 1845-55. Some variants. Made in flint, clear. Rare in color.

Items	Clear
Bar Bottle, blob top	120.00
Bowl, 9" d	90.00
Compote, cov, ls, 7" d	110.00
Creamer	110.00
Egg Cup	60.00
Goblet, knob or straight stem	100.00
Lamp, oil, 9" h	155.00
Pitcher, water	118.00
Spill Holder	90.00
Spooner	48.00
Sugar Bowl, cov	100.00
Sugar Bowl, open	60.00
Tumbler, footed	75.00
Vase, 10" d	75.00
Whiskey, flat	90.00
Wine	55.00

Snail

Compact, Double Snail, Small Comet, Duncan's Pattern Line No. 360

Manufactured by George Duncan and Sons, Pittsburgh, PA, c1880, and by United States Glass Company, Pittsburgh, PA, after the 1891 merger. United States Glass Company production expanded this clear pattern by the addition of ruby staining. Made in non-flint, clear, clear with etched designs, and clear with ruby staining. Add 30% for copper wheel engraved pieces.

Items	Clear	Ruby Stained
Banana Stand, hs, 9" or 10" d	160.00-175.00	230.00-260.00
Bowl, cov, 7" or 8" d	72.00	55.00
Bowl, oval, 7" or 8" l	30.00	55.00
Bowl, oval, 9" l	36.00	—
Bowl, round, 7" or 8" d	30.00	55.00
Bowl, round, 9" d	36.00	
Bowl, round, deep, 10" d	45.00	55.00
Bowl, round, shallow, 10" d	45.00	—
Butter Dish, cov	90.00	172.00
Cake Basket, pewter handle, 9" or 10" d	100.00-115.00	—

Items	Clear	Ruby Stained
Cake Stand, hs, 9" or 10" d	100.00-115.00	—
Celery Tray	45.00	—
Celery Vase	48.00	100.00
Cheese, cov	115.00	—
Compote, cov, hs, 6" d	60.00	—
Compote, cov, hs, 7" or 8" d	60.00-95.00	120.00-145.00
Compote, cov, hs, 10" d	130.00	—
Compote, open, hs, 6", 7", 8", 9" or 10" d	36.00-60.00	—
Compote, open, hs, twisted stem, scalloped, 9" d	90.00	—
Cracker Jar, cov	100.00	—
Creamer, individual, table size or tankard	72.00-85.00	85.00-95.00
Cruet, os	120.00	290.00
Custard Cup	36.00	—
Finger Bowl	60.00	
Goblet	75.00	115.00
Marmalade, cov	110.00	130.00
Pitcher, milk, tankard	120.00	260.00
Pitcher, water, bulbous or tankard	130.00-145.00	260.00
Plate, 5", 6" or 7" d	45.00-48.00	—
Punch Cup	36.00	—
Relish, oval, 7" l	30.00	—
Rose Bowl, 3" or 7" d	60.00	—
Rose Bowl, 5" or 6" d	55.00	—
Salt, individual or master	45.00	48.00-90.00
Salt Shaker, bulbous or straight sides	75.00	110.00
Sauce, flat or footed, 4" or 4-1/2" d	24.00-30.00	48.00-55.00
Spooner	55.00	90.00
Sugar Bowl, cov, individual	60.00	
Sugar Bowl, cov, table	72.00	120.00
Sugar Shaker	100.00	240.00
Syrup, orig top	130.00	230.00
Tumbler, flat	65.00	75.00
Vase	60.00	110.00
Violet Bowl, 3"	60.00	—
Wine	75.00	—

Spirea Band

Earl, Nailhead Variant, Spirea, Square and Dot, Squared Dot

Manufactured by Bryce, Higbee and Company, Pittsburgh, PA, c1885. Made in non-flint, amber, blue, clear, and vaseline.

Items	Amber	Blue	Clear	Vaseline
Bowl, deep or shallow, ftd, 8" d	30.00	48.00	24.00	36.00
Bowl, flat, 8" d	30.00	48.00	24.00	36.00
Butter Dish, cov	60.00	65.00	45.00	55.00
Cake Stand, hs, 11" d	55.00	65.00	48.00	55.00
Celery Vase	48.00	60.00	30.00	48.00
Compote, cov, hs, 6" d	48.00	72.00	45.00	48.00
Compote, cov, hs, 7" d	55.00	75.00	48.00	55.00
Compote, cov, ls, 6" d	48.00	72.00	45.00	48.00
Compote, cov, ls, 7" d	55.00	75.00	48.00	60.00
Compote, open, hs, 7" d	36.00	45.00	30.00	36.00
Cordial	48.00	45.00	24.00	42.00
Creamer	45.00	55.00	45.00	55.00
Goblet	36.00	45.00	30.00	45.00
Honey Dish, flat	18.00	18.00	12.00	18.00
Pickle Dish	18.00	18.00	12.00	18.00
Pitcher, water	75.00	95.00	45.00	72.00
Platter, oval, 10-1/2" l	36.00	45.00	24.00	36.00
Platter, oval, 11" d	45.00	55.00	30.00	45.00
Relish	36.00	45.00	20.00	36.00
Sauce, flat	12.00	15.00	10.00	12.00
Sauce, ftd	18.00	20.00	10.00	18.00
Spooner	36.00	45.00	24.00	45.00
Sugar, open	35.00	48.00	30.00	35.00
Tumbler	30.00	45.00	24.00	36.00
Wine	48.00	45.00	24.00	36.00

Sprig

Paneled Sprig, Ribbed Palm, Royal

Manufactured by Bryce, Higbee and Company, Pittsburgh, PA, c1880. Made in non-flint, clear. Some deep blue pieces are known, including the pickle jar.

Items	Clear
Berry Bowl, scalloped, 10" d	45.00
Bowl, cov, 6" d	55.00

Items	Clear
Bowl, open, 6" d	30.00
Bread Plate	48.00
Butter Dish, cov	75.00
Cake Stand, hs, 8", 9" or 10" d	45.00-55.00
Celery Vase	48.00
Compote, cov, hs, 6", 7", 8" or 10" d	72.00-90.00
Compote, open, ls, 6", 7" or 8" d	55.00-65.00
Creamer	36.00
Goblet	36.00
Pickle Dish	18.00
Pickle Jar	75.00
Pitcher, water	60.00
Relish	18.00
Salt, individual or master	45.00-60.00
Sauce, flat or ftd, 4" d	12.00-18.00
Spooner	30.00
Sugar Bowl, cov	48.00
Tumbler	30.00
Wine	48.00

Star In Bull's Eye

US Glass Pattern Line No. 15,092

Manufactured by United States Glass Company, Pittsburgh, PA, c1905. Made in non-flint, clear, with or without gilt trim, and sometimes found with rose stain (add 50%). Design can also be found without the "fan" below the loops between the eyes.

Items	Clear w/Gold
Berry Bowl, master	30.00
Butter Dish, cov	45.00
Cake Stand, hs	48.00
Compote, cov, ls	55.00
Compote, open, ls	45.00
Creamer	30.00
Cruet, os	36.00
Goblet	30.00
Pitcher, water	55.00
Spooner	30.00
Sugar Bowl, cov	45.00
Toothpick Holder, double	45.00
Toothpick Holder, single	36.00
Tumbler	24.00
Wine	24.00

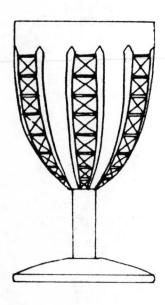

Stars and Stripes

Brilliant, Federal Pattern Line No. 209 and 1903

Manufactured by Jenkins Glass Company, Kokomo, IN, in 1899. Also made by Federal Glass Company, Columbus, OH, c1914. Appeared in 1899 Montgomery Ward catalog as "Brilliant." Made in non-flint, clear.

Items	Clear
Berry Bowl, master	18.00
Butter Dish, cov	36.00
Celery Vase	18.00
Cordial	18.00
Creamer	20.00
Cruet Set	45.00
Fruit Bowl, sq	18.00
Goblet	24.00
Pitcher, water	45.00
Salt Shaker	18.00
Sauce, flat, round or square	10.00
Sherbet, handle	15.00
Spooner	18.00
Sugar Bowl, cov	24.00
Tumbler	18.00
Vase	12.00
Wine	18.00

States, The

Cane and Star Medallion, US Glass Pattern Line No. 15,093

Manufactured by United States Glass Company Pittsburgh, PA, in 1905. Made in non-flint, clear, and clear with gold trim. Many forms also found in emerald green (add 50%).

Items	Clear w/Gold Trim
Bowl, 7" d 3 handles	30.00
Bowl, 9-1/4" d	36.00
Butter Dish, cov	75.00
Celery Tray	24.00
Celery Vase	24.00
Cocktail	30.00
Compote, open, hs, 7" or 9" d	36.00-48.00
Creamer, ph, individual, oval	24.00
Creamer, ph, regular, round	36.00
Goblet	45.00
Jelly Dish, flat	18.00
Pickle Tray	18.00
Pitcher, water, ph, half gallon	55.00
Plate, 10" d	30.00
Punch Bowl, 13"d	90.00
Punch Cup	10.00
Relish, diamond shape	45.00
Salt and Pepper Shakers, pr	48.00
Sauce, flat, tub shape, 4" d	18.00
Spooner	30.00
Sugar Bowl, cov, regular	48.00
Sugar Bowl, open, individual	18.00
Syrup, orig top	75.00
Toothpick Holder, flat, rectangular, curled lip	55.00
Tray, 7-1/4" l, 5-1/2" w	20.00
Tumbler	24.00
Wine	36.00

Stippled Chain

Manufactured by Gillinder and Sons, Philadelphia, PA, c1880. Made in non-flint, clear.

Items	Clear
Bowl, flat	18.00
Butter Dish, cov	60.00
Cake Stand, hs	55.00
Celery Vase	48.00
Creamer	45.00
Egg Cup	24.00
Goblet	24.00
Pickle Tray	18.00
Pitcher, water	75.00
Relish Dish	12.00
Salt, master, ftd	24.00
Sauce, flat or footed, 4" d	12.00-18.00
Spooner	30.00
Sugar Bowl, cov	48.00
Tumbler	24.00

Stippled Forget-Me-Not

Manufactured by Findlay Glass Company Findlay, OH, in the 1880s. Made in non-flint, clear. Also found in amber, blue, and white.

Items	Clear
Bowl, 7" d	55.00
Bread Plate, kittens, tab handles	90.00
Butter Dish, cov	60.00
Cake Stand, hs, 9", 10" or 12" d	45.00-95.00
Celery Vase, 8" h	45.00
Child's Butter Dish, cov	120.00
Child's Creamer	100.00
Child's Mug	75.00
Child's Spooner	110.00
Child's Sugar Bowl, cov	130.00
Compote, cov, hs, 6", 7" or 8" d	60.00
Compote, cov, ls, 6" d	55.00
Compote, open, hs, 6" d	55.00
Compote, open, ls, 6", 7" or 8" d	45.00
Cordial	90.00

Items	Clear
Creamer	36.00
Cup	24.00
Goblet	55.00
Lamp, oil, handle	115.00
Mug	36.00
Pitcher, milk or water	55.00-60.00
Plate, 6" d	36.00
Plate, 7" d, Baby in tub reaching for ball	65.00
Plate, 7" d, star center	36.00
Plate, 9" d, kitten center, handles	65.00
Plate, 9" d, star center	45.00
Relish, oval	18.00
Salt, master, oval	45.00
Salt, master, round, ftd	36.00
Sauce, flat or footed	18.00
Saucer	12.00
Spooner	30.00
Sugar Bowl, cov	45.00
Syrup, orig top	110.00
Toothpick Holder, hat shaped	120.00
Waste Bowl	45.00
Water Tray, aquatic scene	60.00
Water Tray, herons or storks	90.00
Wine	45.00

Stippled Grape and Festoon

Manufactured by Doyle and Company, Pittsburgh, PA, c1870. Reissued by United States Glass Company, Pittsburgh, PA, c1891. Shards have also been found at Boston and Sandwich Glass Company, Sandwich, MA. Made in non-flint, clear. Pieces have applied handles and acorn finials.

Items	Clear
Bowl, 5", 6" or 7" d	30.00
Butter Dish, cov, regular or flange	55.00-72.00
Celery Tray	45.00
Celery Vase, pedestal	55.00
Compote, cov, hs, 6" or 8" d	48.00-55.00
Compote, cov, ls, 6", 8" or 9" d	36.00-65.00
Compote, open, ls	45.00
Cordial	36.00
Creamer	60.00
Egg Cup	45.00
Goblet	32.50
Pickle Tray	36.00
Pitcher, milk, ah, bulbous	90.00
Pitcher, water, ah, bulbous	110.00
Plate, 6" d	45.00
Relish Tray	36.00
Sauce, flat, 4" d	15.00
Spooner, pedestal	36.00
Sugar Bowl, cov, pedestal	72.00
Sugar, open	48.00
Wine	55.00

Stippled Star

Manufactured by Gillinder and Sons, Philadelphia, PA, in the 1870s. Made in non-flint, clear with limited production in blue.

Reproductions: L.G. Wright Glass Company, New Martinsville, WV, reproduced items in amber, amberina, amethyst, blue, clear, green and ruby red, plus added salts to the line with new molds.

Items	Clear
Bread Plate, Mother	48.00
Butter Dish, cov	60.00
Celery Vase	48.00
Compote, cov, hs, 12" d φ	75.00
Compote, open, hs, deep bowl, 7" or 8" d	48.00-55.00
Compote, open, hs, shallow bowl, 7" or 8" d	48.00-55.00
Creamer, applied handle φ	48.00
Egg Cup	45.00
Goblet φ	36.00
Pickle Dish	24.00
Pitcher, water	90.00
Preserve Dish, oval, 8" l	24.00
Sauce, flat or footed, 4" d	10.00-12.00
Spooner	30.00
Sugar Bowl, cov φ	55.00
Wine	45.00

Strawberry

Fairfax, Fairfax Strawberry

Manufactured by Bryce, Walker & Company, Pittsburgh, PA, c 1870. Designed and patented by John Bryce in 1870. Shards have been found at Boston and Sandwich Glass Company, Sandwich MA, and Burlington Glass Works, Hamilton, Ontario, Canada. Made in non-flint, clear and white milk glass.

Items	Clear	Milk Glass
Bowl, oval, 9-1/4" x 6"	36.00	—
Butter Dish, cov	65.00	90.00
Celery Vase	55.00	—
Compote, cov, hs, 8" d	90.00	—
Compote, cov, ls, 8" d	75.00	—
Creamer, ah	75.00	90.00
Egg Cup	40.00	60.00
Goblet	48.00	72.00
Honey Dish	24.00	—
Pickle Tray	24.00	—
Pitcher, water, ah	130.00	145.00
Relish Tray	24.00	—
Sauce, flat	15.00	—
Spooner	48.00	65.00
Sugar Bowl, cov	60.00	90.00
Syrup, orig top, ah	115.00	—
Tumbler, flat	55.00	—
Wine	75.00	—

Strawberry and Currant

Multiple Fruits

Manufactured by Dalzell, Gilmore, and Leighton, Findlay, OH, c1890.

One of a non-flint series of fruit patterns which has become known as Multiple Fruits (Cherry and Fig, Loganberry and Grape, Blackberry and Grape, and Cornucopia with Sprig of Cherries). A Loganberry and Grape jelly goblet, with "U"-shaped bowl is of inferior quality and not part of the pattern. There are matching pieces in all forms, although whether all forms were made in all four patterns is not known. Made in non-flint, clear.

Reproductions: Reproduction goblets and other items are found in clear, opalescent, and colors. L.G. Wright Glass Company, New Martinsville, WV, has also added some additional forms through its reproduction line, including compotes with crimped and ruffled rims, goblets, and wines.

Items	Clear
Butter Dish, cov	60.00
Celery Vase	45.00
Cheese, cov	60.00
Compote, cov, hs, 8"d	85.00
Compote, open, hs	45.00
Creamer	48.00
Goblet φ	45.00
Mug	45.00
Pitcher, milk	48.00
Pitcher, water	60.00
Sauce, ftd	12.00
Spooner	45.00
Sugar Bowl, cov	48.00
Syrup, orig top	95.00
Tumbler	30.00

Strigil

Manufactured by Tarentum Glass Co., Tarentum, PA, in the 1880s. Made in non-flint, clear. May be gilded.

Items	Clear
Bowl, 8" d	24.00
Butter Dish, cov	45.00
Celery Tray	18.00
Celery Vase	30.00
Compote, open, hs	30.00
Creamer, breakfast or table size	20.00
Cruet, os	30.00
Custard Cup	18.00
Egg Cup	24.00
Goblet	48.00
Pitcher, milk or water	36.00-45.00

Items	Clear
Punch Cup	18.00
Sauce, flat	10.00
Spooner	20.00
Sugar Bowl, cov	36.00
Tumbler	20.00
Vase	24.00
Waste Bowl	18.00
Wine	30.00

Sunflower

Lily

Manufactured by Atterbury & Company, Pittsburgh, PA, c1880. Shards have been found at Burlington Glass Works, Hamilton, Ontario, Canada. Made in non-flint, amber, clear, and white milk glass.

Items	Amber	Clear	Milk Glass
Bowl	45.00	30.00	55.00
Butter Dish, cov	95.00	65.00	120.00
Creamer	72.00	48.00	95.00
Pitcher, water	90.00	72.00	120.00
Spooner	45.00	36.00	55.00
Sugar Bowl, cov	65.00	60.00	90.00
Sugar, open	45.00	32.00	48.00

Tacoma

Jeweled Diamond and Fan, Triple X

Manufactured by Greensburg Glass Company, Greensburg, PA, c1884. Production continued by National Glass, Model Flint Glass Company, Albany, IN, c1900. Made in non-flint, clear, amber stained, and ruby stained.

Items	Clear	Ruby Stained
Banana Dish	30.00	65.00
Berry Bowl, master, 7" or 8" d	30.00	55.00
Bowl, oval, 9" or 10" d	30.00-36.00	65.00-72.00
Bowl, square, 7" or 8"w	24.00-30.00	75.00-85.00
Butter Dish, cov	55.00	120.00
Cake Stand, hs, 9" d	48.00	124.00
Celery Tray	30.00	65.00
Celery Vase	55.00	110.00
Compote, open, hs, deep bowl, 7" d or 8" d	60.00	175.00
Compote, open, hs, shallow bowl, 10" d	75.00	190.00
Compote, open, hs, square bowl, 7" w or 8" w	65.00	185.00
Cracker Jar, cov	75.00	240.00
Creamer	45.00	75.00
Cruet, os, large or small	55.00	130.00
Finger Bowl	18.00	45.00
Finger Bowl Underplate	24.00	—
Goblet	30.00	60.00
Ice Cream Dish, 5" d	18.00	—
Pickle Jar, cov	60.00	130.00
Pitcher, water, bulbous	48.00	160.00
Pitcher, water, tankard	60.00	—
Punch Bowl, flat, 12" or 15" d	75.00-95.00	—
Punch Bowl, pedestal, 12" or 15" d	100.00-110.00	—
Rose Bowl, 3-1/2", 4-1/2", 5-1/2" or 6-1/2" d	18.00-36.00	48.00-65.00
Salt, individual or master	12.00-24.00	45.00-65.00
Salt Shaker, straight sides or tapered	18.00	45.00
Sauce, flat, round or square, 4" d or 4-1/2" d	12.00	24.00
Spooner	30.00	65.00
Sugar Bowl, cov	55.00	115.00
Syrup, orig top, tall or squatty	60.00	240.00
Toothpick Holder	60.00	240.00
Tumbler	24.00	48.00
Vase, swung, 8" or 11" h	30.00-45.00	—
Vase, trumpet, 8" or 10" h	30.00-45.00	—
Waste Bowl	118.00	45.00
Wine	24.00	55.00
Wine Decanter, os	72.00	160.00

Teardrop and Tassel

Sampson

Manufactured by the Indiana Tumbler and Goblet Company, Greentown, IN, c1895. Made in non-flint, clear, cobalt blue, emerald green, and opaque Nile green.

Items	Chocolate	Clear	Cobalt Blue	Emerald Green	Nile Green Opaque
Bowl, 5-1/2" d	650.00	40.00	60.00	55.00	—
Bowl, 7-1/2" d	—	48.00	65.00	60.00	90.00
Butter Dish, cov	1,200.00	65.00	115.00	165.00	330.00
Celery Vase	—	48.00	—	—	—
Compote, cov, hs, 7" d	—	90.00	110.00	95.00	130.00
Compote, open, ls, 5" d	—	24.00	—	—	—
Compote, open, ls, 8" d	—	36.00	55.00	45.00	75.00
Creamer	400.00	55.00	120.00	55.00	110.00
Goblet		90.00	130.00	190.00	115.00
Jelly Compote, cov	—	75.00	—	—	—
Pickle Dish	350.00	24.00	65.00	48.00	65.00
Pitcher, water	—	60.00	160.00	160.00	1,200.00
Relish Dish, oval	400.00	30.00	70.00	50.00	70.00
Salt Shaker	—	60.00	90.00	72.00	85.00
Sauce, 4" d	235.00	18.00	24.00	24.00	—
Sauce, 4-1/2" d	250.00	20.00	30.00	30.00	—
Spooner	350.00	36.00	55.00	45.00	75.00
Sugar Bowl, cov	565.00	72.00	145.00	85.00	110.00
Tumbler	—	48.00	60.00	55.00	75.00
Wine	—	75.00	95.00	85.00	112.00

Tennessee

Jewel and Crescent, Jeweled Rosette

Manufactured by King, Son & Company, Pittsburgh, PA, and continued by United States Glass Company, Pittsburgh, PA, in 1899, as a part of the States series. Made in non-flint, clear, and clear with colored jewels.

Items	Clear	Colored Jewels
Berry Bowl, master	24.00	36.00
Bowl, cov, 6", 7" or 8" d	45.00-60.00	—
Bowl, open, 8" d	45.00	48.00
Bread Plate	48.00	90.00
Butter Dish, cov	65.00	—
Cake Stand, hs, 8", 9-1/2" or 10-1/2" d	45.00-55.00	—
Celery Vase	45.00	—
Compote, cov, hs, 5" d	48.00	65.00
Compote, cov, hs, 6", 7" or 8" d	55.00-72.00	—
Compote, open, hs, 5", 6", 7", 8", 9" or 10" d	30.00-75.00	—
Compote, open, ls, 7" d	45.00	—
Creamer	36.00	—
Cruet, os	75.00	—
Goblet	48.00	—
Mug	48.00	—
Pitcher, milk or water	65.00-75.00	—
Relish	24.00	—
Salt Shaker	36.00	—
Sauce, flat	18.00	24.00
Spooner	45.00	—
Sugar Bowl, cov	55.00	—
Syrup, orig top	110.00	—
Toothpick	90.00	100.00
Tumbler	45.00	—
Wine	75.00	100.00

Texas

Loop with Stippled Panels, US Glass Pattern Line No. 15,067

Manufactured by United States Glass Company, Pittsburgh, PA, c1900, in the States pattern series. Made in non-flint, clear, clear with gold, and rose stained. Occasionally pieces are found in ruby stained.

Reproductions: Reproduced in solid colors by Crystal Art Glass Company, Cambridge, OH, and Boyd Glass Company, Cambridge, OH.

Items	Clear w/Gold	Rose Stained
Bowl, cov, 6", 7" or 8" d	90.00-115.00	120.00-148.00
Bowl, open, flared, scalloped, 7-1/2", 8-1/2" or 9-1/2" d	36.00-45.00	55.00-60.00
Bowl, open, flared, smooth rim, 7-1/2", 8-1/2", or 9-1/2" d	45.00	60.00
Bowl, open, straight-sided, 6", 7" or 8" d	18.00-30.00	45.00-55.00

Items	Clear w/Gold	Rose Stained
Bread Tray	45.00	100.00
Butter Dish, cov	90.00	130.00
Cake Stand, hs, 9", 9-1/2", 10", 10-1/2" or 11" d	75.00-100.00	130.00-155.00
Celery Tray	36.00	60.00
Celery Vase	48.00	100.00
Compote, cov, hs, 6", 7" or 8" d	72.00-90.00	130.00-190.00
Compote, open, hs, 5", 7-1/2", 8-1/2" or 9-1/2" d	55.00-75.00	90.00-120.00
Creamer, individual φ or table	24.00-55.00	55.00-100.00
Cruet, os	72.00	175.00
Goblet	115.00	150.00
Horseradish, cov	60.00	—
Jelly Compote, 5" d	55.00	110.00
Olive Dish, scalloped rim	24.00	55.00
Pickle, 8-1/2" l	30.00	60.00
Pitcher, water, ah, bulbous	260.00	600.00
Pitcher, water, ph, tankard	130.00	480.00
Plate, 9" d	45.00	72.00
Relish Tray	30.00	55.00
Salt, master, ftd	60.00	100.00
Salt Shaker, tall or squatty	90.00	160.00
Sauce, flat, round, flared rim, 4-1/2" d	18.00	30.00
Sauce, flat, straight-sides, scalloped or smooth rim, 4" d	12.00	24.00
Sauce, footed, round, smooth rim, 4" d	24.00	30.00
Sauce, footed, round, straight-sides, flared rim, 5" d	24.00	30.00
Spooner	45.00	95.00
Sugar Bowl, cov, individual φ	55.00	—
Sugar Bowl, table, cov	90.00	130.00
Syrup, orig top	90.00	190.00
Toothpick Holder	30.00	115.00
Tumbler	48.00	120.00
Vase, 6-1/2", 8", 9" or 10" h	30.00-48.00	—
Water Bottle	100.00	160.00
Wine φ	90.00	148.00

Texas Bull's Eye

Bryce's Filley, Bull's Eye Variant

Manufactured by Bryce Bros., Pittsburgh, PA, c1875-1880; A. J. Beatty & Sons, Steubenville, OH, c1888; and United States Glass Company, Pittsburgh, PA, after 1891. Canadian makers include Diamond Glass Company, Montreal, Quebec, c1902, and Burlington Glass Works, Hamilton, Ontario, where shards have been found. Made in semi-flint, which has no bell tone, but some lead content, in clear only.

Items	Clear
Butter Dish, cov	65.00
Castor Bottle	75.00
Castor Set, silver plate holder	160.00
Celery Vase	45.00
Champagne, 5" h	48.00
Cordial	45.00
Creamer	45.00
Egg Cup	36.00
Goblet	36.00
Lamp, oil, 5-1/2" h	100.00
Pitcher, water	65.00
Sauce, flat	10.00
Spooner	30.00
Sugar Bowl, cov	55.00
Tumbler, 3-3/4" h	60.00
Wine, 3-9/16" h	30.00

Texas Star

Swirl and Star, Snowflake Base

Manufactured by Steimer Glass Company, Buckhannon, WV, c1903-08. Body of pieces are paneled. Pattern appears on the base, which is frosted around the design. Made in non-flint, clear.

Reproductions: The wine has been reproduced and is usually easily identified by poor frosting.

Items	Clear
Bowl, 9-1/2" d	55.00
Butter, cov	65.00
Cake Plate, hs, 11" d	48.00
Celery Tray	24.00
Cruet	60.00
Pitcher, water, ah, tankard	72.00
Punch Bowl	130.00

Items	Clear
Punch Cup	15.00
Salt and Pepper Shakers, pr	65.00
Syrup, orig top	60.00
Sugar Shaker	48.00
Toothpick	45.00
Tumbler	24.00
Wine φ	24.00

Thistle

Early Thistle, Scotch Thistle

Manufactured by Bryce, Walker & Company, Pittsburgh, PA, in 1872. Shards have been found at Burlington Glass Works, Hamilton, Ontario, Canada. Made in non-flint, clear.

Reproductions: Reproductions of this pattern are confined to the goblet. These are generally smaller and marked with an "R" within a large shield.

Items	Clear
Bowl, cov, 8" d	72.00
Bowl, open, 8" d	36.00
Butter Dish, cov	65.00
Cake Stand, hs, large	90.00
Compote, cov, hs, 6" or 8" d	75.00
Compote, cov, ls, 8" d	90.00
Cordial	72.00
Creamer, ah	75.00
Egg Cup	48.00
Goblet φ	55.00
Pickle Dish, tapered at one end	30.00
Pitcher, milk, ah, quart	130.00
Pitcher, water, ah, half gallon	120.00
Relish Tray, oval	30.00
Salt, master, ftd	45.00
Sauce, flat, 4" d	15.00
Spooner	45.00
Sugar Bowl, cov	75.00
Sugar Bowl, open, buttermilk type	48.00
Syrup, orig top	120.00
Tumbler, flat or footed	48.00-55.00
Wine	60.00

Thousand Eye

Banded Thousand Eye, Three Knob, Adams Pattern Line No. 130

Manufactured originally by Adams & Company, Tarentum, PA, in 1875. The Richards & Hartley Glass Company, Pittsburgh, PA, began production in 1888. The pattern was reissued by United States Glass Company, Pittsburgh, PA, at Factory "A" and Factory "E," c1891. Shards have also been found at the Burlington Glass Works, Hamilton, Ontario, Canada. This popular pattern was made in two forms: Adams & Company used a three knob stem finial, while Richards & Hartley created a plain stem with a scalloped bottom. Made in non-flint, amber, apple green, blue, clear, and vaseline. Some opalescent colors were also made.

Reproductions: Reproductions have been made using original molds and newly created molds. Colors used to make reproductions include amber, amberina, amethyst, apple green, blue, clear, and vaseline. Several companies made reproductions, but Westmoreland Glass Company, Grapeville, PA, is generally credited with some of the early reproductions.

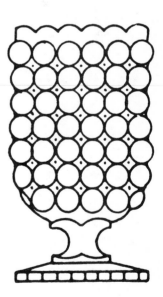

Items	Amber	Apple Green	Blue	Clear	Opalescent	Vaseline
ABC Plate, lock center, 6" d	65.00	72.00	65.00	55.00	—	65.00
Bowl, large, carriage shape	100.00	—	100.00	—	—	100.00
Butter Dish, cov, flat, 6-1/4" or 7-1/2"d	75.00	90.00	85.00	55.00	—	110.00
Butter Dish, cov, footed	100.00	110.00	110.00	75.00	—	112.00
Butter Dish, cov, square, flat	115.00	120.00	120.00	90.00	—	124.00
Cake Stand, hs, 10" or 11" d	60.00	95.00	65.00	36.00	—	100.00
Celery Vase, hat shape	60.00	75.00	72.00	45.00	—	65.00
Celery Vase, 7" h	60.00	72.00	60.00	55.00	85.00	65.00
Christmas Light	36.00	55.00	45.00	30.00	—	48.00
Cologne Bottle	30.00	55.00	45.00	24.00	—	55.00
Compote, cov, hs, 6" d	65.00	72.00	65.00	30.00	—	65.00
Compote, cov, hs, 7" d	72.00	75.00	72.00	36.00	—	72.00

Items	Amber	Apple Green	Blue	Clear	Opalescent	Vaseline
Compote, cov, hs, 8" d	75.00	85.00	75.00	45.00	—	75.00
Compote, cov, hs, 9" d	85.00	90.00	85.00	48.00	—	85.00
Compote, cov, hs, 10" d	90.00	95.00	90.00	55.00	—	90.00
Compote, cov, hs or ls, sq, 8" w	115.00	120.00	120.00	—	—	115.00
Compote, open, hs, 6" d	45.00	48.00	48.00	30.00	—	48.00
Compote, open, hs, 7" d	55.00	60.00	55.00	45.00	—	55.00
Compote, open ,hs, round, 8" d	48.00	60.00	55.00	45.00	118.00	60.00
Compote, open, hs, sq, 8" w	48.00	60.00	60.00	48.00	—	65.00
Compote, open, hs, 9" d	60.00	72.00	65.00	48.00	—	65.00
Compote, open, 10" d	65.00	75.00	72.00	55.00	—	72.00
Cordial φ	45.00	65.00	48.00	30.00	—	72.00
Creamer, 4" h	45.00	48.00	48.00	30.00	—	48.00
Creamer, 6" h	48.00	90.00	65.00	45.00	100.00	90.00
Creamer and Sugar Set	—	160.00	—	120.00	—	—
Cruet, os, 6" h φ	48.00	72.00	60.00	45.00	—	72.00
Egg Cup	75.00	100.00	85.00	55.00	—	110.00
Goblet φ	48.00	55.00	48.00	45.00	—	55.00
Honey Dish, cov, 6 x 7-1/4"	100.00	115.00	110.00	85.00	—	115.00
Inkwell, sq, 2" w	55.00	—	90.00	45.00	—	95.00
Jelly Glass	30.00	36.00	30.00	18.00	—	30.00
Lamp, kerosene, hs, 12" h φ	124.00	160.00	136.00	120.00	—	148.00
Lamp, kerosene, hs, 15" h	160.00	165.00	145.00	112.00	—	160.00
Lamp, kerosene, ls, handle	112.00	118.00	112.00	110.00	—	124.00
Mug, 2-1/2" h φ or 3-1/2" h	30.000	36.00	30.00	24.00	—	45.00
Nappy, 5" d	45.00	—	48.00	36.00	—	55.00
Nappy, 6" d	48.00	—	55.00	45.00	—	65.00
Nappy, 8" d φ	55.00	—	60.00	55.00	—	72.00
Pickle Dish	30.00	36.00	36.00	24.00	—	36.00
Pitcher, milk, cov, 7" h	100.00	110.00	120.00	85.00	—	115.00
Pitcher, water, quarter gallon	85.00	100.00	95.00	65.00	148.00	95.00
Pitcher, water, half gallon φ	95.00	115.00	100.00	75.00	195.00	100.00
Pitcher, water, 1 gallon	110.00	120.00	115.00	100.00	—	115.00
Plate, sq, folded corners, 6" w φ	30.00	36.00	36.00	30.00	—	36.00
Plate, sq, folded corners, 8" w φ	36.00	36.00	36.00	30.00	—	36.00
Plate, sq, folded corners, 10" w φ	45.00	60.00	48.00	30.00	—	45.00
Platter, oblong, 11" l, 8" w	48.00	60.00	55.00	48.00	—	55.00
Platter, oval, 11" l	90.00	95.00	65.00	48.00	—	90.00
Salt and Pepper Shakers, pr, banded	72.00	85.00	75.00	72.00	—	75.00
Salt and Pepper Shakers, pr, plain φ	60.00	72.00	65.00	48.00	—	72.00
Salt, individual	95.00	115.00	110.00	60.00	—	110.00
Salt, master, open, carriage shape	75.00	100.00	90.00	60.00	—	90.00
Sauce, flat, 4" d φ	12.00	24.00	18.00	10.00	—	18.00
Sauce, footed, 4" d	18.00	30.00	18.00	12.00	48.00	24.00
Spooner	45.00	60.00	48.00	36.00	72.00	55.00
String Holder φ	45.00	72.00	55.00	36.00	—	55.00
Sugar Bowl, cov, 5" d	65.00	90.00	72.00	60.00	95.00	72.00
Syrup, orig pewter top	95.00	120.00	85.00	65.00	—	85.00
Toothpick, hat shape φ	45.00	65.00	72.00	36.00	—	55.00
Toothpick, plain φ	45.00	60.00	65.00	30.00	—	48.00
Toothpick, thimble shape	65.00	—	—	—	—	—
Tumbler φ	36.00	75.00	45.00	30.00	—	36.00
Water Tray, round, 12-1/2" d	75.00	95.00	75.00	65.00	—	72.00
Water Tray, oval, 14" l	75.00	95.00	90.00	72.00	—	90.00
Wine φ	45.00	60.00	48.00	24.00	—	48.00

Three Face

The Sisters, Three Sisters, Three Graces, Three Faces, Duncan Pattern Line No. 400

Manufactured by George A. Duncan & Son, Pittsburgh, PA, 1878 to 1886. Designed by John E. Miller, a designer with Duncan, who later became a member of the firm. Miller's design was patented June 18, 1878, as patent No. 10,727. Made in non-flint, clear, and clear with acid finish.

Reproductions: *Three Face* has been heavily reproduced by L. G. Wright Glass Company, New Martinsville, WV, and other companies as early as the 1930s. Imperial Glass Company, Bellaire, OH, was commissioned by the Metropolitan Museum of Art, NY, to reproduce this interesting pattern. These pieces bear the "M.M.A" monogram.

Items	Clear
Biscuit Jar, cov	360.00
Bowl, hs, beaded or smooth rim, 6" d	160.00
Bowl, ls, plain rim, 6" d	145.00
Butter Dish, cov φ	148.00
Cake Stand, hs, 9" d φ, 10", 11" or 12-1/2"	160.00-230.00
Celery Vase, plain or scalloped	115.00
Champagne, hollow stem φ	260.00
Champagne, solid stem	130.00
Champagne, saucer type	160.00
Claret	120.00
Compote, cov, hs, beaded or plain rim, 7" d φ	175.00
Compote, cov, hs, beaded or plain rim, 8" d	190.00
Compote, cov, hs, beaded or plain rim, 9" d	210.00
Compote, cov, hs, beaded rim, 10" d	230.00
Compote, cov, ls, 4" d	160.00
Compote, cov, ls, 6" d φ	172.00
Compote, open, hs, 7", 8" or 9" d	90.00-145.00
Compote, open, ls, 6" d	90.00
Creamer, face under spout φ	145.00
Creamer, without face under spout	130.00
Goblet φ	100.00
Jelly Compote, open, Paneled Huber top	100.00
Lamp, oil, peg, plain foot, 3 sizes φ	230.00
Lamp, oil, pressed design on foot, 6 sizes	260.00
Marmalade Jar	240.00
Pitcher, milk, ah, quart	260.00
Pitcher, water, ah, half gallon	390.00
Salt and Pepper Shakers, pr φ	90.00
Salt, individual φ	45.00
Sauce, ftd φ	30.00
Spooner φ	95.00
Sugar Bowl, cov φ	130.00
Wine φ	160.00

Three Panel

Paneled Thousand Eye, Thousand Eye Three Panel, Richards & Hartley Pattern Line No. 25

Manufactured by Richards & Harley Company, Tarentum, PA, 1888, and by United States Glass Company, Pittsburgh, PA, in 1891, at Factory "E." Shards have been found at Burlington Glass Works, Hamilton, Ontario, Canada. Made in non-flint, amber, blue, clear, milk glass, and vaseline.

Items	Amber	Blue	Clear	Vaseline
Bowl, deep, 8-1/2" d	30.00	48.00	24.00	55.00
Bowl, deep, 9-1/2" d	45.00	55.00	30.00	60.00
Bowl, deep, 10" d	48.00	60.00	45.00	65.00
Bowl, flared, 8" d	36.00	55.00	30.00	60.00
Bowl, scalloped rim, 7" d	30.00	48.00	24.00	55.00
Bowl, scalloped rim, 8" d	36.00	55.00	30.00	60.00
Butter Dish, cov, flanged cover	55.00	60.00	48.00	60.00
Butter Dish, cov, regular cover	48.00	55.00	45.00	55.00
Celery Vase, flared rim	60.00	65.00	36.00	70.00
Celery Vase, plain rim	55.00	60.00	30.00	55.00
Celery Vase, ruffled top	65.00	65.00	45.00	70.00
Compote, open, ls, 7"	45.00	65.00	45.00	65.00
Compote, open, ls, 8" d	48.00	72.00	48.00	72.00
Compote, open, ls, 9" d	55.00	75.00	55.00	75.00
Compote, open, ls, 10" d	60.00	85.00	60.00	85.00
Creamer	48.00	55.00	30.00	60.00
Cruet, os	260.00	275.00	110.00	290.00
Goblet	45.00	48.00	30.00	45.00
Mug, large	45.00	55.00	30.00	45.00
Mug, small	36.00	48.00	24.00	48.00
Pitcher, milk, quart	118.00	145.00	115.00	150.00
Pitcher, water, half gallon	120.00	130.00	90.00	140.00
Salt Shaker, orig top	65.00	72.00	36.00	75.00
Sauce, ftd	18.00	18.00	12.00	18.00
Spooner	42.50	55.00	36.00	55.00
Sugar Bowl, cov	65.00	72.00	55.00	85.00
Tumbler	45.00	48.00	24.00	50.00
Wine	45.00	48.00	30.00	85.00

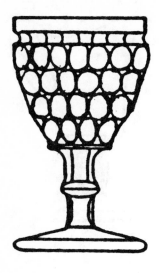

Thumbprint, Early

Argus, Argus Thumbprint, Giant Baby Thumbprint

Manufactured by Bakewell, Pears and Company, Pittsburgh, PA, c 1850-60. Made by several other factories in various forms. Made in flint, clear. Rare examples are found in color and milk white.

Reproductions: Fenton Art Glass, Fenton, OH, produced a similar pattern in non-flint, clear, and colors.

Items	Clear
Ale Glass	48.00
Banana Boat	160.00
Beer Mug, ah	55.00
Berry Set, master bowl and six sauces	215.00
Bitters Bottle	148.00
Bowl, 6" d	45.00
Butter Dish, cov, flat φ or footed	65.00-90.00
Cake Stand, hs φ	60.00
Castor Bottle	65.00
Celery Vase, patterned base	120.00
Celery Vase, plain base	110.00
Champagne	120.00
Claret	85.00
Cologne Bottle	110.00
Compote, cov, hs, 4", 8", 10" or 13-1/2" d	95.00-190.00
Compote, cov, ls, 7" d φ	120.00
Compote, open, hs, 7" d	75.00
Compote, open, scalloped top, flared, 8" d	130.00
Cordial	100.00
Creamer φ	72.00
Decanter, os, quart, plain or pattern base	100.00-130.00
Egg Cup	48.00
Goblet φ	60.00
Honey Dish	12.00
Paperweight, solid	35.00
Pickle Dish	30.00
Pitcher, water, ah, half gallon φ	240.00
Plate, 8" d φ	60.00
Punch Bowl, 13-1/2" d, 12-1/2" h φ	190.00
Relish Dish φ	30.00
Salt, master, ftd	45.00
Sauce, flat φ	18.00
Spooner	55.00
Sugar Bowl, cov φ	75.00
Syrup, orig top	190.00
Tumbler, flat φ or footed φ	60.00-72.00
Tumble Up, water bottle and tumbler	160.00
Water Bottle	120.00
Whiskey, flat or footed	55.00-60.00
Wine, plain stem φ or knob stem	90.00

Torpedo

Pigmy

Manufactured by Thompson Glass Company, Uniontown, PA, c1889. Made in non-flint, clear, and ruby stained. A black amethyst master salt ($160) is also known.

Items	Clear	Ruby Stained
Banana Stand, hs, 9-1/2" d	90.00	—
Berry Bowl, master	55.00	75.00
Bowl, cov, 7" d, 7-1/4" h	75.00	—
Bowl, cov, 8" d	85.00	110.00
Bowl, open, 4" d	—	40.00
Bowl, open, 7" d	20.00	—
Bowl, open, 8" d	24.00	—
Bowl, open, 9" d	24.00	55.00
Butter Dish, cov, quarter pound, flanged base	100.00	130.00
Butter Dish, cov, table size	90.00	120.00
Cake Stand, hs, 9" or 10" d	95.00-100.00	—
Celery Vase, scalloped top	48.00	55.00
Compote, cov, hs, 6-1/2" or 13-3/4" d	100.00-175.00	—
Compote, open, hs, 8-1/2" d	60.00	—
Creamer, breakfast, tankard; or table size	60.00-65.00	85.00-90.00
Cruet, os, ah	95.00	—
Cup and Saucer	72.00	—
Decanter, os, 8" h	100.00	130.00
Finger Bowl	65.00	115.00
Fruit Bowl, ruffled rim, 5-1/2" or 10-1/2" d	24.00-36.00	—
Goblet	55.00	100.00
Honey Dish, flat	18.00	—
Jelly Compote, cov, hs, 4" d	75.00	—
Jelly Compote, open,	30.00	—
Lamp, oil, finger, handle, 3" h	90.00	—
Lamp, oil, plain base, pattern on bowl, 8" h	100.00	—

Items	Clear	Ruby Stained
Marmalade Jar, cov	100.00	112.00
Pickle, Castor, silver plated holder	130.00	230.00
Pitcher, milk, ah, 8-1/2" h	90.00	160.00
Pitcher, water, ah, 10-1/2" h	100.00	190.00
Punch Cup	30.00	—
Rose Bowl	55.00	—
Salt, individual or master	24.00-45.00	55.00-75.00
Salt shaker, single, 2 types	60.00	75.00
Sauce, flat, collared base, 3-1/2" d, 4" d, or 4-1/2" d	18.00	24.00
Sauce, footed, 3-1/2" d, 4" d, or 4-1/2" d	24.00	30.00
Spooner, footed, scalloped top	55.00	—
Sugar Bowl, cov	75.00	—
Syrup, orig top	115.00	190.00
Tray, 11-3/4", clover shaped	90.00	—
Tumbler	55.00	72.00
Vegetable Bowl, flared rim, 7" or 8" d	30.00-36.00	75.00-85.00
Vegetable Bowl, flared rim, 9" or 9-1/2" d	45.00-48.00	—
Water Tray, 10" d	100.00	—
Wine	110.00	118.00

Tree of Life

Portland's

Manufactured by Portland Glass Company, Portland, ME, c1870. Made in flint, and non-flint, in amber, clear, dark blue, green, light blue, purple, and, yellow. Color is rare. A blue finger bowl in a silver plated holder is valued at $190.

Reproductions: Reproductions of *Tree of Life* were made by L. G. Wright Glass Company, New Martinsville, WV, 1968. Colors of these reproductions include amber, blue, and clear.

Items	Non-Flint
Bowl, berry, oval	36.00
Butter Dish, cov	65.00
Celery Vase, silver plated frame	65.00
Cologne Bottle, faceted stopper	55.00
Champagne	65.00
Compote, open, hs, 8-1/2" d	130.00
Compote, open, hs, 10" d	112.00
Compote, open, ls, 10" d	60.00
Creamer, applied handle	85.00
Creamer, molded handle	60.00
Creamer, silver plated holder	90.00
Egg Cup	36.00
Epergne, sgd "P.G. Company Patd"	130.00
Finger Bowl, underplate	72.00
Fruit Dish, silver plated holder	110.00
Goblet, clear shield on side	60.00
Goblet, plain φ	45.00
Goblet, regular, sgd "P.G. Flint"	75.00
Ice Cream Tray	60.00
Lemonade	60.00
Mug	60.00
Pitcher, milk or water, applied handle	115.00
Pitcher, milk or water, molded handle	75.00
Plate, 6" d	30.00
Sauce, flat, 3-3/4" d φ	15.00
Sauce, leaf shape	18.00
Spooner	45.00
Sugar Bowl, cov	85.00
Sugar Bowl, silver plated holder	90.00
Toothpick Holder, footed, scalloped	60.00
Tumbler, ftd	48.00
Vase	60.00
Water Tray	110.00
Wine φ	65.00

Tree of Life with Hand

Pittsburgh Tree of Life

Manufactured by Hobbs, Brockunier & Company, Wheeling, WV, c1875-80. Made in non-flint, clear.

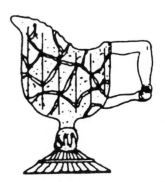

Items	Clear
Berry Bowl, master	30.00
Bowl, oval, 8" or 10" l	30.00-45.00
Butter Dish, cov	90.00
Cake Stand, hs, 10" d	120.00
Celery Vase	48.00
Compote, cov, hs, 6" d	75.00
Compote, open, hs, 10-1/2" d	95.00

Items	Clear
Compote, open, ls, 5" d	75.00
Creamer, signed	75.00
Goblet, signed	48.00
Ice Cream Tray	48.00
Pitcher, water	160.00
Plate, 6" d	45.00
Punch Cup	18.00
Sauce, shell shape, flat or ftd	24.00-30.00
Spooner	45.00
Sugar Bowl, cov	75.00
Tumbler	36.00
Wine	45.00

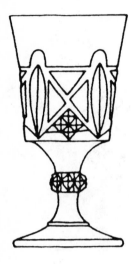

Triple Triangle

Manufactured by Doyle and Company, Pittsburgh, PA, in 1890. Continued by United States Glass Company, Pittsburgh, PA, after 1891. Made in non-flint, clear, and ruby stained.

Reproductions: Only the goblet and wine have been reproduced in this popular pattern. They are usually easily identified by poor staining and lack of quality.

Items	Clear	Ruby Stained
Bowl, rect, 8", 9" or 10" l	24.00-30.00	48.00-55.00
Bowl, round, 6" or 7" d or 8" or 9"	18.00-24.00	36.00-48.00
Bread Plate, rect	48.00	110.00
Butter Dish, cov, handle	48.00	95.00
Celery Tray	36.00	55.00
Creamer, ph	45.00	65.00
Cup	18.00	36.00
Goblet φ	30.00	55.00
Mug	12.00	45.00
Pickle Tray, boat shape	12.00	30.00
Pitcher, water	75.00	145.00
Sauce, flat, 5" d	12.00	24.00
Spooner, handled	24.00	65.00
Sugar, handled, cov	48.00	90.00
Tumbler	24.00	90.00
Wine φ	24.00	55.00

Truncated Cube

Thompson's #77

Manufactured by Thompson Glass Company, Uniontown, PA, c1894. Made in non-flint, clear, and ruby stained. Also found with copper wheel engraving.

Items	Clear	Ruby Stained
Berry Bowl, 4" or 8" d	30.00-60.00	48.00-120.00
Butter Dish, cov	60.00	120.00
Celery Vase	48.00	95.00
Creamer, individual or regular	24.00-45.00	48.00-85.00
Cruet, ph, os	45.00	85.00
Decanter, os, 12" h	72.00	124.00
Goblet	36.00	72.00
Pitcher, milk, ah, quart	60.00	120.00
Pitcher, water, ah, half gallon	72.00	124.00
Salt Shaker, single	18.00	36.00
Sauce, flat, 4" d	36.00	72.00
Spooner	36.00	72.00
Sugar Bowl, cov, individual or regular	24.00-36.00	48.00-72.00
Syrup, orig top	48.00	95.00
Toothpick Holder	36.00	72.00
Tumbler	30.00	60.00
Water Tray	24.00	48.00
Wine	30.00	60.00

Tulip with Sawtooth

Tulip

Manufactured in flint by Bryce Brothers, Pittsburgh, PA, c1854. Later made in non-flint by United States Glass Company, Pittsburgh, PA, c1891. Shards have been found at Burlington Glass Works, Hamilton, Ontario, Canada. Made in flint and non-flint, clear. Rare pieces found in milk white, opalescent, or color.

Reproductions: Reproduction goblets and wines have been made from new molds and are found only in non-flint.

Items	Flint	Non-Flint
Bar Bottle, pint	90.00	95.00
Butter Dish, cov	130.00	95.00

Items	Flint	Non-Flint
Celery Vase	100.00	30.00
Champagne	90.00	—
Compote, cov, hs, 6", 7-1/2" or 8-1/2" d	110.00-115.00	—
Compote, cov, ls, 8-1/2" d	100.00	—
Compote, open, hs, 8" d	—	72.00
Compote, open, ls, ruffled, 6" d	75.00	—
Compote, open, ls, 8" or 9" d	90.00-95.00	—
Creamer	100.00	—
Cruet, os, applied handle	72.00	—
Cruet, os, pressed handle	—	48.00
Decanter, os, handle	160.00	—
Decanter, os, no handle	160.00	65.00
Egg Cup	48.00	—
Goblet φ	75.00	45.00
Honey Dish, flat	12.00	—
Mug	95.00	—
Pitcher, water	160.00	—
Plate, 6" d	72.00	—
Pomade Jar	75.00	—
Salt, master, plain edge	30.00	18.00
Sauce, flat	18.00	12.00
Spooner	45.00	24.00
Sugar Bowl, cov	115.00	—
Tumbler, bar	100.00	30.00
Tumbler, footed	60.00	—
Wine φ	55.00	30.00

Two Panel

Manufactured by Richards & Hartley Glass Company, Tarentum, PA, 1880, and by United States Glass Company, Pittsburgh, PA, in 1891. Made in non-flint, amber, apple green, blue, clear, and vaseline.

Reproductions: The goblet and wine have been reproduced in original colors using a new mold in the early 1960s.

Items	Amber	Apple Green	Blue	Clear	Vaseline
Bowl, 5-1/2" l	45.00	48.00	48.00	18.00	30.00
Bowl, 8" l	45.00	48.00	48.00	24.00	45.00
Bowl, 10" l, 8-1/2" w, 3" h	45.00	60.00	48.00	30.00	36.00
Butter Dish, cov	60.00	65.00	65.00	36.00	48.00
Celery Vase	55.00	60.00	60.00	30.00	48.00
Compote, cov, hs, oval, 6-12" l	65.00	100.00	100.00	45.00	90.00
Compote, cov, hs, oval, 8" l	100.00	100.00	115.00	45.00	115.00
Compote, cov, hs, oval, 9" l, 7-3/8" w, 12-3/4" h	—	120.00	—	—	—
Creamer, ph, 6"	72.00	75.00	75.00	45.00	55.00
Goblet φ	36.00	75.00	75.00	45.00	55.00
Lamp, oil, finger	75.00	90.00	75.00	60.00	75.00
Lamp, oil, hs	100.00	130.00	120.00	55.00	118.00
Marmalade Jar, cov	90.00	115.00	120.00	55.00	120.00
Mug	36.00	45.00	48.00	24.00	36.00
Pickle Dish	30.00	36.00	45.00	30.00	45.00
Pitcher, water	72.00	72.00	75.00	45.00	60.00
Platter	30.00	36.00	36.00	24.00	36.00
Salt, individual	18.00	20.00	18.00	7.50	18.00
Salt, master	24.00	30.00	24.00	12.00	15.00
Salt Shaker	48.00	55.00	48.00	30.00	36.00
Sauce, flat, oval	12.00	12.00	12.00	10.00	12.00
Sauce, footed, oval	15.00	17.50	18.00	12.00	15.00
Spooner	55.00	60.00	55.00	30.00	45.00
Sugar Bowl, cov	75.00	85.00	80.00	48.00	72.00
Tumbler	45.00	55.00	45.00	18.00	48.00
Waste Bowl	48.00	55.00	48.00	24.00	36.00
Water Tray	60.00	65.00	65.00	55.00	60.00
Wine φ	48.00	55.00	48.00	24.00	36.00

U. S. Coin

American Coin, Coin, Frosted Coin, Silver Age, US Glass Pattern Line No. 15,003

Manufactured by United States Glass Company, Pittsburgh, PA, in 1892 for three or four months. Production was stopped by the United States Treasury because real coins, dated as early as 1878, were used in the molds. The 1892 coin date is the most common. Lamps with coins on font and stem would be 50% more. Made in non-flint, clear, frosted, and gilted.

Reproductions: Reproductions by A. A. Importing Co., Inc., St. Louis, MO, have been made from new molds, c1978-81.

Items	Clear	Frosted
Ale Glass	275.00	375.00
Bowl, cov, 6" d φ	235.00	375.00
Bowl, cov, 7" d	275.00	335.00
Bowl, cov, 8" d	235.00	375.00
Bowl, open, flat, 6" d	225.00	230.00
Bowl, open, flat, 7" d	265.00	310.00
Bowl, open, flat, 9" d	225.00	335.00
Bread Plate φ	210.00	335.00
Butter Dish, cov, dollars and halves	275.00	475.00
Cake Plate	110.00	275.00
Cake Stand, hs, 10" d	235.00	480.00
Celery Tray	275.00	—
Celery Vase, quarters	145.00	375.00
Champagne	—	480.00
Claret	—	475.00
Compote, cov, hs, 6" or 7" d	375.00-360.00	575.00-600.00
Compote, cov, hs, quarters and dimes, 8" d	—	425.00
Compote, open, hs, quarters and dimes, 7" d	275.00	360.00
Compote, open, hs, quarters and halves, 7" d	235.00	375.00
Compote, open, hs, 8-3/8" d, 6-1/2" h	—	255.00
Creamer φ	375.00	720.00
Cruet, os	400.00	600.00
Epergne	600.00	1,200.00
Goblet	360.00	475.00
Goblet, dimes	—	575.00
Lamp, round font	300.00	475.00
Lamp, square font	330.00	720.00
Mug, handle	275.00	360.00
Pickle	275.00	—
Pitcher, milk, ph, quart	660.00	720.00
Pitcher, water, ph, half gallon	445.00	925.00
Salt Shaker, orig top	125.00	175.00
Sauce, flat, 4" d or 4-1/2" d	125.00	175.00
Sauce, ftd, 4" d, quarters	125.00	210.00
Spooner, quarters φ	235.00	335.00
Sugar Bowl, cov φ	235.00	445.00
Syrup, orig top, dated pewter lid	—	535.00
Toothpick Holder φ	215.00	300.00
Tumbler φ	145.00	245.00
Waste Bowl	235.00	275.00
Water Tray	300.00	—
Wine	235.00	400.00

United States Rib

New York State, US Glass Pattern Line No. 15,061

Manufactured by United States Glass Company, Pittsburgh, PA, c1891. Made in non-flint, clear and emerald green with gilding. Examples are found in clear with ruby staining. Expect to pay 200% of the values shown for clear for ruby stained.

Items	Clear	Emerald Green
Berry Bowl, master	30.00	45.00
Butter Dish, cov	45.00	75.00
Celery Vase	35.00	45.00
Creamer, individual or table size	25.00-35.00	35.00-45.00
Cruet, os	55.00	95.00
Custard Cup	10.00	15.00
Goblet	45.00	65.00
Lemonade Cup	10.00	15.00
Olive Dish, tab handle	15.00	20.00
Pitcher, water	65.00	85.00
Punch Bowl, stand	300.00	600.00
Relish Tray, rect	15.00	25.00
Sauce Dish, sq	8.00	10.00
Spooner	35.00	45.00
Sugar Bowl, cov, table size	45.00	65.00
Sugar Bowl, open, individual	25.00	35.00
Toothpick Holder	35.00	65.00
Tumbler, water	25.00	35.00
Vase, 9" h	15.00	20.00

United States Sheraton

Greek Key

Manufactured by United States Glass Company, Pittsburgh, PA, in 1912. Made in non-flint, clear, and can be found trimmed with gold or platinum. Some pieces are marked with the intertwined United States Glass trademark.

Items	Clear
Bon Bon, ftd, 6" w	25.00
Bowl, flat, 8" l	18.00
Bowl, ftd, sq, 6" or 8" w	25.00-30.00
Bureau Tray	42.00
Butter Dish, cov	45.00
Celery Tray	42.00
Compote, open, 6" d	20.00
Creamer, after dinner, tall, sq ft	20.00
Creamer, large; or berry, bulbous, sq ft	25.00
Cruet, os	35.00
Finger Bowl, underplate	30.00
Goblet	75.00
Iced Tea Tumbler	25.00
Jelly Compote, open, 4" w	17.50
Marmalade Jar	45.00
Miniature Lamp	75.00
Mug	25.00
Mustard Jar, cov	42.00
Pickle	15.00
Pin Tray	17.50
Pitcher, water, one half gallon; or squat, medium	42.00
Pitcher, water, tankard	45.00
Plate, sq, 4-1/2" or 9" w	10.00-15.00
Pomade Jar	20.00
Puff Box	20.00
Punch Bowl, cov, 14" d	125.00
Ring Tree	35.00
Salt, individual	20.00
Salt Shaker, squatty or tall	20.00-25.00
Sardine Box	45.00
Spooner, handle	25.00
Spooner, tray	20.00
Sugar Bowl, cov, individual or regular	25.00-30.00
Sundae Dish	15.00
Syrup, orig top, glass lid	45.00
Toothpick Holder, lay down	45.00
Tumbler	20.00

Utah

Frost Flower, Twinkle Star

Manufactured by United States Glass Company, Pittsburgh, PA, and Gas City, IN, in 1901 in the States Pattern series. Made in non-flint, clear, and clear with frosting. Add 25% for frosting.

Items	Clear
Bowl, cov, 6", 7" or 8" d	30.00
Bowl, open, 6" or 7" d	25.00
Bowl, open, 8" d	20.00
Butter Dish, cov, small or large	42.00-45.00
Cake Plate, 9" d	30.00
Cake Stand, hs, 7" d	45.00
Cake Stand, hs, 8" d	30.00
Cake Stand, hs, 10" d	42.00
Castor Set, 2 bottles	55.00
Celery Vase	30.00
Compote, cov, hs, 5", 6" or 7" d	55.00-75.00
Compote, open, hs, 6", 7", 7-1/2", 8", 9" or 10" d	30.00-55.00
Condiment Set, salt and pepper shakers, holder	65.00
Creamer	42.00
Cruet, os	55.00
Goblet	35.00
Pickle Tray	20.00
Pitcher, water, 3 pints; or half gallon	65.00
Salt Shaker, orig top	30.00
Sauce, flat, 4" d	10.00
Spooner	25.00
Sugar Bowl, cov	45.00
Syrup, orig top	75.00
Tumbler	25.00
Wine	35.00

Valencia Waffle

Block and Star #1

Made by Adams & Company, Pittsburgh, PA, c1885. Reissued by United States Glass Company, Pittsburgh, PA, after 1891. Made in non-flint, amber, apple green, blue, clear, and vaseline.

Items	Amber	Apple Green	Blue	Clear	Vaseline
Berry Bowl	25.00	35.00	30.00	20.00	25.00
Bread Plate	42.00	45.00	42.00	35.00	45.00
Butter Dish, cov	80.00	90.00	65.00	55.00	42.50
Cake Stand, hs, 10" d	85.00	55.00	65.00	42.00	55.00
Celery Vase	42.00	40.00	45.00	30.00	35.00
Castor set, complete	85.00	110.00	90.00	75.00	85.00
Compote, cov, hs, 7" d	85.00	110.00	110.00	75.00	90.00
Compote, cov, ls	55.00	75.00	85.00	42.00	55.00
Creamer, ph	45.00	—	65.00	42.00	32.50
Dish, 7" d, 8" d, or 9" d	30.00	—	35.00	15.00	30.00
Goblet	55.00	85.00	55.00	42.00	45.00
Pickle Jar, cov	75.00	85.00	40.00	42.00	65.00
Pickle Dish	30.00	30.00	35.00	25.00	30.00
Pitcher, milk	75.00	85.00	80.00	55.00	75.00
Pitcher, water	90.00	85.00	80.00	55.00	75.00
Relish or Pickle	30.00	30.00	35.00	25.00	30.00
Salt, individual	45.00	—	—	—	—
Salt Shaker	30.00	42.00	45.00	25.00	45.00
Sauce, flat, sq, 4" w	15.00	—	25.00	10.00	15.00
Sauce, ftd, sq, 4" w	20.00	—	20.00	15.00	25.00
Spooner	42.00	—	45.00	30.00	45.00
Sugar Bowl, cov	55.00	—	75.00	45.00	65.00
Syrup, orig top	125.00	135.00	135.00	85.00	—
Tray, 10-1/2" l, 8" w	—	45.00	—	—	—
Tumbler	35.00	—	42.00	20.00	35.00

Valentine

Non-flint pattern made by United States Glass Company, Pittsburgh, PA, 1891-95. Made in non-flint, clear.

Reproductions: Degenhart Glass Company, Cambridge, OH, created reproduction toothpick holders from new molds in many colors, including clear and opalescent shades. They are usually signed with the Degenhart logo.

Items	Clear
Berry Bowl	110.00
Butter Dish, cov	110.00
Cologne Bottle, os	110.00
Creamer, 4-1/2" h	110.00
Goblet	135.00
Pitcher, water	250.00
Sauce, flat, 4-1/2" d	30.00
Spooner	75.00
Sugar Bowl, cov	135.00
Toothpick Holder φ	110.00
Tumbler	110.00

Vermont

Honeycomb with Flower Rim, Inverted Thumbprint with Daisy Band, US Glass Pattern Line No. 15,060

Manufactured by United States Glass Company, Pittsburgh, PA, 1899-1903, as part of its States series. Made in non-flint, clear, and green. Both clear and green are found with gold trim. Rare examples in blue, clear with amber stain, clear with ruby stain, and clear with green stain. Very rare in custard (usually decorated), milk glass, and blue.

Reproductions: Toothpick holders have been reproduced by Crystal Art Glass Company, Cambridge, OH, and Mosser Glass Company, Cambridge, OH, and Degenhart Glass Company, Cambridge, OH, who marks its colored line.

Items	Clear w/Gold	Green w/Gold
Basket, handle	42.00	65.00
Berry Bowl	35.00	65.00
Butter Dish, cov	55.00	110.00
Card Tray, small, medium or large	25.00-30.00	35.00-45.00
Celery Tray	42.00	45.00
Compote, cov, hs	80.00	135.00
Compote, open, hs	45.00	90.00

Items	Clear w/Gold	Green w/Gold
Creamer, ph, 4-1/4" h	42.00	80.00
Finger Bowl	35.00	65.00
Goblet	55.00	75.00
Pickle Tray	30.00	42.00
Pitcher, water	75.00	135.00
Salt Shaker	30.00	45.00
Sauce, footed	25.00	30.00
Spooner	35.00	110.00
Sugar Bowl, cov	45.00	115.00
Toothpick Holder φ	42.00	75.00
Tumbler, footed	30.00	55.00
Vase	30.00	65.00

Victoria

Manufactured by Bakewell, Pears and Company, Pittsburgh, PA, in the early 1850s. Made in flint, clear.

Items	Clear
Berry Bowl, master	35.00
Butter Dish, cov	125.00
Cake Stand, hs, 9" or 15" d	115.00-125.00
Celery Vase	85.00
Compote, cov, hs, 8" d	120.00
Compote, open, hs, 10" d	110.00
Creamer	90.00
Goblet	85.00
Pitcher, water	175.00
Spooner	80.00
Sugar Bowl, cov	110.00
Sweetmeat, cov, 6" d	110.00

Viking

Bearded Head, Bearded Prophet, Hobb's Centennial, Old Man of the Mountain

Manufactured by Hobbs, Brockunier, & Company, Wheeling, WV, in 1876, as its Centennial pattern. The pattern was designed and patented by John H. Hobbs, Nov. 21, 1876. The molds are documented as being made by Stephen Hopkins. No tumbler or goblet originally made. Made in non-flint, clear, and clear with frosting. Rare in opaque white.

Items	Clear
Apothecary Jar, cov	80.00
Bowl, cov, oval, 8" or 9" l	80.00-90.00
Bread Plate, oval	115.00
Butter Dish, cov	110.00
Casserole, cov	110.00
Celery Vase	65.00
Compote, cov, hs, oval, 9" l	120.00
Compote, cov, hs, round, 7", 8" or 9" d	115.00-125.00
Compote, cov, ls, round, 9" d	110.00
Compote, open, hs	85.00
Creamer, 2 types	75.00
Cup, ah, ftd	45.00
Egg Cup	55.00
Marmalade Jar, cov	110.00
Mug, ah	75.00
Pickle Dish, oval	30.00
Pitcher, water	135.00
Relish Tray	30.00
Salt, master	55.00
Sauce, ftd	25.00
Spooner	45.00
Sugar Bowl, cov	90.00

Waffle

Paneled Waffle

Manufacturing attributed to Boston and Sandwich Glass Company, Sandwich, MA, c1850. Made in flint, clear. Rarely found in milk white or colors.

Items	Clear
Bowl, 8" oval	45.00
Butter Dish, cov	125.00

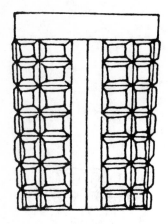

Items	Clear
Celery Vase	90.00
Champagne	125.00
Claret	125.00
Compote, cov, hs, 6", 7", 8" or 9" d	120.00-155.00
Compote, cov, ls, 6", 7", 8" or 9" d	120.00-155.00
Compote, open, ls, 6", 7" or 8" d	85.00-95.00
Cordial	125.00
Creamer, ah, pedestal	135.00
Decanter, os, pint or quart	120.00-125.00
Egg Cup, footed	55.00
Goblet	85.00
Lamp, oil, finger, ah	135.00
Lamp, oil, tall	175.00
Mug, ah	135.00
Pickle Dish, oval	25.00
Pitcher, water, ah	190.00
Relish Tray, oblong, scalloped rim	65.00
Salt, master, cov, ftd	135.00
Salt, master, open, ftd	42.00
Sauce, flat, 4" d	30.00
Spillholder	110.00
Spooner	90.00
Sugar Bowl, cov	120.00
Tumbler	90.00
Whiskey	125.00
Wine	75.00

Waffle and Thumbprint

Bull's Eye and Waffle, Palace, Triple Bull's Eye

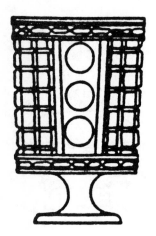

Manufactured first by the New England Glass Company, East Cambridge, MA, c1868 and by Curling, Robertson & Company, Pittsburgh, PA, c1856. Shards have been found at the Boston and Sandwich Glass Company, Sandwich, MA. Made in flint, clear. Rare examples known in canary-yellow and milk white.

Items	Clear
Bitters Bottle	250.00
Bottle, ftd	125.00
Bowl, rect, 7" l, 5" w	42.00
Butter Dish, cov	120.00
Celery Vase	120.00
Champagne	135.00
Claret	125.00
Compote, cov, hs, 6" d; or ls, 6" d	175.00
Compote, open, ls, 6" d	115.00
Cordial	125.00
Creamer, ah	135.00
Decanter, os, pint or quart, blown	125.00-165.00
Egg Cup	65.00
Flip	135.00
Goblet, bulbous, heavy or knob stem	90.00
Lamp, oil, hand, ah, orig burner, 9-1/2" h	125.00
Lamp, whale oil, orig burner, 11" h	200.00
Pitcher, water, ah	450.00
Salt, master	65.00
Spooner	65.00
Sugar Bowl, cov	135.00
Sweetmeat, cov, hs, 6"	175.00
Tumbler, ftd	110.00
Whiskey	110.00
Wine	100.00

Washington

Manufactured by United States Glass Company, Pittsburgh, PA, as part of its States series. Made in clear, frosted with colored floral decoration (add 25%), and ruby stained (add 40%). Rare in custard and milk glass. A very rare covered sugar is known in emerald green, $120.

Items	Clear
Bowl, flat, oblong, 6", 8" or 10" l	35.00-75.00
Bowl, round, 3", 3-1/2", 4", 4-1/2", 5", 6", 7" or 8" d	25.00-42.00
Butter Dish, cov	85.00
Cake Stand, hs, 10" d	75.00
Celery Tray	65.00
Champagne	42.00
Claret	42.00
Compote, cov, hs, 5", 6", 7" or 8" d	80.00-90.00
Compote, cov, ls, 5", 6", 7" or 8" d	65.00-90.00
Compote, open, hs, 5", 6", 7" or 8" d	45.00-65.00
Compote, open, ls, 3-1/2", 5", 6", 7" or 8" d	25.00-42.00

Items	Clear
Cordial	75.00
Creamer, individual; table; or tankard, pint	65.00
Custard Cup	25.00
Fruit Bowl, hs, 7-1/2", 8-1/2" or 9-1/2" d	55.00-75.00
Goblet, small or large	45.00
Jelly Compote, cov, hs, 4-1/2" d	80.00
Jelly Compote, open, hs, 4-1/2" d	45.00
Lemonade Cup	25.00
Oil Bottle	75.00
Olive Dish, oval	42.00
Pickle Dish, oval	42.00
Pitcher, milk, tankard, quart, 3 pints, or half gallon	90.00-110.00
Pitcher, water, tankard, quart, 3 pints or half gallon	90.00-500.00
Powdered Sugar, cov	120.00
Salt, individual or master	35.00
Salt Shaker	65.00
Spooner	65.00
Sugar, cov, table	85.00
Sugar, open, individual	45.00
Toothpick Holder	45.00
Tumbler	45.00
Wine	45.00

Washington

Early Washington, Leafy Panel and Thumbprint

Manufactured by New England Glass Company, East Cambridge, MA, c1869. Made in flint, clear.

Items	Clear
Ale Glass	135.00
Bitters Bottle	110.00
Bowl, cov, 5", 6", 7" or 8" d	110.00-135.00
Bowl, flat, 5", 6", 7" or 8" d	45.00-75.00
Bowl, oval, 7", 8", 9" l, 6" w or 10" l	45.00-75.00
Butter Dish, cov	200.00
Celery Vase	120.00
Champagne	135.00
Claret	145.00
Compote, cov, hs, deep bowl, 6", 7", 8", 9" or 10" d	135.00-200.00
Compote, cov, hs, shallow bowl, 6", 7" or 8" d	135.00-165.00
Compote, cov, ls, deep bowl, 6", 7", 8" or 9" d	135.00-180.00
Compote, open, hs, deep bowl, 6", 7", 8", 9" or 10" d	75.00-135.00
Compote, open, hs, shallow bowl, 6", 7" or 8" d	75.00-100.00
Compote, open, ls, deep bowl, 6", 7", 8", 9" or 10" d	75.00-135.00
Compote, open, ls, shallow bowl, 6", 7" or 8" d	75.00-100.00
Cordial	175.00
Creamer	265.00
Decanter, bar lip, pint or quart	175.00-190.00
Decanter, os, pint or quart	300.00
Egg Cup	110.00
Goblet, lady's, small or gentleman's, large	125.00-150.00
Honey Dish, 3-1/2" d	42.00
Juice Glass	90.00
Lamp	175.00
Lemonade Glass	110.00
Mug	110.00
Pitcher, water, half gallon or 3 pint	375.00-400.00
Plate, 6" or 7" d	85.00-90.00
Salt, individual	30.00
Salt, master, flat or footed	80.00-90.00
Sauce, flat, 4" d or 5" d	35.00
Spooner	110.00
Sugar Bowl, cov	135.00
Syrup, orig top	250.00
Tumbler	110.00
Wine	135.00

Washington Centennial

Chain with Diamonds

Manufactured by Gillinder & Company, Philadelphia, PA, c1876 for the Centennial celebration. Shards have been found at Burlington Glass Works, Hamilton, Ontario, Canada. Made in non-flint, clear.

Items	Clear
Bowl, oval, 7", 8" or 9" l	35.00
Bowl, round, 7", 8" or 9" d	35.00
Bread Plate, "Carpenter's Hall," "George Washington" or "Independence Hall	125.00

Items	Clear
Butter Dish, cov	115.00
Cake Stand, hs, 8-1/2" or 10" d	65.00-85.00
Celery Vase	55.00
Champagne	90.00
Compote, cov, hs, 8" or 9" d	110.00-115.00
Compote, open, hs, 8" or 9" d	65.00-75.00
Creamer, ah	115.00
Egg Cup	65.00
Goblet	65.00
Pickle, fish shape	35.00
Pitcher, milk, ah, quart	150.00
Pitcher, water, ah, half gallon	130.00
Relish, claw handle, dated	75.00
Salt, individual, 2" d; or master	30.00-45.00
Salt Shaker, orig top	90.00
Sauce, flat	20.00
Spooner	45.00
Sugar Bowl, cov	100.00
Syrup, orig top	175.00
Tumbler	55.00
Wine	75.00

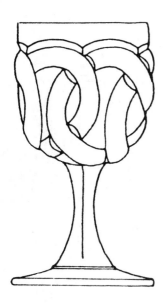

Wedding Ring

Double Wedding Ring

Original manufacturer unknown. Flint production is dated to c1860 while non-flint production dates to c1870. Made in flint, clear only.

Reproductions: The toothpick holder, frequently seen in muddy purple, not originally made. It has now been reproduced in various colors. Dalzell/Viking Glass Company, New Martinsville, WV, c1989, has issued several flat pieces in colors and clear that were not produced earlier, including a sherbet and toothpick holder.

Items	Flint
Butter Dish, cov	125.00
Celery Vase	115.00
Champagne	120.00
Cordial	110.00
Creamer	110.00
Decanter, bar lip or os	135.00
Goblet, plain stem φ or faceted knob stem	90.00
Lamp, oil, finger, orig burner and chimney, 5" h	110.00
Pitcher, water	250.00
Relish	85.00
Sauce, flat	42.00
Spooner	115.00
Sugar Bowl, cov φ	125.00
Syrup, ah, orig top	125.00
Tumbler, flat	110.00
Wine φ	135.00

Westmoreland

Spector Block

Manufactured by Gillinder and Sons, Philadelphia, PA, 1889. Patented by Thomas W. Mellor. Made as late as 1907 by United States Glass Company, Pittsburgh, PA. Made in non-flint, clear.

Items	Clear
Butter Dish, cov	65.00
Celery Tray	30.00
Cologne Bottle, os	42.00
Compote, cov	85.00
Creamer	35.00
Cruet	45.00
Goblet	55.00
Pitcher, water	85.00
Plate, 7" d	35.00
Sauce	15.00
Spooner	30.00
Sugar Bowl, cov	55.00
Syrup, orig top	85.00
Tumbler	42.00
Wine	42.00

Westward Ho!

Pioneer, Tippecanoe

Manufactured by Gillinder and Sons, Philadelphia, PA, c1879. Molds made by Jacobus, which also made *Classic*. Made in non-flint, clear with an acid finish (frosting) as part of the design. Some forms of this pattern were originally made in milk glass and those are considered to be rare.

Reproductions: *Westward Ho!* has been reproduced since the 1930s by L.G. Wright Glass Company, New Martinsville, WV, Westmoreland Glass Company, Grapeville, PA, and several others. Reproductions can be found in several colors and clear. Examples of original *Westward Ho!* Will show fine details, frosting that is used to highlight the pattern rather than cover up inadequate details.

Items	Clear
Bowl, ftd, 5" d	135.00
Bread Plate	250.00
Butter Dish, cov φ	250.00
Celery Vase φ	135.00
Compote, cov, hs, 5" d φ, 6" d φ or 9" d φ	235.00-350.00
Compote, cov, ls, 5" d φ, 6" d φ or 8-1/2" d	175.00-275.00
Compote, open, hs, 5" d φ or 8" d φ	125.00-135.00
Compote, open, hs, oval, 9" d	150.00
Compote, open, ls, 5" d φ	125.00
Creamer φ	120.00
Goblet φ	125.00
Marmalade Jar, cov	275.00
Mug, 2" h or 3-1/2" h	235.00-250.00
Pickle Dish, oval	90.00
Pitcher, milk, ph, quart	395.00
Pitcher, water, ph, half gallon, 9-1/2" h φ	450.00
Platter, oval, 13" l, 9" w	150.00
Sauce, ftd, 3-1/2", 4" d φ, 4-1/2" d φ or 5" d φ	42.00-55.00
Spooner φ	110.00
Sugar Bowl, cov φ	250.00
Wine φ	275.00

Wheat and Barley

Duquesne, Hops and Barley, Oats and Barley

Manufactured by Bryce Brothers, Pittsburgh, PA, c1880. Later made by United States Glass Company, Pittsburgh PA, after 1891. Made in non-flint, amber, blue, clear, and vaseline.

Reproductions: Only the creamer and goblet have been reproduced. Reproductions are documented in amber, blue, clear, and canary-yellow. The knot at the top of the design on reproductions tends to be more open and less detailed.

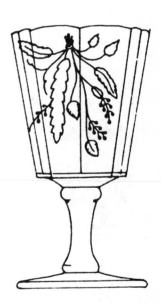

Items	Amber	Blue	Clear	Vaseline
Bowl, cov, 6" or 7" d	42.00	45.00	30.00	42.00
Bowl, cov, 8" d	45.00	55.00	35.00	45.00
Bowl, open, 6" or 7" d	30.00	35.00	15.00	35.00
Bowl, open, 8" d	35.00	42.00	25.00	42.00
Bread Plate	65.00	55.00	45.00	75.00
Butter Dish, cov	65.00	85.00	45.00	80.00
Cake Stand, hs, 8" d	42.00	55.00	30.00	42.00
Cake Stand, hs, 9" d	45.00	65.00	35.00	45.00
Cake Stand, hs, 10" d	55.00	75.00	42.00	55.00
Compote, cov, hs, 6" d	55.00	75.00	45.00	55.00
Compote, cov, hs, 7" d	65.00	80.00	55.00	65.00
Compote, cov, hs, 8" d	75.00	80.00	65.00	75.00
Compote, open, hs, shallow bowl, 6" d	42.00	55.00	35.00	45.00
Compote, open, hs, shallow bowl, 7" d	45.00	65.00	42.00	55.00
Compote, open, hs, shallow bowl, 8" d	55.00	75.00	45.00	65.00
Compote, open, hs, shallow bowl, 10" d	65.00	80.00	55.00	75.00
Creamer φ	42.00	55.00	35.00	45.00
Goblet φ	45.00	47.50	35.00	55.00
Jelly Compote, open, hs	45.00	55.00	42.00	45.00
Mug, ph	42.00	55.00	30.00	45.00
Pitcher, milk, ph, quart	115.00	110.00	55.00	120.00
Pitcher, water, ph, half gallon	110.00	120.00	65.00	125.00
Plate, 7" d	30.00	42.00	25.00	35.00
Plate, 9" d, closed handles	35.00	45.00	30.00	55.00
Relish	30.00	42.00	25.00	35.00
Salt Shaker	35.00	42.00	30.00	25.00
Sauce, flat, handle, 4" d	20.00	25.00	15.00	25.00
Sauce, footed, 4" d	25.00	25.00	15.00	25.00
Spooner	42.00	55.00	30.00	42.00
Sugar Bowl, cov	55.00	75.00	45.00	42.00
Sweetmeat, cov, hs, handle, 6" d	65.00	80.00	42.00	65.00
Syrup, orig top, half pint	250.00	280.00	110.00	250.00
Syrup, orig top, pint	275.00	295.00	150.00	275.00
Tumbler, flat or footed	42.00	45.00	20.00	42.00

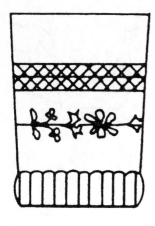

Wildflower

Adams Pattern Line No. 140

Manufactured by Adams & Company, Pittsburgh, PA, c1885, and by United States Glass Company, Pittsburgh, PA, at Factory "A," c1891-1900. Made in non-flint, amber, apple green, blue, clear, and vaseline.

Reproductions: This pattern has been heavily reproduced. Reproductions date as early as 1936. L. G. Wright Glass Company, New Martinsville, WV, and Crystal Art Glass Company, Cambridge, OH, Summit Art Glass Company, Akron, OH, and Mosser Glass Inc., Cambridge, OH, have issued items from new molds and in additional colors. Careful study of the details usually reveals poorly molded vines and flowers on reproductions.

Items	Amber	Apple Green	Blue	Clear	Vaseline
Bowl, round, 6" d	35.00	45.00	45.00	30.00	35.00
Bowl, square, 6" w, 7" w, or 8" w	35.00	45.00	45.00	30.00	30.00
Bowl, square, 9" w	42.00	55.00	55.00	35.00	35.00
Butter Dish, cov, collar base	55.00	75.00	75.00	45.00	65.00
Butter Dish, cov, flat	45.00	65.00	65.00	42.00	55.00
Cake Basket, oblong, metal handle	115.00	110.00	120.00	75.00	110.00
Cake Plate, square, 10" w	42.00	42.00	65.00	35.00	42.00
Cake Stand, hs, 10-1/2" d	75.00	115.00	110.00	65.00	75.00
Champagne φ	55.00	80.00	75.00	35.00	65.00
Celery Vase	80.00	85.00	80.00	45.00	80.00
Compote, cov, hs, oblong, 8" l	115.00	110.00	110.00	75.00	110.00
Compote, cov, hs, round, 8" d φ	115.00	110.00	110.00	75.00	110.00
Compote, cov, hs, square, 8" w	110.00	120.00	125.00	80.00	115.00
Compote, cov, ls, 7" d φ	—	—	100.00	—	—
Compote, cov, ls, 8" d φ	—	—	110.00	—	—
Creamer φ	45.00	75.00	65.00	55.00	60.00
Dish, square, 6-1/2" w	30.00	42.00	42.00	25.00	30.00
Goblet φ	42.00	55.00	55.00	35.00	55.00
Pitcher, water	80.00	120.00	90.00	55.00	100.00
Platter, oblong, 10" l	55.00	65.00	55.00	42.00	42.00
Platter, oblong, 11" l, 8" w, deep scalloped edges	—	—	65.00	—
Relish Tray	30.00	25.00	30.00	20.00	30.00
Salt, master, turtle shape φ	65.00	75.00	75.00	42.00	55.00
Salt Shaker	45.00	80.00	55.00	30.00	65.00
Sauce, flat, round, 3-1/2" d or 4" d	15.00	25.00	25.00	15.00	15.00
Sauce, footed, round, 3-1/2" d or 4" d φ	20.00	20.00	20.00	20.00	20.00
Spooner	42.00	45.00	42.00	30.00	55.00
Sugar Bowl, cov φ	65.00	65.00	75.00	42.00	65.00
Syrup, orig top	135.00	175.00	155.00	90.00	175.00
Tumbler φ	55.00	45.00	45.00	35.00	45.00
Water Tray, oval	75.00	85.00	85.00	55.00	80.00
Wine φ	65.00	65.00	65.00	35.00	65.00

Willow Oak

Acorn, Acorn and Oak Leaf, Bryce's Wreath, Oak Leaf, Stippled Daisy, Thistle and Sunflower, Willow and Oak

Manufactured by Bryce Brothers, Pittsburgh, PA, c1885, and by United States Glass Company, Pittsburgh, PA, at Factory "B," in 1891. Made in non-flint, amber, blue, canary, and clear.

Items	Amber	Blue	Canary	Clear
Berry Bowl, master	35.00	55.00	65.00	30.00
Bowl, cov, 8" d	35.00	55.00	60.00	30.00
Bread Plate, 9" d	55.00	75.00	85.00	45.00
Butter Dish, cov	80.00	90.00	115.00	55.00
Cake Stand, hs, 8-1/2" d	80.00	90.00	100.00	65.00
Cake Stand, hs, 9" d	85.00	100.00	110.00	75.00
Celery Vase	65.00	85.00	110.00	45.00
Compote, cov, hs, 6" or 7-1/2" d	75.00	90.00	115.00	55.00
Compote, cov, hs, 9" d	80.00	100.00	110.00	65.00
Compote, open, 7" d	42.00	55.00	60.00	35.00
Creamer	55.00	75.00	85.00	42.00
Finger Bowl	45.00	55.00	75.00	42.00
Goblet	55.00	75.00	85.00	42.00
Mug, hs	45.00	65.00	55.00	42.00
Pitcher, milk, ph, quart	75.00	85.00	110.00	65.00
Pitcher, water, ph, half gallon	80.00	85.00	110.00	75.00
Plate, 7" d	45.00	65.00	75.00	35.00
Plate, 9" d	32.50	45.00	55.00	35.00
Plate, 11" d	55.00	65.00	80.00	42.00
Salt Shaker	35.00	55.00	80.00	30.00
Sauce, flat, handle, sq	25.00	30.00	28.00	15.00
Sauce, footed, 4" d	30.00	35.00	42.00	25.00
Spooner	45.00	55.00	60.00	42.00
Sugar Bowl, cov	68.50	100.00	110.00	55.00
Tumbler	42.00	45.00	65.00	35.00
Waste Bowl	45.00	55.00	75.00	42.00
Water Tray, 10-1/2" d	45.00	75.00	85.00	42.00

Windflower

Manufactured by McKee & Bros. Glass Company, Pittsburgh, PA, in the late 1870s. Made in non-flint, clear.

Items	Clear
Bowl, oval, 8" l	42.00
Butter Dish, cov	75.00
Celery Vase	55.00
Compote, cov, hs, 7" or 8" d	90.00-100.00
Compote, cov, ls, 7" or 8" d	100.00-110.00
Compote, open, ls, 7" or 8" d	45.00-55.00
Creamer, ah	55.00
Egg Cup	45.00
Goblet	50.00
Pickle Dish, oval	25.00
Pitcher, water, ah	90.00
Salt, master, ftd	35.00
Sauce, flat	25.00
Spooner	42.00
Sugar Bowl, cov	85.00
Sugar Bowl, open	45.00
Tumbler	55.00
Wine	65.00

Wisconsin

Beaded Dewdrop, US Glass Pattern Line No. 15,079

Manufactured by United States Glass Company, Pittsburgh, PA, at Factory "U," (Gas City, IN) in 1903. One of the States series patterns. Made in non-flint, clear.

Reproductions: The toothpick holder has been reproduced in colors by Crystal Art Glass Company, Cambridge, OH, and also by Degenhart Glass, Cambridge, OH. Degenhart's reproductions were marked with a "D" within a heart mark. After Degenhart's death, the company was purchased by Boyd's Crystal Art Glass Inc., and it continued production, changing to a "B" within a diamond mark. Guernsey Glass Company, also of Cambridge, OH, also created toothpick holders in many colors.

Items	Clear
Banana Stand	110.00
Bon Bon, cov	35.00
Bowl, cov, oval, handle, 6" l	55.00
Bowl, oval, 7-1/2" l, 4-1/2" w	30.00
Bowl, round, 6", 7" or 8" d	45.00-65.00
Butter Dish, cov, quarter pound, flange	90.00
Butter Dish, cov, table size, double handles; or flat, flange	110.00
Butter Dish, open, table size, double handles	85.00
Cake Stand, hs, 6-1/2", 8-1/2", 9-1/2" or 11-1/2" d	55.00-85.00
Celery Tray	55.00
Celery Vase, pedestal	65.00
Compote, cov, hs, 5", 6", 7" or 8" d	65.00-110.00
Compote, open, hs, 5", 6", 7", 8", 9" or 10" d	42.00-110.00
Compote, open, ls, 5" or 7" d	42.00-45.00
Condiment Set, individual size creamer, cov sugar, salt and pepper shakers, tray	125.00
Condiment Set, salt and pepper shakers, mustard, horseradish, tray	150.00
Creamer, individual	45.00
Creamer, table	75.00
Cruet, os	115.00
Cup and Saucer	75.00
Custard Cup	15.00
Dish, cov, oval, handle, 6" l	75.00
Dish, open, round, 7" d	85.00
Goblet	90.00
Marmalade Jar, straight sides, glass lid	135.00
Mug	45.00
Mustard Jar, cov, bulbous	65.00
Olive, handle, 5-1/2" d	45.00
Pickle Dish, rect	30.00
Pickle Jar, cov	125.00
Pitcher, milk, ph, footed, quart	80.00
Pitcher, water, ph, footed, half gallon	100.00
Plate, square, 6-3/4" w	35.00
Preserve, oblong, 8" l	60.00
Punch Cup	20.00
Relish	35.00
Salt Shaker, orig top, bulbous or tapered	42.00
Sauce, flat, 4" d	15.00
Sherbet Cup	20.00
Spooner	42.00

Items	Clear
Sugar Bowl, cov, table	80.00
Sugar Bowl, open, individual	42.00
Sugar Shaker, orig top	125.00
Sweetmeat, cov, ftd, 5" d	55.00
Syrup, orig top	150.00
Toothpick Holder, kettle φ	80.00
Tumbler	55.00
Vase, 6" h	45.00
Wine	110.00

Wyoming

Bull's Eye, Enigma, US Glass Pattern Line 15,081

Manufactured by United States Glass Company, Pittsburgh, PA, at Factory "U" (Gas City, IN) and Factory "E" (Tarentum, PA), c1903, as one of the States series patterns.

Items	Clear
Bowl, flat, scalloped rim, 6", 7" or 8" d	25.00-35.00
Butter Dish, cov	75.00
Cake Plate	80.00
Cake Stand, 9" d, 10" d, or 11" d	100.00
Compote, cov, hs, 6", 7" or 8" d	85.00-110.00
Compote, open, hs, deep bowl, 6", 7" or 8" d	42.00-55.00
Compote, open, hs, saucer bowl, 8", 9" or 11" d	85.00-110.00
Creamer, cov, individual, tankard	75.00
Creamer, open, individual, tankard	45.00
Creamer, open, table	55.00
Goblet	90.00
Mug	65.00
Pickle Dish, oval, handles	30.00
Pitcher, milk, ph, quart	90.00
Pitcher, water, ph, 3 pint	110.00
Preserve Dish, oval, 8" l	30.00
Relish Tray	25.00
Salt and Pepper Shakers, pr	65.00
Sauce, flat, 4" d	15.00
Spooner, pedestal	42.00
Sugar Bowl, cov	65.00
Syrup, glass cov, small	90.00
Tumbler	80.00
Wine	110.00

X-Ray

Manufactured by Riverside Glass Works, Wellsburg, WV, 1896-98. Made in non-flint, clear, and emerald green, Royal Purple (dark amethyst), and rare in canary-yellow. Riverside also produced a jelly compote, water pitcher and tumbler in clear with a marigold luster (not carnival), and enameled flowers. An emerald green rose bowl is also known. Pieces can be plain or with gold trim. Prices are for pieces with gold trim.

Items	Royal Purple	Clear	Emerald Green
Berry Bowl, beaded rim, 8" d	125.00	35.00	65.00
Bread Plate, 8" d	225.00	42.00	75.00
Butter Dish, cov	200.00	55.00	110.00
Celery Vase	190.00	35.00	75.00
Compote, cov, hs	110.00	55.00	90.00
Compote, open, ls, 7" d	290.00	—	—
Creamer, individual, breakfast	185.00	25.00	42.00
Creamer, regular	140.00	42.00	85.00
Cruet Set, cruet, os, four- leaf clover tray	650.00	135.00	375.00
Goblet	220.00	30.00	45.00
Jelly Compote	125.00	35.00	55.00
Pitcher, water	250.00	55.00	110.00
Salt Shaker	80.00	15.00	25.00
Sauce, flat, 4-1/2" d	50.00	10.00	15.00
Spooner	120.00	35.00	55.00
Sugar Bowl, cov, regular	170.00	45.00	65.00
Sugar Bowl, open, individual, breakfast	220.00	30.00	32.50
Syrup, orig top	200.00	250.00	290.00
Toothpick Holder	125.00	35.00	75.00
Tumbler	120.00	20.00	35.00

Yale

Ball and Fan, Crow-foot, Turkey Track

Manufactured by McKee & Brothers Glass Company, Jeannette, PA, patented in 1887. Made in non-flint, clear.

Reproductions: Cake stands and goblets have been reproduced in clear and colors.

Items	Clear
Berry Bowl, master, 10-1/2" d	30.00
Butter Dish, cov	65.00
Cake Stand, hs φ	80.00
Celery Vase	45.00
Compote, cov, hs	75.00
Compote, open, hs or ls, scalloped rim	35.00
Creamer	42.00
Goblet φ	42.00
Pitcher, water	90.00
Relish, oval	15.00
Salt Shaker	42.00
Sauce, flat	15.00
Sauce, footed	20.00
Spooner	30.00
Sugar Bowl, cov	45.00
Syrup, orig top	90.00
Tumbler	30.00

Zipper

Cobb, Late Sawtooth

Manufactured by Richards & Hartley Glass Company, Tarentum, PA, c1888. Made in non-flint, clear. Rare pieces are known in amber and possibly other colors.

Items	Clear
Bowl, 7" d	25.00
Butter Dish, cov	55.00
Celery Vase	35.00
Cheese Dish, cov	80.00
Compote, cov, hs, 8" d	65.00
Compote, cov, ls, 8"d	55.00
Compote, open, hs	42.00
Creamer, ph, low or high foot	42.00-45.00
Cruet, os	65.00
Dish, 9-3/4" l, 6" w	30.00
Goblet	30.00
Marmalade Jar, cov	55.00
Pitcher, milk, ph, quart	45.00
Pitcher, water, ph, half gallon	55.00
Relish, 10" l	25.00
Salt, individual	8.00
Sauce, flat or footed	10.00-20.00
Spooner	35.00
Sugar Bowl, cov	45.00
Tumbler	30.00

Zipper Block

Cryptic, Iowa, Nova Scotia Ribbon and Star, Duncan & Sons Pattern Line 90

Manufactured by George A. Duncan & Sons, Pittsburgh, PA, c1887. Reissued by United States Glass Company, Pittsburgh, PA, at Factory "D," c1891. Shards have been found at Trenton Glass Works, Trenton-New Glasgow, Nova Scotia, as well as the Nova Scotia Glass Company, and Lamont Glass Company, Canada. Made in non-flint, clear, frosted, ruby stained, and frosted with cut stars. Add 20% for frosting. Also found with engraving.

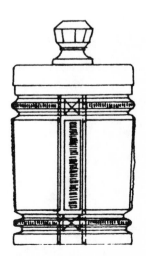

Items	Clear	Ruby Stained
Bowl, cov, round, collared base, 6", 7" or 8" d	55.00-80.00	80.00-110.00
Bowl, flat, round, scalloped rim, 7", 8" or 9" d	25.00-35.00	30.00-55.00
Bowl, oblong, shallow, serrated rim, 6", 7" or 8" l	35.00-45.00	55.00-75.00
Bowl, oval, deep, serrated rim, 7", 8", 9" or 10" l	35.00-55.00	55.00-80.00
Bowl, oval, shallow, 5-1/2", 6-1/2", 7-1/2", 8-1/2", 9-1/2", 10-1/2" or 11-1/2" l	15.00-45.00	35.00-65.00
Bread Plate	35.00	65.00
Butter Dish, cov	110.00	175.00
Celery Vase	55.00	125.00
Cheese Plate, 7" d	42.00	—
Compote, cov, hs, 7" d	80.00	145.00

Items	Clear	Ruby Stained
Compote, cov, hs, 8" d	90.00	135.00
Compote, open, hs, scalloped rim, 7" d	65.00	115.00
Compote, open, hs, scalloped rim, 8" d	75.00	110.00
Creamer	65.00	125.00
Finger Bowl	110.00	165.00
Goblet	55.00	85.00
Ice Cream Plate, 7" d	42.00	65.00
Lamp, oil, orig burner and chimney	110.00	—
Pickle Dish, oblong	35.00	45.00
Pickle Jar, cov	85.00	135.00
Pitcher, milk, ah, quart	125.00	210.00
Pitcher, water, ah, half gallon	135.00	210.00
Plate, 8" d	35.00	—
Salt Shaker	75.00	115.00
Sauce, flat or ftd, 4" d or 4-1/2" d	15.00-25.00	30.00-35.00
Spooner	42.00	85.00
Sugar Bowl, cov, hotel or table	85.00	125.00
Tumbler	42.00	65.00
Waste Bowl	110.00	165.00

Index

The Early American Pattern Glass Society

This society is a non-profit group of collectors and dealers who share a love of pattern glass. The purpose of the society is to foster and encourage the collection, appreciation, study, and documentation of early American pattern glassware, its makers, and its place in American life, past and present. You are invited to become a member of the only glass club devoted exclusively to this American decorative art.

Society Benefits

- Quarterly newsletter with original research articles, glass related articles, reprints, upcoming sales and shows, free want or sale ads, and society news.
- Membership Directory including a list of member pattern glass interests.
- Annual Meeting featuring speakers, auction, and fellowship with other collectors.
- Seminars by nationally recognized experts.
- Contact with other collectors and dealers.

$20 per year, $25 *for two at the same address.*

Mail this Membership Application to the address below.

Name_____

Address_____

City, State_____Zip_____ Phone_____

e-mail address _____

Patterns and/or forms collected:

_____

Are you a dealer? _____Business Name _____

Do you want your address and phone listed in the membership directory?_____

(The society does not share this information beyond its directory, which is for members only)

Please make check for $20.00, ($25 for two persons at the same address) along with suggestions, comments, and ideas to:

Early American Pattern Glass Society
Fred Phelps, Membership Chair
P.O. Box 266
Colesburg, IA 52035
e-mail: fredlmia@email.msn.com